PRACTICAL NARCOTICS
INVESTIGATIONS

PRACTICAL NARCOTICS INVESTIGATIONS

For the Uniformed Officer to the Experienced Detective

James Henning

To order additional copies of this book, contact:
Xlibris Corporation
1-888-795-4274
www.Xlibris.com
Orders@Xlibris.com
25486

Contents

DEDICATION

There are many people who have had a great influence in my career in law enforcement. So I would like to start my dedication to the following individuals: Sheriff Phillip L. Brown and Capt. Sidney E. Pinder (Caroline County Sheriff's Department) for giving me the opportunity to follow my career goals in narcotics and looking out for their deputies; Sgt. Ronald Dixon (Caroline County Sheriff's Department–CID) for being a great supervisor, friend, and always looking out for his men; Sgt. Ronald E. Crouch and Det./Sgt John Wooters (Maryland State Police) for "showing me the ropes"; Det./Sgt. Joe Branham ("Big Brother Joe") and Sgt. Allen McCloud (Maryland State Police) who possess a wealth of knowledge when it comes to any type of investigation and have consistently looked out for me over the years. Cpl. Edward Toatley (Maryland State Police), who lost his life tragically in the line of duty during an undercover operation in Washington DC—you will be missed . . . but never forgotten! And last but not least, a special thank-you to Dep. Eric Peterson, Sgt. Nancy Nagle, Det. Phillip Dixon, Det. Steve Biddle (Caroline County Sheriff's Department), Lt. Frank Ford (Ret.), Tfc. Tyson Bryce, Tfc. Eric Masaracchia (Maryland State Police), Chief Donald Nagle (Federalsburg Police), Chief Rodney Cox (Denton Police), and to all the deputies and detectives of the Caroline County Sheriff's Department who strive for excellence on a daily basis putting their life on the line for the citizens of Caroline County and the state of Maryland.

My personal dedication goes out to my loving wife Pam who has supported me in my law enforcement career and fills my life with joy with every day that passes; to my beautiful "little girl" Kaylie, who has brought so much happiness to my life that goes beyond words; my parents, James and Carol

Henning; brother, Chris Henning, for always being there for me and making me the person I am today; and last but not least, Retired Dep Chief Joseph J. Hock (Anne Arundel County Police), for being there for me when I was growing up and for being a true role model to look up to. I can only hope to be as successful in life and in my law enforcement career as you have been.

Biography

Detective James Henning first started his career in law enforcement in 1996 upon completion of the Anne Arundel County Police Academy, Maryland. After two years of being assigned to Uniform Patrol Division with the Caroline County Sheriff's Department, Maryland, serving under Sheriff Phillip L. Brown, he was transferred by request to the Caroline County Drug Task Force as a detective conducting narcotics investigations throughout the state of Maryland directly working with federal, state, and local jurisdictions in a wide variety of assignments both overt and covert. Detective Henning has taught officers throughout the state of Maryland on criminal procedures and investigative techniques concerning narcotics investigations at all levels. He has received training over the years by the Federal Bureau of Investigation, Drug Enforcement Administration, Army National Guard Counterdrug Task Force, National Drug Intelligence Center, and other allied federal, state, and local law enforcement agencies. He has been declared an "expert" in the field of narcotics investigations concerning a wide range of topics within the Maryland State Judicial System. He is currently attending Johns Hopkins University, Maryland, enrolled in the Police Executive Leadership Program, which is considered to be one of the top law enforcement degree programs in the country to date. Additionally, Det. Henning is a trained crime scene technician, intelligence analyst, and domestic/international terrorism instructor through the Northeast Counter Drug Training Center (SLAT), Pennsylvania. The professional associations Det. Henning belongs to are the International Association of Law Enforcement Intelligence

Analyst (IALEA), National Sheriffs Association, American Deputy Sheriff's Association, and the Fraternal Order of Police. He has been supported over the years by his family, friends, and co-workers who have continued to be the backbone in all his endeavors.

Street-Level Narcotic Tactics

Probable Cause Callouts

1. Planning:

    *   an operational plan (an example is contained at the end of this chapter)
    *   photos of the targeted area
    *   plan for insertion of undercover officers into surveillance post
    *   plan for extraction of undercover officer from surveillance post
    *   if needed, a type of distraction for undercover officers to enter and exit. An example is having an ambulance, with its lights and siren on, go through the area and park just far enough away to get the attention of the individuals in your way of entering or exiting the surveillance post.
    *   determination of perimeters in the area and the manner of approach for the takedown team.
    *   the length of time the operation is to be conducted. You must have undercover officers in place well in advance to allow time to set up equipment and get settled. Prepare yourself though to be in this surveillance location for a very, very long time. Make sure that you go to the bathroom beforehand, it will save you the aggravation later.
    *   retrieve photographs of individuals who are "wanted" that frequent the targeted area. This will assist the officers

doing the surveillance to focus on specific individuals and direct the takedown team to his/her exact location.

*Note: Wearing street clothes or some other outfit that would fit in with the area and not draw attention would benefit the undercover officers in making their entrance and exit from the surveillance post.

2. Personnel: (This is only an example of the personnel needed)

- two to three officers conducting the PC callouts
- four to six officers utilized as the takedown team
- two to three officers as "sweepers," these officers chase down anyone who flees the area.
- two to three officers kept back at a predetermined command post / staging area to begin the booking procedures once each wave of the takedowns (sweeps) have been completed. These officers are usually staged at the police department unless you have access to a mobile command unit.
- two to three officers in patrol vehicles for transportation of the prisoners, although a cargo van would be much more practical if available. Uniformed officers utilizing marked patrol vehicles will also be used to conduct traffic stops on vehicles seen purchasing CDS (controlled dangerous substances) from the runners. We will discuss this later in the scenario section.

3. Equipment:

- notepad
- voice recorder
- pens
- binoculars
- video recorder or video camera
- radios with extra batteries

- a watch or portable clock
- a bag or backpack to carry equipment in
- snacks and drinks

4. Picking a target area that is known for its high drug activity:

- public park
- street corner
- residential "crack" house
- any area that's receiving citizen complaints of drug activity

*Note: If at all possible, when conducting "night time" callouts try and pick a location that is well lit with artificial lighting. This will benefit you later when you write your report and testify in court. Night vision is your only other alternative to insufficient lighting. This is why it is more practical to conduct operations such as this during the daytime hours.

5. Finding a surveillance post:

- business
- abandoned/unoccupied building
- parking lots—utilizing vans or other vehicles as a base
- deer stand/trees
- tower
- rooftops—both residential and/or commercial

*Note: Anything that will allow you a clear and unobstructed field of view yet give you the cover and concealment needed to complete the operation.

6. Identification of "players":

- The Dealer—This individual is the main man on the street. He is the one who has all the CDS for the immediate area; he is the supplier if you will. Sometimes you find more then one dealer in the same area, this only increases your need to be observant. The dealers supply the "runners" who in turn make the sales for the dealer. The dealer is aware of the risk of getting caught with all or some of his CDS by the police. This is where the dealers try to employ tactics to evade police detection and/or apprehension.

*The above-listed photo depicts how street-level drug-dealing occurs. The main dealer is wearing the jacket shown inspecting the CDS. Notice how open the suspect is with the plastic baggie containing the CDS. In addition the individual to the left is scanning the area for the presence of law enforcement.

- The Runner—This individual will either be a user of the CDS and gets a cut of the CDS for every sale he makes. Or he will get a commission from the sale. For instance if the runner makes a $40 sale of crack cocaine then the dealer will give the runner $10 just for finding and making the sale. Some dealers will employ or recruit small children or juveniles to do the "running" due to the fact that the penalty for getting caught by the police is far less harsh than if it were an adult.

* A close-up photograph of the main dealer distributing the crack cocaine to his runners.

- Countersurveillance—These individuals are the eyes and ears for the dealer and the runners. The dealer may recruit individuals hooked on drugs to do this job in exchange for small quantities of CDS and pay them an amount of cash in exchange for the protection they provide. These individuals will strategically place themselves in an area best suitable to observe any police presence or even suspicious behavior from others around them. There are typical characteristics often seen from individuals placed on countersurveillance, which distinguishes them from others in the area. Some of these characteristics are the following:

  1. Stays in one area for a long period of time
  2. Yells to individuals (dealers and/or runners) when police are noticed or seen patrolling nearby. What happens more often than not is that countersurveillance exhibits a specific trait, which is noticeable to the trained officer. It occurs when countersurveillance notices police presence, then yells to the dealer or runners,

and then turns quickly away from where the dealing is occurring. This is done in an attempt to further separate them from the CDS activity happening nearby. Once they feel the police are out of the area and it is safe, they will return to their spot and resume their observations of the area.

3. A dead giveaway is the presence of handheld radios. With the development of the NEXTEL and other "walkie talkie" style cell phones, countersurveillance has a more relaxed appearance yet still accomplishing their job all the same by utilizing this phone as a two-way radio.

4. Also be aware of individuals making animal noises, singing loudly, or shouting out phrases that would in and of itself not seem abnormal but you are able to establish a pattern whenever marked police vehicles drive nearby; ultimately labeling that individual as a member of countersurveillance.

*"Runners" who are obtaining their CDS from the main dealer. As you can see, it is imperative to be in a good surveillance location in order to make these clear observations.

- CDS Buyers—These individuals will come on foot or in vehicle. When a buyer arrives on scene in a vehicle it is very important to get the tag number, a good description of the vehicle, the description and number of occupants, and direction of travel. This will aid the uniform officers in taking down the buyers on a traffic stop once they have left the area.

* A CDS "Runner" distributing CDS to a buyer in a vehicle. This contact is short and to the point.

7. Tactics to evade police detection:

- Hand Signals—Dealers, runners, and buyers will use hand signals to communicate in a discrete yet effective way. The buyer may drive by the runners and hold up four fingers in the air. This is street terminology for $40 worth of cocaine. Although a buyer can hold up any amount of fingers to communicate his needs. Another signal is taking your index finger and pointing it up, then repeatedly make a circular pattern. The runners usually make this signal to the buyers. It is meant for the buyers to drive around the block and come back. This allows the runners to go to their stash spot and retrieve the amount of CDS requested by the buyer. When the buyer returns the runner has the CDS for the buyer without anyone in the vehicle knowing where his drugs are.

- Dealer "Stash" Place—The purpose of a "stash place" is to prevent any drugs on or near the dealer or runners in the event that the police raid the area or take into custody suspected runners and/or dealers; in essence a method of distancing themselves from the CDS. Money obtained from the illegal sales of CDS is also sometimes hidden in the same way. Trash cans, the top of metal fence poles, and trash lying on the ground is some of the many ways that a dealer or runner hides their CDS. Surveillance officers should take their time and watch the dealers or runners go to specific areas just prior to or after a suspected drug transaction. This information will be needed when the takedown team arrives on scene to affect the arrest of individuals.

*Items found in a dealer's stash place that was located in a paper bag and hidden within a community basketball court's trash can. Without the proper surveillance, officers would never have found the items above.

8. Getting started:

- You arrive on scene and take up your surveillance position with a good field of view.
- Next, you need to decide which officer will be the "observer" and which one will be the "scribe" (note taker).The arresting officer will always be the observer since later in court he has to testify to what he had seen.
- Then, you set up your clock (or watch) where the scribe has immediate accesses to it. The need for the clock is to give the scribe the exact time that the observer calls out the actions, traits, and violations, which are occurring. Some officers use a voice recorder to document the violations observed. This is at the discretion of the scribe and the observer. But remember the observer will need the entire tape transcribed for future court purposes later.
- The scribe will mark runners, dealers, and buyers as T1, T2, T3, T4, and so on and so forth. Every time a target (T) is observed making a transaction, signal, or strange behavior (for example, always patting his waistband, which is a subconscious behavior exhibited by individuals carrying guns) you will utilize that individual's target number to refer to him throughout the investigation.

Example: (Identify the physical description of each target first)

1320 T3—B/M, 5' 9", black hat, white T-shirt, blue shorts

1320 T3—pulls out baggie of marijuana and hands to T20

1325 T5—returns to scene and makes contact with T6

—exchanged money and a baggie of cocaine

1325 T6—puts currency and cocaine in front left pocket

1327 T2—returns to vehicle (T1) and leans in to vehicle with a baggie in his hand and gives it to T1
1327 T1—hands T2 money
1327 T2—puts money in his front right pocket

- Now during this time the observer should be talking to his "take down" team leader giving them descriptions of targets, approximate locations of targets, location of countersurveillance, and any stash places observed.
- Now it's time to begin "PC Callouts" are a very, very fast-paced operation. And can get frustrating at times when large groups of runners are making sales quickly. Not to worry, if you had seen them selling or possessing CDS previously in your observation, they are already subject to investigative detention when the "take down" team arrives. The only thing that will weaken your PC on a runner or dealer is if they leave your sight for an extended amount of time or hop in to a vehicle and leave. Now I'm not saying you cannot stop, detain, and search these suspects once they leave your sight, you can! But it will have to take place with in a window of about five minutes after leaving your field of view. Five minutes is just a rule of thumb used, there is no exact time frame, the court will look at the "totality of the circumstance" surrounding the incident to make a determination.
- This is where your uniformed officers come in handy to stop and detain targeted individuals once they have left the area and are out of sight of the other runners and dealers.
- Scenario No.1:

  T1 arrives back on scene and pulls out a baggie with crack in it then hands it to T2. T2 then pulls out money and hands it to T1. This is your basic drug transaction— quick and to the point. Now, based on your observations you can stop, detain, and search both T1 and T2. But make sure to document in your notes and relay this information to the "take down" team standing by. It's important to note that in your charging documents and police report to use the term "(a quantity of) suspected paper currency" in place of "money," until the time you actually know for certain it is US currency. And you wont find this out until the arrest is made. This will save you the headache in court when the defense attorney asks you the ridiculous question: "So, Officer, you stated in the charging documents and police report that you observed at 18:03 hours, my client taking money from the co-defendant in exchange for a package, is that correct? . . . yes . . . well, Officer, are you an expert in the identification of United States currency or other currency for that matter? How do you know for certain it was money? What else are you not sure of?" Well, of course, as police officers we all know how silly these question are, but rest assured questions placed strategically like this could be asked of you while on the stand. This will inevitably "muddy the water" in a trial, especially a jury trial. Phrasing your description of money in this form can avoid these barrage of questions and will cover every type of paper currency, i.e., food stamps, checks, money orders, and actual paper money, etc., all of which have been known to be used as payment in drug transactions.

•   Scenario No.2:

T1 exits 206 Third Street and goes to the park across the street where he meets a group of friends. T1 then produces numerous small baggies of marijuana and hands them to T2, T3, and T4. But there is no money that changed hands between T1 and the others. This is a common transaction among drug dealers. Obviously T2, T3, and T4, are T1's runners and T1 is the dealer. What's even better is that by T1 exiting the residence of 206 Third Street and exhibiting CDS to the others, you now have probable cause for a search and seizure warrant at that residence. By T1 exiting the residence and going straight to the group of friends he has now made the house a part of the probable cause equation. You will need a search warrant though for the house which can be done at a later time.

- Scenario No.3:

While conducting surveillance of the area you notice a late model Ford truck bearing Maryland registration: EER-503, blue in color, operated by a white male, pull on to Fifth Street (the driver of the truck is now labeled as T1). The truck then stops halfway down the road. T2 walks over to the driver's side window and begins to converse with the driver of the truck. T2 then reaches into his front right pant pocket and produces a plastic baggie containing an unknown substance. T2 picks through the baggie and hands T1 an unknown substance. T1 then hands T2 a quantity of suspected paper currency in exchange for the unknown substance. T1 then drives off and turns the corner out of your field of vision. This is when you notify your uniformed officers standing by to conduct a traffic stop of that vehicle. Now, once the vehicle is stopped, you are legally allowed to search the vehicle and the individual and/or passenger(s); (Carroll Doctrine—exception to the written warrant requirement regarding vehicles). As for T2, he is fair game as well. Storm in and take him out!

- Scenario No.4:

During your surveillance operation you observed an individual, later identified as T1, approach T2 at the corner of Fifth and Lincoln streets. A brief conversation ensues where T1 produces a quantity of suspected paper currency and subsequently hands it to T2. At that time T2 crosses the street and meets up with T3. A brief conversation occurs between them both and T2 hands T3 the suspected paper currency. T3 retrieves a plastic bag from his left front pant pocket and hands T2 several small pieces of an unknown substance. T2 then returns back to T1 and hands him the unknown substance. Based on the above observations your takedown team should come on scene and stop, detain, and search T1, T2, and T3 for the previously mentioned CDS violations.

The case of United States v. Green 670 F 2d 148 (D.C. Cir. 1981) clearly described this form of distributing drugs which was termed by the court as a "two-party drug transaction" The court has explained that this is when "a drug transaction involves two people to make a single sale. This occurs when one individual holds the drugs. A second individual—known as a 'runner' receives the money from a customer, carries it to the individual holding the drugs, and returns the purchased drugs to the customer. This form of transaction provides the narcotics dealer some measure of protection from robbery" (*Id. at 1150-1151 n.1*).

9. *Common techniques used to hide contraband on a suspect's person:*

Once the detention/arrest has been made a complete and thorough search must be completed of the suspect's person. This will include a complete strip search to ensure that nothing is overlooked. More specifically the officer should incorporate his/her search in conjunction with their previous observations. For example, during your observation you noticed the suspect reach into his sock and retrieve an object, suspected CDS. This will be your hot spot. When the suspect is apprehended this should be your first place to search. Other common places include the following:

> Mouth—Dealers, runners, and users will transport CDS (commonly crack cocaine) in their mouth. They will insert the CDS between the upper rear or bottom rear cheek portion of their mouth or under their tongue. An individual who stuffs the CDS in the fatty portion of their cheeks can talk clearly and not show any signs on the exterior portion of their face. This only works with small amounts of CDS though

(approximately 0.6 grams and below of crack cocaine.) Larger amounts will result in the bulging of the lower jawline or upper cheeks, giving the officer suspicion that there might be CDS hidden in the suspect's mouth. Although the suspect's mouth might look like that of a chipmunk, with large amounts tucked away, their speech will remain practically unchanged. The tongue, on the other hand, is a dead giveaway. While talking with the suspect you will definitely notice that there is a speech impairment exhibited by the suspect. This is caused by the suspect's tongue not being able to fully utilize the space needed to phonetically speak correctly. In the event that you observe CDS in the suspect's mouth, what I have done in the past is, immediately grab the suspect's Adam's apple and push slightly in and up, this prevents him/her from swallowing. This does not damage or hurt the suspect— just makes them uncomfortable and want to cooperate sooner. Swallowing CDS is of course life threatening for the suspect, and it is your duty too as an officer to first ensure their safety regardless of their reckless manner of evading detection. Second, it's evidence.

Clothing—In today's society it is almost fashionable to have hidden pockets or compartments stitched or placed within the normal fabric of clothing.

- Hats have small pockets sewn on the inside used to hide CDS; or the exterior brim can have a razor blade positioned along the edge used as a weapon.
- Pants/shorts will also have hidden pockets sewn into them. Also, there have been situations where officers reaching into pockets have found themselves cut by razor blades sewn into the sides of the pockets to injure the police.

- Shoes are a very common and accessible way of hiding CDS. One way is to take off your shoe and hide the money or drugs in the front tip of the shoe. Then place your foot back in the shoe to keep it stationary. Another way is to cut a compartment in the heel and place the drugs inside. Once inside the compartment the removable sole used as a cushion in the shoe now acts as a cover to avoid police detection.

- Underwear is used frequently as well to conceal CDS. The most common type I find used to conceal drugs are the "briefs" This is due to the close fit around the suspect's body this style of underwear provides. It keeps the CDS close into the body so it will not fall out the sides. A common style of wearing clothing today is to wear boxers under jeans or shorts. The jeans/shorts will be worn where it is partially falling down exposing the individual's boxers. Don't be fooled, oftentimes they will wear briefs under their boxers to hide the fact that they are wearing this underwear. Again, this affords the suspects to give the appearance that they are wearing the loose-fitting boxers but actually wearing briefs which may contain the CDS underneath. A full strip search would resolve this concealment method quickly.

10. Personnel Documentation

Another important measure in the operation that will save you a lot of aggravation later in court is documenting who the specific officer was that made the detention and search of the target(s) while at the scene. On numerous occasions in court, it has been brought up by the defense (to muddy the waters for the judge and jury of course) the exact officer who stopped and subsequently searched the defendant. A way to ensure you are supplied with this information is by giving each officer two index cards so he/she can put the following information on them:

- the target's full name and address, officers name, department and ID number the time the target was stopped and detained and location
- briefly, what the officer observed during his/her apprehension of the target (i.e., uncooperative, fleeing, tossing CDS, guns, etc).
- the type of CDS or weapon that was found and where in the area or on the targets person it was located.
- the amount of money the target had on his/her person and from what pocket it came from.
- the time Miranda was given and any statements made

The index cards are then given to the seizing officer on scene and forwarded to the observer (case investigator) later to complete his/her police report.

Diagram of a PC Callout Operation

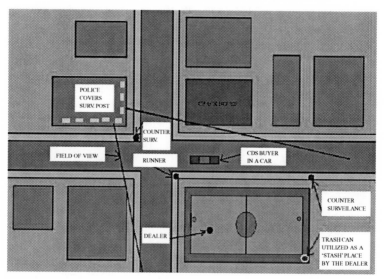

11. Case law:

- Listed below are cases that will explain how and why you can accomplish the above-described operation. These cases will also fall in to the "probable cause," "Investigative Detentions" and "Plain View" doctrine section, which go hand in hand with PC callouts.

Terry v. Ohio
United States Supreme Court
392, U.S. 1,88 S. Ct. 1868 (1968)

Terry v. Ohio is the Supreme Court case, which is the basis for all investigative detentions used in the day-to-day operation of police work.

"The Terry Rule": This rule is made up of three distinct components.

- reasonable suspicion
- the protective frisk
- and the scope of the protective frisk

1. The first component concerns the level of "reasonable suspicion" that must exist before an "investigatory stop" may be conducted. This standard involves a level of belief, which is something less than the probable cause standard needed to support an arrest but more then just a gut feeling. To legally justify such an intrusion the officer "must be able to point to specific and articulable facts which, taken together with rational inferences from those facts," collectively provide "a particularized and objective basis for suspecting the person stopped of criminal activity" Terry at 21, 88 S. Ct. at 1880.

   To determine if this standard has been met in a particular case, the court will give due weight, not to an officer's unparticularized suspicions or gut feelings but to the articulable facts for which the officer is entitled to draw from in light of his or her experience. Your training, knowledge, and experience are what counts here and will most certainly be brought up in court. The officer must be able to articulate specific facts gleaned from the "totality of the circumstances"—the whole picture—from which he or she reasonably inferred that the person confronted was in fact involved in criminal activity.

2. The second component of the Terry Rule involves an inquiry separate from the initial stop and detention. This part of the rule deals with the officer conducting a protective "frisk" of the person detained. This ultimately permits a police officer to conduct a limited search for weapons, a pat down of the outer garments to reveal any hidden weapons when the officer believes that he or she is dealing with an armed and/or dangerous individual, regardless if he or she has probable cause to arrest the individual with a crime—though the officer does not need to be absolutely certain that this individual is armed with a weapon. The main issue is whether a reasonably prudent police officer in the same set of circumstances would be warranted in the belief that his safety or that of others was in danger.

3. The third component deals with the scope of the protective frisk. The purpose of this limited search is not to discover evidence of a crime but to allow the police officer to pursue his investigation without fear that his inquires will be answered with a bullet or knife. The sole justification for the search is the police officer and others nearby—it must be confined in scope to an intrusion reasonably designed to discover guns, knives, clubs, or other hidden instruments for the assault on the police officer.

In reference to PC callouts the Terry Rule simply states that you will need more then just that gut feeling that initially draws the attention of most officers. Build from that feeling and look for indicators that you have been trained on. Accordingly, investigative stops or detentions may only be conducted when an officer has a reasonable suspicion that criminal activity may be afoot. The protective frisk of a suspect's outer clothing may be conducted only when the officer is in possession of additional specific and articulable facts from which he or she can reasonably infer that the individual he or she is confronting is armed and presently dangerous. Moreover, the frisk must be strictly limited in scope— designed solely to uncover hidden weapons. You as a police officer will need to articulate in your report as well as court your reasonable suspicion. An example of what might be articulated is an individual who is acting suspicious, in a high crime / open-air drug market area, and exhibits traits, habits, and actions for which you immediately recognize through your training, knowledge, and experience to be indicative of the drug culture. Now this only allows you to stop the individual, conduct a frisk of his or her outer clothing for weapons (only if you can articulate why), and subsequently determine if criminal activity has occurred or is in the process of occurring. If nothing in your investigation confirms your reasonable suspicion, then further contact should be terminated. But if through your investigation you come in to additional facts for which taken together with your initial reasonable suspicion and that information further supports probable cause, you may arrest that individual and search his entire person as a result.

When conducting PC callouts, for example, the officer is specifically conducting observations of individuals to develop probable cause. After employing the three components listed in the Terry Rule along with your direct observations of what you believe to be controlled dangerous substances and/or the traits, habits, actions, which lead you to believe a drug transaction occurred. It's at that point that the officer has developed more than enough probable cause to stop, detain, and search that individual's entire person and effects (i.e., purses and bags) for controlled dangerous substances. What brings you to the probable cause level is the simple fact that you witnessed, in your presence, what you believed—based on your training, knowledge and experience—to be a crime (the possession or distribution of controlled dangerous substances).

It should be noted that you can, under the Terry Rule, stop and detain an individual and conduct your inquiry without ever performing a protective frisk. It is only when supported by facts such as, but not limited to, high crime areas known for weapons or physical patterns (i.e., repeatedly grasping at waist band) indicating that the individual possesses a gun or knife, that the police officer should proceed with a protective frisk.

United States v. Davis
United States Court of Appeals
458 F.2d 819 (D.C. Cir. 1972)

During the daylight hours, at approximately 6:40 p.m., Officers Gaston and Wingfield, wearing old armed forces jackets over their uniforms, traveling in an unmarked car, observed defendant among a group of five or six "shabbily dressed" men standing on the corner of a "high crime area." According to the officers, the individuals with defendant were "in a kind of a daze . . . in a sleepy mood, twitchy, and a little nervous." Officer Gaston testified that some of them exhibited traits symptomatic of drug addiction such as the "common nod." Based on Officer Gaston's training and experience, he concluded that the members of the group were under the influence of narcotics, demonstrating "the stereotype of what we call junkie."

Defendant then left the group, walked over to a well-dressed man, "furtively" looked about in a nervous and suspicious manner, and "slid" an undetermined amount of paper currency to this man, receiving in exchange a small brown package.

Officer Gaston approached defendant, identified himself as a police officer, and requested that defendant accompany him to the unmarked car. Defendant took several steps in the opposite direction and appeared "as if he was just about to run." However, Officer Wingfield thereafter blocked defendant's path and effected his arrest. Defendant was found to be in possession of seventy-three heroin capsules.

The court noted in the Davis case this was in fact a good arrest. In "viewing the totality of the circumstances, judged in light of the officers' experience . . . there was a reasonable basis for their belief that a crime was being committed" (Id. at 822). Therefore, "the arrest was founded upon probable cause"

"Probable cause exists when known facts and circumstances are sufficient to warrant a man of reasonable prudence in the belief that an offense has been or is being committed" (Id. at 821 citing Beck v. Ohio, 379 U.S. 89, 85 S. Ct. 223 [1964]). Moreover, probable cause is "to be viewed from the vantage point of a prudent, reasonable, cautious police officer on the scene at the time of the arrest guided by his experience and training" Brinegar v. United States, 338 U.S. 160, 175, 69 S. Ct. 1302, 1310 (1949)

A police officer's training, knowledge, and experience reinforce the finding of probable cause and is a legitimate factor for consideration. The Davis court explained "conduct innocent in the eyes of the untrained may carry entirely different messages to the experienced or trained observer" (Id. at 822).

During the officers' testimony in the Davis case they explained that the defendant was seen among several "shabbily dressed" individuals who appeared to be under the influence of narcotics. According to the court, this fact alone does not end the inquiry for the court would never authorize "arrest by association" (Id.).

The officers also testified that the defendant approached an apparently nervous, well-dressed man in an equally nervous manner and subsequently "slid" money to the well-dressed man in exchange for a small package. "Surreptitious passing of a package has been recognized as a possible element in establishing the probable cause mix" (Id.). In addition, the defendant attempted to flee the scene of the crime as the officers identified themselves and made their approach. The Davis case stated "Although flight has been a legitimate factor in a finding of probable cause . . . it has not been considered a reliable indicator of guilt without other circumstances to make its importance less ambiguous."

The final factor is the geographical area of where the crime occurred. Although no presumption of guilt arises from the residents who inhabit a high crime area for which the police know that drug offenses occur, this can still not go unnoticed by the police. This taken with other reliable suspicious circumstances should be looked at as a whole when making a determination of probable cause.

United States v. Green
United States Court of Appeals
670 F.2d 1148 (D.C. Cir. 1981)

Officer Allman, an experienced member of the Third District Drug Enforcement Unit of the Washington DC Metropolitan Police Department was stationed in an undisclosed observation point investigating narcotics activity at the intersection of Fourteenth and V streets, NW. This neighborhood is known as a high crime area, which is used as stomping ground for drug trafficking. At about 11:25 a.m., Officer Allman observed, with the aid of binoculars, three individuals: a man which was later identified as the defendant, Gary Green; a woman who was later identified as Carol Turner; and an unidentified man on the southwest corner of the intersection. During this time Officer Allman observed the unidentified man approach Ms. Turner, engage in a brief conversation, then hand her some paper currency. Turner then walked several feet to Green and handed him the money. Green took the money, stuffed it in his left pant pocket, reached into a paper bag, which was in his left jacket pocket, and appeared to hand a small object from the bag to Turner. Officer Allman was unable to see the exchanged object, which was concealed, in Green's cupped hand and then in Turner's hand. Turner returned to the unidentified man and handed him the object. The unidentified man then received the object and left the area. Officer Allman then saw Green push the top of the brown paper bag back into his left jacket pocket, concealing it from view. Believing that he has just witnessed a typical "two-party drug transaction," Officer Allman radioed the descriptions of Green and Turner to officers awaiting his instructions in an unmarked patrol car two blocks away. Those officers drove to the intersection of Fourteenth and V Street and Officer Willis spotted Green from Officer Allman's description. Green recognized the unmarked patrol car or the officers as they approached. Green then walked quickly into a restaurant, looking back over his shoulder at Officer Willis, who had left the unmarked car to pursue Green on foot Officer Willis saw Green open the restaurant door with his left hand, move five or six feet inside the restaurant, motion with his right hand, and then start to move back out the door. Officer Willis found a brown paper bag lying on the unoccupied counter inside the restaurant, only three to five feet away from Green's position at the time of the confrontation with Officer Willis. The paper bag was within Green's reach and could have been placed on the counter by the movement of Green's right hand that Officer Willis had observed just before Green started out of the restaurant. Officer Willis looked in the brown paper bag and discovered fourteen small packets of heroin. A search of Green's person revealed $242, which was subsequently seized as a result of the above listed events.

The court in this case identified three factors, "especially when observed by experienced police officers in an area noted for the regularity of narcotics trafficking, provided probable cause for arrest" (Id. at 1151). The court noted the following factors:

1. The sequence of events between the three parties, Green, Turner, and the unidentified man, which clearly exhibited a "two-party drug transaction";
2. The movement of the three persons' cupped hands and Green's actions of stuffing the paper bag back into his jacket pocket, which lead the officers to believe that they were attempting to conceal the object of their transaction;
3. And the observation Officer Willis possessed that Green was attempting to flee when pursued.

The court explained though individually these observations would not establish probable cause but only the "totality of the circumstances" approach using all the elements observed would bring an officer—based on his training, knowledge and experience—to this level of probable cause.

The court further explained what probable cause meant in a situation such as this when making a determination:

"Probable cause exists if the totality of the circumstances, as viewed by a reasonable and prudent police officer in light of his training and experience, would lead that police officer to believe that a criminal offense has been or is being committed."

Illinois v. Wardlow
United States Supreme Court
528 U.S. 119, 120 S. Ct. 673 (2000)

In Illinois v. Wardlow a caravan of four police vehicles, converged onto an area known for heavy narcotics trafficking, and the officers anticipated encountering a large number of people in the area, including drug customers and individuals serving as lookouts. As the caravan passed the area where defendant Wardlow was standing and holding an "opaque bag," Wardlow looked in the direction of the officers and fled. It was at that moment, the United States Supreme Court held, that that officers were "justified in suspecting that Wardlow was involved in criminal activity," and were permitted to stop him and investigate further.

All too often officers are faced with individuals fleeing the area at the mere sight of a police presence. When conducting PC callouts, be prepared for this very situation to occur—because it will. If the takedown team converges on an area to get one, two, or three suspected drug dealers, the majority of the time others standing nearby who have not been targeted for the takedown will flee the area as well. These are individuals who have not displayed any contraband during your observations but nonetheless are still in an area considered a high crime district. Whereby their mere actions of fleeing the area reveals that they have something or done something they don't want you to find out about giving the officers reasonable suspicion needed to conduct an investigative detention.

In the event that this occurs, takedown officers should stop, detain, and investigate as to the individual's relative connection to criminal activity. The majority of the time while these individuals are running from you they will attempt to discard or eat the evidence before you can detain them—so be alert!

The U.S. Supreme Court though would not adopt a bright-line rule authorizing the temporary detention of just anyone who flees at the mere sight of a police officer. That the threshold would still need to add up to reasonable suspicion which would be needed to support such a detention. The "Terry Stop" would be determined by "looking at the totality of the circumstances—the whole picture" of what occurred.

In Terry v. Ohio, the court held that an officer may, consistent with the Fourth Amendment, conduct a brief investigatory stop when the officer has a reasonable, articulable suspicion that criminal activity is afoot. While reasonable suspicion is a less demanding standard than probable cause, the officer must be able to articulate more than an inchoate and unparticularized suspicion or "hunch" of criminal activity.

The court explained that an individual's presence in an area of expected criminal activity, standing alone, is not enough to support a reasonable particularized suspicion that the person is committing a crime. But in the same token, officers are not obligated to ignore relevant characteristics of a location in determining whether the circumstances are sufficiently suspicious to allow further investigation.

In this case it was not simply Wardlow's presence in an area of heavy drug dealing that aroused the officer's suspicion but his unprovoked flight upon noticing the police. And an officer developing a reasonable articulable suspicion, "nervous, evasive behavior" may be considered as a major factor in the equation.

The court stated: "Headlong flight—wherever it occurs—is the consummate act of evasion: it is not necessarily indicative of wrongdoing, but it is certainly suggestive of such. In reviewing the propriety of an officer's conduct, courts do not have available empirical studies dealing with inferences drawn from suspicious behavior, and we cannot reasonably demand scientific certainty from judges or law enforcement officers where none exists."

The court further noted in its holding "that this decision is entirely consistent with Florida v. Royer, 460 U.S. 491, 103 S. Ct. 1319 (1983), where it was held that "when an officer, without reasonable suspicion or probable cause, approaches an individual, the individual has a right to ignore the police and go about his business, and any refusal to cooperate, without more, does not furnish the minimal level of objective justification needed for a detention or seizure." Although unprovoked flight is simply not a mere refusal to cooperate, flight, by its very nature, is not "going about one's business"; in fact, it is just the opposite.

Simply put, the sudden, unprovoked flight of a person in a high drug-trafficking area, at the sight of a police officer or police vehicle, is enough reasonable suspicion that criminal activity may be afoot and subsequently authorizes the police to conduct a temporary investigative detention (Terry Stop) of that person until the officer can prove through his inquiry otherwise.

United States v. Smart
United States Court of Appeals
98 F. 3d 1379 (D.C. Cir. 1996)

In the third week of September, Officer Michael Tuz of the Metropolitan Police Department set up an observation post in the area of the 1500 block of Howard Road, SE, "to investigate illegal narcotic activity." After observing, through binoculars, "an apparent narcotic transaction" in a nearby building, Officer Tuz noticed a man, later identified as Antonio Smart, walk over to a grassy strip near several trees and a building, where he reached down and picked up a plastic bag from the ground alongside the building. The plastic bag contained a "chunk of white—a white substance." Although the officer was about thirty feet away, the binoculars made it appear as though Smart were right next to him.

After Smart picked up the bag, he "walked around the building and into a nearby parking lot, where he was out of Officer Tuz's line of sight. Officer Tuz radioed to a nearby arrest team that the suspect was a black man, wearing a black jacket, black shirt, and a black pair of pants, and would be in the first parking lot near the street" Less than a minute later, Officer Chris Huxoll spotted Smart standing "midway" in the parking lot. Although there were a few other people standing in the area, Smart was the only person in the parking lot who matched Officer Tuz's description.

Officer Huxoll drove up to Smart in an unmarked car, identified himself as a police officer, and told Smart to put his

hands up. Huxoll then walked Smart over to the police car.
Before Huxoll could frisk Smart, however, Smart put his hands
on his waistband. Officer Huxoll again asked Smart to put up
his hands. At first Smart complied; he then immediately put his
hands back on his waistband, at which point Officer Huxoll
placed his hand on top of Smart's hand. Huxoll felt a hard object
and knew it was a gun. A scuffle ensued and several other
officers assisted in taking Smart into custody. The officers
recovered a 9-millimeter semi-automatic handgun from Smart.
A search incident to Smart's arrest disclosed a bag containing
over twenty-five grams of crack cocaine and fifty-six small
ziplock bags in the pockets of his coat, a pager, and $580 in
small bills. While Smart was in the parking lot, Officer Tuz
identified him as the individual he had seen earlier.

As a result of these events, the court explained that the
legality of a stop or frisk is evaluated under the "totality of the
circumstances approach." And in this case, the court determined
that under the circumstances, the officers' stop and frisk of
Smart was reasonable and proper.

The court further stated: "The government contends that
the Terry Stop was justified because it was based on a reasonable
suspicion supported by articulable facts that Smart was involved
in criminal activity. The reason Officer Tuz set up the
observation post at that location was to investigate illegal
activity. Prior to observing Smart pick up the plastic bag, Officer
Tuz had observed an apparent narcotic transaction in the
building across the street. Furthermore, Officer Huxoll's
subsequent stop of Smart was also justified. Smart was the only
person in the area that matched the description of a black man
wearing all black in the exact location specified by Officer
Tuz. The inclusion of a specific time and specific location is
what makes the government's contention persuasive."

All in all, the stop and frisk (search) conducted by the
officers in this case were entirely proper, and the evidence seized
was properly admitted.

California v. Hodari D.
United States Supreme Court
499 U.S. 621, 111 S. Ct. 1547 (1991)

Officers McColgin and Pertoso were patrolling a high-crime area in Oakland, California, in an unmarked car. The officers were dressed in street clothes but were wearing jackets with "Police" embossed on both front and back. As they turned onto Sixty-third Avenue, "they saw four or five youths huddled around a small red car parked at the curb." When the youths saw the officers' car approaching, they panicked and took flight.

Hodari and a second youth ran west through an alley; the others fled south. The red car also headed south at a high rate of speed. The officers gave chase. McColgin remained in the car and continued south on Sixty-third Avenue; Pertoso left the car and pursued Hodari. Hodari circled the block in one direction and ultimately emerged on Sixty-second Avenue running north. Officer Pertoso circled in the other direction and emerged on Sixty-second Avenue running south. Looking behind him as he ran, Hodari did not turn and see Pertoso until the officer was almost upon him, whereupon he tossed away what appeared to be a small rock.

A moment later, Pertoso tackled Hodari. Pertoso then handcuffed Hodari and radioed for assistance. Hodari was found to be carrying $130 in cash and a pager; the rock he had discarded was later determined to be crack cocaine. The Supreme Court of the United States found this to be a good arrest, which fell with in the meaning of the Fourth Amendment.

According to the Supreme Court, Officer Pertoso's pursuit did not constitute a "show of authority" by simply directing Hodari to halt, since Hodari did not comply with that direction, "he was not seized until he was tackled" An arrest requires either physical force and/or submission to the assertion of authority.

The word "seizure" means the laying on of hands or the application of physical force to restrain the individual's movement. This does not apply to the police when they yell, "stop in the name of the law!" at an individual who continues to flee. Moreover, for legal purposes, an attempted seizure taken on by police is not a seizure according to the constitution and therefore is not considered a formal arrest under the meaning of the law.

In the above-listed cases we have covered a portion of investigative detentions, which is in line with PC callouts. The second portion of the operation involves the "Plain View Doctrine."

The Plain View Doctrine, which was originally brought forth by Coolidge v. New Hampshire, 403 U.S. 443, 91 S. Ct. 2022 (1971), and then modified by Texas v. Brown, 460 U.S. 730, 103 S. Ct. 1535 (1983), which allows an officer to seize evidence of a crime, any contraband, or other items subject to seizure without first obtaining an arrest warrant. So long as the officer has the justification to be lawfully in the area where he observes the evidence to be seized, a warrantless seizure of that evidence may be immediately effected.

The police may seize an item under the Plain View Doctrine when three conditions are met:

1. The officer must "lawfully make the initial intrusion" or "lawfully be in the viewing area";
2. The officer must discover the incriminating evidence "inadvertently," i.e., he may not know in advance that the evidence is in a particular location nor intend to seize it beforehand; and
3. It must be "immediately apparent" to the officer that the items observed may be evidence of a crime, contraband, or otherwise subject to official seizure.

The Plain View Doctrine has established the general rule "that if, while lawfully engaged in an activity in a particular place, police officers perceive a suspicious object, they may seize it immediately" Brown at 1541. However, holding a law enforcement officer to the "immediately apparent" condition implies "an unduly high degree of certainty as to the incriminating character of the evidence" (Id. at 1542). Since the evidence is in plain view, it should be sufficient to merely require the officers to have probable cause to associate the items with criminal activity (Id).

Justice Rehnquist explained that "probable cause is a flexible, common sense standard" (Id. at 1543). Justice Rehnquist further explained that "It merely requires that the facts available to the officer would warrant a man of reasonable caution in the belief that certain items may be contraband or stolen property or useful as evidence of a crime; it does not demand any showing that such a belief be correct or more likely true than false. A practical, non-technical probability that incriminating evidence is involved is all that is required."

In respect to the type and style of containers commonly utilized by users and dealers of controlled dangerous substances, the Supreme Court in United States v. Ross, 456 U.S. 798, 102 S. Ct. 2157 (1982), established a distinction between "worthy" and "unworthy" containers (Id. at 822, 102, S. Ct. at 2171).

"Worthy containers" are based on the proposition that the Fourth Amendment protects only those containers that objectively manifest an individual's reasonable expectation of privacy. For example, a paper bag stapled shut and marked "private" might be found to manifest a reasonable expectation of privacy.

"Unworthy containers" as found in the Supreme Court case Texas v. Brown was a green, opaque party balloon, observed with the help of a flashlight and from a vantage point where the officer was lawfully allowed to be (outside Brown's vehicle during a traffic stop). The balloon in question came into the officer's plain view when Brown withdrew his hand from his pant pocket and subsequently had caught between his fingers the plastic balloon. As a result, the officer immediately recognized through his training, knowledge, and experiences this container to be a common method of storing and containing controlled dangerous substances (Id. at 822 n.30, 102 S. Ct. at 2171 n.30).

In addition, the Supreme Court declared that the officer possessed probable cause to believe that the balloon in Brown's hand contained an illicit substance. [The officer] testified that he was aware, both from his participation in previous narcotics arrests and from discussions with other officers, that balloons tied in the manner of the one possessed by Brown were frequently used to carry narcotics. "The fact that [the officer] could not see through the opaque fabric of the balloon is all but irrelevant; the distinctive character of the balloon itself spoke volumes as to its contents—particularly to the trained eye of the officer.

Brown at 742-43, 103 S. Ct. at 1543-44. [Emphasis added] Thus, there may exist a group of containers—e.g., filled opaque balloons—"which may be less worthy than others." It is significant to note that in addition to the opaque, green party balloon, the officer in Brown also observed "several small plastic vials, quantities of loose white powder, and an open bag of party balloons in the interior of the open glove compartment. These additional observations, according to the Court, "revealed further suggestions" that the party balloon contained an illicit substance (Id. at 743, 103 S. Ct. at 1543-44).

In association with PC callouts, the training, knowledge, and experience of an officer, his/her observations conducted of that individual (i.e., nervousness, patterns, traits/habits associated with the drug culture) taken with the immediately apparent fact that the individual is in possession of evidence or a container in which you know through your training, knowledge, and experience to commonly contain controlled dangerous substances (i.e., plastic baggie, film container, etc.) the officer can make the apprehension, detention, and subsequent search to retrieve said evidence of what he/she believes to be the fruit of the crime.

United States v. Prandy-Binett
United States Court of Appeals
995 F. 2d 1069 (D.C. Cir.1993)

In United States v. Prandy-Binett, 995 F. 2d 1069 (D.C. Cir. 1993), the court addressed the question whether a narcotics officer's observation of a small rectangular block wrapped in silver duct tape, in the possession of the defendant Prandy-Binett, gave the detective probable cause for an arrest. The court advised here that "some opaque containers induce assumptions about their contents. Refrigerators contain food. Under the hoods of automobiles are engines. These are predictions based on experience." The expertise and training of the officer making the observations is what brings it to the level of probable cause.

In its discussion of whether, under the circumstances presented, the detective's observations of the rectangular block wrapped in silver duct tape provided them with probable cause for an arrest, the court stated:

Somewhere between "less than evidence which would justify [a] conviction" and "more then bare suspicion," probable cause is satisfied. The precise point is indeterminate. We are concerned not simply with probabilities but with conditional probabilities: if one event occurs, how likely is it that another event will occur? This is why the detective's observations up to the time the block slipped out of the perfume bag cannot be disregarded. It is why in similar cases we ask, although sometimes tacitly, what is the probability that a train passenger arriving at Union Station from New York City will be carrying cocaine? Quite low, we trust, despite New York's status as a source city for narcotics. Is the probability increased if the passenger moves quickly through the station after leaving the train? Greater if the passenger also gives apparently deceptive answers when the police question him? Greater still if the passenger opens his bag and refers to a package wrapped in duct tape inside a fancy perfume bag as a "gift" Neither courts nor law enforcement officers, nor anyone else for that matter, can quantify any of this. A mathematician could not perform the calculations because there is no way of assigning probabilities to the individual events. The information is simply unavailable, as will doubtless be true in every Fourth Amendment case. Still, we are convinced that, up to the sighting of the duct tape package, the conditional probability was low, much to low to have satisfied the Fourth Amendment in light of the interests it protects"

The critical question in this case was whether the detective's "inference of narcotics from the appearance of the wrapped block" enhanced the probability of Prandy-Binett's possession drugs (Id. at 1071). In this respect, the court observed:

Upon seeing the kilo-sized rectangular package wrapped in duct tape sticking out of the perfume bag, Det. Centrella and his partner immediately concluded that it held narcotics. Det Centrella testified: "As soon as I saw that, in my mind, that's drugs."

There was first the block's bulk. The weight of consumer goods in this country is usually described in pounds and ounces. Perhaps because of foreign influence, this weight of illicit narcotics is usually measured—in statutes and on the street—in terms of the metric system. The evidence showed that in the drug trade a kilogram of cocaine or heroin is a standardized unit of exchange, commonly referred to as a "kilo brick" or simply a "kilo" (a kilogram equals 2.2046 pounds). Det. Centrella was quite familiar with the bulk package containing one kilogram of cocaine. During his time as a police officer he had received training on such containers and personally seized such containers on numerous occasions. Both Det Centrella and his partner, an experienced narcotics officer who had undergone training at the Drug Enforcement Administration, thus had good reason for believing that the wrapped block in Prandy-Binett's gym bag was about that size of a package containing one kilogram of cocaine.

The second consideration was the rectangular shape of the object. The portion protruding from the perfume bag was consistent with what the detectives knew to be the standard configuration, the typical "kilo brick." The bag itself, roughly four inches wide and between six and ten inches deep, was the right size for holding a kilo of narcotics so packaged. The bricklike shape of the object thus further alerted the detectives, in light of their training and experience, to the possible presence of narcotics.

The third factor was [the] wrapping—silver duct tape (over plastic). Traffickers use duct tape because fingerprints are difficult to lift from its surface and because some criminals believe—erroneously—that it masks the odor of the drugs for police dogs. Det Centrella testified in court that he had seen this type of packaging for cocaine on numerous occasions in the past, which was similar in appearance to the one found in Prandy-Binett's bag.

Accordingly, the court concluded that, under the "totality of the circumstances" of this case, the detectives' observation of Prandy-Binett's possession of the rectangular package wrapped in duct tape provided probable cause for his arrest.

Special Case Law Notes

Field Test of CDS Not Necessary for PC

United States v. Russell
United States Court of Appeals
655 F. 2d 069 (D.C. Cir.1981)

In this case the court rejected the defendant's contentions that the police needed to field-test the controlled dangerous substance prior to making an arrest. According to the court, probable cause merely "rests on a 'reasonable probability' that a crime has been committed, not on certainty that illegal activity is afoot" (Id. 1263-1264). The court further concluded that it would "unduly retard legitimate law enforcement methods if" it were to hold that prior to making an arrest for a violation involving the possession of a controlled dangerous substance, officers were required to conduct a field test of the suspected CDS (Id. at 1264).

This is not to say that an officer should not conduct a field test of the seized controlled dangerous substance. On the contrary, this just makes the probable cause against the defendant that much more stronger. A rule of thumb is if you have the test available use it, if not just articulate your training and experience in drug work when completing the charging documents.

Nondislosure of Police Surveillance Location

United States v. Green
"Suppression Hearing"
United States Court of Appeals
670 F.2d 1148 (D.C. Cir. 1981)

During the suppression hearing in Green, supra, Officer Allman testified that he was in a "hidden observation post" near Fourteenth and V streets, NW. The Defense counsel attempted to disclose this observation post. The prosecution objected and was sustained.

Agreeing with the district court, the circuit court held that "the policy justifications analogous to those underlying the well-established informers privilege" (see McCray v. Illinois, 386 U.S. 300, 87 S. Ct. 1056 (1967), supported a qualified privilege protecting police surveillance locations from disclosure" Green at 1155. Further, "Like confidential informants, hidden observation posts may often prove to be useful law enforcement tools, so long as they remain secret. Just as the disclosure of an informer's identity may destroy his future usefulness in criminal investigations, the identification of a hidden observation post will likely destroy the future value of that location for police surveillance. The revelation of a surveillance location might also threaten the safety of police officers using the observation post or lead to adversity for cooperative owners or occupants of the building. Finally, the assurance of nondisclosure of a surveillance location may be necessary to encourage property owners or occupants of the building. Finally, the assurance of nondisclosure of a surveillance location may be necessary to encourage property owners or occupants to allow the police to make such use of their property" (Id.).

As a result, the court in Green was persuaded "to recognize what might be termed a 'surveillance location privilege'" (Id.). The court did however recognize that a criminal defendant has a strong interest in the effective cross-examination of an adverse witness while at a suppression hearing. A defendant's competing interest in the location of the surveillance post may establish whether the observing officer's view was open or obstructed, whether the angle of the officers view made the observations easy or difficult, and whether the distance from the criminal activity enhances or detracts from an officer's claimed observation or detail (Id. at 1156).

The balancing of this issue should be held on a case-by-case basis, the main issue focusing on whether the disclosure of the "hidden surveillance location" is needed in making a determination of probable cause. At all such hearings, however, the location of the surveillance post should not be disclosed to the defendant or the public. (See Hicks v. United States, 431 A. 2d 18 (D.C 1981) The trial court may exercise its discretion to conduct in camera proceeding if the surveillance location is material and relevant to the determination of probable cause and if the evidence creates a substantial doubt about the credibility of the observer.

The "Fellow Officer" Rule

Karr v. Smith
United States Court of Appeals
774 F. 2d 1029 (10th Cir. 1985)

This pertains to PC callouts because the observer is relaying his/her observations of the suspect's committing the CDS violations to the takedown team who is coming in to make the detention and subsequent arrest.

"Under the 'fellow officer' rule, 'probable cause is determined by the courts on the basis of the collective information of the police involved in the arrest, rather than exclusively on the extent of the knowledge of the particular officer who may actually make the arrest'" (Id. At 1031).

The courts will determine the existence of probable cause under this rule when "the collective information of . . . law enforcement officers involved in an arrest can form the basis for probable cause, even though that information is not within the knowledge of the arresting officer'" (Karr at 1031).

(INSERT YOUR DEPARTMENT NAME HERE)

Operational Plan

OPERATIONAL DATA		
CASE #:	CASE AGENT:	START DATE:
RELATED CASE NUMBERS:	ASSISTING CASE AGENTS:	START TIME:
1.	1.	
2.	2.	END DATE:
3.	3.	
4.	4.	END TIME:
5.	5.	

TYPE OF OPERATION		BRIEFING LOCATION DATA
☒ SEARCH WARRANT	☒ SURVEILLANCE OPERATION	BREIFING LOCATION:
☒ P.C. CALL OUT	☒ CI CONTROLLED PURCHASE	
☒ P.C. RIP	☒ HAND TO HAND PURCHASE	SECONDARY STAGING LOCATION:
☒ BUY / BUST	☒ FELONY VEHICLE STOP	
☒ BUY / WALK	☒ OTHER	TARGET LOCATION:
*OTHER:		BOOKING LOCATOIN:

SUPPORT PERSONNEL			
NAME	AGENCY	CELL PHONE	ASSIGNMENT
1.			
2.			
3.			
4.			
5.			
6.			
7.			
8.			
9.			
10.			

SUSPECT INFORMATION

NAME:				ALIAS:			

AGE:	SEX:	RACE:	HEIGHT:	WEIGHT: LBS.	HAIR:	EYES:	COMP:

STREET ADDRESS:	CITY:	STATE:

HANGOUTS/ SECONDARY ADDRESS:

SCARS/ MARKS/ TATTOOS:

OTHER INFORMATION/ DESCRIPTION/ BASIS FOR CAUTION:

SUSPECT PHOTO

VEHICLE INFORMATION

MAKE:	MODEL:	YEAR:	

REGISTRATION NUMBER:	STATE REG:	COLOR:

REGISTERED TO SUSPECT: ☒ YES ☒ NO

RENTAL CAR: ☒ YES ☒ NO

RENTED IN SUSPECTS NAME: ☒ YES ☒ NO

P.C. TO SEARCH VEHICLE IF FOUND OPERATING AND NOT LISTED ON AGREEMENT

SPECIAL VEHICLE IDENTIFICATION CHARACTERISTICS:

VEHICLE PHOTO

TARGET LOCATION INFORMATION

ADDRESS/ TARGET LOCATION:	CITY:

DESCRIPTION OF RESIDENCE OR AREA:

PRIMARY ENTRANCE /APPROACH:

SECONDARY ENTRANCE/APPROACH:

COUNTER SURVEILLANCE AT THE RESIDENCE OR WITHIN THE AREA:
☒ YES ☒ NO

DOGS/PETS AT THE RESIDENCE OR WITHIN THE AREA:
☒ YES ☒ NO

SMALL CHILDREN AT THE RESIDENCE OR WITHIN THE AREA:
☒ YES ☒ NO

OTHER PERTANENT INFORMATION ON THE RESIDENCE OR AREA:

LOCATION PHOTO

SPECIAL EQUIPMENT NEEDED	SPECIAL UNITS NEEDED	TYPE OF DRUGS EXPECTED
☒ BALISTIC SHEILD ☒ RAM ☒ HIT KIT ☒ LAP TOP ☒ FIRST AID KIT ☒ BINOCULARS ☒ NIGHT VISION ☒ DIGITAL CAMERA ☒ VIDEO CAMERA ☒ WIRELESS SURVEILLANCE	☒ S.W.A.T. TEAM ☒ K-9 UNIT ☒ CRIME SCENE TECH. ☒ COMPUTER CRIMES ☒ STATES ATTNY. ☒ C.I.D. ☒ ASSET FORFEITURE ☒ AVIATION SUPPORT ☒ FEDERAL AGENCY LIST: ▨	☒ MARIJUANA ☒ POWDER COCAINE ☒ CRACK COCAINE ☒ PCP (PHENCYCLIDINE) ☒ MDMA (ECSTACY) ☒ LSD (D-LYSYERGIC ACID) ☒ METHAMPHETAMINE ☒ PERSCRIPTION MEDICATION ☒ OTHER: ▨

CLOSEST HOSPITAL	CASE BACKGROUND
HOSPITAL NAME:	
ADDRESS:	
PHONE NUMBER:	

SCENARIO #1

SCENARIO #2

SCENARIO #3

OP'S PLAN PREPARED BY:	DATE:
OP'S PLAN APPROVED BY:	DATE:

"Trash Rips"
Operations and Procedures

"Trash Rip" operations can result in a wealth of information that provides both intelligence—meant to corroborate tips from informants—and result in evidence needed for probable cause. Be sure to consult with your local prosecutor's office to inquire on the law in your state in reference to "trash rips." Some states such as Hawaii prohibit searching a suspect's trash even if it is placed outside the curtilage of the home. The following procedures will ensure the proper way of conducting "trash rip" operations:

FIRST, KNOW YOUR TARGET AND NEIGHBORHOOD: Once you receive the tip begin your standard background checks: MVA (Motor Vehicle Administration), wanted checks, criminal histories, etc. Also find out the day and approximate time trash is picked up. You can usually find this out from the local police department or by calling the department of public works who handles that specific town or county. During this stage of the operation your main concern is to determine who resides at the residence, if there is pedestrian traffic in the area, or countersurveillance, and dogs!

SECOND, CONDUCT CURSORY SURVEILLANCE: At least two weeks prior to conducting the "trash rip," drive by the residence and make note where the trash cans are positioned. People normally keep their trash cans alongside of their residence or in the backyard prior to collection. This drive by surveillance should be conducted one to two days prior to the designated pickup day during the two-week period. When it comes time for collection, people usually put their trash out the night before. For this reason the investigator needs to respond during the late-night hours the day before trash collection or in the early morning hours on collection day. The purpose of all this is to first, document that the trash cans are normally kept at or near the residence; and second, that on trash day the suspect brings the trash cans from the residence to the curb for collection by refuge personnel. Over the two weeks prior surveillance conducted, you're actually showing a normal course of conduct exhibited by the suspect relating to the "abandonment" of his trash. By the suspect placing his trash at the "public" curbside (public roadway or sidewalk), where it could be easily obtained by an officer in an area he is lawfully allowed to be, the trash now becomes abandoned property accessible to citizens and law enforcement alike. The documentation of these events over the course of your surveillance is imperative and will be included in your probable cause for a search warrant if evidence from the operation is obtained. Another thing to do is to prepick a location to go through the trash that you retrieve. Try to pick a place with a substantial amount of light that is in a secluded area. Some places you can use are schools, churches, or industrial parks. All are fairly secluded and usually have adequate lighting to visually inspect the contents of the trash bags.

THIRD, CONDUCT THE TRASH RIP: Just as you previously made your observations during your cursory surveillance, respond to the suspect's residence doing a drive by first to confirm that the suspect put his trash out in the normal spot along the curbside. Have your partner drop you off down the road from the suspect's house so you can make your silent approach; although not too far because you have to carry trash bags all the way back. Once at the trash cans, quietly remove any loose material such as glass bottles, cans, etc., which would cause excessive noise during the removal of the bags. Make note though of loose boxes or debris that may have addresses or names written on them (i.e., pizza boxes, postal boxes, etc.), you will need all this later in the investigation. Once you have the trash bags return quietly to your getaway vehicle parked up the road.

FOURTH, MATERIALS NEEDED AND WHAT TO LOOK FOR: Once you received the trash and quietly made it to the getaway car, make your way to the predestinated area you have chosen to inspect the trash. You will need the following when conducting your inspection:

* a flashlight
* evidence bags
* rubber or latex gloves
* extra trash bags (make note of the color garbage bags used by the suspect—i.e., black, white, or clear. You will need to place the trash from the suspect's bag into a bag of the same color. Because you need to return the trash in the same colored bag to avoid possible detection by the suspect later)

Note: It is important to note in your search and seizure warrant "if" the trash bags were tied tightly at the top in a secure knot or some other method—i.e., twist ties. Also whether or not the trash bags had any exterior damage to them exposing the contents (i.e., slight damage, moderate damage, extensive damage, or no damage) This curtails the defense's anticipated contention that anyone walking by could have tossed the CDS item or evidence in the bag. In addition, make note as to where in the bag the item was located (i.e., bottom, middle, or top). Proper documentation of the location of evidence within the trash bag will prevent the defense's follow-up argument that someone (other than the defendant) untied the trash bag and placed the item inside. The jury or judge hopefully would see through this most ridiculous smoke screen and realize that it is impractical to dig to the bottom of a trash bag and place the item inside—especially while not being noticed!

During your inspection of the trash bags you will look for the following commonly found items:

- ***Plastic baggies with their corners ripped off:*** This is indicative of drug distribution by which the drug dealer places the drugs in the plastic baggie and positions it in one of the bottom corners. Once in this position the suspect then twists the plastic baggie around the drugs then rips off the remaining plastic baggie. The suspect then ties the twisted end in a knot or sometimes burns the ends to secure the contents within. The dealer will then throw the remaining plastic baggie in the trash. This remaining part of the plastic baggie is what speaks volumes as to the suspect distribution activities. The picture below shows what the investigator is looking for.

PLASTIC BAGGIE WITHOUT CORNER

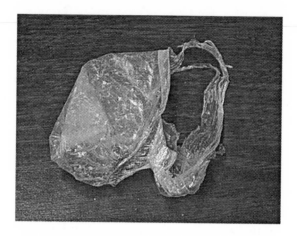

Make note of the white powder substance within the plastic bags shown above. Both field-tested positive for the presence of cocaine utilizing a cocaine swab (NIK swab).

KNOTTED PORTION OF PLASTIC BAGGIE

This knotted end that had been cut from a plastic baggie indicates that the suspect is most likely a user of the substance. Again, this field-tested positive for the presence of cocaine utilizing a cocaine swab. In addition, notice the clean cut above the knot. This indicates that the original supplier of the substance placed the cocaine in the corner of the plastic baggie, knotted

it to seal the contents, and then used scissors to cut the excess away.

- **Plastic baggies with CDS residue:** Users and dealers alike will discard plastic baggies that once contained CDS, either because they used the contents or transferred the CDS from the original package into smaller portions meant for distribution. For example: You rip the suspect's trash and subsequently find a gallon-size freezer bag with marijuana residue in it. It is a known fact that user quantities of marijuana come in small sandwich-sized plastic baggies. And that large plastic bag containers are commonly used for larger distribution quantities of marijuana. I have found through my experience that plastic freezer bags are used to contain at the most one pound of marijuana and at the least a quarter pound. Both amounts are indicative of a quantity to reasonably conclude an intent to distribute. Any less amounts are not practical due to the excess room in the freezer bag making it bulky and harder to conceal. The picture below shows the types of baggies the investigator is looking for.

PLASTIC BAGGIES

- **_Soda cans, plastic bottles, and smoking paraphernalia:_**
  Users of CDS are very adaptive in their methods of
  inhaling their drugs. Commonly found products of their
  ingenuity are soda cans with small holes poked in the
  top portion of the can that is dented inward slightly to
  provide a base for the CDS to remain stationary. On the
  left or right side of the can will be one small hole poked
  in the side. This hole is called a "shotgun hole." The
  purpose of this hole is to allow the smoke from the CDS
  to build up within the can by the user placing his thumb
  over top of it. The user then begins to inhale through the
  standard opening of the can; this causes a vacuum to
  build up within. Once the user feels the smoke entering
  their lungs they let go of their thumb that is covering the
  "shotgun hole" and receive a quick and heavy blast of
  the substance they are inhaling; hence the term "shotgun
  hole." It is also important to note the side that the
  "shotgun hole" is on. If the hole is on the left side this
  means that the user is predominantly left handed and
  vice versa if the hole is on the right side. When you have
  the suspect in custody and he is signing papers, make
  note of which hand he is using to write with. This is
  usually their strong hand. Follow up by asking them
  which hand is their strong hand. You will find that if
  they are right handed then the "shotgun hole" will also
  be on the right side and the opposite if left handed. The
  "shotgun hole" area is an excellent place to look for latent
  prints due to the thumb covering a larger area then other
  fingers, allowing for easier identification of ridge detail
  within the print. Often when the investigator is inspecting
  the trash they will not find the soda can in the manipulated
  form that the suspect used to inhale the substance. The
  suspect will commonly crush the can to prevent civilians
  or law enforcement alike from immediately noticing that
  the object is CDS paraphernalia.

Plastic soda bottles are used and constructed in the same way as cans but because of being made of plastic and easily melted by heat, a hole is cut on the side of the bottle and covered with aluminum foil that have tiny holes poked in it. The foil is indented slightly to allow for the CDS to remain stationary during use.

Cardboard cylinders from toilet paper or paper towels will also be used to make CDS smoking devices. They are converted in the same manner as the above plastic soda bottle. Due to cardboard being easily ignited a small hole is cut in the side of the cylinder. This hole is then covered with aluminum foil that has small holes poked in it acting as a screen to prevent heated debris from the CDS to be inhaled. The only difference in the above two devices is that a "shotgun hole" does not need to be added. The suspect will use the one open end to inhale from and the other as the "shotgun hole" They just cover the opposite end with their hand and when a sufficient vacuum has built up the user then uncovers the "shotgun hole" to complete the cycle.

The pictures below shows what the investigator is looking for.

ALUMINUM CANS

PLASTIC SODA BOTTLES

CARDBOARD INSERTS

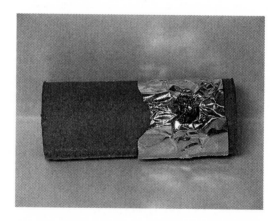

Note: It is imperative that the investigator use gloves when conducting their inspection. This is because there is a possibility of latent prints on the plastic baggies, containers, cans, plastic bottles, or other evidence found within. Although not required, it's wise to fingerprint any evidence obtained from the suspect's trash just to have that extra step when it comes to trial. You can bet that the defense will try to make it look like your hiding something or lazy if you don't at least try.

- ***Discarded Marijuana Cigarettes (Roaches):*** Marijuana users will, as a matter of habit, smoke their marijuana cigarettes then put them out in an ashtray or some other container (i.e., soda cans, beer cans, plastic bottles, etc). This discarded smoked portion of the marijuana cigarette (roach) will contain small amounts of marijuana that can be field-tested to confirm its identity. The picture below shows what the investigator is looking for.

MARIJUANA CIGARETTES

- ***Straws:*** Plastic straws are a common form paraphernalia used in the consumption of powder cocaine. These straws will be cut short, usually to a length of two and half to three inches long. Oftentimes the straw will still contain traces of powder cocaine that can be field-tested. I have found that rolling up a NIK Swab for cocaine and inserting it in the ends of the straw will normally give you the positive result you're looking for. This is due to minuet traces of powder cocaine residue left along the inner walls of the straw after use. The picture below shows what the investigator is looking for.

STRAWS

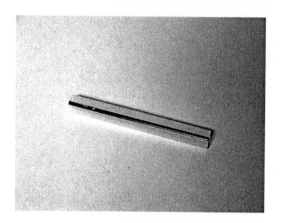

- ***Pieces of Steel Wool (Choy):*** Steel wool is frequently used in crack pipes to act as a filter and keep the crack cocaine stationary during consumption. It is a misconception within the drug community that the steel wool filters impurities. The fact is that no filtering properties occur by the use of steel wool. This steel wool is often referred to as *"choy"* on the street and will be found in all of your glass crack pipes known on the street as a "straight hitter" After repeated use of the glass pipe, carbon builds up within the steel wool and needs to be replaced with a fresh supply. The old steel wool is usually discarded in the trash without any thought, where it is ultimately retrieved by law enforcement and used as probable cause for a search warrant. Normally new steel wool is either copper colored or has a metallic finish to it. Old steel wool is blackened with carbon and sometimes has an oxidized layer surrounding it. The picture below shows what the investigator is looking for.

STEEL WOOL

STEEL WOOL-"CHOY"

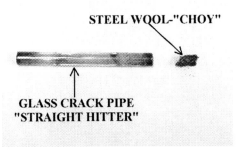

**GLASS CRACK PIPE
"STRAIGHT HITTER"**

- *Documents:* This is one of the most important articles of evidence you will retrieve from your trash rip. The intelligence gathered from documents discarded by the suspect is invaluable. Some of the documents you will find are:

1. *Financial Records and Receipts:* These records will give you the banks your suspect is using, account numbers, investment accounts, and balance information that can be used in financial investigations.

   In addition, receipts for custom car parts, vacations, or other items are very pertinent as well and should be kept to show what the suspect is purchasing with his money. Sometimes the receipt will list the method in which the purchase was made, whether by check (check number), credit card, or cash. Pay attention to the partial credit card account numbers listed on the discarded receipts because you can compare this to bank statements retrieved from the trash. Microsoft Excel is an excellent program to organize financial records once you have enough information on the suspect's purchases, account balances, and legitimate yearly income (if any at all). Excel or most spreadsheets can capture the required information and break it down into graphs/charts or visual exhibit, which makes it a lot easier for the judge or jury to see and understand.

2. *Postal Addresses:* The addresses of individuals who live at the residence can only expand on your criminal investigation. By obtaining the names and information concerning these individuals the investigator can run criminal histories on each person and reveal whether or not they have a history for drug violations or acts of violence. Both pieces of information can and will be used in your probable cause statement to obtain a search warrant. Further, the names of individuals gathered from mail and correspondence will independently corroborate information from your confidential informant or anonymous tip.

3. *Personal Letters and Notes:* It is no secret that individuals involved in drugs have dysfunctional relationships either with family members or friends. On numerous occasions I have found boyfriends or girlfriends who write to their significant other and complain about their drug use and how it affects their relationship. The same goes with friends who either are looking to get "high" with them or complaining about their use. These notes and letters are priceless when it comes time for trial because it shows predisposition in an unbiased manner.

DOCUMENTS

4. *Tobacco Shavings:* This is the tobacco that is discarded from a cigar. Once the tobacco is removed from the cigar it is replaced with quantities of marijuana. The cigars wrapping is then resealed with the marijuana inside and subsequently smoked. This is commonly referred to as a "blunt" on the street. As a result of constructing this smoking device the now-loose tobacco shavings are thrown away in the trash. When an investigator observes this, red lights should immediately start going off. In reality, there is absolutely no other reason the tobacco from a cigar should be removed, but to replace it with a controlled substance, i.e., marijuana or PCP "flakes" or "greens" (PCP laced with marijuana or parsley flakes). Officers on traffic stops should pay close attention for loose tobacco shavings in vehicles as well. I found you can be almost certain that the suspect in possession of these shavings is a marijuana user.

TOBACCO SHAVING

FIFTH, WRITE THE SEARCH WARRANT: If you have received numerous tips on the suspect or the suspect has a criminal history for drug violations, then one trash rip is enough, due to your investigation having numerous pieces of information all corroborating themselves independently. You don't want to chance the suspect or another individual in the area seeing what you're doing because this will surely jeopardize the investigation. But to be sure, check with your local prosecutor's office to get their thoughts on the expectations that the judges have pertaining to this type of operation. If the need for more financial information or the suspect has no CDS-related history or other tips concerning illicit activities then subsequent trash rips would need to be conducted to show a continuing course of conduct. Included at the end of this section is a sample search warrant based on a trash rip operation.

CASE LAW

California v. Greenwood
Supreme Court of the United States
486 U.S. 35, 108 S. Ct. 1625 (1988)

Police received information that the defendant Greenwood was involved in the trafficking of controlled dangerous substances. As a result, police began surveillance of the defendant's home. After confirming that vehicular and foot traffic matched the profile of an individual dealing in drugs, the police made arrangements for the local trash collectors to turn over the bags belonging to the defendant and to ensure that the neighbor's trash bags would not be mixed up with the defendants. The trash collectors retrieved the garbage left on the curbside in front of the defendant's residence and subsequently turned them over to the police for inspection. As a result of the inspection of the defendant's garbage numerous items indicative of narcotics use were located.

A search-and-seizure warrant was obtained to search the defendant's residence. The search revealed quantities of cocaine and hashish, which resulted in the defendant's arrest.

After being released on bail for the previous narcotics violations, the police again received complaints that the defendant was engaged in CDS activity. This time the police responded to the defendant's residence and retrieved the garbage bags left at the curbside for collection. Once again, police located items to indicate narcotic use within the garbage. Another search warrant was obtained for the residence where evidence of narcotic use and trafficking were found. The defendant was subsequently placed under arrest once again.

The United States Supreme Court found that "the warrantless search and seizure of the garbage bags left at the curb outside the Greenwood house would violate the Fourth Amendment only if [defendant] manifested a subjective expectation of privacy in [his] garbage that society accepts as objectively reasonable . . . . It may well be that [Greenwood] did not expect that the content's of [his] garbage bags would become known to the police or other members of the public" (*Id.*). This subjective assumption of privacy does not end the inquiry into the Fourth Amendment. "An expectation of privacy does not give rise to Fourth Amendment protection, . . . unless society is prepared to accept that expectation as objectively reasonable" *(Id.)*.

In this case, it can be concluded that the defendant "exposed [his] garbage to the public sufficiently to defeat [his] claim to Fourth Amendment protection. It is common knowledge that plastic garbage bags left on or at the side of a public street are readily accessible to animals, children, scavengers, snoops, and other members of the public" (*Id* at 1628-1629). In addition, Greenwood placed his garbage "at the curb for the express purposes of conveying it to a third party, the trash collector, who might himself have sorted through [the defendant's] trash or permitted others, such as the police, to do so" (*Id.* at 1629).

"Accordingly, having deposited [his] garbage 'in an area particularly suited for public inspection and, in a manner of speaking, public consumption, for the express purpose of having strangers take it,' [the defendant] could have had no reasonable expectation of privacy in the inculpatory items that [he] discarded" (*Id.*). All in all, the court concluded "that society would not accept as reasonable [the defendant's] claim to an expectation of privacy in trash left for collection in an area accessible to the public [.]" (*Id.*).

EXAMPLE OF "TRASH RIP" SEARCH AND SEIZURE WARRANT

APPLICATION AND AFFIDAVIT FOR SEARCH AND SEIZURE WARRANT

TO: The Honorable _____, Judge of the Circuit/District Court for Caroline County, State of Maryland.

Application is herewith made for a search-and-seizure warrant in that there is probable cause to believe that evidence relating to the crimes of distribution of controlled dangerous substances, possession of controlled dangerous substances with the intent to distribute and possession of controlled dangerous substances, as defined in the Maryland Code Annotated Criminal Law Article, Title 5 et seq. and Common Law Conspiracy to commit said crimes, dealing generally with controlled dangerous substances as amended and revised are being violated in and upon a certain residence identified as 121 Church Street, Apartment C, Greensboro, Caroline County, Maryland. The residence is described as a white colored, two story, multifamily home, with three separate entrances to each apartment. Directions to said residence is from Maryland Route 404, Denton, travel north on Maryland Route 313 toward the town of Greensboro, for approximately six miles. Make a left on to Sunset Avenue and travel for approximately one-fourth mile. Turn right on to Church Street; said residence is the first residence on the left side of Church Street, behind the Greensboro Town Post Office, with the door marked "121 C."

Said residence is further described as having an alleyway that runs along the south side of the property. The main door leading to Apartment C is located on the south side of said residence facing the alleyway on the first floor with "121 C" inscribed in black on the front of the door. The door is described as a white-colored door with an exterior light affixed above it. Apartment C is a second-floor apartment that is accessed through said door. The front of the residence has a covered porch with white-colored wooden post spaced evenly across the entire length. There are also two brick chimneys on both the north and south side of said residence which has a gray-colored shingled roof. Furthermore, the dwelling afore described can be positively identified by your affiant Henning.

Expertise

The name of your affiant is James Henning, detective, Caroline County Sheriff's Department, currently assigned to the Caroline County Drug Task Force. Your affiant has been a police officer for over four and a half years and has completed the basic training requirements for the Maryland Police Training Commission at the Anne Arundel County Police Academy, Davidsonville, Maryland, in which a portion of the training involved the identification and detection of controlled dangerous substances. Your affiant attended a one-day seminar on Drug Interdiction / Hidden Compartments in vehicles, sponsored by the United States Department of Justice—Drug Enforcement Administration (DEA), Maryland State Police and the Virginia State Chesapeake Bay Bridge Tunnel Police Academy. Your affiant also has completed fifty-six hours of instruction in Basic Criminal Investigation Techniques through Eastern Shore Criminal Justice Academy. Your affiant annually attends eighteen hours of in-service training for law enforcement officers, which included search and seizure law, Maryland case law, and various criminal law updates. Your affiant attended a total of 160 hours (four weeks) in Basic Drug Investigators school sponsored by the United States Department of Justice—Drug Enforcement Administration (DEA), which included confidential sources, case initiation and development, conspiracy investigations, domestic drug trends, diversion investigations, drug field testing, drug identification and pharmacology, street drugs and trafficking patterns, postal drug investigation, interview and interrogation, asset forfeiture and sharing, clandestine laboratory investigations, highway interdiction, tactical street operations, and vehicle containment and arrest. Furthermore your affiant is a graduate of the "Top Gun" Academy, for undercover drug investigators, sponsored by the Army National Guard, Multijurisdictional Counter Drug Task Force, which included but not limited to confidential informant and source management; case initiation, development, and investigation; Maryland case law; search and seizure Law; undercover surveillance techniques; conspiracy investigations; domestic drug trends; diversion investigations; drug field testing; drug identification and pharmacology; street drugs and trafficking patterns; postal drug investigations; interview and interrogation; asset forfeiture and sharing; clandestine laboratory investigations; highway interdiction; tactical street operations; and vehicle containment and arrest.

Your affiant, Detective James Henning has authored and assisted in the execution of numerous search-and-seizure warrants during his tenure as a law enforcement officer. Your affiant Henning has also made controlled purchases and hand-to-hand drug transactions of controlled dangerous substances. Your affiant Henning has successfully arrested and obtained convictions for numerous persons concerning violations of the Controlled Dangerous Substance Laws and had been considered an "expert" on numerous occasions in the area of controlled dangerous substance investigations throughout the Maryland State Judicial system.

Furthermore, your affiant receives training on a daily basis working on drug investigations for the Caroline County Drug Task Force.

BASIS FOR APPLICATION

In support of this application, and the basis for probable cause, your affiant deposes and says:

1) During the month of December 2000, your affiant personally spoke with a citizen source of information, hereinafter referred to as CS, in reference to John Doe selling

quantities of suspected cocaine to the Denton, Caroline County, Maryland area. The CS is physically known to your affiant, which has been established through investigation and subsequent face-to-face conversations. As a result of this conversation, the CS explained that it has personally observed Doe with ten ounces of cocaine in the recent past while at Doe's residence of 121 Church Street, Apartment C, Greensboro, Caroline County, Maryland.

Although this CS has never given information to a law enforcement agency before, your affiant has personally confirmed that the CS is gainfully employed and has been for a number of months, ultimately proving to be a lawfully contributing citizen of society.

The CS advised that it is familiar with the actions, traits, habits, and terminology of controlled dangerous substances. That the CS is familiar with the appearance, prices, and packaging of controlled dangerous substances for street-level sales, and that the knowledge and familiarity learned by the CS was obtained partly by the CS having personally used, distributed, and purchased controlled dangerous substances in the past.

Further, all information received from the CS concerning Doe has been successfully corroborated by your affiant either through surveillance or other investigative resources and has successfully proven to be a credible and reliable confidential informant.

2) During the month of March 2001, your affiant personally spoke with a confidential informant, hereinafter referred to as CI No.1. Said CI is physically known to your affiant, which has been established through investigation and subsequent face-to-face conversations. As a result of this conversation, the CI explained that it has personally observed John Doe, white male in his twenties, bring into Greensboro, Caroline County, Maryland, approximately six ounces of cocaine on a weekly basis. Doe would then distribute the cocaine from his apartment located at 121

Church Street, Apartment C, Greensboro, Caroline County, Maryland, directly to the street-level dealers as needed. The CI explained that Doe would commonly utilize rental vehicles to retrieve the cocaine from an unknown location in the city of Philadelphia, Pennsylvania. Then subsequently smuggle the cocaine back in a spare tire, which would be placed in the trunk of the rental car for transport.

Members of the law enforcement community have physically known this CI for approximately two years, whom for reasons of personal safety, security, and ongoing criminal investigations shall remain unnamed throughout this affidavit. During that time, this CI has given information, which has led to the issuance of two criminal arrest warrants for CDS violations, resulting in successful convictions. The CI is familiar with the use, packaging, and appearance of controlled dangerous substances, which has been verified by members of the Caroline County Drug Task Force through their training and experience. This CI has never given any fraudulent information to members of the Caroline County Drug Task Force, which all information received has been verified through a separate and independent investigation. As a result all information has been successfully corroborated and proven to be true and correct to the best of our ability. Your affiant does believe based on your affiant's experience with this CI, that this CI is proven to be a credible and reliable confidential informant.

3) During the month of April 2001, your affiant personally spoke with a confidential informant, hereinafter referred to as CI No.2, in reference to John Doe selling quantities of suspected cocaine to the Denton, Caroline County, Maryland area. Said CI is physically known to your affiant, which has been established through investigation and subsequent face-to-face conversations. As a result of this conversation, the CI explained that it has personally observed Doe with eight ounces of cocaine in the recent past while at Doe's residence of 121 Church Street,

Apartment C, Greensboro, Caroline County, Maryland. The CI stated that Doe routinely makes "runs" (street terminology for retrieving/transporting quantities of controlled dangerous substances to and from various locations) on a weekly basis in his new Acura Legend, which is black in color. Further, Doe's vehicle has a hidden compartment in it, which is controlled by a hydraulic system, securing a steel-vault-type container under the backseat, said the CI.

Although this CI has never given information to a law enforcement agency before, your affiant has personally checked the records of the National Crime Information Center (NCIC), the Criminal Justice Information System (CJIS—only used in Maryland), and local police department's criminal databases, and learned that this CI has never been arrested or charged with any offenses by a law enforcement agency. In addition to being a registered voter, your affiant has also determined that the CI is gainfully employed and has been for a number of months, ultimately proving to be a lawfully contributing citizen of society. Further, all information received from the CI concerning Doe has been successfully corroborated by your affiant either through surveillance or other investigative resources and has successfully proven to be a credible and reliable confidential informant.

4) On April 11, 2001, members of the Caroline County Drug Task Force, and I, responded to the Greensboro, Caroline County, Maryland area to conduct surveillance on the residence of 121 Church Street, Greensboro, Caroline County, Maryland. During this time while at our surveillance location, I observed a large amount of foot traffic going to and from the residence of 121 Church Street, Greensboro, Maryland. These individuals would arrive on foot or in their vehicles and subsequently enter the residence from a side entrance that faces an alleyway, which runs along the south side of said residence. Then shortly there after the individuals would exit the residence and leave the

area. This pattern continued steadily throughout the entire time we were conducting surveillance of the residence (1.5 hours). Through investigation it was learned that this was the apartment of John Doe.

5) I know—based on my training, knowledge, and experience—that individuals involved in the distribution of controlled dangerous substances will often have a high volume of people responding to and from their residence for the purposes of purchasing controlled dangerous substances. That these individuals will stay at the dealer's residence for short periods of time to complete the transactions then exit the residence and leave the area.

6) During the month of May 2001, I conducted cursory surveillance of 121 Church Street, Greensboro, Caroline County, Maryland. I found that the residents along Church Street, Greensboro, Caroline County, Maryland, usually set their household garbage out along the roadside that runs along the front of said residence to be taken away on Tuesday(s) of each week. I noted that the household garbage containers utilized by the residents of 121 Church Street, Greensboro, Caroline County, Maryland, would normally be placed at the roadside along the front of said residence for collection on Tuesdays; which is outside the curtilage of the residence along a public access roadway.

7) On May 1, 2002, members of the Caroline County Drug Task Force and I responded to the residence of 121 Church Street, Greensboro, Caroline County, Maryland, for the purposes of retrieving the trash from said residence. Upon arrival I noted that the garbage container utilized by 121 Church Street, Greensboro, Caroline County, Maryland, had been placed at the edge of the roadway along the front of said residence, where the garbage is commonly recovered by refuse collection personnel. I found that there were two garbage bags that were tied in a knot at the top, with no exterior damage exposing the contents. It should be noted that in order to retrieve the garbage bag I had to travel on

the public roadway and did not leave the boundaries of the pavement of that public roadway.

8) A search of the household garbage retrieved by me revealed three miscellaneous documents with the name John Doe written on it and the address of **121 Church Street, Apt C, Greensboro** along with the phone number **410-482-7404** In addition two of the documents had Doe's full name written on them with an address of **PO Box 564, Greensboro, Maryland**. Further inspection of the garbage bags revealed thirteen plastic baggies containing suspected cocaine residue. Each of the plastic baggies had their corners cut or twisted off.

9) The manner in which the plastic baggies were found indicated to me based on my training, knowledge, and experience that they had been used in the production and packaging of controlled dangerous substances specifically for the illicit purposes of street-level sales and distribution of same.

10) A portion of the above-described plastic baggies containing suspected cocaine residue was field-tested utilizing the NIK Swab field test kit which produced a positive result for the presence of cocaine—a schedule II controlled dangerous substance.

11) Surveillance conducted by members of the Caroline County Drug Task force, and the plastic baggies containing the suspected cocaine residue located in Doe's household garbage, independently corroborated the information given by both CI No.1, CI No.2, and the citizen source of information, in reference to illicit CDS activity occurring at the apartment of John Doe located at 121 Church Street, Apartment C, Greensboro, Caroline County, Maryland.

12) On June 18, 2001, I caused an inquiry through the Greensboro Post Office in reference to subscriber(s) / box holder information at the residence of 121 Church Street, Apartment C, PO Box 564, Greensboro, Caroline County, Maryland, 21639. As a result of this inquiry I received the following information:

Name: **Doe, John**
Address: **PO Box 564**
121 Church Street, Apartment C
Greensboro, Caroline County,
Maryland, 21639

13) On June 18, 2001, as a result of obtaining the above listed information, I caused a computer inquiry through the Maryland Motor Vehicle Administration (MVA), Federal Bureau of Investigation (FBI), and the Criminal Justice Information System (CJIS), concerning the suspect John Doe, with the following results:

MVA:
Doe, John
121 C. Church Street, Greensboro, Maryland, 21639
White Male, 5' 11", 170 lbs.
DOB: 11/25/81, Soundex No.: D-565-098-603-901
Valid class "C", Maryland driver's license.
CRIMINAL: No adult criminal history listed.

14) On June 18, 2001, I caused a computer inquiry through the Caroline County Department of Emergency Management, Residential Database for the owner/occupants of the apartment for 121 Church Street, Apartment C, Greensboro, Maryland, 21639, with the following results:

Name: **John Doe**
Address: **121 Church Street, Apartment C,**
Greensboro, Maryland, 21639.
Phone No.: **410-482-7404**

15) On June 18, 2001, I caused an inquiry through the Caroline County Emergency Management, Bell Atlantic ANI database concerning the phone number **(410-482-7404)**,

which was listed on a miscellaneous document found in John Doe's household garbage. As a result I obtained the following subscriber information:

Phone No.: **410-482-7404**
Name: **J. Doe**
Address: **121 Church Street, Apartment C, Greensboro, Maryland, 21639**

16) During the month of June 2001, I conducted cursory surveillance of 121 Church Street, Greensboro, Caroline County, Maryland. I found that the residents along Church Street, Greensboro, Caroline County, Maryland, usually set their household garbage out along the roadside that runs along the front of said residence to be taken away on Tuesday(s) of each week. I noted that the household garbage containers utilized by the residents of 121 Church Street, Greensboro, Caroline County, Maryland, would normally be placed at the roadside along the front of said residence for collection on Tuesdays, which is outside the curtilage of the residence along a public access roadway.

17) On June 26, 2001, members of the Caroline County Drug Task Force and I, responded to the residence of 121 Church Street, Greensboro, Caroline County, Maryland, for the purposes of retrieving the trash from said residence. Upon arrival I noted that the garbage container utilized by 121 Church Street, Greensboro, Caroline County, Maryland, had been placed at the edge of the roadway along the front of said residence, where the garbage is commonly recovered by refuse collection personnel. I found that there were two garbage bags that were tied in a knot at the top, with no exterior damage to the bag exposing the contents. It should be noted that in order to retrieve the garbage bag I had to travel on the public roadway and did not leave the boundaries of the pavement of that public roadway.

18) A search of the household garbage retrieved by me revealed three miscellaneous documents with the name John Doe written on them, and two other documents with the name Mary Jane. All the documents seized displayed the address of **PO Box 564, Greensboro, Maryland,** which I learned through previous investigation is registered to 121 Church Street, Apartment C, Greensboro, Caroline County, Maryland, 21639. Further inspection of the household garbage bags revealed one pack of EZ Wider rolling papers, eight plastic baggies containing suspected cocaine residue, each of the plastic baggies had their corners cut or twisted off. In addition, there were three suspected marijuana cigarettes containing suspected marijuana, and four plastic ziplock freezer bags containing suspected marijuana residue located as well. One of the plastic ziplock freezer bags was a gallon-size bag, which contained suspected marijuana residue. I also observed four empty boxes of small sandwich bags, each box once containing one hundred and fifty sandwich bags and loose cigar tobacco shavings scattered throughout both trash bags.

19) The manner in which the plastic baggies were found indicated to me—based on my training, knowledge, and experience—that they had been used in the production and packaging of controlled dangerous substances specifically for the illicit purposes of street-level sales and distribution of same. The gallon-size ziplock freezer bag containing suspected marijuana residue, indicated to me that it had contained a large quantity of marijuana. It has been my experience through previous controlled dangerous substance investigations that quantities of marijuana are typically package in plastic baggies proportionate to the amount of marijuana being sold. Based on this fact, the amount of marijuana that once was contained in the gallon-sized freezer bag indicated to me intent to distribute same. The fact that four sandwich bag boxes were found empty, each having the capacity of one hundred and fifty bags

each box; which is a total of six hundred sandwich bags, and that these sandwich bag boxes once contained the exact same size, style, and shape as the baggies found in John Doe's household garbage containing suspected cocaine residue and their corners were cut and/or twisted off, indicated to me that the plastic bags were used in the production, distribution, and sales of controlled dangerous substances. Furthermore, I have found on numerous occasions that EZ Wider rolling papers, as well as other brands of cigarette rolling papers, have all to often been used as paraphernalia for the specific purposes of the inhalation and abuse of marijuana.

20) A portion of the above-described plastic baggies containing suspected cocaine residue were field-tested utilizing the NIK Swab field test kit, which produced a positive result for the presence of cocaine, a schedule II controlled dangerous substance. Both the plastic ziplock bags containing suspected marijuana residue and the suspected marijuana cigarettes were field-tested utilizing the ODV reagent field test kit, which produced a positive result for the presence of marijuana, a schedule I controlled dangerous substance.

21) On June 26, 2001, I caused an inquiry through the Greensboro Post Office in reference to subscriber(s) / box holder information at the residence of 121 Church Street, Apartment C, PO Box 564, Greensboro, Caroline County, Maryland, 21639. As a result of this inquiry I received the following information:

Name: **Mary Jane**
Address: **PO Box 564**
121 Church Street, Apartment C
Greensboro, Caroline County,
Maryland, 21639

22) On June 26, 2001, as a result of obtaining the above-listed information, I caused a computer inquiry through the

Maryland Motor Vehicle Administration (MVA), Federal Bureau of Investigation (FBI), and the Criminal Justice Information System (CJIS), concerning Mary Jane, with the following results:

MVA:
Mary Jane
25879 Bursville Road, Denton, Maryland, 21629
White female, 5' 01", 106 lbs.
DOB: 12/31/80, Soundex No.: J-425-403-564-998
Valid class "C", Maryland driver's license.
CRIMINAL: No adult criminal history listed.

23) On July 1, 2001, I caused an Internet computer inquiry through *www.yahoopeoplesearch.com* for any or all information listed to John Doe, which produced the following results:

NAME: John Doe
ADDRESS: Greensboro, Maryland
PHONE No.: 410-482-7404

24) Your affiant avers that based upon the aforementioned investigation conducted from information supplied by CI No.1, CI No.2, and the confidential source of information pertaining to the illegal distribution of marijuana, cocaine, and the illicit abuse of controlled dangerous substances concerning John Doe; the previously mentioned surveillance conducted on the residence of 121 Church Street, Apartment C, Greensboro, Maryland, demonstrating a large amount of individuals frequenting said residence and subsequently observing patterns indicative of the distribution and sales of controlled dangerous substances; the aforementioned suspected cocaine, marijuana, and related paraphernalia used in the packaging, distribution, and sales of controlled dangerous substances located in the household garbage on two separate occasions; and your affiant's training,

experience, and knowledge as a member of the Caroline County Drug Task Force; that probable cause exists for a search-and-seizure warrant, and that the laws relating to the illegal distribution and possession with intent to distribute controlled dangerous substances, as hereinbefore cited, are being violated and will continue to be violated in and upon the premises and persons, located at 121 Church Street, Apartment C, Greensboro, Caroline County, Maryland.

25) Further, your affiant avers that controlled dangerous substance traffickers maintain books, records, receipts, notes, ledgers, airline tickets, money orders, and other papers relating to the transportation, ordering, sale, and distribution of controlled substances; that controlled dangerous substance traffickers commonly "front" (provide drugs on consignment) CDS to the clients. That the aforementioned books, records, receipts, notes, ledgers, etc., are maintained where the traffickers have ready access to them; that it is common for drug dealers to secrete contraband, proceeds of drug sales, and records of drug transactions in secure locations within their residences and/ or their businesses for their ready access and to conceal from law enforcement authorities. That the persons involved in drug trafficking conceal in their residences and businesses caches of drugs, amounts of currency, financial instructions, precious metals, jewelry, and other items of value and/or proceeds of drug transactions; and evidence of financial transactions relating to obtaining, transferring, secreting, or the spending of large sums of money made from engaging in narcotics trafficking activities; that when drug traffickers amass large proceeds from the sale of drugs that the drug traffickers attempt to legitimize these profits. Your affiant knows that to accomplish these goals, drug traffickers utilize, domestic banks and their attendant services, securities, cashier's checks, money drafts, letter of credit, brokerage houses, real estate, shell corporations, and business fronts.

26) Therefore, as a result of your affiant's involvement in this investigation, and your affiant's expertise in the investigation of narcotics and dangerous drugs, your affiant believes there is presently concealed within the aforesaid premises and vehicle(s) listed in the heading of this affidavit those items which have been previously mentioned as commonly found among drug traffickers, and ultimately constitute evidence that relate to the illegal distribution and possession with intent to distribute controlled dangerous substance, monies, records or accounts, ledgers, books, receipts, bank statements, and other proceeds as defined in the Maryland Code Annotated Criminal Law Article, Title 5 et seq. and Common Law Conspiracy to commit said crimes, dealing generally with controlled dangerous substances as amended and revised.

27) That electronic equipment, such as computers, telex machines, facsimile machines, currency counting machines, telephone answering machines, cell phones, pagers, PDAs/ computers, and related manuals are used to generate, transfer, count, record and store the information described above. Additionally, computer software, tapes and discs, *and the contents therein,* that contain the information generated by the aforementioned electronic equipment will need to be seized and examined, including but not limited to any and all electronic data processing and computer storage devices, such as central processing units; internal and peripheral storage devices such as fixed disks, external hard disks, floppy disk drives and diskettes, tape drives and tapes, optical storage devices, optical readers and scanning-devices; CD-ROM drives and compact disks and related hardware; digital cameras and digital storage media; operating logs; software and operating instructions or operating manuals; computer materials; software and programs used to communicate with other terminals via telephone or other means; and any computer modems, monitors, printers, etc., *that may have been used while engaging in the distribution of cocaine and or any other*

CDS-related activity, as defined in the Annotated Code of Maryland, as amended and revised.

28) In addition, you're affiant knows that CDS traffickers commonly maintain addresses and/or telephone numbers in books, papers, cell phones, pagers, PDAs or computers, which reflect names, address and/or telephone numbers of their associates in the trafficking organizations. Furthermore, your affiant Henning knows through training, knowledge and experience that drug traffickers take or cause to be taken photographs, or videographic images of themselves, their associates, their property, and their product, and that these traffickers usually maintain these photographs or videographic images in their possession.

29) Also, in support of this application, your affiant Henning avers that these individuals involved in the use and sales of controlled dangerous substances will also use their vehicles and/or outbuildings to conceal controlled dangerous substances not only from the police, but also from other dealers and addicts at the residence. That it has been your affiant's experience in searching residences and persons for drug violations, that your affiant, and other law enforcement officers have on numerous occasions found controlled dangerous substances in outbuildings and vehicles located at the residence, where the vehicles were either registered to or under the immediate control of the residence.

30) That the prior experience of your affiant indicates that narcotic/drug dealers/users have, carry, and use firearms to protect their operations. This protection is both from the police and other drug dealers/users who may try to seize the drugs or moneys gained from the operation. These firearms include handguns, rifles, shotguns, and semi/fully automatic weapons, and related equipment such as, but not limited to, ammunition, magazines, bayonets, bipods, tripods, ocular and laser-sighting scopes, etc. These weapons allow the drug dealer/user to operate freely and openly, also enabling them to retaliate against anyone they feel

threatened by. The possession of these weapons is an extension of the narcotic operation and/or conspiracy being conducted.

Your affiant, therefore prays that a search-and-seizure warrant be issued authorizing him, with the necessary and proper assistance, to:

A. Enter and search, the premises and outbuildings identified as 121 Church Street, Apartment C, Greensboro, Caroline County, Maryland (as completely described above); as well as any motor vehicles that are located at/or under the immediate control of on said property.

B. Search the persons and clothing of:

  1) John Doe: White Male, 5' 11", 170 lbs., DOB: 11/25/81;
  2) Mary Jane: White Female, 5' 01", 106 lbs., DOB: 12/31/80

As well as any other persons found in or upon said premises who may be participating in violations of the statutes hereinbefore cited, and who may be concealing evidence, paraphernalia, and controlled dangerous substances.

C. Open and search any safes, boxes, bags, luggage, compartments, or things in the nature thereof, found in or upon said premises, persons, outbuildings, and vehicles.

D. Seize all evidence, paraphernalia, controlled dangerous substances, papers, evidentiary items, books, records, receipts, notes, ledgers, and other papers relating to the transportation, ordering, purchase, and distribution of controlled dangerous substances. Papers, tickets, notes, schedules, receipts, and other items relating to domestic and international travel. Books, records, receipts, bank statements and records, money drafts, letters of credit, money order and cashier's checks, receipts, passbooks, bank checks, safe deposit box keys, and other items evidencing the obtaining, secreting, transfer, and/or concealment of assets and the obtaining, secreting, transfer, concealment and/or expenditure of money. United States currency, precious metals, jewelry, and financial instruments, including stocks and bonds in amounts indicative of the proceeds of illegal narcotics trafficking. Photographs of co-conspirators, of assets, and/or controlled substances. Indicia of occupancy, residency, and/or ownership of the premises described above, including, but not limited to, utility and telephone bills, canceled envelopes, and keys. Receipt for items evidencing the expenditure of the proceeds of drug distribution including, but not limited to, clothing, furniture, and electronic equipment. Receipts, bills, and money used in or incidental to the conduct or operation of controlled dangerous substance violations found in or upon said premises, outbuildings, and vehicles.

E. Search and seize any weapons such as handguns, rifles, shotguns, ammunition, and related equipment such as, but not limited to, magazines, bayonets, bipods, tripods, ocular and laser-sighting scopes, etc., in addition to any and all electronic equipment, such as, but not limited to, computers, telex machines, facsimile machines, currency counting machines, telephone answering machines, pagers, PDAs, cell phones, and related manuals used to generate, transfer, count, record and/or store the information described above. Additionally, computer software, tapes and discs, *and the contents therein,* that contain the information generated by the aforementioned electronic equipment will need to be seized and examined, by persons qualified to do so, and in a laboratory setting, including but not limited to any and all electronic data processing and computer storage devices, such as central processing units, internal and peripheral storage devices such as fixed disks, external hard disks, floppy disk drives and diskettes, tape drives and tapes, optical storage devices, optical readers and scanning-devices, CD-ROM drives and compact disks and related hardware, digital cameras and digital storage media, operating logs, software and operating instructions or operating manuals, computer materials, software and programs used to communicate with other terminals via telephone or other means, and any computer modems, monitors, printers, etc., *that may have been used while engaging in the distribution of controlled dangerous substances, and or any other controlled dangerous substance related activity;*

F. Arrest all persons found in or upon said premises who are participating in violations of the statutes hereinbefore cited.

G. Bring said persons, evidence, and paraphernalia before me, subscriber, or some other judge that of the state or county aforesaid, to be dealt with and disposed of according to law.

SUBSCRIBED AND SWORN TO, this _____ day of July in the YEAR OF OUR LORD, Two Thousand and One.

Affiant
Detective James A. Henning No. 0140
Caroline County Sheriff's Department—CID
Caroline County Drug Task Force

Before me, a district/circuit court judge of the State of Maryland, in and for Caroline County, this _____ day of July 2001, personally appeared Detective James A. Henning, personally known to me or properly identified, and he made oath that the contents of the a foregoing application and affidavit are true and correct to the best of his knowledge.

Time   Judge

Informant Operations

Procedures and Management

Informants play a major role in the day-to-day operations concerning drug investigations. Historically, it is the hard to get information rendered by these individuals that has resulted in the successful conclusion of many, many drug cases. One of the first objectives in developing an informant is to prove his or her reliability. The most common way an informant's reliability is established is to corroborate information received and document the informant's *past use*. An investigator who has a network of good, reliable, and credible informants, who provide information on a frequent basis, will inevitably be on top of things in his or her area, in most cases before it even happens. Although there are various types of informants, the ones that are in trouble with the law are the most likely candidates because of their close proximity to crime. With the proper handling and the identification of their motives, an informant can strike a lethal blow to the criminal underworld.

DEFINITION OF INFORMANTS: Any non-law enforcement person who, by reason of his familiarity or close association with criminals, supplies periodic, regular, or constant information about criminal activities to a police officer.

Types of Informants: There are six general types of informants used in police work:

INFORMANT

Along with the above-listed definition, an informant of this nature is few and far between. This is due to the fact that they will actively help the undercover officer to infiltrate a criminal organization, do "hand-to-hand" drug buys with suspects and even testify in a court of law as to the events that had taken place, all this to make the states case. When managing an informant of this caliber, the investigator must determine his or her motives. There are also some cases where informants who have severe charges placed against them will testify for greater consideration during sentencing. Through more often then not they are just "wannabes" looking for the thrill of being an undercover cop! This is not saying that they are not useful; on the contrary, they are the best an investigator can have. But when the case is done, due care in seeing that his or her safety is monitored is a must. After all they stuck their neck out for your case; it's only fair to make sure that nothing is happening to them as a result.

UNWITTING INFORMANT (U/W or UI)

This type of informant is used in an investigation by an undercover officer and doesn't even know he's assisting, hence the word "unwitting." This occurs when an undercover officer befriends an individual during the course of an investigation and subsequently infiltrates an organization, obtains information, or gets introduced into other criminal suspects.

Because the source of this information does not know he or she is providing information to the police and may be making statements against penal interest, this informant's information is considered "highly reliable." The information obtained from this informant is best used as probable cause and further it is irrelevant whether this informant is a witness to the actual crime or not! Although if the unwitting informant is an accomplice to the crime, his or her information alone is not enough to convict. There must be independent corroboration of the identity of the accused as having committed the crime in question.

If utilizing an informant of this nature, the officer should err on the side of caution. The possibility of suspicions being aroused by the unwitting informant is more likely to occur as time passes due to the undercover officer not actively being seen committing crimes as the unwittings would do. This is an art in and of itself when an officer takes on this feet because of the acting ability needed to consistently mislead the criminals into thinking they are like them.

The unwitting's suspicions can be remedied by staging a fake drug deal or other crime between two undercover officers for the unwitting's benefit. This will surely ease the suspicions and tensions of the unwitting—and it's business as usual!

CONFIDENTIAL INFORMANT OR COOPERATING INDIVIDUAL (CI):

A confidential informant is an individual who for whatever motive he/she has, wishes to cooperate with the police. This informant wants to remain confidential throughout the investigation and not have to testify or divulge their identity to the suspect. Unlike the "informant," the confidential informant will give information and only conduct "controlled purchases" from suspects. This manner of investigation enables the police to make the purchases of drugs for probable cause reasons to obtain a search warrant and not to actually charge the suspect for actual distribution. Utilizing this method enables the confidential informant to remain just that—confidential, because the suspects are not being charged with the distributions. We will talk about controlled purchases later in this text.

ANONYMOUS SOURCE OF INFORMATION (ASOI):

An anonymous source of information is an individual who wishes to remain anonymous even from the police. These informants do not conduct any type of purchase of drugs to assist the police or testify in a court of law. Only information is given concerning a suspect and/or actions conducted by the suspect. This informant is your anonymous callers/tipsters, or anonymous letters that are sent out to inform investigators about an area to be targeted (house, neighborhood, store, etc.) or a specific suspect or group. Because the source of the information is unknown, its reliability is suspect. Just an anonymous tip received by police (on its face) will not be the basis of a police action except a furtherance or initiation of an investigation. An anonymous tip can be used as a basis for reasonable articulable suspicion that can be used in conducting an investigatory stop (Terry Stop)" (Millwood v. State, 72 Md App 82 [1987]. This case dealt with an anonymous tip combined with the police officers observations, information, and experience with CDS-related investigations.) To utilize this information the investigator will actively need to corroborate the information received in order to use it in a report, affidavit, or a court of law. An uncorroborated tip is as useful as a rock! Unless the information received is otherwise confirmed to be accurate. Also refer to Watkins v. State, 7 MdApp 151 (1969) and Whitely v. Warden, 401 US 560 (1971)

CONFIDENTIAL SOURCE OF INFORMATION (CSOI):

This can be an individual or business that is known to the investigator but wishes to remain confidential throughout investigation. These informants do not conduct any type of purchase of drugs to assist the police. Only information is given concerning a suspect, group, or area that will further investigative leads into a case.

When dealing with sources of information it is safe to assume that an ordinary citizen presumably has no ties or connections with the criminal underworld. Therefore the court will likely assume based on common experience that such a person, regarded as a law-abiding citizen, is motivated by the same factors as law enforcement officials and considered "highly reliable" Although this does not mean that information obtained from a citizen source can be used for all purposes. Like all information obtained from informants it should be:

- fresh (recent),
- corroborated to the best of the officers ability,
- personally observed by the citizen source (the citizen personally observed the contraband or crime that occurred),
- and a basis for the informant's belief that a criminal act occurred (this can be accomplished by inquiring on the citizen sources past drug use or knowledge/experience with drugs or the impression that the suspect left the source with based on traits, habits, and actions symbolic of criminal mischief.)

Information from a citizen informant may be used for an investigatory stop if corroborated and the citizen source has been proven reliable in the past. Refer to Millwood v. State, 72 MdApp 82 (1987).

Also a citizen informant's information can provide probable cause if corroborated and the citizen informant has been proven reliable in the past. Refer to Watkins v. State, 7 MdApp 151 (1969) and Whitely v. Warden, 401 US 560 (1971)

An example of a CSOI is when the manager of a trailer park gives you numerous tag numbers of individuals frequenting a residence suspected of dealing drugs. Of course surveillance will be needed to corroborate what information the manager gives you, but nonetheless the information furthers your investigation. Some other examples of confidential sources of information are the following:

1. Citizens known to the investigator who routinely give information that can be used in your case,

2. Store owners,
3. Apartment managers,
4. Inmates in prison (watch their motives though!)

SOURCE OF INFORMATION (SOI):

Any person who is not a law enforcement officer that is known and provides information to an investigator. A source of information is not expected to become a witness to the case. This informant does not actively seek out criminal cases and is not usually associated with the criminal element. This type of informant was created for the mere means of description, accountability, and a way to document credibility. Some forms of investigative sources are as follows:

1. Rental car agencies,
2. Insurance agencies,
3. Federal, state, and local Information agencies.

MOTIVES OF INFORMANTS

As mentioned previously an informant's motive should always be considered when evaluating the information you are receiving. There are many forms of motivation informants project—it is your job to determine which one they possess in order to avoid any problems in an investigation.

A. *Fear:* Some people will become informants for the simple fact that they are afraid of the police catching them committing crimes or the actions performed by their criminal associates.
B. *Avoidance of Punishment:* A person who has been arrested for a minor crime may look for leniency if he or she gave up information. This pertains to the type of informant previously mentioned—arrested informants.

C. *Revenge:* A person may desire to be an informant to get back at his associates for a wrong they had committed against him/her. This person's story will need extra corroboration due to the fact that they will often exaggerate or give information concerning a case, which is completely erroneous. Their motivation is to get even for the wrong committed against them.

D. *Gratitude:* In this case, the informant wishes to cooperate as an expression of his appreciation for an officers interest and for the criminal and/or his family while he/she is in custody or jail.

E. *Gain:* An informant who has a special interest in the case will provide information that will help your case and at the same time getting the informant what he/she would need.

F. *Reformed:* This type of informant feels remorse for his/her actions and wishes to make things right and clear their guilty conscious.

G. *Competition:* These informers are often individuals who you know to be drug dealers themselves and supply information about their competition. This is done to eliminate the competitor and take over his territory, which will increase the informer's profits. Be aware though that false information is often provided to the investigator to divert suspicion from themselves or to attempt to gain information from the police as to what they know about him.

H. *Demented*: Some informers will need to be looked at very carefully due to their personality they exhibit. These are the individuals who call about every little thing—even if it does not pertain to your case. These persons are more of a bother than a value. But take their information and check it out. In some cases their information is useful and maybe that tip that brings you over the edge.

DEVELOPING INFORMANTS

- *Traffic Offenses / Civil Citations:*

    1. DWI/DUI (The prosecuting attorney may frown on this if the individual is an excessive repeat offender),
    2. Speeding tickets,
    3. "Must appear" violations,
    4. Underage drinking.

- *Criminal Arrests:*

    1. Drug violations,
    2. Any crime committed where the victim is the state. *Sometimes you can utilize informants who have minor criminal charges placed on them and have a victim involved, although this is not often practiced. In exchange for the informant's cooperation a lesser sentence can be sought out. Of course if restitution is an issue, the informant will have to pay the appropriate balance in order to be considered.

- *Wives or Girlfriends:*

    1. These individuals will need to be spoken to *quickly* while they are still angry at their boyfriends or husbands. Take advantage of the females' state of mind because if they make up before you retrieve the necessary information you are hard pressed to have another chance until the next argument. Some states have a law allowing the spouse to not testify against their husband. It is for this reason you should retrieve a written statement of the information given to you by the scorned wife at the time of initial contact. Then if the wife goes to court and invokes her right not to testify, you can introduce her written statement into evidence.

- *Attorneys:*

  1. Some attorneys will bring their clients to you if you have a good reputation of taking care of their interest when it is time for court. But leave the negotiating to the attorneys, that's what they get paid for. As a rule of thumb explain to the attorneys: *"anything done by your client will be brought before the state's attorney for consideration—but no promises will be made."*

SPECIAL CONSIDERATIONS WHEN HANDLING INFORMANTS:

- *Female Informants:* There should be no personal contact with female informants unless it is for official business and not without at least one other officer present. If at all possible have a female officer accompany you during your meeting. And all meetings should be conducted in a public place. Though there is a need for developing a rapport with informants, the female informant must be closely limited and carefully controlled due to sexual innuendos commonly used by female informants to befriend the investigator. And relationships between the officer and the female informant go without saying— *never* engage in a sexual or otherwise type of relationship with a female informant. The supervisor should have strict guidelines prohibiting close relationships or socializing between officers and female informants.

- *Drug Addicts:* One of the most effective informants is a drug addict. They commonly obtain firsthand information on how, when, and where individuals, stash houses, and types of organizations involved in the distribution of controlled dangerous substances go about their business. Because of their association with drugs they are in a position to introduce undercover officers into other drug users and their suppliers without arousing suspicion. Unfortunately, drug addicts also pose a serious threat to an investigator's safety. They have set up officers to fail in their investigation or participate in attempts to frame them. In addition, they are in a position to use the police to carry out personal vendettas against another individual by spreading false information, which would result in the investigation to fail. If this should occur, no future use of that informant should take place.

• *Payment to Informants:* Before paying informants for any information or action performed toward an investigation, the investigator should look at the information received and determine its value in the investigation. If only receiving information from an informant the investigator must ensure that the information received is valid and creditable before any payment is made. Once you have validated all the information received or the informant conducted a proper assignment, he or she should be paid in cash with the informant signing a receipt (Informant Contact Sheet) in the presence of two officers, who also should sign the receipt to verify that the receipt is valid. This receipt will then be placed in the informant's file for future auditing procedures. Refer to the example of an Informant Contact Sheet at the end of this chapter.

• *Juveniles:* When working with juveniles the investigator must have a signed parental permission slip from the juvenile's guardian. At no time is a juvenile to be placed in a situation where weapons are known to be present or the risk of serious bodily injury may occur. In essence, treat this kid as if he or she were your own. Refer to the example of a parental permission slip/contract at the end of this chapter.

OPERATING PROCEDURES
FOR MANAGING INFORMANTS

A. You meet with an informant and determine his/her motives and found that their information concerning your target is correct. Now you are ready to sign him up as an informant. Follow the procedures listed below as a guide to signing up informants. (Follow your department's policies and procedures in this instance. In the event that you do not have a policy try this and see if it suits your needs.)

- *Open an Incident Report:* Categorize the report as "CI Debriefing." Fill out your standard information in each field of the incident report. The IR should not have anything specific about the informant. Do not list the name, physical description of the informant/suspect, or any specific addresses. Next, in the narrative section write:

   "On *(insert date)*, I, Detective John Doe No. 0744, met with an individual who desired to become a confidential informant and assist with CDS related investigations in the Caroline County, Maryland, area."

   The narrative is short and to the point. This is because a standard incident report, or any police report for that matter, is part of public information. This means that any person, including the bad guys, are able to get a copy of your report. To get around this try the "confidential memorandum" approach. Refer to the example of an Informant debriefing incident report at the end of this chapter.

- *The Confidential Memorandum:* The confidential memorandum is just as it sounds—confidential. This means that only law enforcement personnel are able to view this report. Further, the chances of a defense attorney to actually be able to obtain this document are slim to none due to what is called the "informer's privilege." The benefit of this report is that it is not part of public record. In both the incident report and the confidential memorandum the CI's name is *never* to be used. In its place when talking about the CI refer to him or her as just that "CI." Another important fact is that you never refer to the CI in your debriefing report as a he, she, him, or her. You will refer to the CI as "it" in an effort to hide the CI's sex and cause more confusion to the defense should this report have to be called in to court. Refer to the example of an informant debriefing confidential memorandum at the end of this chapter. Now is the time to start your debriefing report (confidential memorandum). Some things you will include would be the following:

5. Introduction:

    A. Identify yourself,
    B. Your current assignment,
    C. And list everyone present during the debriefing.

Note: As mentioned earlier in the text, if the CI is the opposite sex of the investigator, then there should be a witness present during the interview and any subsequent contact.

6. Identify how the CI was developed (refer to the types of informants section). Listed below are four of the most common informants you will run into:

    A. Criminal Arrest

        1) Identify the arresting officer and their agency/unit;
        2) Briefly list the circumstances of their arrest, i.e., a traffic stop which lead to a CDS arrest etc.;

*Note:** If a resisting arrest is the cause of the informant's problems the investigator should consult with the original arresting officer before interviewing the CI out of courtesy.

3) List the charges pending against the CI in your debriefing report.

B. A Volunteer

1) Identify motives (refer to motives of informants section)

C. Mercenary

1) Explain in detail any financial agreements made for cooperation. For example:

   A. Payment value for controlled buys
   B. Payment value for introductions
   C. Payment value for information

2) All financial arrangements must be approved by the appropriate unit or section supervisor.

D. Vengeance

1) Identify motives (refer to motives of informants section)

   Note: You will have a lot of prisoners who display vengeance to past or present criminal associates. This is due to them feeling forgotten about and used. All the more reason to check and recheck any information this potential informant gives you to ensure the informant is not just giving you what you would like to hear just so you will pull his associate up or raid their residence.

Remember: corroborate every bit of information given to you to the best of your ability.

7. Document the fact that **no promises** have been made.

   A. Document the potential of a formal contract between the informant and the prosecuting attorney (if applicable).

   1) Contact the local prosecuting attorney if the suspect is attempting to work off charges. A local prosecuting attorney should prepare/approve formal contracts.

8. Document known criminal activity involving suspects and groups to include *all* potential targets and their associates.

   A. Identify all suspects and associates

   1) Full description, personal identifiers and ethnicity;
   2) Indicate all criminal activity being conducted by the suspect and associates;
   3) Known hangouts;
   4) List vehicle information, telephone numbers, cell phones, and pagers, etc.;
   5) Any violence associated with the target or associates

   B. Identify the Crime

   1) CDS activity connected to the targets and their associates:

   A. List the type of drug
   B. List the quantities
   C. Prices

D. Supplier information
E. Packaging methods
F. Concealment methods
G. Identify customers
H. Weapons
I. Animals at residence (i.e., dogs, snakes)
J. Violence
K. Children present at residence (include age)
L. Spouses

2) Other criminal activity connected to the targets and their associates:

A. Homicide information
B. Shootings
C. Theft
D. Auto theft
E. Firearms violations
F. Anything else

9. Corroborate information received from the informant concerning the named targets and associates.

A. Conduct investigative checks

1) NCIC and your statewide criminal database
2) Wanted checks
3) The Motor Vehicle Administration
4) And your local intelligence databases
5) Anything else that would corroborate the CI's statements.
    *Include your original printouts in your debriefing case file.

10. Indicate what type of cooperation the CI is willing to provide.

    A. Information only
    B. Controlled buys
    C. Introductions

- *Confidential Informant History Sheet:* A crucial part of the informant process is the "Confidential Informant History Sheet." This sheet should include a picture of the CI, a thumbprint, and any and all personal information pertaining to the informant. In addition this sheet will have the number given to the informant (i.e., CI-0386) so you can reference your CI numbers to that particular individual. This is needed in case the CI has turned up dead, the CI rips you off for your buy money, or if the CI has just plain vanished without a trace. Refer to the example of a Confidential Informant History Sheet at the end of this chapter. Further, turn in with this sheet the following original printouts:

  1. Wanted checks (stating that the CI *is* or *is not* wanted)
  2. Criminal history
  3. Driving record
  4. Any vehicles registered to the CI
  5. Parole and probation checks
  6. If applicable, juvenile records

- *Confidential Informant Contact Sheet*: Next you should complete a "Confidential Informant Contact Sheet." This is a form that documents the information received from the CI and anything good or bad surrounding the CI's information. This sheet is completed every time you have contact with your CI, i.e., the phone or personal contact. This form also acts as documentation of the payments and/or the quantity of CDS bought or seized as a result of the CI's cooperation. In essence, this form is a running record showing the credibility of your confidential informant. These sheets may save your case when the defense challenges the credibility and reliability of your informant's information. These contact sheets can also dispel the defenses contention that your informant was paid an enormous amount of money to "set up" (as they like to put it) their client. This form should not be displayed to the defense unless the informant is testifying. This is due to the informant's signature on the sheet showing that they received their payment. Remember if it is not documented it never happened! Refer to the example of a Confidential Informant Contact Sheet at the end of this chapter.

• *Confidential Informant Catalog:* A binder should be kept to categorize and correlate the CI number to the specific individual's name. This is a quick and easy way to look up basic information about a CI. In addition, this catalog should also indicate whether a CI is an "active CI" or a "deactivated CI." An "active CI" is an individual who continuously or periodically does investigations or gives information to the police. A "deactivated CI" is an individual who once was in the active status and conducted investigations with police, but has since ceased to continue on a regular basis to give information or cooperate in any manner. A CI audit should be done on a six-month cycle. This audit is performed to "deactivate" any CI who is not participating actively or periodically in police investigations. The supervisor should review the CI catalog and make up a list of the active CIs. This list is then given to the perspective investigator for whom the CI belongs to. The investigator will make the determination on whether or not to "deactivate" a CI or not. If an investigator "deactivates" a CI, the investigator needs to accomplish the following:

1. Do an informant contact sheet filled out with the pertinent CI information and include in remarks the following: "Biannual CI Wanted and Criminal Check"

2. Complete a confidential memo explaining specifically why this informant is being "deactivated." (Refer to examples of these memos at the end of this chapter.)

3. In addition to that, the investigator should conduct and submit a wanted check on the CI prior to "deactivation"

If an investigator is keeping a CI on "active status," then the investigator needs to:

1. Do an informant contact sheet filled out with the pertinent CI information and include in remarks the following: "Bi-annual CI Wanted and Criminal Check."

2. Submit an updated criminal history, motor vehicle check, and wanted check.

This all gets submitted to the supervisor who in turn places this paperwork in the CI's personal file and subsequently checked off in the catalog as in "active status" or "deactivated status" In the event that a CI wishes to cooperate again, after being "deactivated," the investigator needs to go through the CI personal file and deactivation memos prior to re-activating a CI. This is done to ensure that the CI has not been "black listed" (determined to be uncredible or reliable) for some reason.

EIGHT STEPS OF SUCCESSFULLY MANAGING INFORMANTS:

1. *IDENTIFYING AND SCREENING POTENTIAL INFORMANTS:* This will be determined by the officer's experience handling informants over his career. The main objective is to be able to weed out the informants who just "talk the talk" and who can actually do what they say.

2. *RECRUITMENT:* By developing a rapport with people and explaining the benefits of cooperating with law enforcement, you will eventually have a network of informants and sources that will supply you with information almost daily. In addition, clearly explain your payment policy for information/cooperation supplied by the informant. If this is an arrest, be sure to explain in detail what the prosecutor is willing to do for the informant if they cooperate (refer to developing informants).

3. *ESTABLISHMENT:* Document the informant's or source's track record of information supplied to the police. Completing "CI contact sheets" on informants will establish a true picture of the informant's performance and will prove invaluable in court if the informant is required to testify. It's important to maintain your CI files accurately by completing annual background checks as well as contact sheets to document their performance.

4. *TRAINING:* Yes, informants will need to be trained on how to complete the task given. They do not know the laws like you do, so you will need to educate them on how to complete the task given. Once an informant is properly trained and has completed several investigations for you, they will then become self-motivated and skilled on generating cases on their own by identifying potential targets.

5. *DEVELOPMENT:* Every informant/source has limitations. You must be able to identify and work with the informant's limitations. For instance, if the informant does not feel comfortable going into suspects' houses to complete controlled buys, then you will need to adapt to this and come up with an alternative plan of action.

6. *MAINTENANCE:* The maintenance of an informant will need to constantly be assessed. If the informant is a constant source of information, be sure not to "burn" them in an investigation. They are no good to you if they cannot interact within the community. By not exposing

the informant/source to certain situations will help to prevent them from being restricted and perform to their maximum potential.

7. *UTILIZATION:* Never let an informant go stale. Always *motivate* them to find new cases for you on their own or at your direction. Contact them by phone or in person at least once a month if you have not worked with them for a while. The informant that goes by the wayside is a waste of investigative resources. It will take more time and effort later to develop a rapport with the informant later than if you had continually kept in contact with them. Remember, informants are what makes an investigator successful and on top of his game. So take care of them, and they will take care of you.

8. *CONTROL:* This has to be the most important aspect of managing informants. The amount of control an investigator has over his informants can make the investigator a success or land him/her in the hot seat with the administration or, even worse, criminally. Under no circumstances should the informant be allowed to run any aspect of the investigation regardless of how insistent or argumentative the informant may be. They must realize right from the start that *you're the boss* and that there are reasons that things are done the way they are done! Lose control of an informant during an investigation and you can kiss your case goodbye, if not then it will sorely embarrass you later in court.

THE INFORMANT CONTRACT

*   A contract between the informant and the police should be completed on every CI if possible. The informant contract should spell out the expectations of the CI's capacity and desired outcome of future investigations. The following is what each contract should cover among other details that the prosecutor sees fit:

1. That the defendant (the CI) understands that only productive results will benefit him/her and not simply good faith, efforts, and attempts.
2. That the defendant be truthful and submit to a polygraph examination and random urinalysis upon demand.
3. The defendant may be released from any and all obligations at their pleasure. In this event the state reserves the right to not be bound to their part of the agreement, and there will be no retribution against the CI unless they jeopardize the subsequent investigation or other investigations known to the defendant during his/her involvement with the police.
4. The objectives of the investigation such as persons, type of drugs, etc.
5. The methods to be used such as controlled buys, informant testimony, recorded conversations, written statements, etc.
6. And include an agreement, which releases the law enforcement agency from liability in the event of the informant being hurt while actively working with the police or even claiming workman's compensation or unemployment benefits.

*An example of an informant contract is included at the end of this chapter.

FIRST-TIME INFORMANTS OR CITIZENS

• Sometimes prosecutors and officers think that an individual giving information or doing buys and who has never been an informant before or given information as a source can't be used in the probable cause in a search warrant. This is not the case. In the event that you have an individual who wishes to provide information or participate actively in an investigation, all that is needed is the background of this individual along with corroboration of the information received. If the informant does not have a criminal background put that in the affidavit. Further, if the informant is gainfully employed, even a registered voter, and seems to be a productive citizen in society put that in the affidavit as well. If the individual is a first-time informant who has a criminal record, is not employed, and does not have a steady residence but still wants to remain anonymous throughout the investigation, then the officer will need to submit a lot of corroborative detail in the affidavit in order to satisfy the judge and ultimately surpass a possible suppression hearing that could be brought forth later at trial.

EXAMPLE OF CONFIDENTIAL INFORMANT (CI) AND CITIZEN/CONFIDENTIAL SOURCE (CS) FIRST-TIME NARRATIVE FOR AFFIDAVIT—CLEAN RECORD

"During the month of December 2002, your affiant personally spoke with a confidential informant, hereinafter referred to as CI, in reference to John Doe selling quantities of suspected cocaine to the Denton, Caroline County, Maryland area. Said CI is physically known to your affiant, which has been established through investigation and subsequent face-to-face conversations. As a result of this conversation, the CI explained that it has personally observed Doe with eight ounces of cocaine in the recent past while at Does residence of 123 Shore Highway, Denton, Caroline County, Maryland. The CI stated that Doe routinely makes 'runs'—street terminology for retrieving/transporting quantities of controlled dangerous substances to and from various locations-on a weekly basis in his new Acura Legend, which is black in color. Further, Doe's vehicle has a hidden compartment in it, which is controlled by a hydraulic system, securing a steel-vault-type container under the backseat, said the CI." (Make sure to put in as much personal information about the suspect within the narrative of the CI or CS's statement. This demonstrates their "inside" information concerning the suspect and only further corroborates other aspects of the investigation.)

"Although this CI has never given information to a law enforcement agency before, your affiant has personally checked the records of the National Crime Information Center (NCIC), the Criminal Justice Information System (CJIS-only used in Maryland), and local police department's criminal databases, and learned that this CI has never been arrested or charged with any offenses by a law enforcement agency. In addition to being a registered voter, your affiant has also determined that the CI is gainfully employed and has been for a number of months, ultimately proving to be a lawfully contributing citizen of society. Further, all information received from the CI concerning Doe has been successfully corroborated by your affiant either through surveillance or other investigative resources and has successfully proven to be a credible and reliable confidential informant."

EXAMPLE OF CONFIDENTIAL INFORMANT (CI) AND CITIZEN / CONFIDENTIAL SOURCE (CS) FIRST-TIME NARRATIVE FOR AFFIDAVIT—BAD RECORD

"During the month of December 2002, your affiant personally spoke with a confidential informant, hereinafter referred to as CI, in reference to John Doe selling quantities of suspected cocaine to the Denton, Caroline County, Maryland, area. Said CI is physically known to your affiant, which has been established through investigation and subsequent face-to-face conversations. As a result of this conversation, the CI explained that it has personally observed Doe with eight ounces of cocaine in the recent past while at Doe's residence of 123 Shore Highway, Denton, Caroline County, Maryland. The CI stated that Doe routinely makes 'runs'—street terminology for retrieving/transporting quantities of controlled dangerous substances to and from various locations—on a weekly basis in his new Acura Legend, which is black in color. Further, Doe's vehicle has a hidden compartment in it, which is controlled by a hydraulic system, securing a steel-vault-type container under the backseat, said the CI." (Make sure to put in as much personal information about the suspect within the narrative of the CI or CS's statement. This demonstrates their "inside" information concerning the suspect and only further corroborates other aspects of the investigation.)

"Although this CI has never given information to a law enforcement agency before, your affiant has personally confirmed that the CI is gainfully employed and has been for a number of months, ultimately proving to be a lawfully contributing citizen of society.

The CI advised that it is familiar with the actions, traits, habits and terminology of controlled dangerous substances. That the CI is familiar with the appearance, prices, and packaging of controlled dangerous substances for street-level sales, and that the knowledge and familiarity learned by the CI was obtained partly by the CI having personally used, distributed, and purchased controlled dangerous substances in the past.

Further, all information received from the CI concerning Doe has been successfully corroborated by your affiant either through surveillance or other investigative resources and has successfully proven to be a credible and reliable confidential informant."

EXAMPLE OF CONFIDENTIAL INFORMANT (CI) AND CITIZEN / CONFIDENTIAL SOURCE (CS) (PAST USE/ OR CURRENT USE) NARRATIVE FOR AFFIDAVIT

"During the month of July 2001, your affiant personally spoke with a confidential information, hereinafter referred to as CI. Said CI is physically known to your affiant, which has been established through investigation and subsequent face-to-face conversations. As a result of this conversation, the CI explained that it has personally observed Ricky Clark, white male in his midtwenties, bring into Federalsburg, Caroline County, Maryland, approximately a one-fourth to a one-half kilogram of cocaine (over sixteen ounces of cocaine) on a weekly basis. Clark would then distribute the cocaine from the Brooklyn area directly to the street-level dealers as needed. The CI explained that Clark would commonly utilize rental vehicles to retrieve the cocaine from an unknown location in the city of Philadelphia, Pennsylvania. Then subsequently smuggle the cocaine back in a spare tire, which would be placed in the trunk of the rental car for transport." (Make sure to put in as much personal information about the suspect within the narrative of the CI or CS's statement. This demonstrates their "inside" information concerning the suspect and only further corroborates other aspects of the investigation.)

"Members of the law enforcement community have physically known this CI for approximately two years, whom for reasons of personal safety, security, and ongoing criminal investigations shall remain unnamed throughout this affidavit. During that time, this CI has given information, which has led to the issuance of two criminal arrest warrants for CDS violations, resulting in successful convictions. The CI is familiar with the use, packaging, and appearance of controlled dangerous substances, which has been verified by members of the Caroline County Drug Task Force through their training and experience. This CI has never given any fraudulent information to members of the Caroline County Drug Task Force, which all information received has been verified through a separate and independent investigation. As a result all information has been successfully corroborated and proven to be true and correct to the best of our ability.

Your affiant does believe based on your affiant's experience with this CI, that this CI is proven to be a credible and reliable confidential informant."

Note: Officers should always include in their affidavit when utilizing informants who have worked for the police in the past/present the following information:

1. How often the informant has been used;
2. The nature or character of the investigations the informant has been used (i.e., drugs, burglary, stolen property, arson, etc.);
3. How many times the information given by the informant has proved to be true and correct;
4. Whether the information has led to the arrest of the subject of the information;
5. Whether the subsequent prosecution led to a conviction and if applicable any seizures of assets (do not name what assets seized).

EXAMPLE OF ANONYMOUS SOURCE (CALLER/ LETTER) NARRATIVE FOR AFFIDAVIT

"During the month of July 1999, your affiant received a phone call from an individual who wished to remain anonymous. The anonymous source of information, herein after referred to as ASOI, explained that Jeremy Klein who lives on Baltimore Avenue, Ridgely, Maryland, was currently growing quantities of marijuana in one of his outbuildings. The ASOI went on to state that it has personally observed Jeremy Klein recently sell approximately one hundred marijuana plants from his Baltimore Avenue residence. The plants were allegedly being transported in a large van from Jeremy Klein's residence to an unknown out-of-county location to be processed and packaged for distribution." (Make sure to put in as much personal information about the suspect within the narrative of the CI or CS's statement. This demonstrates their "inside" information concerning the suspect and only further corroborates other aspects of the investigation)

"The ASOI explained that it is familiar with the actions, traits, habits and terminology of controlled dangerous substances. That the ASOI is familiar with the appearance, prices, and packaging of controlled dangerous substances for street-level sales, and that the knowledge and familiarity learned by the ASOI was obtained partly by the ASOI having personally used, distributed, and purchased controlled dangerous substances in the past."

Note: If the information is obtained from an anonymous caller, try and corroborate the caller's knowledge on the suspect and the drugs allegedly used or distributed. In turn document this information in the narrative. Use the questions below as a guide.

1. Have they ever used drugs?
2. What kind of drugs and how often did or do they (the anonymous caller) use? Is it occasionally, socially, or are they addicted?
3. And most importantly how did they come about their information? Through personal observations or knowledge, rumor (hearsay), or other method?

EXAMPLE OF CONFIDENTIAL SOURCE (CALLER/ INPERSON) NARRATIVE FOR AFFIDAVIT

"During the month of July 2001, I received information from a confidential source of information, hereinafter referred to as CSOI, who advised your affiant that Ricky Clark, white male in his midtwenties, brings in to Federalsburg, Caroline County, Maryland, approximately a one-fourth to one-half kilogram of cocaine (over sixteen ounces of cocaine) on a weekly basis. Clark would then distribute the cocaine from the Brooklyn area directly to the street-level dealers as needed. The CSOI explained that Clark would commonly utilize rental vehicles to retrieve the cocaine from an unknown location in the city of Philadelphia, Pennsylvania. Then subsequently smuggle the cocaine back in a spare tire, which would be placed in the trunk of the rental car for transport.

Members of the law enforcement community have physically known this CSOI, whom for reasons of personal safety and security shall remain unnamed throughout this affidavit, for approximately two years. During that time, this CSOI has given information, which has led to the issuance of two criminal arrest warrants for CDS violations. The CSOI is familiar with the use, packaging, and appearance of controlled dangerous substances, which has been verified by members of the Caroline County Drug Task Force through their training and experience. This CSOI has never given any fraudulent information to members of the Caroline County Drug Task Force, which all information received has been verified through investigative corroboration. Your affiant does believe based on your affiant's experience with this CSOI, that this CSOI is proven to be a credible and reliable source of information."

EXAMPLE OF SOURCE OF INFORMATION NARRATIVE FOR AFFIDAVIT

On February 16, 2000, I spoke with the management of Enterprise Leasing-Easton satellite office who explained that the renter of the vehicle listed under Maryland registration No.: HXP-625 was Sydney Jacobs. As a result I received the following information from the rental agreements:

- Name: Sydney Carl Jacobs
- DOB: 09-10-72, Height: 5' 09", Weight: 185lbs.
- Soundex No.: J-520-149-067-704
- Address: 108 Forest Park Apartments, Preston, Maryland
- Home Phone No.: 410-234-3285

EXAMPLE OF UNWITTING INFORMANT NARRATIVE FOR AFFIDAVIT

"During the week of March 26, 2000, your affiant made contact, via telephone, with an unwitting suspect, herein after referred to as U/W. The purpose of this conversation was to make an additional purchase of marijuana. During this time, a drug conversation ensued where the U/W explained that they could get me the marijuana I was asking for, but I would have to pick the U/W up in Ridgely, Caroline County, Maryland, and take the U/W to their supplier's residence on Holly Road in Ridgely to purchase the marijuana."

Note: When dealing with unwittings in reports, replace the unwitting's name with U/W or U/I. This is done to avoid a potential retaliation against the unwitting by the main target for his or her stupidity and further afford the undercover officer a little more anonymity in the investigation.

THE PROTECTION OF THE INFORMANT'S IDENTITY IN COURT

The court system of the United States has continuously upheld the confidentiality of the use of informants in law enforcement operations as a necessary evil in the fight against crime. This has been termed the "informer's privilege." This allows the government to withhold from disclosure the identity of persons who furnish information of violations of law to officers who enforce that law. "The purpose of the privilege is the furtherance and protection of the public interest in effective law enforcement. The privilege recognizes the obligation of citizens to communicate their knowledge of the commission of crimes to law-enforcement officials and, by preserving their anonymity, encourages them to perform that obligation" *Roviaro v. United States, 353 U.S 53, 59, 77 S. Ct. 623, 627*

(1957). "The scope of the privilege is limited by its underlying purpose. Thus, where the disclosure of the contents of a communication will not tend to reveal the identity of an informer, the contents are not privileged" *(Id.* at 60, 77, *S. Ct.* at 627). "Likewise, once the identity of the informer has been disclosed to those who would have cause to resent the communication, the privilege is no longer applicable. A further limitation on the applicability of the privilege arises from the fundamental requirements of fairness. Where the disclosure of an informer's identity, or of the contents of his communication, is relevant and helpful to the defense of an accused, or is essential to a fair determination of a cause, the privilege must give way. In these situations the trial court may require disclosure and, if the Government withholds the information, dismiss the action" (Roviaro at 60-61, 77 *S.* Ct. at 627-628).

It is important to note though that there is no fixed rule pertaining to disclosure of an informant. "The problem is one that calls for balancing the public interest in protecting the flow of information against the individual's right to prepare his defense" *(Id.* at 62, 77 *S. Ct.* at 628-629). Consequently, a court's decision to compel the disclosure of an informant's identity will depend on "the particular circumstances of each case, taking into consideration the crime charged, the possible defenses, the possible significance of the informer's testimony, and other relevant factors" *(Id.* at 62, 77 *S. Ct.* at 629).

With the proper handling and documentation of interactions between suspects and the informant, law enforcement can utilize this technique in court to assist in the apprehension and convictions of criminals. An informant's identity should not be disclosed unless the court finds it absolutely necessary, and then only to the proper parties involved. The court should not disclose the identity of the informer if it would create an immediate danger to their life or in the long run cut off a credible and reliable source of information. The informant's rule of protection against disclosure was also mentioned in the case of

Wilson v. United States, which sums it all up in the following statement provided by the court:

"*It is the right and the duty of every citizen of the United States to communicate with executive officers of government charged with the duty of enforcing the laws all the information which he or she has of the commission of an offense against the law of the United States, and such information is privileged as a confidential communication which the courts will not compel or permit to be disclosed without the consent of the government. Such evidence is excluded, not for the protection of the witness but for the policy of law . . . however, a trial court must dispose of a case before it if what is asked is essential evidence to vindicate the innocence of the accused of lessen the risk of false testimony, or is essential to the proper deposition of the case, disclosure will be compelled*" (Id.).

As in most states, Maryland has a specific rule pertaining to the disclosure of informants. Refer to your state's court rules and trial procedures, which can be easily obtained through your state's or district attorney's office.

Maryland Rule 4-263 (c)(2): *Matters not subject to discovery by the defendant.* This rule does not require the state to disclose the identity of a confidential informant so long as the failure to disclose the informant's identity does not infringe on a constitutional right of the defendant and the state's attorney does not intend to call the informant as a witness.

SPECIAL ISSUES CONCERNING THE DISCLOSURE OF INFORMANTS

- *IN CAMERA HEARINGS:* A mechanism whereby a judge can review evidence or documents and make a determination as to whether the evidence or documents must be disclosed to the defense. In applying the balancing test as mentioned in *Rovario v. United States, 353 US 53 (1957),* a judge may conduct an in camera hearing to ascertain the identity of the informant and the nature of the informant's role in a case in order to determine whether disclosure of the informant's identity is required. (*Warrick v. State*, 46 *Md* 696 [1992]).

- *ENTRAPMENT:*

  A. The "Origin of Interest" Test: (*Dravo v. State*, 46 *MdApp* 622 (1980)

     1. Did the agent of the police induce the accused to commit the offense for which the accused is charged? And if so
     2. Was the accused ready and willing without persuasion and was he awaiting any propitious opportunity to commit the offense?

  B. The defense must show by a preponderance of the evidence that the police or their agent induced the defendant to commit the offense. If this if proven, the State must then show beyond a reasonable doubt that the *defendant's conduct was due to his own predisposition* (*Kenney v. State*, 62 *MdApp* 555 [1985]).
  C. An entrapment defense requires an admission by the defendant that he committed the crime because he must show not only that the police or their agent induced him to commit the crime but that he succumbed to said inducement (*Adcock v. State*, 66 *MdApp* 454 [1986]).
  D. If an informant is acting as an agent of the police, the disclosure of his identity may be required in an entrapment defense if the assertion is that the informant induced the defendant to commit the crime and the defendant succumbed to said inducement when he was not otherwise predisposed to commit the crime.

- *BRADY ISSUE: (Brady v. Maryland,* 373 *US* 83 [1963])

  A. The prosecution is required to turn over all information to an accused upon request, which may tend to negate or mitigate the guilt or punishment of the accused.
  B. If the defense can articulate grounds for believing that the identity of an informant will reveal exculpatory evidence pursuant to Brady, the disclosure of the informant's identity may be required.

- *WHEN DISCLOSURE IS REQUIRED*
  The following options should be decided on a case-by-case basis:

  1. Enter a *Nolle Prosequi* (drop the case) to protect the identity of the informant.
  2. Provide the defense with the informant's identity and follow up with witness protection measures on the informant's behalf.
  3. Bargain with the defense to take a plea to a lesser charge or sentence in exchange for not revealing the informant's identity.

DOCUMENTS REQUIRED WHEN THE INFORMANT IS DISCLOSED

- all reports and notes regarding the information furnished by the informant, who has led to arrests, seizures, etc.
- all reports regarding those arrests based on information from the informant in question.
- all reports regarding those seizures based on information from the informant.
- all search warrants and affidavits and returns to search warrants, which was the result of information from this informant.

- the "rap sheet" (past criminal arrest) showing all felony convictions as to the informant who is referred to in the affidavit.
- police reports of any cases pending against the informant at the time the information was given by the informant.
- all pay vouchers/contact sheets concerning compensation or expenses to the informant for information supplied in the investigation.
- all promises, representations, assurances, or contracts whether or not reduced in writing, given in exchange for information supplied by the informant.

As you can see, documentation of the informant throughout the entire time they are assisting you is imperative. The above documentation should be clear and concise in the event that your informant is required to be disclosed by the court.

THE POLICE OFFICER AND PROSECUTOR RELATIONSHIP

As a police officer you should take every possible step as to not disclose the identity of the confidential informant. But this does not mean keeping secrets from the prosecutor. On the contrary, the prosecutor will need to know the following information in order to complete their mission.

1. If there is an informant, say so.
2. If the informant is being paid, say so.
3. If the informant has issues that may or may not come up in court, explain them.
4. Detail the informant's involvement for the prosecutor.
5. If the informant is not really anonymous, do not represent the informant as an anonymous informant. Legally, an anonymous informant and a confidential informant pose

very different problems for a prosecutor in terms of suppression and discovery issues.

6. It will help the prosecutor if the police officer keeps good records regarding informants in order to provide information concerning the informant's actions, past proven reliability, compensation/motivation, and whereabouts. Records also will help the police officer if these become issues at any disclosure hearings or at trial.

PREPARING THE TESTIFIYING INFORMANT FOR THE COURTROOM

• Make certain in advance that the informant is going to testify and that it is documented in a written contract between the informant's attorney and the prosecuting attorney.

• Prepare for this while the case is occurring not after the arrest has been made. To reduce the likelihood of the testimony being required of the informant, officers should conduct the following procedures:

1. The investigators should corroborate as much of the informant's testimony as possible. Using, body wires, tape recordings, surveillance, written statements, photo lineups, other observations or physical evidence.

   It should be done throughout the investigation especially after each contact. This is done in an effort to not only corroborate the investigators observations but also refresh the informant's recollection as to what transpired during the operation for the criminal trial. In addition, the written statement or tape recording given by the informant as the case unfolds will lock them into testimony if they later chose not to cooperate in the case or lie on the witness stand. It's important to note that if an informant fails to cooperate as required and refuses to testify on the stand as to the events that occurred they can still be compelled to testify according to the law. This is due to the fact that an informant, who is acting as an agent of the police, has no Fifth Amendment right against self-incrimination. Due to the fact that it's not the informant that has charges against him/her, it's the suspect on trial. Not only can they be held in contempt of court, but it would certainly cancel out any contract set forth regarding consideration in the informants case; therefore, charges are brought back full force on the informant and rightfully so!

2. All currency paid to the informant should be properly documented (i.e., on the Confidential Informant Contact Sheet) in the event that the defense files for disclosure during the discovery process. This is due to the defense attempting to show that the informant was paid an enormous amount of money to set up or "entrap" the defendant. Adequate records and a proper method of payment will invalidate this defense.

INFORMATION AND CASE LAW DEALING WITH "INFORMANTS" *AND* "CONFIDENTIAL INFORMANTS"

The courts have routinely recognized that an informants reliability can be adequately established if, during the course of an investigation, the informant supplies information concerning his/her *own name* to the police and includes a "statement against his penal interest," *United States v. Harris* 403 *U.S.* 573, 583, 91 *S. Ct. 2075, 2081-82 (1971)*. "Common sense in the important daily affairs of life would induce a prudent and disinterested observer to credit these statements. People do not lightly admit crime and place critical evidence in the hands of the police in the form of their own admissions" (*Id. at 583, 91, S. Ct.* 2082). In addition, the court pointed out in *United States v. Clark*, 24 *F.*3d 299, 303 (D.C. Cir. 1994): "Officers could reasonably believe that precisely because [the informant] was actively engaged in drug trafficking, he would know—and thus be able to identify—the source of his trading goods; furthermore, because he was seeking leniency at the hands of the law, [the informant] would have little reason to prove himself an unreliable informant"

Methods used in qualifying an informant

There are two basic methods of proving an informant's truthfulness and reliability before you reach the probable cause threshold:

- *Predicting future actions* of the suspect; or
- *A great amount of detail* concerning the suspect, the suspect's current personal life, or any other facts that shows a strong basis for the informant's knowledge of that particular suspect. (commonly used with first-time informants)

Both of which will need to be independently corroborated by the police to establish the truthfulness and "basis of knowledge" that the informant possess. Refer to *U.S. v. Reyes (First-Time Informant)* in this chapter for an example of "a great amount of detail" involving a confidential informant's tip.

Establishing the "Reliability" of an Informant

The most common way "reliability" is established is by documenting the *past use* of the particular informant and the *number of times* the information relayed by that informant proved not only to be true and correct but also led to the arrest and successful prosecution of the subject of the information. Anything less then that will not pass judicial review. Just putting in your affidavit that the informant is credible and reliable will not cut it. An officer will need to articulate the following in their affidavit or police report to qualify the informant properly:

- how often the informant has been used;
- the nature or character of the investigations in which the informant has previously supplied information (i.e., burglary, narcotics, arson, etc.);
- how many times the informants information proved to be true and correct;
- whether the information led to the arrest of the subject of the information; and
- whether the subsequent prosecution of those subject to the informants information were in fact convicted

Establishing the "Basis of Knowledge" of an Informant

The informant's "basis of knowledge" may be established by *documenting* the informant's personal observations (so long as you are vague enough that it does not disclose the identity of your informant). This in essence establishes how and when the informant came by their information, and would show what precisely the informant personally saw, heard, smelled, tasted, or touched. The information obtained from the informant's knowledge would be:

1. The description of the target's residence;
2. Exactly where in the residence the suspect keeps or conceals the evidence or contraband (only put in affidavit if testifying informant);
3. What the evidence or contraband looked like;
4. How it was packaged (only put in affidavit if testifying informant);
5. The name and physical description of the subject and/or others who may also live at, or frequent the target premises, etc.

Although, the above information is necessary when establishing the informant's credibility, reliability, and basis of knowledge the more specific you are in your search warrant affidavit about the informant's observations, the greater the chance the target will figure out who the informant is. When using a testifying informant this does not matter. Only when a confidential informant is being used is when you need to avoid exact descriptions of where evidence is located or statements made by the suspect.

The degree of information received from the informant's detailed description not only fortifies the reliability of the information but also constitutes a material consideration in the "totality of the circumstances approach" in making a determination by a judge for probable cause.

The final part of the "totality of the circumstances approach" requires the police to conduct an independent investigation to corroborate as much of the information given by the informant as possible. This not only establishes the truthfulness of the informant but displays that the informant has firsthand knowledge of the suspect's operation or at least in a personal position to gain that knowledge. The court in *Jones* stated that when making a determination of the information which has been obtained from an informant, "[I]t is enough, for the purposes of assessing probable cause, that [corroboration] through other sources of information reduced the chances of a reckless or prevaricating tale" further providing "a substantial basis for crediting the hearsay" (*Jones v United States*, 362 *U.S.*, at 269, 271)

When dealing with confidential informants there are certain situations in which an officer can act simply on the word of the informant's proven credibility and reliability, in conjunction with corroboration of the information received. Listed below are various cases, which will guide you through the situations an informant is commonly used when conducting law enforcement operations.

126 JAMES HENNING

Confidential Informants Used for PC to Search Persons or Vehicles

Draper v. United States
Supreme Court of the United States
358 U.S. 307, 79 S. Ct.329 (1959)

This case has become the benchmark for the independent corroboration of an informant's story. *U.S. v. Gates* refers to it as "the classic case on the value of corroborative efforts of police officials" (462 U.S. at 242, 103 S. Ct. at 2334).

In this case, an FBI confidential informant, *personally known* to the agent, explained that:

- Draper (the suspect) had taken up residence at a stated address in Denver and had been selling narcotics in that city.
- Several days later, the CI reported that Draper had gone to Chicago the day before by train, and that he was going to bring back three ounces of heroin.
- The CI stated that Draper would be returning to Denver by train on the morning of one of two specified days.
- The CI gave a detailed physical description of Draper—describing him as a black male, light complexion, approx twenty-seven years old, 5'8", and 160 lbs.
- The CI further *predicted* that he would be wearing a light-colored raincoat, brown slacks and black shoes, that he would be carrying a tan zipper bag, and that he habitually "walked fast" (*Id* at 309, 79 S. Ct. at 331).
- Periodically over a six-month period the CI had given information to the FBI regarding CDS violations, for which he was paid for his assistance.

When a man believed to be Draper appeared at the Denver Union Station as predicted, disembarking from an incoming

Chicago train, having the exact physical characteristics and wearing the precise clothing described by the CI and tended to "walk fast" toward the exit carrying a tan zippered bag as the CI had previously predicted, the FBI agent and a uniformed officer approached Draper, stopped, detained, and searched him. The search incident to the arrest uncovered two envelopes containing heroin and a syringe.

The CI never stated how it knew this information (basis of knowledge). The United States Supreme Court in this case held the tip was detailed enough to support probable cause, based on the fact that each part of the information received from the CI was independently corroborated by the police. Further, the Supreme Court has noted in *United States v. Gates*, 462 U.S. at 233-34, concerning basis of knowledge that "if an unquestionably honest citizen [informant] comes forward with a report of criminal activity—which if fabricated would subject him to criminal liability—we have found rigorous scrutiny of the *basis of his knowledge unnecessary*"

The court in this case stated that the arresting officer "had personally verified every facet of the information given to him by the CI except whether Draper had accomplished his mission and had the three ounces of heroin of his person or in his bag. And surely, with every other bit of the CI's information being thus personally verified, the officer had "reasonable grounds" to believe that the remaining unverified bit of the CI's information, that Draper would have the heroin with him, was likewise true" (Id. at 313, 79 S. Ct. at 333).

Further, the United States Supreme Court's language in *U.S. v. Gates*, 462 U.S. at 244, explained that "innocent behavior [as observed by police in the Draper case, for example:

1. Draper matched the informant's description;
2. Draper arrived in Denver on a train from Chicago;

3. Draper's attire and luggage matched the description given by the informant, and
4. Draper walked rapidly.

[frequently] will provide the basis for a showing of probable cause . . . . In making a determination of probable cause the relevant inquiry is not whether particular conduct is 'innocent' or 'guilty,' but the degree of suspicion that attaches to particular types of noncriminal acts." In *Draper*, all of the independent police observations were of innocent facts.

Additionally in *Gates*, police corroboration of seemingly innocent activity, reduced to very specific details, tend to show the informant's reliability" (Id) Information regarding the informant's veracity (truthfulness), the amount of detail provided by the informant, and police corroboration have all been gathered together in cases in which probable cause existed. When one of these factors was lacking, the others were stronger, so that probable cause could be determined by "the totality of the circumstances."

Confidential Informants Used for PC to Conduct Terry Stop on Both Person and/or Vehicles

Adams v. Williams
Supreme Court of the United States
407 U.S. 143, 92 S. Ct. 1921 (1972)

At approximately 2:15 a.m., Sgt Connolly of the Bridgeport, Connecticut, Police Department was in his patrol car when he was approached by a person (informant) known to him and who provided information in the past. The informant stated "an individual seated in a nearby vehicle was carrying narcotics and had a gun at his waist" (Id. at 1922). "After calling for assistance on his car radio, Sgt. Connolly approached the vehicle to investigate. Connolly tapped on the car window and asked the occupant, Robert Williams, to open the door. When Williams rolled down the window instead, the sergeant reached into the car and removed a fully loaded revolver from Williams's waistband. The gun had not been visible to Connolly from outside the car, but it was in precisely the place indicated by the informant" (Id at 1922-9123). Connolly then placed defendant Williams under arrest for the unlawful possession of the firearm. "A search incident to that arrest was conducted after other officers arrived. They found substantial quantities of heroin on Williams's person and in the car, and they found a machete and a second revolver hidden in the automobile" (Id. at 1923).

The Fourth Amendment does not require a policeman who lacks the precise level of information necessary for probable cause to arrest to simply shrug his shoulders and allow a crime to occur or a criminal to escape. "[Instead, a] brief stop of a suspicious individual, in order to determine his identity or to maintain the status quo momentarily while obtaining more information, may be most reasonable in light of the facts known to the officer at the time" (Id). "When an officer is justified in believing that the individual whose suspicious behavior he is investigating at close range is armed and presently dangerous to the officer or others," *Terry* permits that officer to "conduct a limited protective search for concealed weapons" (Id at 1923).

In this case, Sgt. "Connolly acted justifiably in responding to his informant's tip. The informant was known to him personally and had provided him with information in the past. This is a stronger case than obtains in the case of an anonymous telephone tip. *The informant here came forward personally to give information that was immediately verifiable at the scene" (Id)*. While this informant's previously unverified/corroborated tip may not have been enough for an *arrest or search*, the information certainly carried enough reliability to justify the *temporary investigative detention of defendant.*

In addition, the information supplied also formed the basis of a reasonable cause to suspect that defendant was armed and presently dangerous. "While properly investigating the activity of a person who was reported to be carrying narcotics and a concealed weapon and who was sitting alone in a car in a high-crime area at 2:15 in the morning, Sgt. Connolly had ample reason to fear for his safety. When Williams rolled down his window, rather than complying with the policemen's request to step out of the car so that his movements could more easily be seen, the revolver allegedly at Williams's waist became an even greater threat. Under these circumstances the policeman's action in reaching to the spot where the gun was thought to be hidden constituted a limited intrusion designed to insure his safety, and [the U.S. Supreme Court] conclude [s] that it was reasonable" (Id at 1924).

"Once Sgt. Connolly had found the gun precisely where the informant had predicted, probable cause existed to arrest Williams for unlawful possession of the weapon" (Id). Because the sergeant found the gun in precisely the right place predicted by the informant, the reliability of the informant's report that narcotics may also be found in the vehicle was corroborated, which made the subsequent search of the defendant's vehicle and person for drugs or contraband clearly constitutional.

First-Time Informants Used for PC to Search Persons or Vehicles

United States v. Reyes
United States Court of Appeals
792 F.2d 536 (5th Cir. 1986)

A federal agent, Gordon Ridings, with the United States Customs Service received a phone call from a confidential informant whom was *known to the agent* for over two years.

Up to this point the confidential informant *never gave* Agent Ridings any investigative information. On this particular occasion the confidential informant had explained to Agent Ridings the following:

- a Mexican male named Daniel
- who *had* been staying for the past ten days in Room 414 of the Holiday Inn on Highway 80 between Odessa and Midland, Texas
- was in possession of a large quantity of cocaine
- the confidential informant explained that Daniel was heavily armed and considered dangerous
- Daniel operated a black and silver 1985 Chevrolet Blazer with a temporary California license tag located in the back window.
- the confidential informant stated that it had *personally* seen Daniel with cocaine in his vehicle and his motel room within the previous twenty-four hours

Agent Ridings subsequently relayed this information to Sgt. Dixon of the Odessa Sheriff's Department Narcotics Division. Later that same morning, Sgt. Dixon and Officer Clark traveled to the Holiday Inn in an attempt to corroborate the informant's story before seeking a search warrant. Upon arrival, they immediately observed a Mexican male loading suitcases and gun cases into a vehicle fitting the description given by the informant. "The Blazer was parked in front of Room 414. Dixon entered the motel and requested the records for Room 414 from the motel manager. The manager provided records from September 29 to October 7, . . . and informed Dixon that the occupant's name was Daniel Reyes. The records indicated approximately $600 worth of long distance phone calls made in that period of time. Before leaving the motel, Dixon noticed that the Mexican male he had observed earlier was standing at the front desk. Dixon overheard him say that his name was 'Daniel Reyes and that he would like to check out of room

414.' Dixon and Clark then left the motel area, radioed for assistance, and parked where they could observe the Blazer" (Id. at 538).

Reyes departed from the motel in the Blazer and within ten minutes Dixon and Clark, along with two local police officers who had joined them, stopped him, removed him from the Blazer, and placed him in handcuffs. "The four law enforcement officers then proceeded to search the Blazer, including the suitcases which contained $12,000 in cash, a gun, a shoulder holster, and a smaller locked nylon bag. Dixon then took the keys out of the ignition and opened this bag. Inside were one and one-half pounds of 83 percent pure cocaine, diazepam, and some pills. They also found four handguns, one of which was loaded, a rifle, and a shotgun" (Id.).

In *U.S. v. Reyes* the court found that under the Fourth Amendment, information supplied by a *"first-time informant"* may be used to establish probable cause to search a *motor vehicle* or *person* if the credibility of the informant and the informant's "basis of knowledge" is sufficiently corroborated by the "totality of the circumstances" (Id. at 539, 540).

"numerous detailed facts were supplied by the informant. Specifically, he informed Ridings of"

- the suspect's first name
- where he was staying
- how long he had been there
- the make, year, and color of his vehicle
- the type of contraband; and
- the fact the suspect was armed

Significantly, all this information was based on the informant's personal knowledge, which is evinced by his statement to Ridings that he had seen the cocaine in the Blazer and Room 414 within the past twenty-four hours" (Id)

The court explained that "a citizen does not surrender all the protections of the Fourth Amendment by entering an automobile' . . . The automobile exception to the Fourth Amendment's warrant requirement protects only searches supported by *probable cause*. Only the prior approval of the magistrate is waived; the search otherwise must be such as the magistrate could authorize" (Id).

"The automobile exception applies where there are both exigent circumstances and probable cause to believe that the vehicle in question contains property that the government may properly seize, and in this case, probable cause is based on an informant's tip" (Id. at 538). As result the "totality of the circumstances" test will be applied to determine if the informants tip provided probable cause.

As the United States Supreme Court determined in *Illinois v. Gates*, 462 *U.S.* 213, 103 *S. Ct.* 2317 (1983), "the search for probable cause involves 'a practical, common sense decision whether, given all the circumstances . . . including the "veracity" and "basis of knowledge" of persons supplying *hearsay information*, there is a fair probability that contraband will be found in a particular place'" (Reyes at 539 [quoting *Gates* at 238, 103 *S. Ct.* at 2332]). "Although an informant's veracity, reliability, and basis of knowledge still should be considered, *'a deficiency in one* [piece of information] *may be compensated for, in determining the overall reliability of a tip, by a strong showing as to the other, or by some other indicia of reliability'*" (Id. [quoting *Gates* at 233, 103 *S. Ct.* at 2329]). What the Gates court means is that even if one or two pieces of the informant's information is wrong, you can still continue to establish probable cause by corroborating the other information supplied.

"Although the usual method of proving an informant's reliability is to point to information provided in the *past* that turned out to be truthful, this is not the only method. *An informant's tip can be confirmed by independent police work which corroborates the information received . . . . Additionally, the credibility of an informant's tip is strengthened if it is made in 'great detail,' thus, evincing a strong basis for the informant's knowledge . . . . Moreover, the surrounding facts and information are not to be viewed in isolation but must be viewed in light of their having been evaluated by trained law enforcement officials.* What appears quite innocent to the untrained eye may be significant to the trained law enforcement official . . . . Finally, an informant's tip is buttressed by the fact that it is based on his own personal observation rather then on hearsay" (Id).

"Since Dixon was able to corroborate the informant's tip, the government was justified in believing the statement that cocaine was in the Blazer. Moreover since Dixon personally observed Reyes check out of the motel and pack his belongings into the Blazer, the government could reasonably infer that the cocaine supposedly located in the motel room was transferred into the Blazer. Therefore, when all the information gathered from the informant and Dixon's personal observations is considered in the light of Dixon's extensive narcotic investigation experience, it is clear that the authorities had probable cause to believe contraband was inside that Blazer when Reyes exited the Holiday Inn parking lot" (Id).

Finally, "the exigent circumstances surrounding the investigation were also sufficient to justify a warrantless search of the Blazer. Since the officers were at the motel attempting to corroborate the informant's tip to justify obtaining a search warrant, they cannot be faulted for failing to have one in their possession at that time. More important, the suspicion that Reyes would soon depart was clearly warranted by the fact that immediately after loading the Blazer, he checked out of his room and left the motel in the Blazer. Consequently, the circumstances were sufficiently exigent to justify the search and seizure" (Id)

INFORMATION AND CASE LAW DEALING WITH "ANNONYMOUS SOURCES OF INFORMATION"

Out of all the types of informant information obtained, the anonymous source of information requires the most independent investigation by police to corroborate that information gathered. Simply put, the anonymous source of information does not produce with it the traditional credibility or reliability that is attached to sources of information or informants/sources who are known to officers. As a result the officer must ensure that the following is adhered to:

1. Get as much detail as possible.

    You need this to demonstrate the anonymous sources "basis of knowledge." In essence you're eliciting a prediction of future or current events from the source of information for you to later corroborate independently. The officer should get as much information as possible by asking the following questions:

    A. What have you observed? (or are presently observing)
    B. What is the description and location of the suspect?
    C. How far away their observations were conducted?
    D. What is the location the alleged crime occurred?
    E. What is the location of the suspect?
    F. Can you give a description of any houses or vehicles used in the crime or in the area?
    G. Can you give any information, which would let us know what the suspect plans on doing next or in the future? (i.e., direction of travel or vehicle path the suspect uses to complete a transaction at a meeting spot or residence)
    H. How long ago their observations were made?

*Do not get personal information concerning the anonymous source before asking the above questions. This could frighten them and cause them to hang up to soon.

2. Conduct an independent investigation.

In this phase the investigator needs to corroborate as much of the information given by the anonymous source as possible. It is the independent corroboration of the facts given to the investigator, which establishes a foundation later in court and allows the hearsay information given by the anonymous tipster to be admissible.

"Because the informant is right about some things, he is more probably right about other facts" (Illinois v. Gates, supra, 103 S. Ct. at 2335 [quoting Spinelli v. United States, 393 U.S. 410, 427, 89 S. Ct. 584, 594 (1969) (White, J., concurring)]). Once an officer has personally verified every possible facet of the information contained in the tip, reasonable grounds may then exist to believe that the remaining unverified bit of information—that a criminal offence is occurring or has occurred—is likewise true (Draper v. United States, 358 U.S. 307,79 S. Ct. 329 [1959]). The United States Supreme Court has historically stated that, "such tips, particularly when supplemented by independent police investigation, frequently contributes to the solution of otherwise 'perfect crimes'" (Gates at 2332).

To sum it all up, when utilizing anonymous tips, the officer needs to spend a great deal of time to corroborate as much of the information as possible in order to pass the judicial muster. Remember, they are not considered credible or reliable until your independent investigation proves otherwise. If the anonymous tip predicts the future actions of an individual and through your independent investigation you corroborate the tipster's information to be true and correct. Probable cause has now been established for a search warrant or investigative detention to further investigate. Let's break this down into scenarios supported by actual case law.

Anonymous Tip Resulting in Probable Cause for a Search Warrant

Illinois v. Gates
Supreme Court of the United States
462 U.S. 23, 103 S.Ct.2317 (1983)

On May 3, 1978, the Bloomingdale Police Department received in the mail an anonymous handwritten letter which read as follows:
"This letter is to inform you that you have a couple in your town who strictly make their living on selling drugs. They are Sue and Lance Gates; they live on Greenway, off Bloomingdale Rd. in the condominiums. Most of their buys are done in Florida. Sue, his wife, drives their car to Florida, where she leaves it to be loaded up with drugs, then Lance flies down and drives it back. Sue flies back after she drops the car off in Florida. May 3 she is driving down there again and Lance will be flying down in a few days to drive it back. At the time Lance drives the car back he has the trunk loaded with over $100,000 in drugs. Presently they have over $100,000 in their basement. They brag about the fact they never have to work and make their entire living on pushers. I guarantee if you watch them carefully you will make a big catch. They are friends with some big drug dealers who visit their house often" (Id. at 2325).
Following up on the tip, Detective Mader discovered that a driver's license had been issued to Lance Gates. The detective also ascertained Gates's address and learned from an officer assigned to the O'Hare Airport that L. Gates had made a reservation on Eastern Airlines flight 245 to West

Palm Beach, Florida, scheduled to depart from Chicago on May 5 at 4:15 p.m.

Detective Mader then made arrangements with an agent of the Drug Enforcement Administration (DEA) for surveillance of the May 5 Eastern Airlines flight. "The agent later reported to Mader that Gates had boarded the flight, and that federal agents in Florida had observed him arrive in West Palm Beach and take a taxi to the nearby Holiday Inn. They also reported that Gates went to a room registered to one Susan Gates and that at 7:00 a.m. the next morning, Gates and an unidentified woman left the motel in a Mercury bearing Illinois license plates and drove northbound on an interstate frequently used by travelers to the Chicago area. In addition, the DEA agent informed Mader that the license plate number on the Mercury registered to a Hornet station wagon owned by Gates. The agent also advised Mader that the driving time between West Palm Beach and Bloomingdale was approximately twenty-two to twenty-four hours" (Id. at 2325-26).

Detective Mader incorporated the foregoing facts into an affidavit and submitted it, together with a copy of the anonymous letter, to a judge of the Circuit Court of DuPage County. The judge issued the warrant, authorizing a search of the Gates's residence and their automobile.

At 5:15 a.m. on May 7, "only thirty-six hours after he had flown out of Chicago, Lance Gates and his wife returned to their home in Bloomingdale, driving the car in which they had left West Palm Beach some twenty-two hours earlier. The Bloomingdale police were awaiting them, searched the trunk of the Mercury, and uncovered approximately 350 pounds of marijuana. A search of Gates's home revealed marijuana, weapons, and other contraband" (Id. at 2326).

This is one of the landmark cases the United States Supreme Court used to redefine over a decade of law, which governed the issuance of search warrants in relation to information received from informants **(all informants)**. As a result the courts *now make their determination based on the* "totality of the circumstances" *analysis to determine if:*

- *information supplied by an informant is deemed credible and reliable and;*
- *that the independent investigation conducted by the police had, to the best of their ability, corroborated the informant's statements or predictions.*

Illinois v. Gates established that an officer's independent investigation, which corroborates a **detailed** anonymous tip, may, together with the tip, provide probable cause for the issuance of a search warrant. This can be achieved even in the *absence* of information demonstrating that the anonymous informant was historically honest or the information reliable, or even that the informant had a basis for the information conveyed.

The Supreme Court in Gates held that "*the information contained in the affidavit should be analyzed by reference to the totality of the circumstances presented therein.*" Speaking for the court, Justice Rehnquist elaborated:

"[A]n informant's 'veracity,' 'reliability' and 'basis of knowledge' are all highly relevant in determining the value of his report. We do not agree, however, that these elements should be understood as entirely separate and independent requirements to be rigidly exacted in every case [.] . . . Rather, . . . they should be understood simply as closely intertwined issues that may usefully illuminate the common sense, practical question whether there is 'probable cause' to believe that contraband or evidence is located in a particular place.

Probable cause is a fluid concept—turning on the assessment of probabilities in particular factual contexts—not readily, or even usefully reduced to a near set of legal rules. Informants' tips doubtless come in many shapes and sizes from many different types of persons . . . . Rigid legal rules are ill suited to an area of such diversity" (Id. 2337-39).

What is important to note in this case is that the letter obtained from the anonymous tip, in detail, *described and predicted* the Gates's method of operation, which gave more weight toward the anonymous tipster's credibility. This letter contained details not just too easily obtained facts at the time frame that Gates took their trips but predicted the future actions not easily known to third parties unless having some sort of direct knowledge of their travel plans and method of operations. The subsequent independent investigation, which successfully corroborated the tipster's information, clearly brought officers to the level of probable cause to apply and receive a search and seizure warrant.

Anonymous Tip Resulting in a "Terry Stop" of a Vehicle or Person

Alabama v. White
Supreme Court of the United States
496 U.S. 325, 110 S. Ct. 2412 (1990)

At about 3:00 p.m., Cpl Davis of the Montgomery Police Department "received a telephone call from an anonymous person, stating that Vanessa White would be leaving 235-C Lynwood Terrance Apartments at a particular time in a brown Plymouth station wagon with the right taillight lens broken, that she would be going to Dobey's Motel, and that she would be in possession of about an ounce of cocaine inside a brown attaché case. Cpl Davis and his partner, Cpl P.A. Reynolds, proceeded to the Lynwood Terrace Apartments. The officers saw a brown Plymouth station wagon with a broken right taillight in the parking lot in front of the 235 building. The officers observed [defendant] leave the 235 building, carrying nothing in her hands, and enter the station wagon. They followed the vehicle as it drove the most direct route to Dobey's Motel" (Id. at 2414).

"When the vehicle reached the Mobile Highway, on which Dobey's Motel is located, Cpl Reynolds requested a patrol unit to stop the vehicle. The vehicle was stopped at approximately 4:18 p.m., just short of Dobey's Motel. Cpl Davis asked [defendant] to step to the rear of her car, where he informed her that she had been stopped because she was suspected of carrying cocaine in the vehicle. He asked if they could look for cocaine and [defendant] said they could look. The officers found a locked brown attaché case in the car and, upon request, [defendant] provided the combination to the lock. The officer found marijuana in the attaché case and placed [defendant] under arrest. During the processing at the station, the officers found three milligrams of cocaine in [defendant's purse]" (Id. at 2414-2415).

When an anonymous caller provides police with information consisting of "'a range of details relating not just to easily obtained facts and conditions existing at the time of the tip, but to *future actions* of third parties ordinarily not easily predicted,'" the information contained in the tip demonstrates "inside information," and the anonymous informant's "special familiarity with the suspect's affairs." Thereafter, when significant aspects of the information and predictions in the *anonymous tip* are verified by independent police investigation, reason may then exist "to believe not only that the caller was honest but also that he was well informed, at least well enough to justify . . . [an] investigatory stop [.]"(Id. at 2417).

On another note, if time allowed, officers could have received a search warrant for the vehicle and persons involved. This is basically the same set of circumstances that fell in place in the *Illinois v. Gates* case.

The court in White "conclude[s] that when the officers stopped [defendant], the anonymous tip had been sufficiently corroborated to furnish reasonable suspicion that [defendant] was engaged in criminal activity and that the investigative stop therefore **did not** violate the Fourth Amendment" (Id.) The court further explained that while "not every detail mentioned by the tipster was verified, such as the name of the women leaving the building or the precise apartment from which she left, the officer did corroborate that a woman left the 235 building and got into the particular vehicle that was described by the caller. With respect to the time of the departure predicted by the informant, Cpl. Davis testified that the caller gave a particular time when the woman would be leaving, but he did not state what the time was. He did testify that, after the call, he and his partner proceeded to the Lynwood Terrance Apartments to put the 235 building under surveillance . . . Given the fact that the officers proceeded to the indicated address immediately after the call and that [defendant] emerged not too long thereafter, it appears . . . that [defendant's] departure from the building was within the time frame predicted by the caller. As for the caller's prediction of [defendant's] destination, it is true that the officers stopped her just short of Dobey's Motel and did not know whether she would have pulled in or continued on past it. But given that the four-mile route driven by [defendant] was the most direct route possible to Dobey's Motel, it is reasonable to conclude that defendant's destination was significantly corroborated" (Id. at 2416-2417).

In conclusion, it is significant to address that, "as in Gates, 'the anonymous [tip] contained a range of details relating not just to easily obtained facts and conditions existing at the time of the tip, but to **future actions of third parties** ordinarily not easily predicted.' . . . The fact that the officers found a car precisely matching the caller's description in front of the 235 building is an example of the former. Anyone could give 'predict' that fact because it was a condition presumably existing at the time of the call. *What was important was the caller's ability to predict [defendant's] future behavior, because it* *demonstrates inside information—a special familiarity with [defendant's] affairs.* The general public would have had no way of knowing that [defendant] would shortly leave the building, get in the described car, and drive the most direct route to Dobey's Motel. Because *only a small number of people are generally privy to an individual's itinerary, it is reasonable for the police to believe that a person with access to such information is likely to also have access to reliable information about that individual's illegal activities . . . .* When significant aspects of the caller's **predictions** were verified, there was reason to believe not only that the caller was honest but also that he was well informed, at least well enough to justify the stop" (Id.). (See also *United States v. Hill,* 91 F. 3d 1064, 1069 [8th Cir. 1996], where the court made known the importance of an informant predicting a suspect's future behavior, resulting in the suspect's investigative detention.)

It is important to note that even though this case dealt with an anonymous tip concerning an individual in a vehicle, nothing changes when applying the same concept to an individual on foot. Following the requirements of conducting a complete and thorough investigation (to the best of the officer's ability) in an effort to corroborate the *predictions* relayed by the anonymous tip, will bring the officer to the level of reasonable, articulable suspicion resulting in probable cause needed for the investigatory stop to either confirm or dispel his/her suspicions that criminal activity is afoot. But there must be more to the anonymous tip that would normally be apparent to the average citizen.

In *United States v. Roberson, 90 F. 3d 75 (3rd Cir. 1996)* stated an anonymous tipster making their observations as to what "is apparent to the everyday public" will not pass judicial review. Simply put, the anonymous tip's *predictions of future actions* of a suspect supported by an independent police investigation will get the officer their search warrant or investigative stop *(Terry Stop)* need to further investigate.

United States v. Thompson,
United States Court of Appeals
234 F. 3d. 725 (D.C. Cir. 2000)

This case deals with officers receiving an anonymous tip and actually observing suspicious behavior during the course of investigating the tip, which subsequently resulted in a Terry Stop. This case is how the police should have handled the anonymous tip received in *Florida v. J.L.*, which is included later in this section.

At about 3:20 a.m., Officers Hollaway and Pope of the Metropolitan Police Department, while in uniform, were approached by a middle-aged male who reported that he "just saw" a man with a gun get out of a sport utility vehicle in the parking lot of a Wendy's restaurant, about one hundred yards from where the officers stood. "The informant, who was anxious and agitated, described the suspect as a young black man wearing dark pants and a bright orange shirt"(Id. at 727).

Without asking for the man's identity, the officers immediately drove off (in their separate cars) to the Wendy's restaurant, which was closed at the time. As the officers entered the parking lot, they saw a dark-colored sport-utility vehicle leaving. Officer Holloway then spotted a black male, later identified as the defendant Thompson, wearing a bright orange shirt and standing by himself at the far end of the parking lot with his back against a fence. At the time, there was no one else in the parking lot. "Thompson was looking around the edge of the fence toward a nightclub called the Mirage . . . , 'sort of peeking around as if he was trying to keep his position concealed'"(Id.).

In light of the tip and the circumstances, Officer Holloway exited his patrol car with his weapon drawn and approached. Thompson spotted Officer Holloway when the officer was about five to seven feet from him. Holloway told Thompson to raise his hands to the air and to stop, and Thompson complied. "Thompson at that point said something to the effect of 'you got me' and indicated that he would not put up a fight. At Holloway's instruction, he dropped to his knees. As Holloway assisted him to the ground, the officer felt a weapon toward the front of Thompson's person. At that point, Officer Pope arrived and helped to handcuff Thompson. The two officers then rolled Thompson over and retrieved a 9mm semiautomatic pistol, loaded and cocked, that was sticking out of his waistband" (Id.).

As a result of the court finding the stop and frisk lawful, the court noted that the tip in this case carried with it "indicia of reliability beyond those of the anonymous tip in [Florida v.] J.L.; and the police themselves observed Thompson engaging in suspicious conduct" (Thompson at 729).

The court noted the following differences:

- the tipster here informed the police in person, making his report inherently trustworthier than that of the unidentified caller in [Florida v.] J.L.
- the informant stated that he "just saw" Thompson, indicating that his knowledge was based upon *firsthand observation.*
- and the *suspicious behavior exhibited* from Thompson prior to the police making contact with him.

Looking at these facts "from the perspective of a reasonable police officer," the court found that the officers possessed the necessary reasonable, articulable suspicion need to affect the Terry Stop on Thompson.

The Thompson court went on to explain that "Thompson's furtive conduct was not merely consistent with the tip that he had a weapon; it would have signaled a reasonable police officer that Thompson was positioning himself to use it, perhaps against someone exiting the nightclub toward which he was looking. To ask more of the police in these circumstances—to require them to investigate still further or to watch from a distance—might well preclude them from interceding before the suspect has accomplished his violent, perhaps lethal, purpose. The requirement of reasonable suspicion does not necessitate such forbearance" (Id. at 729-30).

Anonymous Tip Failing to Result in a "Terry Stop" of Vehicle or Person

United States v. Roberson
United States Court of Appeals
90 F.3d 75 (3rd Cir. 1996)

In late September, just after 7:00 p.m., a Philadelphia police dispatcher received an anonymous call reporting that, "a heavyset black male wearing dark green pants, a white hooded sweatshirt, and a brown leather jacket was selling drugs on the 2100 block of Chelten Avenue" (Id. at 75). The call taker had no information concerning the reliability of the caller or the source of the information. The dispatcher had no information concerning the reliability of the caller or the source of the information.

At about 7:18 p.m., the anonymous tipster's report was relayed over the police radio. Officers Nathan and Hellmuth, who were patrolling the general area in a marked police vehicle, responded. Less than a minute after receiving the call, they arrived at the 2100 block of Chelten and saw a man standing on the corner. The man matched the description provided by the caller. This corner, according to the officers, was a "hot spot" where drugs were sold to passing motorist. "Officer Nathan and the man, later to be identified as the defendant Lester Roberson, made eye contact. According to Nathan, the defendant then walked 'casually' over to a car parked facing the wrong way on Chelten Avenue and leaned in as if to speak with the vehicle's occupants. The Police observed no indicia of drug activity" (Id. at 76).

At this point, the officers exited their vehicle, "with guns drawn, and ordered the defendant away from the parked car. As they approached him, they observed the butt of a gun protruding from his pants. They patted him down and seized from his person a 9mm semiautomatic pistol with thirteen rounds of ammunition, two plastic bags containing numerous packets of cocaine, a pill bottle containing forty-seven valium pills, a half-bottle of cough syrup, and $319 in U.S. currency" (Id.). The officers subsequently placed the defendant under arrest.

In the above case the court found that an "anonymous tip" that contains only information that is readily observable to anyone passing by will *not* supply reasonable suspicion to conduct a Terry Stop. This cannot be accomplished without the police making their independent observations of the suspect's conduct or the corroboration of information from which the police could reasonably conclude that the anonymous tipster's allegation of criminal activity was reliable.

In *Terry v. Ohio*, 392 U.S. 1, 88 S. Ct. (1968), the United States Supreme Court held that "a police officer may detain and investigate citizens when he or she has a *reasonable suspicion* that 'criminal activity may be afoot'" (Roberson at 77 [quoting Terry at 30, 88 S. Ct. at 1884]).

To determine whether the anonymous tip provided reasonable suspicion of criminal activity, the court relied on two landmark U.S. Supreme Court cases:

- Illinois v. Gates, 462 U.S. 213, 103 S. Ct. 2317 (1983); and
- Alabama v. White, 496 U.S. 325, 110 S. Ct. 2412 (1990)

As a result of these cases the U.S. Supreme Court adopted the "totality of the circumstances approach" whenever making an evaluation of an anonymous tip. "In concluding that the *Gates* tip provided probable cause and the *White* tip provided reasonable suspicion, the Supreme Court stressed two factors:

1: An officer's ability to corroborate significant aspects of the tip; and

2: The tip's ability to predict future events (Roberson at 77)

Unlike the tips received in *Gates* and *White*, the caller in the *Roberson* case did not supply the necessary information concerning the defendant's future activities.

The court in Roberson explained that the tip contained *no* "details of future actions of third parties ordinarily not easily predicted." Thus, no future actions could be corroborated, and an important basis for forming reasonable suspicion was absent. Moreover, because they were dealing with an anonymous and bare-bones tip, the police has no basis for assessing either the *reliability* of the informant or the grounds [basis of knowledge] on which the informant believed that a crime was being committed—important ingredients in the "totality" (Id. at 80).

The court added, however, that these omissions "probably would not have invalidated the stop, if after corroborating readily observable facts, the police officers had *noticed unusual or suspicious conduct on Roberson's part* . . . . But they did not" (Id.).

Accordingly, the court held that "the police do not have reasonable suspicion for an investigative stop when, as here, they receive a fleshless anonymous tip of drug-dealing *that provides only readily observable information, and they themselves observe no suspicious behavior*" (Id.).

The *Roberson* court did make note that "the police were not powerless to act on the nonpredictive, anonymous tip they received. The officers could have set up surveillance of the defendant . . . . If the officers then observed any suspicious behavior or if they had observed suspicious behavior as they approached the defendant [Roberson] in this case, they would have had appropriate cause to stop—and perhaps even arrest— him. This, however, they did not do. In the absence of any observations of suspicious conduct or the corroboration of information from which the police could reasonably conclude that the anonymous tipster's allegation of criminal activity was reliable, we must conclude that there was no reasonable suspicion to stop the defendant" (Id. at 81).

Florida v. J.L.
Supreme Court of the United States
529 U.S. 266, 120 S. Ct. 1375 (2000)

In this case an anonymous tipster contacted the Miami-Dade Police and made a report that "a young black male standing at a particular bus stop and wearing a plaid shirt was carrying a gun" (Id. at 1377). After about six minutes, two officers responded to the area and observed three black males at the bus stop "just hanging out" (Id.). They noticed that one of the three, defendant J.L., was wearing a plaid shirt, which matched the description given by the anonymous tipster. *"Apart from the tip, the officers had no reason to suspect any of the three of illegal conduct" (Id.)*. One of the officers "approached J.L., told him to put his hands up on the bus stop, frisked him, and seized a gun from J.L.'s pocket" (Id.).

The court made note that the police officer's suspicion that J.L. was armed with a handgun originated "not from any observations of their own but solely from a call made from an unknown location from and unknown caller. Unlike a tip from a known informant whose reputation can be assessed and who can be held responsible if his/her allegations turn out to be fabricated," "an anonymous tip alone seldom demonstrates the informant's basis of knowledge or veracity" (Id.). Although there are certain situations where a sufficiently corroborated anonymous tip can bring an officer to the level of reasonable suspicion, which can result in a Terry Stop of the suspect. Refer to *Alabama v. White* for a case that explains the necessary requirements to conduct a Terry Stop.

In essence, to justify a stop based solely on an anonymous tip, police must take steps to establish the reliability of the tip (i.e., through surveillance of the suspect prior to making their contact). If the anonymous tip is found to be lacking in reliability then the constitutional standard of a "reasonable, articulable suspicion" of criminal activity has not been satisfied. This in turn makes the stop and frisk unjustified and therefore making any evidence found there after inadmissible in court—even if the tip alleges the suspect has a firearm! The officer must make his/her observations prior to the initial contact to establish the tips reliability and gather reasonable, articulable suspicion. The court further noted that this tip did not:

- demonstrate any sort of "*inside knowledge*" about the suspect,
- and the tip did not *predict future movements or actions,* which could have been corroborated by the police.

Without such predictive information, the officers were left with no means of corroborating the tipster's knowledge or credibility.

AN EXAMPLE OF A COMMON "ON-SCENE INFORMANT OPERATION" SCENARIO

All too often at the end of an operation—whether it is a search warrant, a buy bust operation, or a PC arrest—the subject of that arrest will want to immediately cooperate with the police in an effort to gain leniency in court later. In this situation the bad guy has now turned informant and oftentimes will have some very good information concerning his/her supplier that may need to be acted on immediately.

It is important to note that the new informant will also have to agree to testify in court as to the events that will take place, if deemed necessary. After establishing that the informant will testify, you will need to debrief your new informant about his/ her knowledge of drugs and about individuals he/she knows to be in the "drug game" (corroborating the informant's basis of knowledge).

Below I have listed a few things that you will need to know to complete this operation. It is important to note though that you do not need to have all the questions below answered in order to establish the necessary probable cause. Each situation is different and the set of questions below should just be a guide.

1. Who is the supplier and what is his description?

    • Run a criminal history check, a motor vehicle check, and a wanted check through your department's database.
    • Get the most detailed description of what the suspect looks like, i.e., short hair, long hair, white/black, approx. age, height, etc.

2. Where does he live?

    • Run a crisscross directory (a method of determining who resides at a specific address) if available to your department
    • Immediately set up surveillance at the residence so you can get the suspect coming from his residence to make the deal with the informant.

3. What car does he drive?

    • Run a vehicle registration check.

4. Where does he keep his drug stash?

    • If in the car, where at and in what fashion?

5. How long have you been dealing with the supplier?

   • Establishes the history between the informant and the supplier.

6. How do you make contact with the supplier (phone or in person)?

   • Check the phone number through your department's databases, crisscross directory to determine the subscriber of the suspect's phone number to corroborate that it is in fact listed to the suspect's residence or subscribed to in his/her name.

7. How much drugs at one time have you purchased in the past from the supplier?

   • Makes sure that the informant is not overextending himself by ordering more then what would be normal. This will most certainly raise suspicions with the suspect and risk the operation.

8. Where is he at right now?

   • This establishes the informant's inside knowledge of the supplier's personnel schedule.

9. Where do you normally meet to make the deals?

   • Allows surveillance to set up in the area or make additional determinations to ensure a successful outcome.

These are just some of the pertinent questions that you will ask you're new informant. Just remember that the more information you are able to retrieve from the informant, which would have to be subsequently corroborated to form the informants "basis of knowledge," the greater your probable cause will be in the courtroom.

Now, have the CI take the next step while you still have them in the palm of your hands. Call their supplier and place an order of drugs to be brought to your current location. Ensure that the conversation is *recorded* for anticipated trial purposes in the future. Recording the conversation practically ensures a conviction in court. This is all done fairly quickly after the informant's arrest. Time is of the essence if you choose to complete an operation such as this because we all know that word travels fast!

The main probable cause to stop, detain, and subsequently search the suspect will come when your new informant either makes a purchase of CDS in front of you or points out the vehicle your new target is in as he/she makes the delivery to the CI. The CI will then make a positive identification giving the police the probable cause to conduct their search of the supplier and/or their vehicle.

How this all happens is that the courts have routinely recognized that an informant's reliability can be adequately established if, during the course of an investigation, the informant supplies information concerning his/her *own name* to the police and includes a "statement against his penal interest" (United States v. Harris 403 U.S. 573, 583, 91 S. Ct. 2075, 2081-82 [1971]). "Common sense in the important daily affairs of life would induce a prudent and disinterested observer to credit these statements. People do not lightly admit crime and place critical evidence in the hands of the police in the form of their own admissions" (Id. at 583, 91, S. Ct. 2082). In addition, the court pointed out in *United States v. Clark*, 24 F.3d 299, 303 (D.C. Cir. 1994) "Officers could reasonably believe that precisely because [the informant] was actively engaged in drug trafficking, he would know—

and thus be able to identify—*the source* of his trading goods; *furthermore, because he was seeking leniency at the hands of the law, [the informant] would have little reason to prove himself an unreliable informant."*

In *United States v. Reyes*, 792 *F.2d* 536 (5ᵗʰ Cir. 1986), the court found that under the Fourth Amendment, information supplied by a *"first-time informant"* may be used to establish probable cause to search a **motor vehicle** or **person** if the credibility of the informant and the informants "basis of knowledge" is sufficiently corroborated by the "totality of the circumstances" (Id. at 539, 540).

HOW TO CONDUCT A CONTROLLED BUY UTILIZING AN INFORMANT

Conducting controlled buys are the most commonly used method to further narcotics investigations. A controlled buy utilizes confidential informants who either are going to testifying in the case at trial or wish to remain anonymous while assisting in the investigation. An informant that is conducting controlled buys needs to be properly debriefed as to their knowledge of the suspect (refer to a sample debriefing form at the end of this chapter) and their motivation thoroughly identified before the use of this informant. This is all done in addition to formally signing up the informant through your department or unit. Once the above has been accomplished, the following procedures *need to be strictly adhered to* in an effort to ensure that the integrity of the buy is guaranteed.

1. **BREIFING LOCATION:** Set up a meeting with the informant at a predetermined location away from the area where the buy is to take place. Behind shopping centers, community parks, and industrial parks are normally used for meeting spots, but any location that enables you and

the informant anonymity can be used. An important step in conducting a controlled buy is to have the CI physically point out to you the target residence used by the suspect. This eliminates any mistakes later in the investigation when it comes to the proper identification of the residence and provides you with direct knowledge of the location. This preventive measure should be common sense and is a very important step, which should be exercised on every controlled buy.

2. *PAPERWORK/DOCUMENTATION OF CURRENCY:* Complete the proper paperwork prior to the transaction. This is when the CI will sign for the currency to be used for the transaction, which will be captured on the CI Contact Sheet. (A CI Contact Sheet is included at the end of this chapter). Money used to purchase narcotics while conducting controlled or hand-to-hand buys should be copied prior to making the purchase to accurately document the serial numbers. You can do this in the field by writing down the serial numbers of the buy money or making photocopies prior to leaving your office. This is all done to confirm the fact that the money previously documented was the same money used to make the purchase with the suspect. In turn this corroborates informant or officer statements that the defendant was involved in the distribution of controlled dangerous substance, which is evidenced by the documented money in the possession of the suspect.

3. *SEARCHING AND EQUIPING THE INFORMANT:* Next, thoroughly search the informant from head to toe, including hats, pants, shoes, socks, and other garments. Be sure to look in the CI's mouth and between the CI's fingers (web portion). These are common areas of concealment used by individuals to hide controlled dangerous substances. In addition to searching the informant, you will need to search the entire passenger compartment of the informant's vehicle

that it is using. The purpose of searching the confidential informant is to ensure that the informant went into the residence with nothing and exited with the CDS, showing that the only place the informant could have gotten the CDS was from within the residence/vehicle or from the suspects themselves. If you locate CDS on the informant prior to conducting the controlled purchase, you are obligated to place the informant under arrest for possession of the drug and subsequently avoid further use of the informant in future police investigations. Locating CDS on informants prior to a controlled buy shows deception on their part and would jeopardize the investigation if allowed to proceed. In addition to the search, retrieve all personal currency that the informant brought with him or her. This is to ensure that the CI is only sent into the suspect's residence/vehicle with only the amount of currency needed to complete the purchase. This is also the time to outfit the informant with a body wire / Kel Mic (covert listening device) to record all conversations during the time of the transaction. Recording the conversation during the transaction will most certainly cause the CI to be divulged in court. Because of this, only record the conversation during a drug transaction when the informant agrees to testify in open court. Refer to "preparing the testifying informant for the courtroom" within this chapter.

4. ***INSTRUCTING THE INFORMANT:*** Once the informant has been searched, give him specific instructions to go directly to the suspect or the residence/vehicle. Then once the transaction occurs return directly back to you at a predetermined location to be debriefed. It is very important to stress to the informant *not* to have any physical contact with other individuals along the way or when returning. Again, this is to ensure that the CDS in question was in fact purchased from the suspect or the suspect's residence/vehicle. It is also important to instruct the informant not

spend a great deal of time in the suspect's residence, for the informant to get the drugs, then leave the area. Remember, the longer the informant is interacting with the suspect the more the chances that the informant will slip up and cause the suspect to become weary. In addition, the safety of the informant should be held to the standard of a fellow officer placed in the same situation—they are your responsibility.

5   *PRIOR TO INFORMANT ARRIVING:* Have your surveillance team set up at the residence prior to sending the informant. Presurveillance can produce priceless information for the investigation. This will allow you to know if there is anyone home at the suspect's residence, or if there is a lot of foot traffic in and out of the residence (clear indication that the suspect has a ready supply), or if there is countersurveillance in the area that would impede the members of your team from being able to keep steady surveillance of the informant to and from the suspect's residence. A very important aspect of a controlled purchase is to ensure that surveillance units keep a constant eye on the informant's movements to and from the target residence/ vehicle; again to ensure that the CI retrieves the CDS purchased from the suspect's residence/vehicle and is not deviating from the plan of action. If need be, place members of your surveillance team on foot hidden in the area, close to the suspect's residence to ensure that the informant arrived at the point of destination.

6   *COMPLETION OF TRANSACTION:* Once the informant returns to the predetermined location, retrieve the CDS from the CI and conduct a complete and thorough search, again to ensure that there is no excess currency or drugs hidden on their person or in their vehicle that was used for transportation. Once the search is conducted, begin debriefing the informant as to what had occurred. If the informant is being honest he or she will tell the same story

that your surveillance witnessed minus what occurred within the residence. This again corroborates your informant and shows his or her veracity. During your questioning of the informant inquire as to what happened during the transaction while inside the residence (i.e., where the suspect went to retrieve the drugs, how much drugs did they witness at the residence, who was present, what's the layout of the interior like, etc.). This is all documented in your report, while being as vague as possible being careful not to put anything in your report that would disclose your informant's identity and allow the suspect to relate this transaction to your informant.

SAMPLE NARRATIVE USED IN AN INFORMANT CONTROLLED BUY REPORT

Prebuy information identifying what the purpose of the meeting with the CI is about. Also explains that a through search was conducted on the CI, and the vehicle used by the CI. And lastly the fact that official funds were used to make the purchase

During the week of February 16, 2003, members of the Caroline County Drug Task force and I met with said CI at a predetermined location in Caroline County for the purpose of the CI to make a controlled purchase of a controlled dangerous substance from Julie Draper and Steve Doe, while at Apartment 1002, Caroline Apartments, Denton, Caroline County, Maryland. I caused a complete and thorough search of the CI and the vehicle to be used by the CI. No controlled dangerous substances or United States currency were located. The CI was then given an amount of U.S. currency from the task force official advanced funds used for the purchase of controlled dangerous substances.

This paragraph lists the events that the surveillance team observed. Notice how the paragraphs are worded vaguely so not to inadvertently tip off the suspect later at trial or when reading the search warrant. In addition, make note here that there was no other contact between the informant or any other individuals in the area. Lastly explain that a subsequent search was again completed which showed that the informant was free of any additional controlled substances or Currency other then what was purchased from the suspect.

I took up a position where I could maintain surveillance on No. 1000 building of Caroline Apartments and on the CI's path going to and from No. 1000 building of Caroline Apartments, Denton, Caroline County, Maryland. I would like to note that the buildings in the Caroline Apartments complex all have open foyers allowing me an unobstructed view of the CI's path to and from No. 1000 building of Caroline Apartments. The CI was greeted at the door and permitted access into the main entrance of the apartment. Shortly thereafter the CI exited the main entrance of the apartment and left the area, responding to the predetermined location in its vehicle. Upon contact with the CI, it handed me a plastic bag, which contained a quantity of suspected marijuana. At no time did said CI come in contact with any other person prior to or after leaving the apartment. I again caused a complete and thorough search of the CI and the vehicle utilized by the CI, which were found to be free of any controlled dangerous substances or United States currency.

This is where your observations are corroborated by the informant's description of the events that had occurred. Be sure not to be to detailed as to what was said or the exact location of where the drugs were retrieved. Remember that the suspect will be reading this and will try to remember who the informant would be.

I spoke to the CI who advised me that it had entered apartment No. 1002 through the main entrance, where Steve Doe greeted the CI. Once inside the apartment the CI purchased a quantity of marijuana from Steve Doe. The CI then exited and returned directly to the predetermined location to be debriefed. At that time contact with said CI was terminated.

Explain that a field test was completed, list the property held number, and where the CDS was forwarded to.

A portion of the suspected marijuana was field-tested utilizing the ODV filed test system for marijuana, which yielded a positive indication for the presence of marijuana—a schedule I controlled dangerous substance. The suspected marijuana was logged under Maryland State Police property held No. P-179716 and forwarded to the Maryland State Police Crime Lab for further chemical analysis.

(INSERT YOUR DEPARTMENT'S NAME HERE)
CDS Debriefing Information Form

Defendant's Name: _____   Defendant's Address:_____

_____

_____

NickName:_____   Maiden Name:_____

Police Department:_____   Case Number:_____

Arresting Officer:_____   Misc. Numbers:_____

List of Charges: Type of CDS/ Paraphernalia Confiscated:

1. _____   1. _____
2. _____   2. _____
3. _____   3. _____
4. _____   4. _____
5. _____   5. _____

Debriefing Questionnaire:

1. How old were you when you first started using drugs?_____
2. What type of drugs have you used, purchased, or distributed in both the past and present?_____

_____

_____

3. How often do you use these drugs?_____
4. What is the usual amount of drugs you would purchase at a time?_____
5. Have you ever distributed drugs in the past? Yes / No. If so what type of drug and how much drugs would you get at a time?_____

_____

_____

6. What is the *most* amount of drugs you have purchased at one time?_____
7. When was the last time you purchased drugs; and how much?_____
8. When you buy your drugs do you go alone or have you had someone with you? _____
9. Do you drive your own car or do you get a ride from a friend to pick up your drugs?_____

10. Who is the biggest person you know involved in drugs? And what type of drug(s)?_____

11. Have you bought drugs from this person?_____

12. When was the last time you purchased drugs from this person?_____

13. Do you purchase these drugs from this persons home or vehicle?_____

14. Does this person distribute drugs out of their vehicle?_____

15. List the address/directions to this person's home and give a brief description:

_____

_____

_____

_____

_____

16. List the vehicle(s) driven by this person and description; list Maryland or out of state registration if known:_____

_____

_____

17. Does this person have pets? If so what kind and do they bite, bark a lot etc . . . ?

_____

_____

18. Do these pets run free around the yard?_____

19. Does this person have children living at the residence? If so how many and how old?_____

_____

20. Does this person have people act as look outs or use electronic equipment such as police scanners, two way radio=s etc.? If so describe:_____

_____

_____

21. List any other individuals and their address=s who are involved in drugs or you can buy from:

What type of drug their involved in as well.

1. ._____

2. ._____

3. ._____

4. ._____

5. ._____

22. Do you know of any illegal sales of firearms and or crimes, terrorism activities, other then drugs, that have occurred in the past? ☐ Yes ☐ No

23. If so, what, where, when, and who committed this act?_____

_____

_____

_____

_____

24. **NOTES:**_____

_____

_____

_____

SIGNATURE OF OFFICER: _____ **SIGNATURE OF SOURCE:**_____

DATE:_____ **TIME:**_____ **LOCATION:**_____

(INSERT YOUR DEPARTMENT'S NAME HERE)
CONFIDENTIAL INFORMANT AGREEMENT

I, _____ the undersigned, state that it is my intent to associate myself, of my own free will and without any coercion or duress, with the (*insert your department's name here*) as a confidential informant.

As a confidential informant, I understand and agree that I have no police powers under the laws of the state of (*insert your state here*) and have no authority to carry a weapon while performing my activity as a confidential informant. Further, I understand and agree that my only association with the (*insert your department's name here*) is as a confidential informant on a case-by-case or time-by-time basis as an independent contractor and not as an employee of the police department. Any payment I receive from the (*insert your department's name here*) will not be subject to state and federal income tax withholding or social security. I understand that it is my responsibility to report any income and also that I am not entitled to either workman's compensation or unemployment insurance payments for anything I do as a confidential informant.

In consideration for being allowed to associate with the (*insert your department's name here*) as a confidential informant and in consideration for any payment I may receive, I agree to be bound by the following terms and conditions and procedures while so associated.

1. I agree that under no circumstances will I purchase or possess any controlled dangerous substances or suspected controlled dangerous substances without the direction and control of a police officer and then will only make a purchase only with monies supplied by the officer.

2. I agree not to use, sell, dispense, or transfer any controlled dangerous substances except that I may use any

controlled substance prescribed to me by a licensed physician.

3. I agree to maintain a strict accounting of all funds provided to me by the (*insert your department's name here*) and I understand that misuse of (*insert your department's name here*) funds could be grounds for criminal prosecution against me.

4. I agree not to divulge to any person, except the officer with whom I am associated, my status as a confidential informant for the (*insert your department's name here*) unless required to do so in court, and shall not represent myself to other as an employee or representative of the (*insert your department's name here*) nor use the department or any of its officers as personal references or as credit or employment references.

5. I understand that any violation of the above-listed provisions may be grounds for my immediate removal as a confidential informant and that any violation of law may result in my arrest and prosecution.

I understand that association with the (*insert your department's name here*) as a confidential informant may involve strenuous physical activity and may become hazardous to my physical well-being and safety. Nevertheless it is my desire to associate myself with the (*insert your department's name here*), on an independent contractor basis, as a confidential informant. I am associating myself with the (*insert your department's name here*) in this status freely and without any coercion or duress. In consideration for being accepted as a confidential informant, I release and discharge the (*insert your department's name here*), and its elected official, officers, employees, and agents from all claims, demands, actions, judgments, and executions which I may have or acquire and subsequently claim to have against the (*insert your department's name here*) for personal injuries and property damage I sustain which arises out of or in connection with my association with the (*insert your department's name here*). I make this release for myself, my heirs, executors, and administrators. Also, I agree not to maintain any action against the (*insert your government's name here*), (*insert your department's name here*), or its elected officials, officers, employees, or agents for personal injuries and property damage I sustain which arise out of or in connection with my association with the (*insert your department's name here*).

_____

CONFIDENTIAL INFORMANT'S SIGNATURE.

_____

DATE

WITNESSES:

_____

OFFICER'S SIGNATURE

_____

OFFICER'S SIGNATURE

(INSERT YOUR DEPARTMENT/UNIT NAME HERE) CONFIDENTIAL INFORMANT PARENTAL AGREEMENT

I, _____ the undersigned, hereby grant permission for my **(son/daughter),**_____, to associate with and to serve as a confidential informant for the **(insert your department's name here)** This permission is given after consulting with my **(son/daughter)** and members of the **(insert your department's name here)**, and is given of my own free will and without any coercion or duress.

As a confidential informant, I understand and agree that my **(son/daughter)** has no police powers under the laws of the state of Maryland and has no authority to carry a weapon while performing **(his/her)** activities as a confidential informant. Further, I understand and agree that my **(son's/daughter's)** only association with the **(insert your department's name here)** as a confidential informant on a case-by-case or time-by-time basis as an independent contractor, and not as an employee of the police department.

I understand that it is **(his/her)** responsibility to report any income and to pay any state, federal, or social security taxes due and that **(he/she)** is not entitled to either workman's compensation or unemployment insurance payments for anything **(he/she)** does as a confidential informant.

In consideration for being allowed to associate with the **(insert your department's name here)** as a confidential informant and in consideration for any payment **(he/she)** may receive, my **(son/daughter)** agrees to be bound by the following terms and conditions and procedures while so associated.

6. I agree that under no circumstances will **(he/she)** purchase or possess any controlled dangerous substances or suspected controlled dangerous substances without the direction and control of a police officer and then will only make a purchase only with monies supplied by the officer.

7. I agree for my (**son/daughter**) not to use, sell, dispense, or transfer any controlled dangerous substances except that (**he/she**) may use any controlled substance prescribed to (**him/her**) by a licensed physician.

8. I agree for my (**son/daughter**) to maintain a strict accounting of all funds provided to (**him/her**) by the (**insert your department's name here**) and (**he/she**) understands that misuse of (**insert your department's name here**) funds could be grounds for criminal prosecution against him.

9. I agree for my (**son/daughter**) not to divulge to any person, except the officer with whom (**he/she**) is associated, (**his/her**) status as a confidential informant for the (**insert your department's name here**) unless required to do so in court, and shall not represent (**himself/ herself**) to others as an employee or representative of the (**insert your department's name here**) nor use the department or any of its officers as personal references or as credit or employment references.

10. I understand that any violation of the above-listed provisions may be grounds for (**his/her**) immediate removal as a confidential informant and that any violation of law may result in (**his/her**) arrest and prosecution.

I understand that my (**son's/daughter's**) association with the (**insert your department's name here**) as a confidential informant may involve strenuous physical activity and may become hazardous to (**his/her**) physical well-being and safety. Nevertheless, it is my desire to permit my (**son/daughter**) to work with the (**insert your department's name here**) as an independent contractor, as a confidential informant. I am associating my (**son/daughter**) with the (**insert your department's name here**) in this status freely and without any coercion or duress. In consideration for being accepted as a confidential informant, I release and discharge the (**insert your department's name here**), and its elected officials, officers, employees, and agents from all claims, demands, actions, judgments, and executions which I may have or acquire and subsequently claim to have against the **(insert your department's name here)** for personal injuries and property damage my **(son/daughter)** sustains which arises out of or in connection with **(his/her)** association with the **(insert your department's name here).** I make this release for my **(son/ daughter)**, heirs, my executors, administrators, and myself. Also, I agree not to maintain any action against the agencies and governments which make up the **(insert your department's name here)**, or its elected officials, officers, employees, or agents for personal injuries and property damage my **(son/ daughter)** sustains which arise out of or in connection with my **(son's/daughter's)** association with the **(insert your department's name here).**

PARENTAL SIGNATURE OF CONFIDENTIAL INFORMANT   DATE

WITNESSES:
          OFFICER'S SIGNATURE   TIME

EXAMPLE OF CI DEBRIEF MEMO-DRUG USE
(ON AGENCY LETTERHEAD)

April 11, 2004

Caroline County Drug Task Force   IR-04-58-00810
Drug Enforcement Command   CI Debriefing No.93-018
Confidential Memorandum   Initial/Final

==

On April 6, 2004, at approximately 1700 hours, I, Detective James Henning, Caroline County Sheriff's Department-CID (Caroline County Drug Task Force), met with an individual who desired to become a confidential informant. The confidential informant herein referred to as CI has criminal charges pending in Caroline County and wishes to cooperate with the task force for consideration with the Caroline County States Attorneys Office for same. The CI advised that the CI is familiar with individuals who are distributing controlled dangerous substances in the Caroline County area and wished to provide assistance for consideration in sentencing for those charges pending against the CI. The CI was directed that I would research the information that the CI provided and then would contact the assistant state attorney handling the prosecution of the CI's case. I explained that all determination for consideration would be the decision of the state attorney's office. It should be noted that the state attorney's office has authorized the use of the CI and the assistance provided by the CI would be given consideration toward the outstanding criminal charges. In addition a signed confidential informant contract has been obtained and included in this case file.

The CI provided information concerning Connie Parsons, white female, in her mid to late forties, who is distributing quantities of marijuana and cocaine in the Denton, Caroline County Maryland area. The CI stated that the CI has purchased marijuana and cocaine from Connie Parsons in the past and can make controlled purchases of marijuana or cocaine from Parsons at her residence. The CI also advised that the CI may be able to introduce an undercover police officer to Parsons.

The CI also provided information concerning Ray Boyd, white male, in his late teens early twenties, who is distributing quantities of marijuana and cocaine in the Denton Caroline County, Maryland area. The CI stated that the CI has purchased marijuana and cocaine from Boyd in the past and can make controlled purchases of marijuana or cocaine from Boyd at his residence.

The CI advised that the CI began using controlled dangerous substance at the age of sixteen. The drugs the CI admitted to using in the past is marijuana and cocaine. The CI advised that the CI has spent up to $1,000 a week for marijuana and cocaine. The CI advised that the CI is familiar with the actions, traits, habits and terminology of controlled dangerous substances.

The CI is familiar with the appearance, prices, and packaging of controlled dangerous substances for street-level sales, and that the knowledge and familiarity learned by the CI was obtained partly by the CI having personally used, purchased, and distributed controlled dangerous substances in the past.

The CI was instructed not to be involved with CDS or anyone with CDS unless under the direct supervision of an investigator from the task force. The CI agreed to all terms and provisions set forth in regards to cooperating with the Caroline County Drug Task Force. The CI had no other knowledge of illegal gun sales or any other criminal activity taking place in the surrounding area.

Case closed

Det James Henning	No. 0140	Date
Cpl. Ronald E. Crouch	No. 0759	Date
D/Sgt John R. Bounds	No. 0297	Date

EXAMPLE OF CI DEBRIEF MEMO-NO DRUG USE (ON AGENCY LETTERHEAD)

October 29, 2004

Caroline County Drug Task Force   IR-04-07-02476
Drug Enforcement Command   CI Debriefing No.07-93-012
Confidential Memorandum   Initial/Final Report

On October 29, 2004, at approximately 1700 hours, Cpl. Ronald E. Crouch No.0759, Caroline County Drug Task Force (Maryland State Police), Det Kenneth Schmidt No.0108, Caroline County Sheriff's Department-CID (Caroline County Drug Task Force), and I, Det. James A. Henning No.0140, Caroline County Sheriff's Department-CID (Caroline County Drug Task Force), met with an individual who desired to become a confidential informant. The confidential informant, herein referred to as CI, advised that the CI is familiar with numerous individuals who are currently distributing controlled dangerous substances in the Caroline County area.

The CI advised that the CI was interested in assisting the Caroline County Drug Task Force with controlled dangerous substance investigations in the Caroline County area in exchange for payment for services rendered. It should be noted that the state attorney's office has authorized the use of the CI as well as any and all assistance provided by the CI.

The CI advised that the CI has never used controlled dangerous substances at all. The drugs the CI admitted to being exposed to in the past through friends and associates are marijuana, powder cocaine, crack cocaine, LSD, and ecstasy (MDMA). The CI advised that during the CI's exposure to CDS, the CI had been present while CDS transactions occurred and has handled various forms of CDS. The CI advised that the CI is familiar with the actions, traits, habits, and terminology of controlled dangerous substances. That the CI is familiar with the appearance, prices, and packaging of controlled dangerous substances for street-level sales, and that the knowledge and familiarity learned by the CI was obtained partly by the CI having personally observed its associates handling and using controlled dangerous substances in the past.

The CI provided information concerning Michele Butler, white female, in her late teens early twenties, from the Greensboro or Henderson area, who is distributing crack cocaine and powder cocaine in the Caroline County area. The CI stated that the CI has been approached by Butler in the recent past in reference to purchasing CDS and can make controlled purchases of CDS from Butler. The CI also advised that the CI may be able to introduce an undercover police officer to Butler.

The CI was instructed not to be involved with any CDS or anyone with CDS unless under the direct supervision of an investigator from the Caroline County Drug Task Force. Case closed.

Det James Henning	No. 0140	Date

Cpl. Ronald E. Crouch	No. 3718	Date

D/Sgt John R. Bounds	No. 0297	Date

(INSERT YOUR AGENCY NAME HERE)
Confidential Informant History

PHOTOGRAPH (From files if available)	Date:	CI No.
	Name: (Last, First, Middle)	
	Nickname or Alias:	Soc. Sec. No.
	Address:	Telephone: ( )
	City: State:	Place of Birth:
	Type of Activity:	

Sex	Descent	DOB	Hgt.	Wgt.	Hair	Eyes

Complexion, Marks, Scars, Tattoos, etc.
Vehicles:
Assisted: Other agencies (names)

Signature:	
Assumed Name:	
How CI Developed:	Contributing Officer:
Criminal Record: FBI Sheet N/A ☐	In File ☐
Local/State Sheet N/A ☐	In File ☐
Hangouts:	
Associates:	

Miscellaneous Information: (summary of contacts and assessment)	Right Thumb Print: (Where identification is not established by other records)

(INSERT YOUR DEPARTMENT'S NAME HERE)
Confidential Informant Contact Report

Investigator:_____   Date: _____

Informant Number:_____   Time: _____

- ☐ Initial Contact
- ☐ Personal Contact
- ☐ Telephone Contact
- ☐ No Information Received
- ☐ Information Received

- ☐ Controlled Purchase Made
- ☐ Introduction to Suspect/No Purchase
- ☐ Introduction to Suspect/Purchase CDS
- ☐ Informant Paid
- ☐ Other

REMARKS (Explain circumstances surrounding contact, include case number)

_____
_____
_____
_____
_____
_____

Purchase Record Information

Amount of monies given to informant for contraband purchase: $_____

Signature of informant verifying purchase funds received:_____

Contraband Purchased (describe):_____

Stolen Property Purchased (describe):_____

Informant Payment Record

I hereby acknowledge receipt of $ _____ for services rendered.

Date of payment _____ Informant's Signature: _____

Investigator's   Supervisor's
Signature: _____   Signature: _____

Enter the results of the informant contacts/investigation

Date	Case Number	No. of Persons arrested/offense	Search & Seizure Warrants	Contraband Seized	Investigator

(INSERT YOUR DEPARTMENT'S NAME HERE)
Confidential Informant Contact Report
(Example)

Investigator: <u>Detective J.A. Henning</u>   Date: <u>12/30/200</u>

Informant Number: <u>CI No.07-93-002</u>   Time: <u>1200 hrs</u>

☐	Initial Contact	☒	Controlled Purchase Made
☒	Personal Contact	☐	Introduction to Suspect/No Purchase
☐	Telephone Contact	☒	Introduction to Suspect/Purchase CDS
☐	No Information Received	☐	Informant Paid
☒	Information Received	☐	Other

REMARKS (Explain circumstances surrounding contact, include case number)

On 7-22-02, members of the Caroline County Drug Task Force conducted a controlled purchase of cocaine from a residence in the Caroline County area. This was accomplished with the assistance of the above listed CI who made the purchase of the suspected cocaine. The purchased cocaine was tested & proved positive for the presence of cocaine a schedual II CDS. The cocaine has been logged under property held#: P-177293. Refer to confidential memo listed under CIR-02-07-03345 for further information.

Purchase Record Information

Amount of monies given to informant for contraband purchase: $ 50.00

Signature of informant verifying purchase funds received: _____

Contraband Purchased (describe): _____

Stolen Property Purchased (describe): _____

Informant Payment Record

I hereby acknowledge receipt of $ 50.00 for services rendered.

Date of payment 7-22-02 Informant's Signature: _____

Investigator's
Signature: _____   Supervisor's
Signature: _____

Enter the results of the informant contacts/investigation

Date	Case Number	No. of Persons arrested/offense	Search & Seizure Warrants	Contraband Seized	Investigator
7/22/02	CIR-02-07-03345	Pending	Pending	3.5 Cocaine	HENNING

Confidential Informant Contact Report
(Example)

Investigator: <u>Detective J.A. Henning</u>   Date: <u>12/30/200</u>

Informant Number: <u>CI No.-07-93-002</u>   Time: <u>1200 hrs</u>

☐ Initial Contact	☐ Controlled Purchase Made
☐ Personal Contact	☐ Introduction to Suspect/No Purchase
☐ Telephone Contact	☐ Introduction to Suspect/Purchase CDS
☐ No Information Received	☐ Informant Paid
☐ Information Received	☒ Other

REMARKS (Explain circumstances surrounding contact, include case number)

BI ANNUAL CI WANTED AND CRIMINAL CHECK

Purchase Record Information

Amount of monies given to informant for contraband purchase: $ <u>N/A</u>

Signature of informant verifying purchase funds received: _____

Contraband Purchased (describe): _____

Stolen Property Purchased (describe): _____

Informant Payment Record

I hereby acknowledge receipt of $ <u>N/A</u> for services rendered.

Date of payment <u>N/A</u> Informant's Signature: _____

Investigator's
Signature: _____   Supervisor's
Signature: _____

Enter the results of the informant contacts/investigation

Date	Case Number	No. of Persons arrested/offense	Search & Seizure Warrants	Contraband Seized	Investigator
7/22/02	N/A	N/A	N/A	N/A	HENNING

(ON AGENCY LETTERHEAD)
Example of CI Annual Memo-Not Keeping CI

July 22, 2002

Caroline County Drug Task Force
07 Drug Enforcement Command   CI No.07-93-002
Memo to File   Biannual Check

The confidential informant listed under CI No.07-93-002, has not actively participated in CDS-related investigations since last contact. A check through NCIC/MILES revealed no new information concerning the CI's criminal history or wanted status. I am requesting this confidential informant to be deactivated.

Det. James A. Henning No.0140   Date

(ON AGENCY LETTERHEAD)
Example of CI Annual Memo-Keeping CI

July 22, 2002

Caroline County Drug Task Force
07 Drug Enforcement Command   CI No.07-93-002
Memo to File   Biannual Check

The confidential informant listed under CI No.07-93-022 has been actively participating in CDS related investigations in the Caroline County, Maryland area. A check through NCIC/ MILES revealed no new information concerning the CI's criminal history or wanted status. I am requesting this confidential informant to remain on active status to complete future criminal investigations with the Caroline County Drug Task Force.

Det. James A. Henning No.0140 Date

Surveillance
Operations and Techniques

Surveillance is the key to all successful criminal investigations. It is the one of the most single most important factor in ensuring that an individual or group is engaging in criminal activity. In general there are three basic categories of surveillance techniques:

- moving surveillance
- stationary surveillance
- electronic surveillance

Regardless of the type of surveillance the investigator uses, the main goal in any surveillance is to gain intelligence and corroborate information already received (i.e., drug tips). Some of the objectives are to obtain specific details of persons and places suspected of drug trafficking, to verify an informant's information, to collect evidence of crimes, to obtain probable cause for a search warrant, to apprehend a suspect in the commission of a crime, to prevent the commission of a crime, to gain intelligence on a crime for which there are no other sources to corroborate the information received, and to locate suspects wanted for a crime.

Surveillance is also one of the tedious and time-consuming aspects of law enforcement. It takes an investigator who has patience and a strong motivation to ensure the successful outcome of any surveillance undertaken. In addition to patience, investigators must be creative in their efforts to observe criminal suspects and activity covertly. To prepare for a surveillance operation the officers should:

- Study police files for any information pertaining to the case. An example of some of the information the officer must have before conducting a surveillance operation is:

  1. Physical description,
  2. Photographs,
  3. Names,
  4. Addresses,
  5. Physical descriptions of associates,
  6. Vehicle descriptions,
  7. Identifying residence and business addresses,
  8. And other areas the suspect is known to frequent

- The most common equipment needed in a surveillance are:

  1. 35-mm or digital cameras with telephoto lenses (digital cameras I have found are the most practical for surveillances. An officer can zoom in and out and focus on details while sitting at their desk);
  2. Binoculars (preferably high power);
  3. Tape recorders for surveillance notes (digital handheld recorders are the most practical);
  4. Night vision;
  5. Pens/pencils, notebook for the surveillance log;
  6. Cell phone or radio for communication;
  7. And change for payphones, tolls, parking meters and "tags." (A tag is a way of finding out what phone number a suspect had dialed on a public telephone. We will talk more about this later in this section)

- Drive through the area to be targeted and get an idea of surveillance locations for officer's and/or identify where countersurveillance may be placed. Look at the style vehicles and dress that's appropriate for that area and adapt to them. Make sure to note the street names, one-way streets, dead-end streets, and traffic conditions to avoid problems during the operation.

- Lastly, the lead officer should give a briefing of all the information gathered to that point and relay it to the assisting members who will be conducting the surveillance operation. This can be done in an operational plan which contains all the pertinent information that you have gathered during your preliminary measures to ensure that everyone is on the same sheet of music when out in the field. Further, An equipment check is also preferable during this time . . . better to find out in the beginning a member of the team does not have a piece of equipment then out in the field when its needed!

Physical Surveillance Techniques

MOVING SURVEILLANCE

Utilizing mobile surveillance is much more difficult than conducting stationary surveillance. The chances of the target noticing you or your assisting members are much greater. The most common way mobile surveillance is accomplished is by foot or vehicle. Whichever method used, caution on the side of the officers conducting the mobile surveillance should be practiced at all times so that they do not compromise the operation or put themselves or others in a dangerous situation.

1. *One-man foot surveillance:*

During the course of your investigation it may be necessary to conduct surveillance of a target with just one person. Although not the most desired method it still can be effective if conducted properly. When conducting by yourself it is imperative that you keep the suspect in view at all times. If you let the target leave your sight for more than a couple seconds you will probably lose the target altogether or miss an important detail that could make your case. Some methods of completing this task is:

- *Mix in:* Find cover in pedestrian traffic. Mix in with people in the area to afford you the cover you will need.
- *Paralleling:* Another way is to walk even (parallel) with the target from across the street. Staying even with the target will afford you the opportunity to avoid losing him/her when they turn down a street, alley, or enter a building.

Diagram of One-Man Foot Surveillance

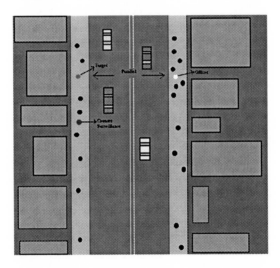

If by chance the target notices you, immediately break off the surveillance. Following through with the surveillance once this happens is not only dangerous for you but will surely blow your investigation wide open. Live to fight another day, pull off and reestablish your surveillance at a later time. You surely will not miss anything because the target will most likely not engage in any criminal behavior if he/she knows he is being watched.

Another thing you need to be aware of is countersurveillance. Don't underestimate the modern criminal. They employ the same type of surveillance tactics that law enforcement use. When this occurs it is like a chess game—who can outsmart who? What's important is to not overreact in an effort to appear normal. Overreactions draw more attention than diverting. Keep your head and wits about you, and it will turn out fine. Some signs and techniques of countersurveillance are:

- Noticing an individual staying back from the main suspect being very alert to the surroundings.
- Any one who continuously makes the same turns and route that the suspect may take over a period of time (i.e., enters the same building, same alley, crosses intersections and street at the same time).
- Look for continuous glances from the suspect to his countersurveillance. Sometimes this will come in the form of a head nod or hand signals.
- A suspect can view reflections in a storefront window as a rearview mirror.
- A suspect may enter a restaurant or store and observe who enters behind him, then leave abruptly midway through the meal or while shopping. If this occurs do not follow the suspect out of the restaurant. Upon entering the restaurant you should have one person stationary waiting to move in the event that the target takes such action. The officer immediately reacting to this while in the restaurant will sorely compromise the surveillance.
- A suspect may drop a worthless piece of paper to see if a suspected surveillance officer picks it up.
- A suspect may drive the wrong way down a one-way street or make an illegal U-turn to see if anyone is following them. This is also termed "heat run." When a suspect conducts a heat run their sole purpose is to locate anyone in the area who even looks suspicious of being a police officer. These are usually done prior to conducting

drug transactions and can span outward to as much as a five-mile radius from where the drug deal is to take place. So be aware of this, and do not have your secondary staging area or takedown team near the location of the transaction.

Along with learning the types of mobile surveillance, members of your team should also have had signals and nonverbal signs in place in the event that your office does not have the budget to get whisper mics/radios or if your radios fail. Some of the signs your unit can use is taking off your hat, tying a shoe, turning up your collar, taking off your sunglasses, or placing a newspaper under your arm. There are many signs your unit can come up with, but make sure that everyone is familiar with each signal to eliminate confusion.

2. *The ABC Method:*

This method is considered the best for foot surveillance. It utilizes three officers, which makes the surveillance much safer and easier to conduct. When using this method each officer will have a turn rotating on "point" (lead). This will be done periodically to avoid detection from the target or countersurveillance. This surveillance method is conducted in the following fashion:

A is the point man who maintains visual contact with the suspect.

B is maintaining visual contact with **A**.

C will commonly be across the street to be on the lookout for countersurveillance that may be mixed in with or tailing officers **A** and **B**. The sole purpose of **C** is to identify this threat.

- When a target is about to reach an intersection or change direction, **C** should reach the intersection first.

- If the target stops, **A** and **B** should continue past the target. **C** then takes the "eyeball" (a term used to distinguish who has visual surveillance of the target). Once the target starts to move again then each officer should pick up their positions where they left off.
- It is important to rotate positions periodically during the surveillance. A signal should be made up to notify each officer of the rotation. A rotation should be **A** continues past the target or crosses the street paralleling the target. **C** takes the spot of **B**, and **B** now becomes **A**. Sounds harder than it is, but with a little practice it will all become second nature when the time comes. Refer to the diagram for the pattern used in this method.

Diagram of ABC Method

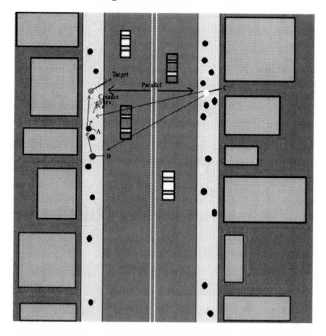

3. The "Lead and Follow" Method:

This method takes a little more time than the ABC method due to the constant fluctuation of positions. This method is good to use if you need to locate a target's hiding place, meeting spot, stash houses, and especially when the target enters department stores. The Lead and Follow method operates in the following fashion:

A. One officer follows behind the target from a safe and inconspicuous distance.

B. Another officer positions himself well ahead of the target who would be walking in the direction toward this officer. This officer is usually on the opposite side of the sidewalk standing stationary, if possible.

C. Once the mobile officer reaches the stationary officer, they then switch positions, and the mobile officer now needs to move ahead of the target to find a stationary position.

4. *Single Vehicle Surveillance:*

When conducting mobile surveillance it is always better to have two or more vehicles to follow a suspect than one. But due to manpower issues sometimes it will become necessary to follow a suspect by yourself. While following the suspect in your vehicle, especially on rural roads, allow some distance between your vehicle and the suspect's. This is done so as to not arouse the suspect's suspicions. In heavy traffic conditions or on a highway, allow at least one vehicle between yours and the suspect's. This will provide you some cover and not raise suspicions. It is better to have a few more cars in front of your vehicle (not too much to where you may lose site of the vehicle) to draw the attention away from you as they periodically turn off in separate directions as the suspect. In the event that you are following a suspect vehicle into a small town be careful that the suspect doesn't notice you. It is easy to draw suspicions on small town streets. The only way to rectify this is to keep your distance.

The vehicle you use for surveillance should not have any distinguishing marks or equipment that can be easily recognized (i.e., bright lights, flashy rims, or running lights). It is also unwise to utilize a vehicle with burned-out headlights or parking lights, which might be noticed by the suspect after seeing your vehicle more than once.

One trick you can do to your vehicle is having two toggle switches inside your vehicle each controlling the power to an individual headlight. In the event that you follow a suspect (at night) and he/she sees your vehicle more than once during the operation. You can turn one headlight off to change your vehicles appearance giving the impression that it is a different vehicle. After a while, switch it to the other headlight to black it out. Then when you have the chance put your headlights back to normal. This tactic will give the illusion at night that there are three different vehicles behind the suspect.

5. *Multiple Vehicle Surveillance (The Leap Frog Method):*

Diagram of Leap Frog Method

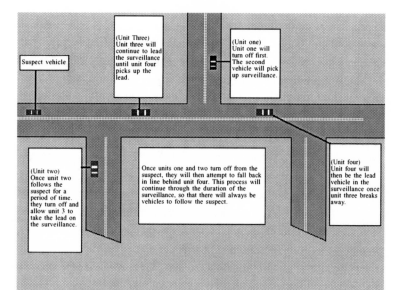

This type of surveillance needs at least two to three vehicles in order to work properly. Conducted properly, the Leap Frog method is a great tool in keeping track of a suspect's vehicle. It is accomplished by assigning each surveillance vehicle with a number (i.e., unit 1, unit 2, etc). This helps the flow of communication between surveillance vehicles in the event split-second decisions are made. Have Unit 1 follow behind the suspect vehicle for a while. Remember try not to arouse the suspicions of the suspect. Unit 2 is to fall in behind or within a reasonable distance behind Unit 1, and so on and so forth for each additional unit assisting. How this works is after Unit 1 tails the suspect for a period of time, he turns off of the suspect. Unit 2 then picks up pace and falls in to position behind the suspect vehicle. It is important that each unit makes sure that the other is in position to take the "eyeball" (visual) of suspect before pulling off. Unit 1 should turn around and aggressively attempt to catch up with Unit 2. Once in position, Unit 2 will pull off and Unit 1 will resume its spot following the suspect. This is done repeatedly throughout your surveillance and is much more effective when utilized with a group of surveillance vehicles.

STATIONARY SURVEILLANCE

Stationary surveillance is the most common method used by law enforcement. Stationary surveillance allows officers continuous observation of the target or the specific location being "staked out." Oftentimes officers interested in establishing who's frequenting a residence, business or specific location utilize this technique to establish probable cause based on observations or simply to gather intelligence to further an investigation.

Stationary surveillance is mostly conducted from two types of surveillance points:

1. *Vehicles* (a vehicle specifically designated for covert surveillance operations that is outfitted with the proper surveillance equipment, or a vehicle inconspicuous to the surrounding area; a "decoy" which is disguised as a

specific company's vehicle—i.e., telephone company, electric company, plumbing company, etc.)

2. *Or basic cover-stationary surveillance, also called a "base"* (i.e., houses, businesses, rooftops, woods, etc.)

Whether conducted from a base or a vehicle, officers engaged in stationary surveillance must maintain a chronological log of all the activity observed during the time of the surveillance: descriptions, times of individuals arriving and leaving, vehicle traffic, and any items brought to or from the location. The surveillance log/notes need to be meticulous in detail, including times, physical description, even the lighting conditions/weather, so that later, whether for court or intelligence purposes, you can have all the information at your fingertips. A surveillance log in the long run can assist in establishing patterns or other illicit activities and behaviors. I'll talk more about note-taking techniques in the PC callout section, which will give you an idea of how detailed an officer should be.

VEHICLES: When conducting stationary vehicle surveillance officers should consider the following:

1. The type of vehicle selected should match its surroundings.
2. In cold or inclement whether, an idling vehicle will emit exhaust fumes (condensation), that can be easily seen by individuals in the surrounding area, which can raise suspicions of the targets you are watching or even the neighbors that live nearby. Another dead giveaway is daytime running lights. If your vehicle has this option take it to a shop and have them set up on a switch so that you can turn them on and off when needed. If neighbors see a vehicle that looks out of place they will contact the local police for a suspicious vehicle in the area. So have a plan of action already in place if this occurs.
3. Go to the bathroom prior to getting into your position. This will save a lot of aggravation in the long run.

4. Come prepared with food, water, and snacks that will last you until your shift is completed.

5. The most important measure in stationary vehicle surveillance is to not move abruptly as to cause the vehicle to shake. This will give away your position as well and can ruin your operation if seen by neighbors or targets.

A van or sport utility vehicle is best suited for this type of surveillance operation. The basic stationary surveillance vehicle should be outfitted with the following features:

- Tinted windows, or windows that are shrouded with blackout curtains. Having both increases your ability to be totally covert during your observation.

- Some way of obscuring the interior of the vehicle from individuals looking in through the front windshield. A great way is draping a black curtain across the front section of the vehicle, separating the front seats from the back portion of the vehicle. A small slit can be made in the curtain to allow officers to peer through and make their observations or take the appropriate photographs. The other way is to buy a sunblock shade for the windshield of the vehicle and cut slits in it to allow officers to peer through or take pictures. The sunblock shade is a more temporary method if switching surveillance vehicles frequently.

- A tripod for spotting scopes or cameras. A lot of camera shops now sell window-mounted tripods that work great in keeping your spotting scopes or binoculars from shaking. They can even be easily moved from one vehicle to another.

- Portable air conditioners can be of great assistance in hot weather. They can be purchased from camping catalogs/stores or through law enforcement catalogs. They are fairly cheap and are cooled utilizing dry ice (the best) or bags of ice purchased at your local convenience store. As mentioned earlier, you do not want to draw attention to yourself by having the surveillance vehicle running. The ability to have a portable air conditioner (although not necessary) can make your surveillance a much more pleasant experience.

A stationary vehicle surveillance technique that has been successful with some agencies is utilizing a "drone" vehicle. A drone is a vehicle that is selected to look inconspicuous in a specific area and is outfitted with a visual covert surveillance system that can capture a specified target area on tape or through wireless video transmissions sent back to a designated location to be viewed in real time.

For example, an old car that would be inconspicuous in the targeted area is outfitted with a pinhole camera system in the headrest, front dash, rear deck, or a stuffed animal, which is set to view the targeted area. The recording/transmitting equipment is locked in the trunk of the vehicle. When it comes time to implant the drone in its designated area the officer drives the vehicle into position, gets out and walks down the road, only to be picked up by other officers and transported back to the surveillance base station.

Wireless technology has come a long way since the days of microwave transmission (direct line of site). Today law enforcement has at their disposal, equipment that operates off various frequencies without being close to the action. The Internet can play a big role in surveillance. There is equipment on the market today that allows an officer to sit at his desk in his office and observe video on his computer from a hidden camera placed at a location miles away and still have the ability to record, zoom, pan, and tilt if needed.

BASIC COVER-STATIONARY SURVEILANCE (BASE): When conducting basic cover-stationary surveillance officers should consider the following:

1. Pick a location that will allow you the best vantage point to view the targeted area. Some examples of locations that can be used are:

   - business
   - abandoned/unoccupied building
   - parking lots—utilizing vans or other vehicles as a base
   - deer stand/trees
   - towers
   - rooftops—both residential and/or commercial

2. Plan on how to covertly enter and exit your base location. You might utilize a form of distraction to allow the undercover officers to enter and exit. An example is having an ambulance, with its lights and siren on, go through the area and park just far enough away to get the attention of the individuals in your way of entering or exiting the base.

3. Always send two officers at a time to a base. This will allow one officer to make the surveillance observations while the other takes notes and watches the other officers back.

1. *Surveillance Note Taking:*

Taking notes during a surveillance operation is one of the most important measures an officer can do to ensure a successful outcome both in the field and later in court. It is imperative that while making observations you are as descriptive as possible. After the fieldwork is done, you will need to refer to these notes to write your reports and articulate what you had seen during the surveillance. This includes the following:

1. The time and date you began your surveillance;
2. The lighting conditions or if conducted during the daylight, dusk, or at night.

3. Who is present with you and actually taking the notes;
4. Mark runners, dealers, buyers, and countersurveillance as T1, T2, T3, T4, and so on and so forth. Every time a target (T) is observed making a transaction, signal, or strange behavior (for example, always patting his waistband, which is a subconscious behavior exhibited by individuals carrying guns) you will utilize that individuals target number to refer to him throughout the investigation.

Example: (Identify the physical description of each target first)

> 1320 T3—B/M, 5' 09", black hat, white T-shirt, blue shorts
>
> 1320 T3—pulls out baggie of marijuana and hands to T2
>
> 1325 T5—returns to scene and makes contact with T6 exchanged money and a baggie of cocaine
>
> 1325 T6—puts currency and cocaine in front left pocket
>
> 1327 T2—returns to vehicle (T1) and leans in to vehicle with a baggie in his hand and gives it to T1
>
> 1327 T1—hands T2 money
>
> 1327 T2—puts money in his front right pocket

Refer to the P.C. callout section for more information on conducting surveillance from stationary locations.

8. *"Tagging"*

Sometimes when conducting physical surveillance, both mobile or stationary, the suspect you are following will stop to make a phone call at a public telephone booth. "Tagging" is a method used to find out who the suspect just called. When the suspect makes his phone call, take up a surveillance position in the area to ensure that he is actually talking on the phone or just trying to see if anyone is following him. If the suspect appears to be having a conversation on the phone wait till he hangs up. Without blowing your cover, immediately respond to the phone booth. Now its time to "tag" the phone:

1. Place the proper amount of change to place a local or long distance call (do not use a calling card). Then dial a number specifically known to you that will pick up the line (answering machine or live person). I have in the past dialed my department's dispatch line. This is due to the fact that there is someone there to answer the line twenty-four hours a day, seven days a week.
2. Document the date and time you dialed your specific phone number.
3. Retrieve the address of where the phone booth is located, the phone number belonging to that phone, and the service carrier (i.e., Verizon, Sprint, Cingular, or some other private carrier).
4. After your surveillance has ended, return to your office and get a subpoena for the phone records. Include in your subpoena all calls made for a twenty-four-hour period on the date your suspect made his call. In addition list in the subpoena the address, phone number, and service carrier for that specific phone booth.

Once you have obtained the phone records belonging to that specific phone booth on the date you witnessed your suspect utilize it, scroll down the records till you see the phone number that you had dialed. The phone number just prior to the one you dialed is the number that the suspect had called.

Now you will run that number to find out the address of that phone number as well as subscriber information which will finally establish whether or not your suspect is talking to others involved in criminal activity or even his stash house or supplier.

SURVEILLANCE ON PRIVATE PROPERTY
(Open Fields Doctrine—Curtilage)

Conducting covert surveillance on a residence can be one of the most important tasks an investigator does to further his/her case. The ability to gain visual vantage points on or near a suspect's property to gather intelligence or probable cause for a search warrant can be absolutely priceless to ensure a successful outcome.

The main objective of going on the property of a suspect is to monitor individuals living at or frequenting the residence/business or observe a criminal violation. The documentation and identification of these individuals living at or frequenting the property can corroborate information already obtained through CI information or other sources. By physically identifying the individuals who are either living at or frequenting said property an officer can effectively establish the probable cause need to complete the investigation at hand.

First let's look at the case law that allows officers to conduct this type of surveillance. The Open Fields Doctrine, which was originally set forth by the U.S. Supreme Court in *Hester v. United States*, 265 U.S. 57, 44 S. Ct. 445 (1924), allows law enforcement officials to enter and search an "open" field without a warrant. Though the term "open field" is not to be taken in a literal sense as it sounds. It need not be "open" or a "field" per se, but the area deemed outside the curtilage of a residence. This means that fields, woods, or any area for that manner owned or rented by the suspect, which is considered not to be within the boundaries of the curtilage, falls in the category of the Open Fields Doctrine. In essence, the rule laid out in *Hester* states that a person may not legitimately demand privacy for activities conducted out of doors in fields, except in the area *immediately surrounding the home.*

But before we can be certain that the Open Fields Doctrine applies we must first determine what is or isn't deemed curtilage, which is protected by the Fourth Amendment of the U.S. Constitution. The Fourth Amendment provides safeguards for people to be secure in their "persons, houses, papers, and effects" from governmental intrusion. This does not pertain to the Open Field Doctrine, due to a "field" is not considered a "house" or personal "effects." The final analysis in the decision process is whether a person has a "constitutionally protected reasonable expectation of privacy" in a particular area.

"Curtilage" is the land adjoining a residence or business (termed *industrial curtilage*) that is routinely maintained by the owners or leases, or within a sectioned off enclosure. Such things as the boundaries of where the lawn has been mowed, planted shrubs, flowers, or other obviously tended to foliage are just a few examples to determine a maintained area. An enclosed area in essence is a fence or barrier surrounding the residence in question.

A basic rule of thumb is, if it looks like the residence is routinely maintaining an area, that is immediately surrounding and associated with that home, then its part of the curtilage. But remember this only pertains to areas within a reasonable circumference around and associated to that particular home. This is due to there being no societal interest in protecting the privacy of a crop cultivation, field irrigation, or wooded area even though they may be used by the owners of the property. They are clearly distinguished separate and apart from curtilage and therefore fall into the category of the Open Fields Doctrine.

The diagrams below are just some examples to assist you in determining a Residence's curtilage.

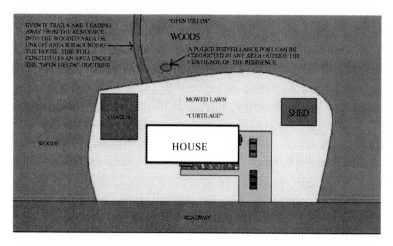

WOODED OR UNKEPT AREA NOT TENDED TO BY THE OWNERS-LAND CONSIDERED "OPEN FIELDS"

MOWED OR KEPT AREA ROUTINLY UTILIZED BY THE OWNERS-LAND CONSIDERED "CUTILAGE"

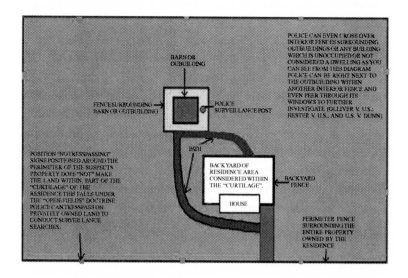

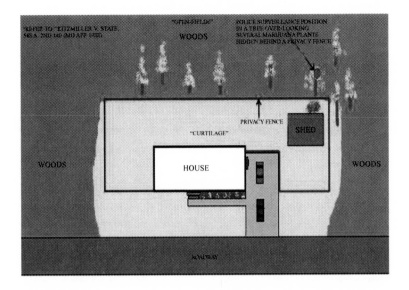

When talking about the Open Fields Doctrine and curtilage, there are three landmark cases that clearly define the meaning of each and further assist law enforcement in making the proper justification. These three U.S. Supreme Court cases are:

Hester v. United States
Supreme Court of the United States
265 U.S. 57, 44 S. Ct. 445 (1924)

This case originally set forth the Open Fields Doctrine, which clearly distinguished areas deemed as open fields and authorized law enforcement personnel to enter upon such lands and make their appropriate observations or seizures without the necessity of obtaining a warrant first. In this, *Justice Holmes* explained that the special and unique safeguards provided by the Fourth Amendment to the people in their "persons, houses, papers, and effects," is not extended to open fields. Open fields are not "houses" nor may they be considered "effects."

Since the beginning of the United States, the home has commanded the sanctity and privacy that is recognized by not only our society but also our Constitution. In turn the privacy of the home has extended to the *"land immediately surrounding and associated with the home"* (Oliver v. United States, 466 U.S. 170, 180, 104 S. Ct. 1735, 1742 [1984]) it is this that is considered the curtilage. *"Open fields do not provide the setting for those intimate activities that the [Fourth] amendment is intended to shelter from government interference or surveillance"* (Id. at 179, 104 S. Ct. at 1741. *"As a practical matter, these lands usually are accessible to the public and the police in ways that a home, office, or commercial structure would not be"* (Id). A clear example of this would be to view such fields from the air by airplane or helicopter.

Oliver v. United States
Supreme Court of the United States
466 U.S. 170, 104 S. Ct. 1735 (1984)

In this instance the Supreme Court of the United States decided on two cases: One from Maine and the other from Kentucky, both factually very similar. Both defendants were growing quantities of marijuana in fields on their property a distance from their residence. While the Kentucky defendant erected a fence around his field with a locked gate and posted No Trespassing signs at various intervals surrounding his property, the Maine defendant utilized chicken wire as his fence and also posted No Trespassing signs on and about his property.

In deciding this case the Supreme Court utilized the Open Fields Doctrine to explain their rational. While reaffirming *Hester v. Unites States,* 265 *U.S.* 57, 44 *S. Ct.* 445 (1924), the court stated, "no expectation of privacy legitimately attaches to open fields" (Id. at 1742). In both cases the defendants attempted to create an expectation of privacy by putting up fencing and No Trespassing signs on and around their property, all to conceal their illicit activities of growing marijuana plants. The government's intrusion upon an area that falls under the category of the Open Field Doctrine is not a "search" within the meaning of the Fourth Amendment, and therefore any contraband or evidence observed or seized may be properly admitted in a court of law.

United States v. Dunn
Supreme Court of the United States
480 U.S. 294, 107 S. Ct. 1134 (1987)

Law enforcement officers from the DEA and the local police department entered on to the defendant's 198-acre ranch property, where they crossed over a perimeter fence that encircled the entire property. The officers noted that there was another fence that encircled the defendant's ranch house and a small greenhouse. There were two barns that were positioned approximately fifty yards from the ranch houses fence, with the front of the larger barn enclosed by a wooden fence. Said barn had an open overhang but locked waist-high gates prevented entry in the barn proper, and there was netting material that was stretched from the ceiling to the top of the wooden gates.

The officers then stood midway between the defendant's ranch house and the two barns. It was at this time one of the DEA agents recognized the odor he had commonly associated with phenylacetic acid emanating from the direction of the two barns. Phenylacetic acid is a precursor used in the production of methamphetamine. *As the officers made their way toward the larger barn they had to cross over a barbed wire fence and a wooden fence that enclosed the entire front portion of the larger barn.* Officers then "walked under the barn's overhang to the locked wooden gates and, shining a flashlight through the netting on top of the gates, peered into the barn. They observed what the DEA agent thought to be a phenylacetone laboratory. After making the previous mentioned observations of the barn and the surrounding area, they subsequently left and later responded back with a search-and-seizure warrant to search the entire residence (ranch house) and outbuildings (barns, sheds, etc.). As a result of the search, chemicals and equipment were found in the barn that contained the suspected phenylacetone laboratory and bags of amphetamines, which were located in a closet in the defendant's residence.

The United States Supreme court explained that the evidence in this case was properly admitted in court and "that the barn and the area around it lay outside the curtilage of the house [.]" (Id. at 1137).

In *Oliver v. United States*, 466 U.S. 170, 104, S. Ct. 1735 (1984), the court explained that "the Fourth Amendment protects the curtilage of a house and that the extent of the curtilage is determined by factors that bear upon whether an individual reasonably may expect that the area in question should be treated as the home itself" (*Dunn* at 1139 [citing *Oliver* at 180,104 S. Ct. at 1742]). The main determination of curtilage is "whether the area harbors the 'intimate activity associated with the sanctity of a man's home and the privacies of life'" (*Dunn* at 1139).

As a result of the previous findings the Supreme Court passed down four factors that can be used in the determination of what actually constitutes "curtilage":

1. **The *proximity* of the area claimed to be curtilage to the home,**
2. **Whether the area is included within an *enclosure* surrounding the home,**
3. **The *nature of the uses* to which the area is put, and**
4. **The *steps taken* by the resident *to protect the area from observation* by people passing by.**

In relation to *Dunn* the above four factors were applied and revealed the following:

1. **PROXIMITY:** The barn's substantial distance from the

fence surrounding the house (fifty yards), and from the house itself (sixty yards), supports no inference that it should be treated as an adjunct of the house;

2. **ENCLOSURE:** The barn was not within the fence surrounding the house; it stands out as a distinct and separate portion of the ranch;

3. **NATURE OF USE:** The barn was not being used for the intimate activities of the home;

4. **PROTECTION FROM OBSERVATION:** Little had been done to protect the barn area from observation by those standing outside, ranch fences were the type to corral livestock not ensure privacy.

In the final opinion of the court they addressed the defendant's contention "that he possessed an expectation of privacy, independent from his home's curtilage, in the barn and its contents" (Id). In this the court explained "the term 'open fields' may include any unoccupied or underdeveloped area outside of the curtilage. An open field need be neither 'open' nor a 'field' as those terms are used in common speech" (Id. at 1141 [quoting *Oliver* at 180, 104 S. Ct. at 1742]). "It follows that no constitutional violation occurred here when the officers crossed over [the defendant's] ranch-style perimeter fence, and over several similarly constructed interior fences, prior to stopping at the barn, nor did they enter any structure on [defendant's] premises. Once at their vantage point, they merely stood outside the curtilage of the house and in the open fields upon which the barn was constructed and peered into the barn's open front. And standing as they were in the open fields, the Constitution did not forbid them to observe the phenylacetone laboratory located in the [defendant's] barn . . . . Under *Oliver* and *Hester*, there is no constitutional difference between police observations conducted while in a public place and while standing in the open fields" (*Dunn* at 1141).

Further, the officers "lawfully viewed the interior of [defendant's] barn, and their observations were properly considered by the magistrate in issuing a search warrant for [defendant's] premises" (Id).

Curtilage of Apartments or Multi-Unit Buildings:

United States v. Acosta
965 F. 2d 1248 (3rd Cir. 1992)

Many times an officer will need to conduct surveillance of multi-family dwellings such as duplexes and apartment units. The following only pertains to apartments or units that are located on the ground floor and have access to an area similar to use as a typical "backyard."

In *Acosta*, the court was faced with the question of whether the first-floor tenants of the three-story multi-unit apartment building, located in an urban setting in Philadelphia, maintained a reasonable expectation of privacy in the fenced-in backyard adjacent to the first-floor apartment.

"[T]he more fundamental question is whether the backyard constitutes curtilage . . . at all.

[A]lthough the *Dunn* factors also apply to determine extent-of-curtilage questions in urban areas, certain factors may be less determinative in a city setting because of the physical differences in the properties . . . . We believe that the weight of the factors is diminished further as applied to apartment dwellings . . . . It seems clear, for example, that 'the configuration of the streets and houses in many parts of the city may make it impossible, or at least highly impracticable to screen one's home and yard from view.' . . . In addition, . . . tenants generally have neither the authority nor the investment incentive to take steps to protect a yard from view by doing such things as erecting a solid fence or planting trees and shrubbery. Instead, the tenant generally takes the property as he finds it, with or without fencing or other types of obstructions in place. In this context, the *Dunn* factors are not as useful analytically as in other settings" (Acosta at 1256).

The *Acosta* court explained that while conducting an inquiry the court will look at whether the particular tenant enjoys any "property interest" in the area that they claim to be within their curtilage; for example whether the tenant's lease gives him a legal interest in the backyard area, or a "right to use" the area (Id.).

In the *Acosta* case, the lease utilized by the defendant did not grant the defendants the right to use the backyard of the first-floor apartment (Id. at 1257). Although they had permission to use it, they hardly did. In addition, "the landlord used the backyard freely, as did his employees. Indeed, the landlord stored his boat in the backyard" (Id.).

Further, "the fact that the defendants had permission to use the yard did not create any legitimate expectation of privacy in it . . . . Defendants' insubstantial privacy interest arising from their authorized but limited use of the yard renders the four *Dunn* factors of insignificant value on this record in deciding the curtilage issue . . . Thus, the [officer's] observations from his vantage point in the yard were constitutionally permissible" (Id.).

Arial Surveillance Observations

Arial surveillance operations are routinely undertaken by law enforcement to enhance observations of a targeted area. Whether this action is the result of a tip on a specific residence or randomly flying to locate evidence of a crime, the United States Supreme Court has routinely recognized the value of such techniques and upheld the use of both helicopters and fixed wing aircraft to accomplish these tasks.

The current FAA (Federal Aviation Administration) regulations on utilizing both aircraft in a low altitude operation is:

- Helicopters: Minimum of ***four hundred feet***

- Airplanes: Minimum of **one thousand feet** in congested areas and *five hundred feet* in more sparsely populated locations.

Peering into a targeted area from the air at the above-listed regulated altitudes makes no difference, whether looking at areas considered "open fields" or the "curtilage" of the residence, law enforcement can utilize this tool to effectively make their observations. In addition, the use of binoculars, cameras, or other visual enhancement equipment can be utilized to assist in such operations (***Dow Chemical v. U.S.*, 476 U.S. 227, 90 L. Ed. 2d 226, 106 S. Ct. 1819 [1986]).**

California v. Ciraolo
Supreme Court of the United States
476 U.S. 207, 90 L. Ed. 2d. 210, 106 S. Ct. 1809 (1986)

The Santa Clara, California, police received an anonymous telephone tip that marijuana was growing in a respondent's backyard, which was enclosed by two fences and shielded from view at ground level. Officers who were trained in marijuana identification secured a private airplane, flew over respondent's house at an altitude of one thousand feet, and readily identified marijuana plants growing in the yard. A search warrant was later obtained on the basis of one of the officer's naked-eye observations; a photograph of the surrounding area taken from the airplane was attached as an exhibit. The warrant was executed, and marijuana plants were seized.

Review by the United States Supreme Court found that "the Fourth Amendment was not violated by the naked-eye aerial observation of respondent's backyard" (Id. 211-215). In addition, the court explained that "the respondent's expectation of privacy from all observations of his backyard was unreasonable. That the backyard and its crop were within the curtilage of respondent's home did not itself bar all police observation. The mere fact that an individual has taken measures to restrict some views of his activities does not preclude an officer's observation from a public vantage point where he has a right to be and which renders the activities clearly visible. The police observations here took place within public navigable airspace, in a physically nonintrusive manner. The police were able to observe the plants readily discernible to the naked eye as marijuana, and it was irrelevant that the observation from the airplane was directed at identifying the plants and that the officers were trained to recognize marijuana" (Id. at 476 U.S. 207, 208). Further, "[A]ny member of the public flying in this airspace who cared to glance down could have seen everything that the officers observed. The Fourth Amendment simply does not require police traveling in the public airways at one thousand feet to obtain a warrant in order to observe what is visible to the naked eye" (Id. 212-215).

Florida v. Riley
Supreme Court of the United States
488 U.S. 445, 102 L Ed. 2d. 835,109 S. Ct., 693 (1989)

A Florida county sheriff's office received an anonymous tip that marijuana was being grown on respondent's property. Officers responded to the defendant's residence and conducted surveillance. The officers observed that the defendant lived in a mobile home located on five acres of rural property. A greenhouse was located ten to twenty feet behind the mobile home. Two sides of the greenhouse were enclosed. The other two sides were not enclosed, but the contents of the greenhouse were obscured from view from surrounding property by trees, shrubs, and the mobile home. The greenhouse was covered by corrugated roofing panels, some translucent and some opaque. At the time relevant to this case, two of the panels, amounting to approximately 10 percent of the roof area, were missing. A wire fence surrounded the mobile home and the greenhouse, and the property was posted with a Do Not Enter sign. When an investigating officer discovered that he could not observe from ground level the contents of a greenhouse home he circled twice over the property in a helicopter at the height of four hundred feet and made naked-eye observations through openings in the greenhouse roof and its open sides of what he concluded were marijuana plants.

After a search pursuant to a warrant obtained on the basis of these observations revealed marijuana growing in the greenhouse, respondent was charged with possession of that substance under Florida law.

The Supreme Court rejected the defendant's motion that the aerial surveillance of the premises violated his rights under the Fourth Amendment. In addition the Supreme Court explained, "We recognized that the yard was within the curtilage of the house, that a fence shielded the yard from observation from the street, and that the occupant had a subjective expectation of privacy. We held, however, that such an expectation was not reasonable and not one "that society is prepared to honor" (Id. at 214) Our reasoning was that the home and its curtilage are not necessarily protected from inspection that involves no physical invasion. "*What a person knowingly exposes to the public, even in his own home or office, is not a subject of Fourth Amendment protection*'" (Id. at 213, quoting *Katz v. United States*, 389 U.S. 347, 35 [1967]). As a general proposition, the police may see what may be seen "*from a public vantage point where [they have] a right to be*" (476 U.S. at 213) Thus the police, like the public, would have been free to inspect the backyard garden from the street if their view had been unobstructed (*Riley* at 488 U.S. 445, 450). "They were likewise free to inspect the yard from the vantage point of an aircraft flying in the navigable airspace as this plane was. "In an age where private and commercial flight in the public airways is routine, it is unreasonable for [the defendant] to expect that his marijuana plants were constitutionally protected from being observed with the naked eye from an altitude of four hundred feet. The Fourth Amendment simply does not require the police traveling in the public airways at this altitude to obtain a warrant in order to observe what is visible to the naked eye" (Id. at 215).

Note: Although aerial photography and visual enhancement devices such as binoculars are allowed to assist officers in their quest for the truth (*Dow Chemical v. U.S. and California v. Ciraolo*), the courts have cautioned officers about using such high-tech equipment, not normally available to the public and the ability to view activities not otherwise visible. In addition the courts have also warned about police flyovers that are to "physically intrusive" (i.e., too low, loud, frequent, prolonged, etc.), which could make this investigative technique a constitutional violation.

Miscellaneous Surveillance Issues

WINDOWS: The courts have routinely explained that as long as a police officer is in an area he has a lawful right to be, the officer may look through windows to observe activity from within. This is due to the fact that anyone who leaves their shades open or utilizes sheer curtains that allow the ability to visually observe activities, cannot reasonably expect privacy within. It should be noted though that "peeking" through slits or under window or door shades is considered an improper search under the Fourth Amendment and subsequently will result in any actions resulting in such observation as inadmissible in a court of law.

FENCES AND WALLS: Courts have varied in their decisions when it comes to privacy created by the erection of walls and fences. In one case an officer received a tip that a quantity of marijuana plants were growing in the defendant's backyard. Acting on this tip the officer responded to the alleyway alongside the defendant's property and looked through a knothole that was in the defendant six-foot privacy fence that bordered his entire backyard. As a result, the officer observed marijuana plants growing in the backyard and subsequently returned with a search and seizure warrant to search the premises. The evidence was suppressed because "peering" through a knothole was considered a warrantless search (*People v. Lovelace*, 116 *Cal. App.* 3d 541, 172 *Cal. Rptr.* 65, [*Cal. App. 5 Dist.* 1981])

Although in a similar case, it was held that there was no search when marijuana plants observed in the defendants backyard where plainly visible to an officer as he stood in a public alleyway. The plants were both over and through cracks in the defendant's fence and clearly seen from where the officer was lawfully standing. The court found that the viewing of this evidence constituted probable cause for a search warrant of the defendant's house (*People v. Reiss*, 129 *Cal. App.* 3d. 550, 181 *Cal. Rptr.* 166 [(*Cal. App. 3 Dist.* 1982])

As you can see the courts vary in their opinions as to the extent of an officer's surveillance techniques, even if he is in a position where he is lawfully allowed to be. Taking that extra step to "peer" through a little knothole in a fence is considered far more intrusive then simply observing suspected marijuana plants coming through and over a fence.

USE OF BINOCULARS: Officers utilize binoculars to help enhance their vision during operations. This equipment can be used to conduct surveillance of residences, buildings, or suspects if what is being viewed can already be seen with the naked eye. It is important to note that there is no limit to the magnification used, just that as long as it can be seen with the naked eye. In addition, the officer would need to be in a position where he is lawfully allowed to be in order for his observations pass judicial review.

SURVEILLANCE FROM NEIGHBORING PROPERTIES: The courts have routinely upheld that officers may conduct surveillance from a neighboring property during the course of a criminal investigation in efforts to gain visual vantage points to view suspected criminal violations, so long as the officer is in a place he is lawfully allowed to be. This is due to two reasons: first, the Supreme Court has stated that whatever a person knowingly exposes to the public, even in there own home or office cannot reasonably expect privacy in hopes that the Fourth Amendment would be insinuated and therefore attached; second, and most importantly, the defendant does not have a Fourth Amendment protection on his neighbor's property, for the simple fact that it is *not his property*!

Case in point, the defendant's neighbor called the police and stated that the defendant was growing marijuana in his backyard, which had a fence around the entire perimeter. The officer acting on the tip responded to the area and took up a surveillance position from a neighbor's second-story window, which was approximately forty feet away. From this vantage point, the officer was able to view a quantity of marijuana plants growing in the defendant's backyard. A search and seizure warrant was obtained for the premises and subsequently resulted in successfully seizing marijuana. At trial the court found this to be a lawful observation and reasoned that "the view of the backyard was vulnerable to observation by any of the petitioner's neighbors, in essence, open to public view" (Dillon v. Superior Court of Santa Barbara County, 7 Cal. 3d. 305, 102 Cal. Rptr. 161, 497 P.2d 505 [Cal. 1972]).

Surveillance Log

TARGET NAME: | **CASE NUMBER:**

| 1. Date: | 2. Start Time: | 3. End Time: | 4. Call No.: |

5. Name of Person Completing Log: | 6. ID No.:

7. Type of Surveillance Conducted: ▦ Moving ▦ Stationary

8. Location(s):

9. Type of activity observed:

10. Any Vehicle Information: (Registration, Color, Make, Model, Describe Driver)

11. Any Person(s) observed: (Description, If known–Name, How did you identify them? . . .)

12. Did anyone take notice of your presence? If so describe how so, and their reaction.

| 13. If necessary continue any entries on additional sheet | 14. Continuation Sheet ▦ YES ▦ NO |

Asset Forfeiture Methods

A large part of narcotics investigations turn up assets that have been illegally gained as a direct result of the sales of controlled dangerous substance. This is a multibillion-dollar-a-year industry. So successfully marketed and distributed, that if legal, it would rank among the top of our nations Fortune 500 companies. The unfortunate side is that the wealth generated by the sales of controlled substances have been contributed to financing other forms of illegal acts such as terrorism, commonly referred to as "Narco-Terrorism." Further, the sales from drugs degrade our society and support the continuation of satellite crimes (crimes that are generated due to drug use or sales) that plague our communities on a daily basis. It is a known fact that to hit the drug dealers hard, you need to seize the assets that they had obtained as a result of their drug sales. There will always be drugs for the dealers to sell—but take their assets and you have hurt them. In essence law enforcement needs to take the profit out of the drug trade to the level that it is more profitable to be legitimate than not. This can be only done through the process of asset forfeiture.

Seizing assets obtained from the sales of drugs should go hand and hand with your drug investigation. Asset investigations can be very difficult to follow, especially if the business, suspected to be used as a front, is claiming to be a cash business. In any asset seizure investigation, no matter if it is large or small, there should be a thorough investigation done to show that the only likely place that the money could have come from is the sales from drugs. In most cases, the seizure of money or other assets (vehicles, homes, etc.) will be fought in both civil and criminal court. Because of asset seizures being civil in nature, the prosecutor's office or your law enforcement agencies' designated civil attorney will need to file for the seized asset within a specified time period. For example, Maryland's guidelines state that an asset (money, vehicle, etc.) needs to be filed in the County *Circuit Court* within forty-five days from the time of the seizure. Make sure that you check with your states guidelines concerning filing for seized assets; as they may vary from state to state. Below we will discuss the many methods of conducting an asset investigation and how to properly document it for trial purposes.

SEIZING ASSETS

There are two basic ways of seizing assets: from the **proceeds** of selling controlled dangerous substances, or the **facilitation** of controlled dangerous substances.

- **PROCEEDS:** This can be described as any asset that was purchased or obtained as a direct result of selling controlled dangerous substances; money falls within this category. For example, a vehicle that was purchased from the money obtained as a result of selling drugs.
- **FACILITATION:** Possibly the most easiest and frequent method of seizing assets is through the facilitation of said asset. Facilitation means when a suspect utilizes an asset to store, contain, or transport, a controlled dangerous substance (i.e., house, car, boat, etc.), whether it was purchased with drug money or not. An example would be when a uniformed officer stops a vehicle and finds over one pound of marijuana hidden in the trunk. This vehicle then would be viewed to have been used to facilitate the drug transaction by enabling the suspect to get from point A to point B.

THE COMPREHENSIVE DRUG ABUSE PREVENTION AND CONTROL ACT OF 1970

This is the primary legal foundation for all the laws regulating the manufacturing and distribution of controlled dangerous substances. In addition, section 881 of this act pertains to the forfeiture of controlled dangerous substances and the various legal actions to be taken by the government to see that the law is carried out effectively. Most states have their own laws regarding forfeiture, but stay along the lines of section 881. For further information on your state's guidelines and laws pertaining to forfeiture, contact your local prosecutor's office for assistance.

SECTION 881 REGARDING FORFEITURES

(a) Subject property: The following shall be subject to forfeiture to the United States and no property right shall exist in them:

(1) All controlled substances, which have been manufactured, distributed, dispensed, or acquired in violation of this subchapter.

(2) All raw materials, products, and equipment of any kind which are used, or intended for use, in manufacturing, compounding, processing, delivering, importing, or exporting any controlled substance or listed chemical in violation of this subchapter.

(3) All property which is used, or intended for use, as a container for property described in paragraph 1, 2, or 9.

(4) All conveyances, including aircraft, vehicles, or vessels, which are used, or are intended for use, to transport, or in any manner to facilitate the transportation, sale, receipt, possession, or concealment of property described in paragraph 1, 2, or 9.

(5) All books, records, and research, including formulas, microfilm, tapes, and data, which are used, or intended for use, in violation of this subchapter.

(6) All moneys, negotiable instruments, securities, or other things of value furnished or intended to be furnished by any person in exchange for a controlled substance or listed chemical in violation of this subchapter, all proceeds traceable to such an exchange, and all moneys, negotiable instruments, and securities used or intended to be used to facilitate any violation of this subchapter.

(7) All real property, including any right, title, and interest (including any leasehold interest) in the whole of any lot or tract of land and any appurtenances or improvements, which is used, or intended to be used, in any manner or part, to commit, or to facilitate the commission of, a violation of this subchapter punishable by more than one year's imprisonment.

(8) All controlled substances, which have been possessed in violation of this subchapter.

(9) All listed chemicals, all drug manufacturing equipment, all tableting machines, all encapsulating machines, and all gelatin capsules, which have been imported, exported, manufactured, possessed, distributed, dispensed, acquired, or intended to be distributed, dispensed, acquired, imported, or exported, in violation of this subchapter or subchapter 2 of this chapter.

(10) Any drug paraphernalia (as defined in section 1822 of the Mail Order Drug Paraphernalia Control Act).

(11) Any firearm (as defined in section 921 of title 18) used or intended to be used to facilitate the transportation, sale, receipt, possession, or concealment of property described in paragraph 1 or 2 and any proceeds traceable to such property.

(b) Seizure procedures: Any property subject to forfeiture to the United States under this section may be seized by the

Attorney General in the manner set forth in section 981(b) of title 18.

(c) Custody of Attorney General: Property taken or detained under this section shall not be repleviable, but shall be deemed to be in the custody of the attorney general, subject only to the orders and decrees of the court or the official having jurisdiction thereof. Whenever property is seized under any of the provisions of this subchapter, the attorney general may—

    (1) place the property under seal;

    (2) remove the property to a place designated by him; or

    (3) require that the General Services Administration take custody of the property and remove it, if practicable, to an appropriate location for disposition in accordance with law.

(d) Other laws and proceedings applicable: The provisions of law relating to the seizure, summary and judicial forfeiture, and condemnation of property for violation of the customs laws; the disposition of such property or the proceeds from the sale thereof; the remission or mitigation of such forfeitures; and the compromise of claims shall apply to seizures and forfeitures incurred, or alleged to have been incurred, under any of the provisions of this subchapter, insofar as applicable and not inconsistent with the provisions hereof; except that such duties as are imposed upon the customs officer or any other person with respect to the seizure and forfeiture of property under the customs laws shall be performed with respect to seizures and forfeitures of property under this subchapter by such officers, agents, or other persons as may be authorized or designated for that purpose by the attorney general, except to the extent that such duties arise from seizures and forfeitures effected by any customs officer.

(e) Disposition of forfeited property:

    (1) Whenever property is civilly or criminally forfeited under this subchapter the attorney general may—

(A) Retain the property for official use or, in the manner provided with respect to transfers under section 1616a of title 19, transfer the property to any federal agency or to any state or local law enforcement agency which participated directly in the seizure or forfeiture of the property;

(B) Except as provided in paragraph 4, sell, by public sale or any other commercially feasible means, any forfeited property which is not required to be destroyed by law and which is not harmful to the public;

(C) Require that the General Services Administration take custody of the property and dispose of it in accordance with law;

(D) Forward it to the Bureau of Narcotics and Dangerous Drugs for disposition (including delivery for medical or scientific use to any federal or state agency under regulations of the attorney general); or

(E) Transfer the forfeited personal property or the proceeds of the sale of any forfeited personal or real property to any foreign country, which participated directly or indirectly in the seizure or forfeiture of the property, if such a transfer—

   (i) has been agreed to by the Secretary of State;

   (ii) is authorized in an international agreement between the United States and the foreign country; and

   (iii) is made to a country which, if applicable, has been certified under section 2291j(b) of title 22.

(2)

(A) The proceeds from any sale under subparagraph B of paragraph 1 and any moneys forfeited under this subchapter shall be used to pay

   (i) all property expenses of the proceedings for forfeiture and sale including expenses of seizure, maintenance of custody, advertising, and court costs; and

(ii) awards of up to $100,000 to any individual who provides original information, which leads to the arrest and conviction of a person who kills or kidnaps a federal drug law enforcement agent.

Any award paid for information concerning the killing or kidnapping of a federal drug law enforcement agent, as provided in clause ii, shall be paid at the discretion of the attorney general.

(B) The attorney general shall forward to the Treasurer of the United States for deposit in accordance with section 524(c) of title 28, any amounts of such moneys and proceeds remaining after payment of the expenses provided in subparagraph A, except that, with respect to forfeitures conducted by the Postal Service, the Postal Service shall deposit in the Postal Service Fund, under section 2003(b)(7) of title 39, such moneys and proceeds.

(3) The attorney general shall assure that any property transferred to a state or local law enforcement agency under paragraph 1A

(A) has a value that bears a reasonable relationship to the degree of direct participation of the state or local agency in the law enforcement effort resulting in the forfeiture, taking into account the total value of all property forfeited and the total law enforcement effort with respect to the violation of law on which the forfeiture is based; and

(B) will serve to encourage further cooperation between the recipient state or local agency and federal law enforcement agencies.

(4)

(A) With respect to real property described in subparagraph B, if the chief executive officer of the state involved submits to the attorney general a request for purposes of such subparagraph, the authority established in such subparagraph is in lieu of the authority established in paragraph 1B.

(B) In the case of property described in paragraph 1B that is civilly or criminally forfeited under this subchapter, if the property is real property that is appropriate for use as a public area reserved for recreational or historic purposes or for the preservation of natural conditions, the attorney general, upon the request of the chief executive officer of the state in which the property is located, may transfer title to the property to the state, either without charge or for a nominal charge, through a legal instrument providing that

(i) such use will be the principal use of the property; and

(ii) title to the property reverts to the United States in the event that the property is used otherwise.

(f) Forfeiture and destruction of schedule I and II substances

(1) All controlled substances in schedule I or II that are possessed, transferred, sold, or offered for sale in violation of the provisions of this subchapter; all dangerous, toxic, or hazardous raw materials or products subject to forfeiture under subsection a2 of this section; and any equipment or container subject to forfeiture under subsection a2 or 3 of this section which cannot be separated safely from such raw materials or products shall be deemed contraband and seized and summarily forfeited to the United States. Similarly, all substances in schedule I or II, which are seized or come into the possession of the United States, the owners of which are unknown, shall be deemed contraband and summarily forfeited to the United States.

(2) The attorney general may direct the destruction of all controlled substances in schedule I or II seized for violation of this subchapter; all dangerous, toxic, or hazardous raw materials or products subject to forfeiture under subsection a2 of this section; and any equipment or container subject to forfeiture under subsection a2 or 3 of this section which cannot be separated safely from such raw materials or products under such circumstances as the attorney general may deem necessary.

(g) Plants:

(1) All species of plants from which controlled substances in schedules I and II may be derived which have been planted or cultivated in violation of this subchapter, or of which the owners or cultivators are unknown, or which are wild growths, may be seized and summarily forfeited to the United States.

(2) The failure, upon demand by the attorney general or his duly authorized agent, of the person in occupancy or in control of land or premises upon which such species of plants are growing or being stored, to produce an appropriate registration, or proof that he is the holder thereof, shall constitute authority for the seizure and forfeiture.

(3) The attorney general, or his duly authorized agent, shall have authority to enter upon any lands, or into any dwelling pursuant to a search warrant, to cut, harvest, carry off, or destroy such plants.

(h) Vesting of title in United States: All right, title, and interest in property described in subsection a of this section shall vest in the United States upon commission of the act giving rise to forfeiture under this section.

(i) Stay of civil forfeiture proceedings: The provisions of section 981(g) of title 18 regarding the stay of a civil forfeiture proceeding shall apply to forfeitures under this section.

(j) Venue: In addition to the venue provided for in section 1395 of title 28 or any other provision of law, in the case of property of a defendant charged with a violation that is the basis for forfeiture of the property under this section, a proceeding for forfeiture under this section may be brought in the judicial district in which the defendant owning such property is found or in the judicial district in which the criminal prosecution is brought.

[(k)](l) Functions. The functions of the attorney general under this section shall be carried out by the postal service pursuant to such agreement as may be entered into between the attorney general and the postal service.

Money Seizures

Steps to Complete

1. *DOCUMENT WHERE THE CURRENCY WAS FOUND:* This should be done in your police report as well as through photographs. If you locate the currency hidden in the lining of a suitcase, this needs to be document in both ways so a record has been created. More specifically, if the drugs were found in close proximity to the currency itself then a nexus can be made and should be viewed as such later in court.

   • Note the location of the currency in your report
   • Photograph the location where it was found

2. *DESCRIBE THE CURRENCY:* Take note on how the currency is found/secured and the denomination amounts

it consists of. If you find $260 on a suspect, and it is made up of mostly $10s and $20s that are sectioned into groups ($10s with $10s, $20s with $20s, etc.), this is consistent with standard denomination amounts commonly seen in drug distribution practices. The currency is sectioned into numerical groups to easily allow the dealer to see how much money they have at any given time. In addition, note how it is secured. Currency is commonly found on dealers secured with rubber bands wrapped around it, paper clips, or stuffed in envelops to mention a few. There may be times when you locate currency on suspected drug dealers that are not sectioned into denomination groups or secured at all. This does not mean that it is not proceeds from drug sales. Traits, habits, and actions in this manner vary from area to area. The details listed above are just commonly seen in drug distribution cases, but not in every instance. It's just important to recognize details such as these in the event that it becomes an issue later in court— so document every aspect.

- document the type of denominations—i.e., $5, $10, $20
- document if it is sectioned out into specific denomination groups.
- document the way it was secured—i.e., rubber bands, paper clip, etc.

3. *COUNTING THE MONEY:* This is the most important step of seizing money. The seizing officer should count the money seized first. Then let a second officer count the money again. After both officers have counted the money, compare the amount counted from each officer. If there is a discrepancy in the amount, start the process again until both officers come out with the same numbers. Never count or handle money seized from a suspect while alone if possible. Always have a witness while handling,

counting, and securing the currency. This should eliminate any accusations of corruption and theft on law enforcements part. *do not* initially count the money in front of the suspect(s). This is due in part because oftentimes drug dealers do not know exactly how much they have on their person or in their possession. By counting the money first, this gets a true and accurate count, which then can be compared to what the suspect says he has. It has been my experience while seizing money from drug dealers that about 99 percent of the time they will *not know* the amount of money seized and will almost certainly give you a "ball park" figure/ estimate. This is another indicator that should most certainly be documented in the officer's report. Normal law-abiding citizens know how much money they have in their possession, or at least come very close to the exact amount. Drug dealers, on the other hand, often throw a number out and hope it sticks. After the two officers have confirmed the amounts and the suspect had given his "ball park" figure to the officer on the scene, the seizing officer should count the money in front of the suspect letting him/her know the exact amount seized. It is imperative that this is done correctly because it will most certainly come back to haunt you later if there is a mistake. Lastly, officers should not mix money with dope. Always change gloves or wash your hands thoroughly before handling seized money. This is to prevent cross contamination so that later an accurate K9 scan or Ion Scan (detects microscopic particles of controlled dangerous substances) can be completed properly and subsequently give true and accurate results.

4. *PHOTOGRAPH THE MONEY:* The officer should photograph the money with it spread out on a table to properly depict the amount seized.

•   Photograph the money spread out on a table

5. *QUESTIONS TO ASK THE SUSPECT:* The following questions are used as just a guide for the officer to use to support his/her investigation. Not all questions will be applicable to every situation. The officer can pick from the questions below, then go more in depth into a specific line of questioning according to the information received. A good idea is make up a cheat sheet with the following questions on it and keep copies with you when you go on operations. This will guide you through the questioning and allow you to fill in the answers or make notes where appropriate.

     Where did you obtain the money? Often the suspect will state that they received the money from another individual. If this is the case get the name, address (location), and phone number where they can be reached. It would be wise to send an officer immediately to speak with this person that allegedly gave the suspect the money to prevent them from getting a story together. This should be done in person if possible so the officer will be able to put a face with the name. If the suspect explains that the money was from their bank account, be sure to find out what bank it was from and the date of withdrawal You will need this information to subpoena the bank for the records that reflect the suspect's account information.

     Do you work? If so, where?

     How are you paid—paycheck, cash (under the table), or direct deposit?

     Where did you cash your last paycheck? Contact the business that cashed the check for the suspect and attempt to confirm or dispel that the suspect did cash a check at that location, and get the amount that the check was for.

     What is your paycheck schedule? (i.e., weekly, biweekly, monthly, salary, commission based, etc.) This will be needed to do a debt-to-income ratio analysis later.

How long have you been employed at your current job?

Are you currently collecting unemployment? If so, from where, and how much? Contact your local unemployment office *(***Department of Labor, Licensing, and Regulation Department***)* to corroborate how much the suspect is drawing each pay period.

Do you receive any other form of income? If so, from where and what is the payment schedule? (child support, government assistance, roommates, etc.)

Do you have a bank account (checking/savings)? If so, where? You will need this information to subpoena bank account records to analyze later. The purpose of this is to see how much the suspect is depositing and withdrawing from the account.

If you don't have a bank account (checking), then how do you pay your bills? Do you use money orders to pay bills? If so, where do you obtain the money orders? Contact the business or post office where the suspect received the money order. Oftentimes they can tell you how many money orders that the suspect purchases and the common amounts that each are for.

If you don't have a bank account where do you normally keep your money and how do you record it?

What are your monthly bills/debts? (Include utilities, insurance, mortgage, loans, average food expenses, etc.) This is a very important aspect of your investigation. You will need to have a running total of the suspect's monthly expenses to properly analyze their financial stability. Financial programs such as Quicken, Microsoft Money, Excel or any spreadsheet program will enable you to keep a running total of all expenses paid out on a monthly basis by the suspect and even display it in graphs (which is great for court purposes). With the information obtained from the questions above, you will be able to do a *debt-to-Income ratio (net worth) analysis* on the suspect, which will show that he/she does or does not have a positive cash flow to support the money seized or the assets in their possession. In other words, the suspect is spending more then he is making. A basic debt-to-income ratio analysis example is included in this chapter.

The above questions should be asked of the suspect to get a basis of what direction you need to take to confirm or dispel that the currency seized is from the sales of controlled dangerous substances. Most likely the suspect will only give answers to some of the above questions or none at all. In the event that the suspect fails to cooperate with your investigation to establish the legitimacy of the currency, it should be documented in your police/seizure report that the suspect refused to cooperate or was vague on his/her answers. The questions above are just basic inquires which should be expanded upon as you speak with the suspect. Once you get the answers to some or all of the above questions, you will then need to attempt to corroborate the information by talking to employers or subpoenaing bank information to mention a few. Now that the questions have been asked it's time to do the legwork to confirm the suspect's story.

6. *K9 SCAN OF MONEY:* It has been proven scientifically that a positive alert to U.S. currency by a properly trained narcotics detection canine indicates that the currency had recently, or just prior to packaging, been in close or actual proximity to an amount of narcotics, and is not the result of any alleged innocent environmental contamination of circulated U.S. currency by microscopic traces of cocaine, like the defense so eloquently leads the courts to believe. The study that defense attorneys are relying upon is quite flawed and is based upon relatively small samples of currency. The experiment utilized only 135 bills, which was analyzed by a gas chromatograph/mass

spectrometer (a machine that measures particles of a specific substance) not with drug detection canines. The fact that such a small sample of currency was used as a basis for such a broad statistical conclusion that all circulated currency in the United States is tainted with controlled dangerous substances is not scientific evidence or even considered remotely accurate. Records kept since 1989, by the Metro-Dade Police Department in Miami, Florida, has over seventy-plus reports of *non-alerts* by drug detection canines who have scanned hundreds even thousands of dollars in individual cases separate and apart from each other. This is a far greater spectrum of currency found in the general circulation than 135 dollars used to conduct the study that is so commonly referred to by defense attorneys throughout the country. This clearly blows the previous study out of the water by showing that enormously large random samples of United States currency have proven not to be detected for the presence of controlled dangerous substances.

Research has shown to a reasonable scientific certainty that a narcotics detection dog alerts to the odor of *methyl benzoate* as the dominant odor of illicit cocaine and not the pure cocaine itself. That this dominant odor found in cocaine is the chemical, methyl benzoate, which is considered a highly volatile substance associated with the manufacturing of cocaine and has been shown to evaporate quickly when handled and/or exposed to air, while pure cocaine hydrochloride has almost no gaseous odor and is transferred rather easily by physical contact. The very processes, which result in the contamination of currency by cocaine (including the handling and mechanical currency counting apparatuses), tend to dissipate the cocaine odor chemical, methyl benzoate, which in turn would not trigger an alert by a drug detection canine. Although methyl benzoate can be found in some perfumes, the quantity is so minuet compared to the many other gaseous substances contained in perfume that a narcotics detection dog trained to alert to cocaine would not alert to perfume.

In addition, cocaine is considered to be a local anesthetic and as such blocks the transmission of nerve impulses to the brain. Therefore cocaine, in all actuality would block the transmission of the olfactory (smell) nerve fibers in a canine during a scan, which would subsequently result in a non-alert to the currency in question.

Further, in support of the above facts there have been numerous studies throughout the nation exhibiting non-alerts by trained narcotics canines in regards to large amounts of circulated U.S. currency; a fact that is inconsistent with the theory that all U.S. currency is contaminated with so much cocaine that narcotics detection canines will always alert to money. Prof. Kenneth G. Furton, Ph.D., Florida International University, has written several published research papers on this mater. Prof. Furton's scientific experiments was conducted over a two-year period involving over thirteen drug detection canines (not a machine like a gas chromatograph/mass spectrometer) of various breeds and ages; which has provided an accurate and accepted scientific basis to be used in court. Prof. Furton's scientific research in this matter, has been used in trials as evidence to show that currency suspected of being involved in the distribution of controlled dangerous substance and has subsequently received a positive alert by a drug detection canine, shows that the currency had recently, or just before being packaged, been in close or actual proximity to an amount of narcotics. For this reason, prosecutors should not accept any further evidence or testimony supporting the "contaminated money theory," but rely only on qualified testimony and scientific research, such as the studies conducted by Prof.

Furton, when involved in trials that pertain to a drug detection canine alerting to circulated United States currency.

HOW TO SCAN SEIZED MONEY WITH A K9

- While at the scene of an incident have a drug detection canine respond to your location.
- Once the money is seized retrieve three paper bags, placing the seized money in one of them.
- Lay the three paper bags down on the ground with at least five feet between each. Two of the bags should be empty with the third containing the seized currency.
- Document the date and the time the scan was conducted by the canine.
- If the canine alerts on the paper bag containing the seized currency, document the time of the alert, and the confirmation from the handler that their canine did display a positive alert.
- Ensure that the K9 officer submits a scan report to you at a later date to include with your seizure report. If you do not have the K9 handler's credentials for both the handler and canine, you will need to get copies of them and keep them on file and/or submit with your report.

7. *CURRENCY USED IN A CONTROLLED BUY/HAND TO HAND:*

As mentioned in the informant operations chapter, money used to purchase narcotics while conducting controlled or hand-to-hand buys, should be copied prior to making the purchase to accurately document the serial numbers. This is to confirm the fact that the money previously documented was the same money used to make the purchase with the suspect. In turn this corroborates informant or officer statements that the defendant was involved in the distribution of controlled dangerous substance, which is evidenced by the documented money in the possession of the suspect.

Be sure to go through each serial number of the currency seized and compare it to the previous documented serial numbers that were used to make the controlled or hand-to-hand purchases. If any of the serial numbers matched the currency seized from the suspect, note this fact in your police report. In addition, if the currency that you had previously documented is found mixed in with other seized currency of the suspect, the entire amount can be seized. This is a pretty much a sure win in court when it comes time for a forfeiture hearing.

VEHICLE SEIZURES

1. *PICTURES*: As soon as practicable, you need to take at least four photographs of the vehicle. The pictures should depict each side of the vehicle to document any previous damage before the seizure or that no damage was sustained when the vehicle was seized.
2. *ODOMETER*: Document the odometer reading on the vehicle at the time it was seized. This should be included within your report for future reference and to defeat the claim of alleged misuse of the vehicle by law enforcement personnel.
3. *VEHICLE INVENTORY*: When the vehicle is seized, a thorough inventory of its interior should be conducted. A vehicle inventory is conducted to prevent the claim of lost or stolen property, ensure the safety of officers in control of the vehicle, and to protect any valuables that may be present. Once the inventory is completed and all the miscellaneous items are found in the vehicle, a list should be made to document those items. A copy of this list, along with the items found during the inventory

should be turned over to the suspect or his/her designee, but only upon their signature at the bottom of the inventory stating that they received all items placed on the list. *Do not* disconnect stereos, speakers, or anything aftermarket that is attached to the vehicle. A rule of thumb is anything attached to the vehicle, stays with the vehicle. In addition, you may find during your inventory search controlled dangerous substances or other forms of evidence that were not found during your initial search. All additional evidence that is found during your inventory search should be processed and logged in the same fashion as the other evidence initially found. It is important to note that the United States Supreme Court requires all law enforcement agencies to have in place a policy regarding departmental procedures when conducting a vehicle inventory. That if no written policy in the form of a general order or similar correspondence is established by the officers department then any item of evidence found during the inventory of the suspect's vehicle will not fall within the exception of the Fourth Amendment and would be subsequently prevented from being presented at trial (Florida v. Wells, 495 U.S. 1, 110 S. Ct. 1632 [1990]). In addition, when conducting inventory searches of vehicles you can only search in areas that are readily accessible to the occupants or owner. For instance, you can search the entire passenger compartment's open area, any normal storage compartments (center consol storage, glove compartments, trunks, etc.), even locked or sealed containers found within the vehicle; so long as your departments policy allows you to (Colorado v. Bertine 497 U.S. 367, 107 S. Ct 738 [1987]). You cannot go looking in the engine compartment, under the dashboard or inside the gas tank, this would be deemed out of the scope of the standard inventory practice. An inventory search is to just do a basic inventory of all items that were present within the vehicle upon its seizure.

Any further in-depth search of the vehicle would require a search warrant.

4. *FILING FOR THE VEHICLE:* Every state has a set of procedures on how to file in court for seized assets. You will need to make contact with your local prosecutor's office to find out your states time limits on filing for these assets seized. In Maryland, the courts require the state to file within forty-five days of the seizure. If the petition for forfeiture is not filed within the specified time limit the asset seized will need to be given back to the suspect.

5. *QUESTIONS TO ASK THE SUSPECT:* The following questions are used as just a guide for the officer to use to support his/her investigation. Not all questions will be applicable to every situation. The officer can pick from the questions below, then go more in depth into a specific line of questioning according to the information received.

- *Who owns the vehicle? Is the vehicle co-owned? If so, by whom?*
- *When did you purchase the vehicle? Where did you purchase the vehicle? How much did you pay for the vehicle, including down payment and taxes?*
- *Is the car paid off? If so, when was it paid off?*
- *Do you make payments on the vehicle? If so, how do you make your payments? (Checks, money orders, cash, etc)*
- *Who is the vehicle financed through?*
- *What insurance company carries the vehicle? Whose name is on the insurance policy?*
- *Do you normally operate the vehicle? If not, who does? (Name, address, and phone number)*

6. *VEHICLE SEIZURE INVESTIGATION:* You will need to conduct an investigation surrounding the actual or alleged ownership of the vehicle in question. The main goal of this investigation is to show who actually owns

the vehicle regardless of whose name is on the title and
to find the financial aspects surrounding the vehicle.
Oftentimes drug dealers will have vehicles titled and
registered in another person's name. In order to seize the
vehicle you will need to show that the suspect financed
and primarily benefits from the vehicles use. This can
be done in a variety of ways. Some of the steps you will
need to take to prove your case are listed below.

- *Motor Vehicle Administration:* Request a title search
  on the vehicle. This will show you:

  1. Who the vehicle is titled to, and their personal
     information,
  2. The amount that the vehicle was purchased for,
     including the down payment and the amount paid
     on taxes and tags,
  3. Who the vehicle is financed with, including the
     term of the loan, and the percentage rate,
  4. It will show you if there is no lean on the vehicle
     and if the vehicle was paid off in cash—displaying
     the amount of cash paid out.
  5. Where the vehicle was purchased from—either a
     dealer or from an individual sale.

     The above information will be used to further a
     financial investigation on the titled owner whether
     it's in your suspect's name or not.

- *Financing Institution:* Here you will most likely need
  a subpoena to retrieve the information you are
  seeking. If you are asking for this information prior
  to the suspect's arrest, make sure that you put in a
  nondisclosure statement in the subpoena to avoid the
  financial institution from notifying the suspect of your

investigation. The information you will be inquiring about is:

1. Who makes the payments on the vehicle loan?
2. How are the payments made (cash; money orders; if checks, find out whose name is listed on them)?
3. How much has been paid on the loan, and how much is left to satisfy the loan?
4. Was there a cosigner on the loan? If so, what is their information?
5. What is the payment schedule for the loan?
6. Did the suspect or the individual who is named on the loan place anything down as collateral security? If so, what is it? And what is the value?
7. Get from the institution a copy of the suspect's or titleholder's loan paperwork, as well as their account payment history pertaining to the loan. This will be used to compare to other account information found in the financial investigation. For example, if the vehicle loan is in another person's name and the car payment is $700 a month. Compare your suspect's bank account history with the payment history of the vehicle loan. Look for any withdrawals for $700 or checks written to the titled party in that amount. This would clearly show that the suspect is actually paying for the vehicle and not the titleholder.

• *Dealership/Seller:* By interviewing the dealer who sold the vehicle to the suspect or titleholder, you will be able to obtain added information as to the sale of the vehicle. Oftentimes drug dealers will go to the auto dealership with the person who the vehicle will be titled in. Commonly the suspect is the one who test-drives the vehicle instead of the title owner. After all it's going to be his car, he's just using this other party to title the car in their name to avoid police detection. Most automobile dealers will keep good notes on conversations that had occurred during sale. For example, they will often write down who was the most involved in the conversation of the sale, i.e., the suspect is doing all the talking and negotiating the sale, where the titleholder, who is buying the car, just sits there listening. They also will document either in writing or by making photocopies of the person's driver's license whenever a person test-drives a vehicle. This shows that even though the titled party is buying the vehicle, it was test-drove by the suspect. Usually a person who buys a car would be the one who test-drives it, not his alleged friend. With this all documented in your police report it will be easily shown in court that the suspect was the actual buyer of the vehicle and that the title holder is just a front to avoid police detection. Dealers also keep meticulous records on the maintenance of vehicles serviced by them. If the suspect is using a dealership to do the maintenance of the vehicle, you will need to obtain these records. They will show the dates that the vehicle was serviced, the work done on the vehicle, the name of the person brining the vehicle in for service, a full description of the vehicle and its condition, and whether the bill was paid by cash, check, money order, or credit card.

• *Surveillance:* This is most important. You will need to conduct surveillance of the suspect operating the vehicle on numerous occasions. A surveillance log should be established to document the dates, times, and activities of the suspect while he/she is operating the vehicle. Photographs of the suspect on various occasions operating the vehicle will also assist in documenting its true ownership. This is all done to show that the person benefiting from this vehicle is only the suspect, who has been observed through surveillance, on numerous occasions, to solely operate the vehicle or operates the vehicle the majority of the time.

- *Purchased Accessories for the Vehicle:* We all know that drug dealers love the lavish lifestyle, which is also reflected in their assets. Go into any open-air drug market and you will see many flashy and intricately detailed vehicles with thousands of dollars in aftermarket accessories. For example, stereo systems, special chrome rims or tires, and other forms of cosmetics to alter its factory appearance, all to make the vehicle original to their specific taste. If targeting a seized vehicle, take note as to the accessories that are placed on the vehicle. You can get an estimated value of the accessories that a vehicle has by searching through automotive accessories catalogs or the Internet. Also look for receipts by doing trash rips, search warrants, or while searching the suspect's vehicle that would show the various accessories purchased for the vehicle. This will allow you to document for your financial investigation the amount of money spent toward the vehicle. In addition, if you can prove that the suspect is outfitting the vehicle with accessories, this would show that he/she is primarily benefiting from the vehicle and not the person titled to the vehicle.

- *Police Reports and Traffic Tickets:* Often reports from police departments and traffic tickets are used to document a connection between the suspect and the vehicle in question. Several reports and/or traffic tickets showing that the suspect was operating the vehicle on numerous occasions can also be used to display primary ownership of the vehicle over a period of time. Traffic ticket information or vehicle equipment repair orders, can be obtained by making an inquiry through the Motor Vehicle Administration. You can find out what vehicle the suspect was driving when given the traffic ticket. This information may also be accessed through your counties district court records or the courts archives.

- *Vehicle Indemnity Form:* As previously mentioned, drug dealers will have their vehicles registered in other people's names to avoid police detection and hide their illegally gained assets. In some cases the individual that the vehicle is registered to does not even know that the suspect is using it for illegal acts. In this case the vehicle cannot be seized by law enforcement unless you can prove that the owner of the vehicle was somehow involved or had knowledge that the vehicle was being used for the unlawful act. In the same token, finance companies also have an interest in the vehicle while the suspect is being financed through them. This is commonly referred to as the "innocent owner defense." To get around this problem, you can use what is called a Vehicle Indemnity Form. This form is made in triplicate and given to both the suspect and owner of the vehicle or financial institution who is financing the vehicle. By giving this form to all parties involved, it officially notifies the owners of the vehicle that it was seized pursuant to a controlled dangerous substance investigation. Further, that it is being returned to the owner under one circumstance; that if the vehicle or any other vehicle owned by them is loaned out to the same suspect who used the vehicle to traffic drugs, then they would have forfeited all ownership rights to the vehicle and would subsequently be subject to civil forfeiture. More specifically they would have waived all innocent owner privileges pertaining to the vehicle in question. Often finance companies will either demand the remaining balance of the vehicle loan from the suspect, or reposes the vehicle to prevent a future loss due to possible civil forfeiture brought on by law enforcement. The Vehicle Indemnity Form should be kept on file in the event that a forfeiture hearing occurs at a later date. An example of a Vehicle Indemnity Form has been included at the end of this chapter.

VEHICLE CIVIL SEIZURE WARRANTS

Vehicle seizure warrants are civil in nature. They are primarily used to seize illegally gained assets obtained through proceeds or due to the suspect using the vehicle to facilitate a transaction, etc A vehicle seizure warrant should only be used if the vehicle is not named in a search and seizure warrant and is stored, hidden, or kept on privately owned property. For example: you have already served a search warrant on the suspect, which had listed his vehicle as one of the items to be searched and seized as a result of the investigation. While at the scene of the search warrant, you are unable to locate the vehicle due to the suspect allegedly hiding it from police. Two months later you observe the suspect's vehicle *parked in the backyard* of one of his known associates. You would then use a "vehicle seizure warrant" (either for proceeds or facilitation) to seize the vehicle. It is important to note that any civil seizure warrant sought, can only be signed by a circuit court judge, and who is sitting in the county for which the item to be seized is located. In other words, if the item you are looking to seize is located in Queen Anne's County, you cannot get a circuit court judge from Caroline County to sign your seizure warrant. You will need to have the sitting judge for Queen Anne's County (the county that the item is located in) sign the seizure warrant for it to be a valid legal court order. Remember that you must display your financial analysis investigation in your vehicle seizure warrant when dealing with a proceed situation. Your financial analysis investigation should be able to clearly show the judge that proceeds from the sales of controlled substances and/or unexplained income, were used to finance and/or maintain the vehicle. For facilitation situations, explain in your warrant how the suspect used the vehicle to facilitate the controlled substance violation. Sample copies of a vehicle seizure warrant for both proceeds and facilitation are included at the end of this chapter for your review.

As explained above, you will need a seizure warrant if the vehicle is located on private property. But what if the vehicle is located on a public street, parking lot, or at a business? The United States Supreme Court has made it very clear in *Florida v. White*, 526 *U.S.* 559, 119 S. Ct 1555 (1999) when it overturned the state court's decision, holding that the Fourth Amendment doesn't require law enforcement to get a seizure warrant before seizing property in a public place if they believe that they have probable cause that the item in question is forfeitable contraband (i.e., vehicle) (Id. 119 S. Ct. at 1557). In *Florida v. White*, officers had observed the defendant on three separate occasions deliver cocaine using his vehicle. After several months had past, officers arrested White and seized his vehicle, believing that they had probable cause under state forfeiture laws that the vehicle was used to facilitate the prior CDS transactions. The arrest of White and the subsequent seizure of his vehicle all occurred at his employment, which was in a public place. Officers then completed an inventory search of the vehicle and found crack cocaine in the ashtray (you can look here in an inventory search because often people will keep change in their ashtray which would need to be logged on your inventory list). The Supreme Court stated in *White* that although the police lacked the probable cause necessary to believe that the vehicle contained contraband, "they certainly had probable cause to believe that the vehicle itself was contraband under Florida law" (Id. 1559).

RESIDENCE SEIZURES

Residence seizures are the most complicated of all. There is a lot of research and inspection that needs to be done prior to a seizure of a residence. When you are faced with this situation, it would be wise to contact your local Drug Enforcement Administration office and have them connect you with their Asset Seizure Department. The federal government does an excellent job in asset forfeiture investigations. There are some requirements that need to be met prior to their acceptance, such as: The value of the home needs to be above a certain amount, any renovations that need to be made in order to make the residence habitable must not exceed the assessed value (i.e., asbestos removal), etc. Some of the basic documents you must have for the federal government to accept your proposed seizures are:

- certified copies of the deed to the residence (county court house),
- the state's assessment value of the property (Assessment Office),
- pictures of the residence to forward with your paperwork,
- and any reports involving the suspect or the residence in question.

As with vehicle seizures, residences are sometimes rented out to suspects who will use them as a base of operation to distribute their drugs or as a "stash house." If this is the case, you will need to issue to all parties involved a Residence Indemnity Form. This is very similar to the Vehicle Indemnity Form which explains that the residence was seized pursuant to a controlled dangerous substance investigation and that it is being returned to the owner under one circumstance; that if the residence in question or any other residence owned/financed/ or rented by them is given to the same suspect who used the residence to store and contain controlled dangerous substances, then they would have forfeited all ownership rights to the residence and would subsequently be subject to civil forfeiture. More specifically they would have waived all innocent owner privileges pertaining to the residence in question no matter if a mortgage was on the property or not. The Residence Indemnity

Form should be kept on file in the event that a forfeiture hearing occurs at a later date. An example of a Residence Indemnity Form has been included at the end of this chapter for your use.

DEBREIFING INFORMANTS IN ASSET INVESTIGATIONS

Questioning informants about your suspect's financial background can provide an insight into how your suspect's operation works. The questions should be asked in a way to obtain every detail of how the assets are obtained and hidden. Below is a list of questions that should be asked to retrieve the information you will need to complete your asset investigation. To make things easier, you can place these questions on a cheat sheet and just fill the answers in when debriefing informants The following questions should be used as a basis of questioning when debriefing informants about asset investigations:

A. *Who are the members of the suspect organization?*

B. *How do you know this?*

C. *Do you have any evidence that you can give to corroborate your information?* (i.e., phone/address book, toll records, photographs, etc)

D. *What role does each member have in the organization?*

E. *Who are the key people in this organization?*

F. *Do you know any of their friends, family, and girlfriends/ boyfriends? If so what are their names, addresses, or phone numbers.*

G. *What is the main purpose of the suspect's organization?* This is important to know because individuals who launder money have different records then drug traffickers. This is all critical to know for your affidavit wording.

H. *What is the approximate amount of drugs that the suspect is distributing per week, month, or year?*

I.   *What are the expenses incurred by the suspect?*

- money given to his members,
- money paid toward a stash house,
- expenses on rental cars,
- daily, monthly, or yearly living expenses,
- money spent on cell phones or prepaid cell cards, etc.

J.   *Do you know the purity of the drugs received from the source?* This will let you know how far up the scale the suspect is. The higher the purity of the drugs means that the suspect is close to the initial source. If the drugs have a lower purity rate, this likely shows that the drugs have changed hands a couple times before the suspect had received it. The lower the purity rate of the drugs means that it has been diluted with a cutting agent.

K.   *On what days are collections of drug proceeds made?*

L.   *Who are the collections made from?*

M.   *Who makes the collections?*

N.   *What denominations of currency are collected?*

O.   *Once the money is collected, what does the suspect do with it?*

P.   *Is there a specific location that the suspect uses to count his/her money?*

Q.   *Once the money is received is it converted to larger bills? Or is the money converted to money orders, checks, or other financial instruments?*

R.   *Is the money deposited into banks or through other financial institutions? If so, what are the names and addresses of the institutions? Do you know the account numbers used for the accounts?*

S.   *Are there "front" companies used to launder the money? If so what is the name(s) and addresses(s)?*

T.   *What assets does the suspect own?*
    For example, if real estate:

- *Who owns the property?*
- *When was it bought?*
- *Who was it purchased from?*
- *How was it paid for?*

U. *What trips has the suspect taken? How did he arrange to take these trips (travel agency, internet agency, or independently)? If an agency was used, what's the name of the company or the web address?*

V. *How does the suspect pay for his lifestyle? Through credit cards, cash checks?*

The questions listed above should be asked of your informant to gain as much knowledge as you can into how the suspect operates. In addition, you will always need to corroborate the information that your informant is telling you. Any questions that the informant cannot answer should be found through your investigation of the suspect/organization.

Asset Investigation Techniques

The purpose of the asset investigation is to ensure that the proper documentation is obtained to show in court that the currency seized was most likely the proceeds from illegal sales of controlled dangerous substances. The below listed methods can also be used to complete an investigation prior to the suspect's arrest or the seizure of their assets. For example, if you notice that a suspect is spending a great deal of money on cars, houses, or other material items, then the following basic investigative methods should be conducted to corroborate the fact that the money was obtained by selling CDS or confirm that it was not. It is important to note that if an asset investigation is conducted prior to having contact with your suspect, be careful not to ask business or institutions that my intentionally or inadvertently notify the suspect that the police were inquiring about him/her.

Work History: Contact the suspect's current employer. Inquire as to how long they have worked there. In addition, ask about the suspect's hourly wage, salary, or pay schedule. Find out what their last paycheck amount was and when was it distributed out, if they have direct deposit and their date of hire/fire, etc. You most likely will need a subpoena from your prosecutor's office to obtain this information. If that is the case, the officer making the inquiry will need to word their subpoena in a specific way to ensure that all information is obtained to complete their investigation. Refer to the "subpoena language section" in this chapter for specific examples that you can use to obtain employment/payroll records from any business. The information obtained from subpoenaing the suspect's employer will confirm or dispel the suspect's story concerning his/her employment. If getting work history information prior to arresting the suspect is the goal then you will need to run a Wage Records Check through your state's Department of Labor, Licensing, and Regulation Department. This will provide you the employers, name, address, telephone number, and the employee's quarterly wages without tipping anyone off.

Financial Institutions / Bank Accounts: By obtaining the suspect's bank account information you can get the following information:

- *Signature Cards*: This shows who can sign on the account. Great way of identifying co-conspirators.
- *Bank Account Statements:* Monthly schedule of the deposits, withdrawals or any other form of transaction made will reflect a summarized history of that account.
- *Account Control:* Provides the names of the company or persons who control the account. This may provide previously undisclosed relationships with other persons and entities.
- *Canceled Checks:* Which allow you to trace them back to their ultimate disposition, can uncover assets

purchased, as well as third parties or co-conspirators who receive payments by check.

- *Deposit Slips:* Can be traced to their initial source, show evidence of receipts, lead to third parties or can show undisclosed assets.
- *Credit/Debit Memos:* These show wire transfers in and out, loan proceeds or repayment, the purchase of CDD or securities, and payments to or receipts from other accounts with the same financial institution, etc.

This can be done after the seizure of the money occurs or before. One way of getting bank information before you make a seizure is to conduct a trash rip. Refer to the "Trash Rip Operations" section in this text on how to conduct a trash rip Another way is to develop a working relationship with employees of the local banks in your area. Ask them to contact you directly when they notice any suspicious transactions concerning individuals that utilize their institution. They can record the tag numbers of people that come through the drive thru windows and/or tip you off with a name. In any event you will need a subpoena to receive any account information from a financial institution. Further, in this chapter you are given examples of specific language needed to put in your subpoenas for the various information you are seeking. Once you have identified the suspect's accounts and determined that there is illegal proceeds being held within them, you can then write a seizure warrant to have the financial institution write out a check in the amount contained in the suspect's account, made payable to your department and subsequently placed into an interest bearing escrow account until after the suspect's trial. A sample seizure warrant for bank accounts/safe deposit box is included at the end of this chapter for your use.

Some other ways you can find out about suspects and their assets is through the following reports that are generated by financial institutions.

Currency Transaction Report (CTR): It is important to note that cash transactions of $10,000 or more involving a financial institution must be reported to the IRS in the form of what is called a currency transaction report (CTR). CTRs capture the identity of the person or persons involved, the financial institution, and account information to mention a few. The financial institution files the CTR with the information given by the person making the transaction. But the bad guys then began to catch on and attempted to avoid the CTR by making multiple deposits in amounts under $10,000. This is commonly referred to as "smurffing" the system. The federal government then realized what these individuals were doing and subsequently revamped the CTR reporting system by enacting "31 USC 5324," which carries with it five to ten-year penalties. By doing this, any individual with a cash transaction of $3,000 or more must provide the information needed to file a CTR. Recognizing that legitimate business routinely makes large cash deposits of over $10,000, financial institutions are permitted to exempt some business's from filing a CTR, which are established over a period of regular deposits. In addition, CTRs are now used in casinos to document individuals that exhibit suspicious transactions. These reports are called CTR-Cs (Casino).

Suspicious Activity Report (SAR): Due to the constant adaptation of career criminals, FinCEN and the Board of Governors of the Federal Reserve System, created what is called a suspicious activity report (SAR). Unlike a CTR, where a report is generated when a transaction exceeds $10,000 or more, a SAR has no threshold. So in essence anyone who they know, suspect, or have reason to suspect that a crime has occurred or that a transaction is suspicious can file a SAR. In addition, SARs are now used in casinos to document individuals that exhibit suspicious transactions. These reports are called SAR-C (Casino)

IRS Form 8300: Converting cash into tangible assets through retail businesses is a common method to launder money. An IRS form 8300 is used by businesses when the following occurs:

- one lump sum of more then $10,000 is received (8300 must be filed with IRS within fifteen days of cash being received);
- installment payments that cause the total cash received within one year of the initial payment to total more than $10,000, or;
- other previously unreported payments that cause the total cash received within a twelve-month period to total more than $10,000.

The information obtained from the Form 8300 is similar to the CTRs. This form has been very successful in targeting car dealerships and real estate brokers suspected of catering to the illegal drug trade.

Note: In addition to coin and currency, cash also refers to cashiers checks, bank drafts, traveler's checks, and money orders with a face value of $10,000 or less. Cashiers checks, bank drafts, travelers checks are considered cash in this sense only when two or more of these instruments are presented in connection with cash in an amount exceeding $10,000. To inquire if your suspect has had a CTR, SAR, or 8300 filed on him/her, make contact with their financial institution, your local IRS office, or FinCEN (refer to the below FinCEN caption for further details). They all will be able to give you a wealth of financial information concerning your target. Remember to be aware of who you are speaking with at financial institutions. Suspects have been known to have connections with tellers or other employees within the local banking system. Further, included at the end of this chapter is a sample Suspicious Transaction Matrix, used to keep track of CTRs, SARs, and 8300s.

Income Tax Returns: A good way of proving whether a suspect can afford the lifestyle he or she is living is through their income tax records. This will show you exactly how much the suspect is claiming to make in that specified year. By completing a debt-to-income ratio analysis of the suspect you will be able to compare this to their filed tax information to see if he/she could or could not afford the lifestyle or assets they have. In Maryland, only a court order from a circuit court judge can retrieve this information and the state attorney's office must apply for it, *not* the officer. It is important to inquire with your prosecutor's office to determine what action is needed to obtain a tax return court order. In addition to contacting your prosecutor's office, you will need to make contact with your states taxation office to find out how far back your state holds tax records on file. In most states they hold tax records that go back several years. A sample of a petition and order for state income tax records is included at the end of this chapter. When attempting to obtain the suspect's federal income tax information, you will need to make contact with your local United States Attorney's Office to obtain what is called a federal "Exparte Order." Most of the time though, the state income tax records will suffice. If you need more detailed information concerning the suspect's financial status, then applying for the federal returns may be what you need; due to it giving a much more detailed itemization of their financial makeup.

Registrar of Wills (Probate and Death Records): This is usually a local/county government department that captures assets given out to beneficiaries. The purpose of contacting this department is to confirm that the suspect has not received assets left to them due to a will or to locate previously undisclosed assets that were dispersed to your suspect. This is manly done to document that a check has been made and subsequently include in your financial investigation report so later in court the suspect does not come up with the story on the day of trial the he/she had received the money through an inheritance.

Financial Crimes Enforcement Network (FinCEN): Just as the name suggests, this is an intelligence network made up of federal, state, local, and international law enforcement agencies, which have combined together to investigate financial crimes. This should be your first step in investigating an asset/ forfeiture case due to the amount of information that can be gained. The databases that are used by FinCEN are:

Law Enforcement Databases

- Drug Enforcement Administration
- Federal Bureau of Investigation
- U.S. Postal Inspection Service
- Immigration and Naturalization Service
- U.S. Department of Agriculture
- Internal Revenue Service
- DCII (Defense Clearance and Investigative Index
- TECS II (this includes NCIC/NLETS)
- Bureau of Alcohol, Tobacco, and Firearms
- U.S. Customs Service
- U.S. Secret Service

Commercial Databases

- D&B World Base
- Lexis-Nexis
- AutoTrack
- NASD
- CDB Infotek
- Equifax (credit information)

Note: FinCEN's commercial database has a wide spectrum of information that can assist you in your investigations. The commercial database will give you the following information.

1. *Credit Information*

  - Identifies the location of the suspect; or

- May identify other names or social security numbers used on credit applications.

2. *Property Information*

   - Identifies ownership of the property in question (Not all states have coverage on this so the search result may vary depending on what state the query is made)

3. *Business Records*

   - Shows ownership or control over the business
   - Can identify associates (business partners)
   - The information obtained can be used to uncover suspected money laundering investigations.

4. *Other database queried would produce*

   - Corporate/limited partnerships
   - Bankruptcy filings people finder
   - UCC filings
   - Liens and judgments
   - Aircraft locator (FAA)
   - Watercraft locator (Coast Guard)
   - Motor vehicle records
   - People and business finder information
   - Professional licensing
   - Docket information

Financial Databases

- Currency Transaction Report (CTR)
- Currency Transaction Report—Casino (CTR-C)
- Foreign Bank Account Report (FBAR)

- Report of International Transportation of Currency or Monetary Instruments (CMIR)
- Suspicious Activity Reports (SAR)

There are two types of investigative reports that are produced by FinCEN:

1. *Targeted Reports:* These reports tend to have a faster turnaround rate. To obtain a report in this manner you will need to have the suspect identified prior to sending off your request for assistance. The information most needed in your request would be the suspect's name and social security number. This report is the style you most often will use in your asset investigations.

2. *Developed Subject Report:* This report is more time intensive to complete due to the detail that has to go into it to convert the unknown structure of your target's financial status into a flowing report that details his/her financial history with explanation. This should only be used for larger scale financial cases. In addition, if you have a significant case that you feel warrants direct analytical support from FinCEN, then you will first need to obtain the approval of the director or assistant director. This can be done on letterhead from your agency directed to FinCEN.

To request the assistance from FinCEN you will need to fill out and submit via mail or fax, a Request for Research form. You can obtain this form by calling your state/local coordinator (every state has an assigned coordinator most likely located in your state police agency), your local IRS field office, or contacting FinCEN at the following phone number: 1-800-SOS-BUCK; fax number: 703-905-3526; or Web site: www.fincen.gov. In addition to the Request for Research form, a Request Memo should be forwarded as well. The Request

Memo should contain the following to give as much detail as possible concerning your suspect and the investigation:

- Who is making the request?
- Are you working with another agency?
- Who is the subject of the request? (Include some or all of the following: address, aliases/nicknames, social security number,
- DOB, business name and/or locations, etc.)
- What information do you want?
- What information do you have concerning the suspect or affiliations?
- What specific crime or violation is involved?
- How do you need the information prepared? (reports, flowcharts, timelines, etc.)
- When do you need this information?
- How did you identify the subject?

Complete the Request for Research form and the Request Memo in its entirety and forward it to FinCEN for further disposition. A sample Request Memo is included at the end of this chapter.

A *free* database computer program that FinCEN distributes out to law enforcement is called ASIS (Analytical System for Investigative Support). This program is a Microsoft Access Database Shell that assists law enforcement agencies with the organization and presentation of major complex case to the court. ASIS was developed to capture, maintain, and store large amounts of information involving a single case. Once you have the information documented and stored under the ASIS program, you can send your ASIS case diskette to FinCEN attn: The ASIS department. It is at this location they can place your data in a graphical format (flowchart, timeline, etc.), so it's easier to look at or generate reports.

Report of International Movement of Currency or Monetary Instruments (CMIR): By transporting large amounts of cash outside to a country with more relaxed banking regulations is probably the easiest way to hide drug proceeds. The cash can then be spent or transferred back into the country to make appear legal. In order to create a paper trail in this sort of situation, whenever there is the exportation or importation of a item of monetary value or cash of $10,000 or more, a Report of International Movement of Currency or Monetary Instruments is completed—commonly known as CMIRs. A CMIR is a U.S. Customs form that is routinely utilized in day-to-day travels. This can prove to be invaluable to uncovering drug organizations through asset disbursement methods both into and out of the country. This form identifies the person traveling, the person for whom the currency is being shipped to, the type and amount of currency or monetary instrument, as well as any other individuals involved in the activity. To find out if your suspect has filed a CMIR, contact your local Customs office or submit a FinCEN request asking for a any CMIRs that your suspect may have been the subject of.

Department of Human Resources (Welfare): This department is worth its weight in gold. Not only can you find out where a suspect is living, but they can also tell you whether your suspect is receiving financial assistance, food stamps (which it is known that users trade food stamps for drugs), or medical assistance. Regarding financial investigations the user can get a running total of how much financial assistance a person has received during a given period of time.

Department of Labor, Licensing, and Regulation (Wage Records Check): This will be one of the primary financial checks that you will conduct to find out if your suspect has a job or not. In reference to unemployment, employers are required to pay unemployment tax for each of their employees, which through this database will allow you to see if the suspect is currently on unemployment and from which business he/she is collecting it from. In addition, there is a separate wage record account that is set up for each of the business's employees, which reveal the quarterly contributions made by the business to the employee. Further benefits of using this system are:

- to locate a suspect's current place of employment,
- uncovering a suspect's prior employer,
- find wages paid out to the subject on a quarterly basis,
- get the subject's current home address (if the suspect is receiving an unemployment check from his previous employer),
- or to obtain a list of employees at a certain business.

Lottery Winnings: A technique used by drug dealers to hide money obtained through the sales of controlled dangerous substances is to keep old lottery tickets with their money. Some of the tickets may be winners and some may not. Suspects may also pay for "old" winning lottery tickets that had a substantial value to them from other individuals. The suspects in turn will then keep those tickets with their drug money. This is all done to portray an alibi in an attempt to cover the fact that the money found is actually from the sales of drugs. To get around this you will need to seize the lottery tickets (along with the money) and contact your state's lottery commission. Every lottery commission has a security section that will assist you in this investigation. Give security the lottery numbers that the suspect is claiming to be winning numbers. In a matter of seconds they will be able to tell you if in fact those tickets were winners or not, the amount each was worth, who the winnings were paid out to, and the date that the winnings were claimed. This method is also used for scratch-off game tickets sponsored through the state lottery commission.

Department of Assessments and Taxation (Land/Residence Value): This can be a wealth of knowledge in a variety of ways. There is a lot of information contained in these records concerning the property owned by your suspect or in whoever's name the suspect has the property. This can be used as a starting point to investigating a residence owned by your suspect. The next step to take is to go to your county circuit court and pull the land deed records for the property. This will have additional financial information on the property and your suspect. The assessment record will tell you:

- who sold the property and who bought the property,
- what was the selling price and when it was purchased,
- the assessed value of the property (A state assessment tends to always be on the low side. If filing for this property federally you will need to give them this approximate value of the property to get them started. This is due to certain monetary thresholds they need to meet before any action can be taken.)
- and the dimensions of the property and any structures built on it.

The majority of states have this information on the interment. Just plug in your address and up comes all the assessment information you will need. In Maryland, you can access this information at *www.dat.state.md.us*

UCC Filings (Uniform Commercial Code): UCC Filings are a way for a creditor (the seller of expensive tangible or intangible property) to protect their investment in the transaction. The creditor is also referred to as a secured party. For example if the creditor were to file a UCC Agreement and the debtor (the buyer of the tangible or intangible property) subsequently goes bankrupt, the creditor, which is now the secured party due to the UCC filings, will get paid first before all other creditors. It's important to note that UCC Filings information pertains to both individual filings and business filings. *Tangible property* includes things like furniture, automobiles, jewelry, equipment, etc. *Intangible property* includes things like notes, contract rights, leases, etc. As an investigator you can use UCC fillings to find a suspect's assets, who the suspect's business associates are (co-owners of tangible or intangible property), to provide a starting point for net worth methods of proof, as well as their financial relationships. The UCC Filings database will contain the following information:

- the debtor's name,
- the creditor's name,
- date/time the UCC was filed,
- amounts financed.

In order to obtain UCC copies filed with your state, get on the Internet and conduct a search through your state's government Web site. By conducting this search, you can see if your suspect has any involvement in UCC Filings. In Maryland, you can find UCC Filings on the Internet at the Maryland Department of Assessments and Taxation (*www.dat.state.md.us*) You will not be able to obtain a list of the items purchased over the Internet. You will need to request the information by sending a UCC Filings Request Letter to receive the information you need. When sending your request letter, you will need to include the Film/Folio numbers which can be found during your UCC Filings Internet search. These numbers will allow the UCC department to find the records needed to fulfill your request.

Corporate Charters: All incorporated businesses record what is called an Article of Incorporation with the Corporate Charter Division of your state. Articles of Incorporation contain certain information about the individuals involved in that business as well as the business itself. In addition, the Corporate Charter Division also records identifying information about unincorporated businesses such as proprietorships and partnerships. As with UCC Filings, some states may have this information on a database via the Internet through your state's Corporate Charter Division, but wont list all of the below information. You will need to send a request letter to your states Corporate Charter Division and ask for a certified copy of the business in question. By researching a businesses corporate charter you can retrieve the following information:

- verify the company's name, and if a sole proprietorship it will display the name it trades under;
- determine if the business is in "good standing," for example if the business is active, dissolved, merged, or forfeited;
- locate a business's address for both corporations and unincorporated businesses;
- the name of the person who formed the business;
- find out the point of contact name and address for the corporation, this will be the resident agent's information. If your suspect is connected to this business it may be listed as the resident agent;
- the date the corporation was formed and the nature of the business

   Note: The resident agent is the official contact person for the business in the event that legal papers need to be served.

Personal Property Returns: Corporations and unincorporated businesses are obligated to pay personal property tax annually on their furniture, fixtures, equipment, and tools. The personal property returns tell a wealth of information concerning a business. It will tell you the following information:

- the current officers and director's names of the business (if a corporation), which reflect who is running the business;
- the nature of the business;
- financial information about the business, its assets and liabilities;
- and the owner's name, the trade name that the business operates under, and addresses for the unincorporated businesses.

   To obtain a certified copy of this document you will need to make contact with your state's personal property unit/division which will most likely be found in the assessment and taxation department of your state's government. Send this department a request letter to obtain the personal property tax information concerning the business in question. Refer to a sample Personal Property Request Letter at the end of this chapter.

Business License: Not all businesses are required to have a business license to operate. Only businesses that have *an inventory of products to sell* require one. Some examples of businesses that need to have a business license are coin-operated vending machine companies, chain stores, cleaning/pressing companies, construction firms, restaurants, and storage warehouses. The benefits to the investigator of researching a business license is that you can receive the following information:

- locate a businesses address and telephone number,
- the owner's name and social security number,
- and the type of business it conducts.

Credit-Reporting Agencies: By making contact with credit-reporting agencies, you will be able to find out who your suspect has his/her credit accounts with and how much each is for. In addition, you will be able to obtain personal financial information about your suspect. Once you identify the suspect's credit accounts you can then contact each creditor and make inquires as to payment schedule, amounts paid out by the suspect, items purchased (this will assist you later to identify assets and subsequently seized them), etc. Below is a list of the three main credit-reporting agencies that will be able to supply you with the information you are seeking. Fax your subpoena or court order to the credit agency and then send the hard copy via mail. The turnaround rate for records to be returned is usually seven to ten working days. For basic information about your suspect, you can use a subpoena. For more in-depth financial information on the suspect and account information, you will need to have a court order. Per section 604 of the Fair Credit

Reporting Act (15 U.S.C. § 1681 et seq.), you will need to have a signed court order to retrieve the suspect's full credit history. The Fair Credit Reporting Act prohibits consumer-reporting agencies, such as the ones listed below, from furnishing credit or consumer reports to anyone, even law enforcement or grand juries, except only when a court order is issued. In addition, your local prosecutor is the only person who can petition the court for a suspect's credit history. It's important to note that any inquiry to the credit-reporting agency will be reflected on the suspect's credit report unless otherwise ordered by the court not to be. Be aware that it may tip off your suspect if this nondisclosure statement is not included in your petition to the court. Refer to the end of the chapter for an example of a Petition and Court Order for credit history records. Remember that only your local prosecutor's office can petition the court for these records.

1. *Experian*

   - Phone Number: 972-390-4041
   - Mail subpoena / court order requests to:
   Experian
   Attn: CASS Department-Subpoena Request
   PO Box 1240, Allen, Texas 75013

2. *Trans Union*

   - Phone Number: 714-680-7241
   - Mail subpoena / court order requests to:
   Trans Union
   555 West Adams Street
   4th Floor, Chicago, Illinois 60661

3. *Equifax* (This is the most popular reporting agency and should be queried first)

- Phone Number: 770-752-1286 / 678-795-7972
- Mail subpoena / court order request to:
Equifax
211 Perimeter Center Parkway,
Suite 300, Atlanta, Georgia 30346

Bankruptcy Records (Federal Bankruptcy Court):
Information concerning your suspect's assets and financial
makeup can be found in bankruptcy records, which are a matter
of public record. This information can be accessed by telephone
through your local Federal Bankruptcy Court. The phone
number can be found in the government section of your local
phone book. Although If you want documents pertaining to
your suspect then you will need to got the court and request
them in person; but be prepaid for a small fee. If you learned
that your suspect has filed bankruptcy in the past then you
can access this information to reveal assets at the time the
suspect had filed bankruptcy and creditors at the time of
bankruptcy, which provides an excellent starting point for
net worth purposes. This will usually lead to angry creditors
and/or hidden assets that the suspect might still have in their
possession.

Civil Court Records: These records can be accessed through
your local county court house where civil cases are filed. By
researching civil actions pursued, or brought against your
suspect, you will be able to identify any monetary settlements,
either given to, or paid out by your suspect. Civil court records
can also reveal previously unknown addresses, social security
numbers, affiliations with other persons or entities, etc. You
can obtain these records by going to your county court house
(usually circuit court), in the county that the suspect resides in,
and ask the court clerks to run your suspect's name or business
in their database. In addition, this is a way of corroborating that
a suspect is telling the truth or lying about money he/she claims
was obtained as a result of a settlement.

Divorce/Separation Records: Often divorces and separations are not pleasant. And both parties usually air "dirty laundry" about the other which is all documented in the form of hidden transactions, assets, or other affiliations with persons or entities. This in turn gives you a host of information that uncovers the financial status concerning your suspect and any assets that he/she may have or gain as a result of a divorce. These records can be accessed through the county of which the divorce is filed in. Contact the clerk of the court to make your inquiries and to received the information you are seeking.

Judgment Indexes: This is a list of civil judgments that can be used to reveal any previously undisclosed assets that may have been used by your suspect to satisfy a judgment placed against him/her. It also discloses past creditors who have filed against the suspect or previously undisclosed affiliations to other persons or businesses. These records can also be accessed through your county court house through the clerk of the court.

Money Orders: Money orders are commonly found to be used by drug dealers to transform illegal proceeds obtained from the sale of controlled dangerous substances into apparently legal funds. This is done by the drug dealer taking his drug money to a local convenience store, post office, or bank and turning it in for money orders. The dealer then takes the money order and deposits it into his account or a third party account. By doing this the dealer has just created a paper trail to make it appear that the money in his account was obtained from a legitimate source (the money orders). Oftentimes when a drug dealer tries to hide money like this, the investigator, who usually only has a money order receipt, is unable to find out what account that the money was deposited into. A way to find out what account the money was deposited into is to get the money order receipt and run the receipt numbers through the U.S. Postal Inspector's Office. They in turn will be able to run the money order receipts numbers, which will tell you what account the money was deposited into pertaining to that specific money order. In most instances suspects will purchase several money orders in succession at one time for varied amounts, due to the limitations on the amounts that can be purchased daily by a single individual. So when an investigator finds a single money order receipt, or several receipts, the investigator should also check the receipt numbers five ahead and five behind the receipt numbers you are inquiring about. This will allow you to see if the suspect purchased several money orders at once. When the account(s) are identified, you can begin monitoring it to further your investigation. The main objective here is to obtain the money order receipts, which can be done in several ways:

- *Trash Rips:* By searching the trash of the suspect you can receive numerous financial documents including money order receipts that have been thrown away—if the suspect is using them.
- *Search Warrants:* When searching a suspect's house, be sure to look for money order receipts along with other documents. Money order receipts have been located in a suspect's wallet or purse, mixed in with his/her money or other items.
- *Store, Bank, and/or Post Office Employees:* This is an excellent source of information concerning money order receipts. By developing a relationship with these establishments, you can arrange for them to contact you and document the money order numbers when your suspect makes the purchase. In addition, you can arrange for these employees to contact you whenever they see something suspicious or when an individual engages in frequent use of money orders involving large amounts of currency.
- *Internet:* In today's society almost anything can be done with a computer. Unfortunately this means that methods of evasion that were done physically can now be done virtually. Referring to the use of money orders, a suspect can now go on line and purchase money orders right from their own home. For instance a popular money order

Internet site is www.payko.com, sponsored through Paypal (a large online e-commerce company), www.WesterUnion.com, and www.Payingfast.com to mention a few. The money orders are purchased online by setting up virtual accounts then having the company forward the money order to you or a third party via the mail. In the suspect's mind, the plus side to this is that the suspect does not have to leave the comforts of their home; they can easily make a transaction utilizing modern e-commerce methods to obtain money orders over the Internet. The downside of it all is that by using the Internet you (the police) will be able to establish a more evidentiary paper trail that is commonly generated due to various online company policies. Therefore you should always check computers found while on search warrants for Web sites that cater to specific financial institutions. Once identified you can then subpoena the institution to receive the desired information.

Life Insurance Policies: A life insurance policy is considered an investment, and as with all investments it takes money to start one. On some occasions you may find that drug dealers will hide illegally obtained monies from the sales of controlled dangerous substances placed in interest bearing investment accounts such as stocks, bonds, and life insurance policies. A life insurance policy is an excellent way of hiding illegally obtained money due to some policies allowing you to withdraw money from the insurance in the form of a no interest or low interest loan or even a cash out option after a certain point of the policies maturity. This money in turn can be used to buy assets such as vehicles, homes, etc., which on its face would appear to have come from a legitimate source. But further inspection into the finances surrounding the life insurance shows that unexplained income was used to make monthly, quarterly, or yearly payments to satisfy the policy agreement. Once you have identified that the life insurance policy was obtained from illegal funds, you can then seize the proceeds from the policy through a seizure warrant. When the seizure warrant is given to the insurance company, they will then give you a check, usually within forty-eight hours per court order. The check should be made out to your department to be placed in an interest-bearing escrow account until the case is adjudicated. Some ways of finding out if your suspect has a life insurance policy is through trash rips and search warrants. Both methods can provide your investigation with a wealth of knowledge in to the financial background of your suspect. A sample life insurance seizure warrant is included at the end of this chapter.

Business Deposits: You will find on occasion that drug dealers will place deposits on items such as cars, homes, vacation rentals, layaway items, and other merchandise. The deposits used to secure these items are commonly funded with the proceeds from drug sales. Once your financial investigation is complete and you can prove that the suspect's net worth is in the negative and shows unexplained income, you can subsequently seize these deposits through a seizure warrant. By retrieving documents or deposit receipts from the suspect's trash or from a search warrant executed at their residence, you will be able to identify the various businesses that the suspect has deposits with and approximately how much was paid and when. Refer to the end of this chapter for a sample business/ retail deposit seizure warrant.

Bail Bonds: On many occasions when a drug dealer is arrested they will use money from the sales of controlled dangerous substances to secure their bail. How this commonly occurs is the suspect will contact an associate of theirs to retrieve the amount of currency needed to secure their bail. This associate will then contact another individual to make the actual delivery of the payment. The individual making the payment will usually be a person not involved in drugs and who does not draw attention to themselves. For example, elderly people or family members such as a husband, wife, mother, father, sister, brother, girlfriend, boyfriend, who does not have a tainted history, are some of the usual decoys used by the suspect. Another method used is having these decoys listed on the suspect's accounts so they would be able to have access to the account in circumstances like this if needed. When looking at a situations like this you must first identify the individual who is providing the funds. This can be done through documentation filed when bail is posted. Once you have identified the individual posting the bail you can then begin your financial investigation on them. You can start by running a Wage Records Check on the individual to determine where they work, if they work at all, and if they are on disability or retired, etc. If the individual does not work, or is on disability or retirement, you now have some ammunition against the individual before you talk to them. A person who does not work clearly cannot afford to throw money down in this fashion; and people on disability or retirement are on fixed incomes that would typically prevent them from being able to drop money down in this instance. Next, physically contact the individual and ask them the following questions:

- Did you post bail in the form of cash for the suspect?
- How do you know the suspect? Or what is your relationship?
- **Important:** How did you get the money to pay for the suspect's bail? Did you withdraw money from you bank to get these funds? What bank did you use? And did you use your checking account or savings account? Do you use any other banks or financial institutions? If so, what are their names? How much, if any money, do you keep on hand (meaning outside a financial institution) at any given time (in their wallet or shoebox, etc.)?

These individuals will sometimes tell you they got the money from a bank, or they will explain that they retrieved it from a friend. If the money came from a friend get the name and address / phone number for this other person and conduct the same financial investigation and questions on them. Once you have found the individual's bank, subpoena their account records for the past month to the date that the bail was posted. Look for any withdrawals listed on the statements that would match the suspect's bail amount, or other withdraws that would corroborate the individual's statement. You will most likely find that the person has lied to you about where they had obtained the money. If this is the case, you have just built your probable for a Bail Bonds Seizure Warrant. Document in a seizure warrant the above financial investigation methods conducted on this individual showing that there is no explainable income to support the bail deposit placed for the suspect and/or that the suspect had lied about where the currency actually came from. Once you have your seizure warrant written, serve it on the court or other entity that has the deposit. They will then turn over all proceeds used for the bail deposit and subsequently revoke the suspect's bail causing the suspect to be placed back in jail. Another common mistake that the decoy individual will do is bring large amounts of cash with bank bands still attached to the currency. The bank bands/straps will have the name of the bank where the money came from. This is a good lead on your financial investigation in regards to the individual who posted the bail for the suspect. Refer to the end of this chapter for an example of a Bail Bonds Seizure Warrant.

Child Support Payments: Your local Child Support Services Division is a great resource to uncover how much money the suspect has paid toward child support. This agency keeps a running ledger that lists the following:

- payment amount,
- method of payment (cash, check, or money order),
- schedule of payments,
- the suspect's current job,
- and who the payments are being made to.

The information gained from this agency can be incorporated into other aspects of your financial investigation. Such as comparing child support payments to checking account or withdraw transactions in the suspect's bank account or documenting the amount of "cash" paid out by the suspect to Child Support Services when you know that he has no job.

Subpoena Language Examples

The information presented below is not represented to include all details necessary for the preparation of the subject subpoenas. As the author of this text, I do not claim to be qualified to dispense legal opinion. The intent here is to provide ideas and verbiage that will ensure that the writers of the subpoenas ask for the appropriate information to assist in the investigation. Before you use this text, it is important to ensure that the verbiage and specific requests are consistent with your agency's policy and approved by the prosecuting attorney(s) working with you on your case.

FINANCIAL INSTITUTION RECORDS

To bring with you and produce the following documents for all accounts bearing the signatory authority of (insert suspect's name) and/or in the name(s) or (insert other names used by suspect), and/or bearing the account numbers(s) (insert account numbers), for the period of (insert beginning date here) to (insert ending date here) including but not limited to: (Insert here one or any combination of the below captions that are specific to what you are looking for)

Account Information

- *All documents pertaining to all open or closed checking, savings, NOW (Negotiable Order of Withdraw), time or other deposit or checking accounts in the name of or under signature authority of any of the named parties or entities including, but not limited to, signature cards, corporate board authorization minutes or partnership*

resolutions, bank statements, canceled checks, deposit tickets, items deposited, credit and debit memos, forms 1099, 1089, or backup withholding documents.
What this subpoena will get you:

1. Bank statements which will allow you to get a summarized history of all transactions in the account
2. Any canceled checks which may lead to any assets purchased with the checks
3. All deposit tickets that can be used to trace back to their original source (i.e., cash, or other bank accounts)
4. Information contained in credit/debit memos that will reveal to you the loans proceeds or repayments, wire transfers both in and out, and forms 1099, 1089, or backup withholding documents, etc.

Loans/Mortgages

• *All documents pertaining to open or closed bank loans or mortgage documents, reflecting loans made to or cosigned by any of the named parties or entities including, but not limited to, loan applications, corporate board authorization minutes or partnership resolutions, loan ledger sheets, documents (check, debit memos, cash in tickets, wires in, etc.) reflecting the means by which loan repayments were made, documents (bank checks, credit memos, cash out tickets, wires out, etc.) reflecting disbursement of the loan proceeds, loan correspondence files including, but not limited to, letters to the bank, letters from the bank, notes, memoranda, etc. to file, collateral agreements and documents, credit reports, financial statements, notes or other instruments reflecting the obligation to pay, real estate mortgages, chattel mortgages, or other security instruments for loans, forms 1099, 1089, or backup withholding documents, loan amortization statements.*

What this subpoena will get you:

1. This will give you all loan applications and financial records that may provide you with a starting point for a net worth or expenditures investigation.
2. These records will possibly show undisclosed assets or liabilities listed on financial statements
3. And there may be some discrepancies found on these records in the suspect's income or net worth between what is listed on the financial statements and what is documented elsewhere in the case.
4. Other important items you will receive is all loan ledger sheets, which summarizes the loan amount, payments, and interest charged, and loan amortization schedules, that allow you to compare with actual terms and repayments, against unusual transactions you have found in other accounts,
5. All real estate, chattel mortgages, or other security instruments for loans that may list assets that have been used to secure each loan.

Certificate of Deposits (CDs)

- *All documents pertaining to CDs purchased or redeemed by any of the named parties or entities including, but not limited to, copies of the certificates, corporate board authorization minutes or partnership resolutions, documents (checks, debit memos, cash in tickets, wires in, etc.) reflecting the means by which the CD was purchased, documents (bank checks, credit memos, cash out tickets, wires out, etc.) reflecting disbursement of the proceeds of any negotiated CD, records reflecting interest earned, withdrawn or reinvested, records reflecting rollovers, forms 1099, 1089, or backup withholding documents.*

What this subpoena will get you:

1. Copies of the certificates
2. Will allow you to trace items used to purchase the CD's to their initial source, and all evidence of redemption and disbursement
3. All records reflecting the interest earned, withdrawn, reinvested, roll-overs, and forms 1099,1089, or backup withholding documents

Investment Accounts

• *All documents pertaining to open or closed investment or security custodian accounts, IRA, Keogh, or other retirement plans in the name of or for the benefit of any of the named parties or entities including, but not limited to, documents (checks, debit memos, cash in tickets, wires in, etc.) reflecting the means by which the security was purchased, documents (bank checks, credit memos, cash out tickets, wires out, etc.) reflecting disbursement of the proceeds of any negotiated securities, confirmation slips, monthly statements, payment receipts, safekeeping records and logs, receipts for receipt or delivery of securities, forms 1099, 1089, or backup withholding documents.*
   What this subpoena will get you:

1. Evidence showing the ownership of the securities (investment accounts)
2. Confirmation slips that will show you the dates of any transactions and reveal all receipts and disbursements involving the investment account
3. And will be able to trace all receipts into the suspect's securities accounts and all payments out to their initial source. In addition, this subpoena will give you how

the payments were made and may show evidence of cash expenditures.

Customer Correspondence

- *Customer correspondence files for each of the named parties and entities.*
  What this subpoena will get you:

1. Any correspondence between your suspect and the bank.
2. Previously undisclosed relationships with other persons or businesses.

Checks and Money Orders

- *All documents pertaining to all cashier's checks, manager's checks, traveler's checks, and money orders purchased or negotiated by any of the named parties or entities including, but not limited to, documents (checks, debit memos, cash in tickets, wires in, etc.) reflecting the means by which the checks or money orders were purchased, documents (bank checks, credit memos, cash out tickets, wires out, etc) reflecting disbursement of the proceeds of any negotiated checks or money orders, applications for purchase of checks or money orders, retained copies of negotiated checks or money orders.*
  What this subpoena will get you:

1. Information from this subpoena will allow you to trace all checks from their source to disposition
2. Show you evidence of disbursements
3. Assets that were purchased with the checks

Wire Transfers

- *All documents pertaining to wire transfers sent or received by any of the named parties or entities including, but not limited to, Fedwire, CHIPS, SWIFT, or other money transfer or message documents, documents (checks, debit memos, cash in tickets, wires in, etc. reflecting the source of the funds wired out, documents (bank checks, credit memos, cash out tickets, wires out, etc.) reflecting the ultimate disposition within the bank of the funds wired in, notes, memoranda, or other writings pertaining to the sending or receipt or wire transfers.*
  What this subpoena will get you:

1. This will give you all information on CHIPS (Clearing House for Interbank Payments System) and Fedwire (Federal Reserve Banks), which are the two most commonly used transfer systems to carry out exchanges with other banks. And SWIFT's (Society for Worldwide Interbank Financial Telecommunication), is an international messaging system that carries instructions for wire transfers between pairs of correspondent banks. Allowing you to find the source or destination of the wire transfers along with detailed information concerning the transfer itself.

Safe Deposit Box Information

- *All documents pertaining to current or expired safe deposit box rentals by or under the signatory authority of any of the named parties or entities including, but not limited to, contracts, and entry records.*
  What this subpoena will get you:

1. You will get the identification of all persons having access to the safety deposit box and any contracts that are involved.
2. Any *"entry records"* that were made. This can be compared with surveillance notes to document currency payments made from the box to third parties (i.e., car purchase, property, etc). Or even to document probable cause for a search warrant and/ or forfeiture.

On occasion, drug dealers will hide their assets from law enforcement by placing currency in safe deposit boxes. This is a very safe and secure way of preventing their money from being discovered by police or stolen from rivals. Once you have learned that the suspect has a safe deposit box, and developed probable cause, you will be able to write a seizure warrant for its contents. At the end of this chapter is an example of a safe deposit box /bank account seizure warrant.

Bank Credit Cards

*   *All documents pertaining to open or closed bank credit cards in the name of or under the signatory authority of any of the named parties or entities including, but not limited to, applications for credit, corporate board authorization minutes or partnership resolutions, credit reports, monthly statements, financial statements, charge tickets, documents (checks, debit memos, cash in tickets, wires in, etc.) reflecting payments on the account, and correspondence files.*
    What this subpoena will get you:

1. This you will get all credit applications, which may reveal previously undisclosed assets or credit cards.

2. Monthly statements that can provide you evidence that can be used to investigate all expenditures. And may reveal assets purchased by credit cards
3. All financial statements that can provide you with a starting point to determine net worth or expenditures. This will also allow you to reveal any discrepancies in income or net worth between what is listed on the financial statements and what is documented elsewhere in you investigation.
4. Evidence of payments

Teller Tapes

- *Teller tapes reflecting all transactions between the bank and any of the parties or entities named.*
  What this subpoena will get you:

1. This is a method of tracing and documenting currency transactions, which should be used as a last resort due to it being so time consuming.

CTRs and CMIRs

- *All CTRs (Form 4789) and CMIRs (Form 4790) filed with the Department of the Treasury, Internal Revenue Service, or the U.S. Customs Service by the (insert bank's name here) between (insert beginning date here) to (insert ending date here) concerning currency transactions conducted by or on behalf of the named parties or entities.*
  What this subpoena will get you:

1. Documentation of currency transactions
2. The addresses, identification numbers, and business relationships of customers
3. This may reveal previously undisclosed relationships with other persons or businesses.

4. Or this may provide evidence of cash receipts and expenditures for you to use to show a suspect's net worth or spending methods.

Documents Filed with Federal Authorities

- *Copies of the following documents, if any, filed by the (insert bank's name here) with the aforementioned federal agencies, the Drug Enforcement Administration, the Federal Bureau of Investigation, the Department of Justice, or any bank regulatory agency concerning transactions by, on behalf of, or involving the named parties or entities: Criminal Referral Form (Short Form); Office of the Comptroller of the Currency (OCC)-OCC Form CC-8010-08, Criminal Referral Form (Short Form); the Board of Governors of the Federal Reserve System—Federal Reserve Form FR2230, Report of Apparent Crime (Short Form); Federal Deposit Insurance Corporation (FDIC)-FDIC Form 6710/06*
    What this subpoena will get you:

1. This information may provide previously unknown leads or evidence relating to the investigation.

Exemptions Lists

- *Any and all "exemption lists," requests for exemptions and statements submitted in support or such requests filed with the Internal Revenue Service pursuant to 31 U.S.C. § 103.22 concerning the named parties or entities.*
    What this subpoena will get you:

1. All requests sent to the Internal Revenue Service for exemptions
2. Any written customer statements submitted to the bank in support of exemptions

3. Exemptions may reveal previously undisclosed business practices of the subject or evidence of currency receipts concerning the suspect's business.

Documentation of Telephone and Meeting Conversations

- *Any and all correspondence, letters, or documents reflecting telephone conversations or meetings between the (insert the bank's name here) and any bank regulatory or federal law enforcement agency regarding suspicious transactions, pending investigations or ongoing investigations relating to any of the named parties or entities.*

  What this subpoena will get you: Exactly what the subpoena explains

BUSINESS AND CORPORATE RECORDS

To bring with you and produce the following documents for the period of (insert beginning date here) to (insert ending date here) including, but not limited to, any and all retained copies of documents relating to (insert corporate name here) banking transactions including, but not limited to: (Insert here one or any combination of the below captions that are specific to what you are looking for)

Account Information

- *All documents pertaining to all open or closed checking, savings, NOW (Negotiable Order of Withdraw), time, or other deposit or checking accounts held in the name of, for the benefit of, or under the control of (insert corporate name here) including, but not limited to, retained copies or signature cards, corporate board authorization minutes or partnership resolutions, bank statements, canceled checks, deposit tickets, retained copies of items deposited, credit and debit memos, and Forms 1099, 1089, or backup withholding documents.*

What this subpoena will get you: The same as what a financial institution will give you.

Loans/Mortgages

- *All documents pertaining to open or closed bank loans or mortgage documents, reflecting loans made to, cosigned by, or made for the benefit of (insert corporate name here) including, but not limited to, loan applications, corporate board authorization minutes or partnership resolutions, loan statements, documents (check, debit memos, cash receipts, wire transfer documents, etc.) reflecting the means by which loan repayments were made, documents (checks, debit memos, cash receipts, wire transfer documents, etc.) reflecting the means by which loan repayments were made, documents (bank checks, credit memos, wire transfer documents, etc.) reflecting disbursement of the loan proceeds, copies of loan correspondence including, but not limited to, letters to the bank, letters from the bank, notes, memoranda, etc to the file, collateral agreements and documents, credit reports, financial statements, notes or other instruments reflecting the obligation to pay, real estate mortgages, chattel mortgages, or other security instruments for loans, forms 1099, 1089, or backup withholding documents, loan amortization statements.*

  What this subpoena will get you: The same as what a financial institution will give you.

Certificate of Deposits

- *All documents pertaining to CDS purchased or redeemed by or for the benefit of (enter corporation's name here) including, but not limited to, copies of the certificates, corporate board authorization minutes or partnership resolutions, documents (checks, debit memos, cash receipts, wire transfer documents, etc.) reflecting the means by which the CD was purchased, documents (bank checks, credit memos, wire transfer documents, etc.) reflecting disbursement of the proceeds of any negotiated CD, records reflecting interest earned, withdrawn or reinvested, records reflecting roll-overs, forms 1099, 1089, or backup withholding documents.*

What this subpoena will get you: The same as what a financial institution will give you.

Investment Accounts

• *All documents pertaining to open or closed investment or security custodian accounts, IRA, Keogh, or other retirement plans in the name of, for the benefit of, or under the control of (insert corporation name here) including, but not limited to, documents (checks, debit memos, cash receipts, wire transfer documents, etc.) reflecting the means by which the security was purchased, documents (bank checks, credit memos, wire transfer documents, etc.) reflecting disbursement of the proceeds of any negotiated securities, confirmation slips, monthly statements, payment receipts, safekeeping records and logs, receipts for receipt or delivery of securities, forms 1099, 1089, or backup withholding documents.*

What this subpoena will get you: The same as what a financial institution will give you.

Bank Correspondence

• *Any and all bank correspondence files.*

What this subpoena will get you: Exactly what it says

Checks and Money Orders

• *All documents pertaining to all cashier's checks, manager's checks, bank checks, traveler's checks, or money orders purchased or negotiated by or on behalf of (insert corporation name here) including but not limited to, documents (checks, debit memos, cash receipts, wire transfer documents, etc.) reflecting the means by which the checks or money orders were purchased, documents (bank checks, credit memos, wire transfer documents, etc) reflecting disbursement of the proceeds of any negotiated checks or money orders, applications for purchase of checks or money orders, and retained copies of checks or money orders.*

What this subpoena will get you: The same as what a financial institution will give you.

Wire Transfers

- *All documents pertaining to wire transfers sent or received by or on behalf of (insert corporation name here) including, but not limited to, federal wire, CHIPS, SWIFT, or other money transfer or message documents, documents (checks, debit memos, cash receipts, wire transfer documents, etc.) reflecting the source of the funds wired out, documents (bank checks, credit memos, wire transfer documents, etc.) reflecting the ultimate disposition of the funds wired in, notes, memoranda, or other writings pertaining to the sending or receipt or wire transfers.*

What this subpoena will get you: The same as what a financial institution will give you.

Safe Deposit Box Information

- *All documents pertaining to current or expired safe deposit box rentals in the name of, for the benefit of, or under the control of (insert corporation's name here) including, but not limited to, contracts, and entry records.*

What this subpoena will get you: The same as what a financial institution will give you.

Bank Credit Cards

• *All documents pertaining to open or closed bank credit cards in the name of, for the benefit of, or under the control of (insert corporation's name here) including, but not limited to, applications for credit, corporate board authorization minutes or partnership resolutions, credit reports, monthly statements, financial statements, charge tickets, documents (checks, debit memos, cash receipts, wire transfer documents, etc.) reflecting payments on the account(s).*

What this subpoena will get you: The same as what a financial institution will give you.

Documentation of Corporations Formation

• *All documents relating to (insert corporation's name here) formation including, but no limited to, articles of incorporation, by laws, minute book(s), stock book(s), stock transfer records, and annual reports filed with the state of incorporation.*

What this subpoena will get you:

1. This will generally give you a list of other corporate officers, board members, or partners involved in the business, which allows you to potentially identify possible co-conspirators.
2. Explains the nature of the business

Corporations Financial Performance

• *All documents summarizing annual, quarterly, monthly, weekly, or daily financial performance including, but not limited to, balance sheet, state of operations (profit and loss statement), annual filings with the SEC or other federal or state agencies or regulatory bodies. In addition, trial balances, federal and state income tax returns and quarterly estimated tax returns, sales tax returns, periodic reports required to be filed by the SEC, CFTC, or other regulatory body.*

What this subpoena will get you:

1.   All financial aspects of the business.

Employee Payroll Records

- *With respect to transactions between (insert business/ corporation name here) and (insert the suspect's name here), provide the following documents for the period (insert beginning date here) to (insert ending date here): employment records including, but not limited to, payroll journal, annual recap of wages paid (filed with the Internal Revenue Service), all forms W-2 issued, all forms 940 and 941 filed, all state employment and unemployment returns filed, all checks, or other earned income payments to (insert the suspect's name here), all contracts or other agreements made or entered into between (insert business/corporation name here) and (insert the suspect's name here)*

    What this subpoena will get you: Exactly what it is asking for

Documents Reflecting Any Contact with a Corporation

- *Any and all correspondence, letters, files or other documents reflecting telephone conversations, meetings, contracts, agreements, or transactions between (insert corporation's name) and (insert suspect's name).*

    What this subpoena will get you: Exactly what it is asking for

Documentation of payment to the suspect
kept in ledgers and journals

- *Copies of all documents in (insert corporation's name here) books or original entry containing entries reflecting any and all transactions between (insert corporation's name here) and (insert suspect's name here) including, but not limited to, general ledgers, general journals, summary journals including, but not limited to, sales journals, purchase journals, cash receipts journals, and cash disbursements journals In addition, invoices, sales receipts, purchase orders, receiving reports, and inventory records.*

  What this subpoena will get you:

1. This will give you all ledgers used in payroll for the entire business. You can use this in your financial comparisons to other aspect in your investigation.

CREDIT CARD COMPANY RECORDS
(NOTE: DO NOT USE FOR CREDIT-REPORTING AGENCIES)

To bring with you and produce the following documents for all open or closed credit card accounts bearing the signatory authority of and/or in the name of (insert suspect's name here), and credit card number(s) (insert credit card account numbers here), for the period (insert beginning date here) to (insert ending date here) including, but not limited to, applications for credit, corporate board authorization minutes or partnership resolutions, financial statements, monthly statements, charge tickets, documents (bank checks, personal checks, money orders, wire transfers in, etc.) reflecting payments on the account, and any correspondence files.

SECURITIES FIRM RECORDS
(INVESTMENT ACCOUNTS)

To bring with you and produce any an all retained copies of all documents relating to any and all securities transactions in the name(s) of (insert your suspect's name) or under the account number(s) (insert account numbers here), for the period of (insert beginning date here) to (insert ending date here) including, but not limited to, account statements for all accounts including, but not limited to cash accounts, margin accounts, mutual fund accounts, limited partnership accounts, IRA accounts, Keogh accounts, and cash management accounts. In addition, applications to open all accounts cash received and delivered blotters, confirmation slips, corporate board and partnership resolutions, CTRs and CMIRs, customer correspondence files, payment receipts (currency, check, wire, and securities), securities position records, stock certificate of bonds, and stock delivery receipts.

FINDING THE "NET WORTH"
OF YOUR SUSPECT
(ALSO KNOWN AS A DEBIT-TO-INCOME RATIO ANALYSIS)

When starting a financial investigation, you will need to find the "net worth" of the suspect. The investigator can do this by taking the suspect's *assets* and subtracting them from his *liabilities*, the difference will equal out to be the suspect's *net worth*. If the suspect's net worth is more than their income then something is wrong. This would immediately portray additional income with no known legitimate source. You should consider using a net worth analysis on the suspect when:

- there is no direct link between the subject and the alleged illegal activity that you are investigating,
- the suspect has acquired a great deal of assets or has a dramatic increase in net worth,

- if the suspect appears to be a "high roller" (a person who exhibits a wealthy lifestyle),
- your case needs corroboration or hinges on a weak confidential informants information,
- and lastly when the case involves a small amount of drugs.

To do this you will need to develop a starting point in the investigation from which you will be able to assess the net worth of the suspect. The investigator will need to determine the suspect's net worth by looking at the suspect's assets and liabilities on **December 31 of the previous two years or more.** The easiest way to get this information is by obtaining the suspect's tax records. This will enable you to show a gradual or sharp progression of the suspect's net worth over the targeted period of time. When doing this analysis you are only looking at the suspect's financial history one year at a time.

1. First you need to identify all the *assets* the suspect has on December 31 of the year you are targeting. It's important to use the historical cost of the assets (the cost at the time it was purchased) and not the current market value. For example if you have identified a suspect's assets on December 31, 2001, you will look back to the time the asset was obtained during that year and take the amount that it was purchased for to be placed in your analysis, not the market value listed for the asset on December 31.

   Assets are any items that have substantial value and can be converted into cash. Examples of assets are, but not limited to:

   - checking and savings accounts,
   - the amount of a home or other real estate,
   - original purchase price of vehicles (including fees for tax and tags), etc . . .

REMEMBER WHEN DEALING WITH ASSETS ONLY USE THE INITIAL COST OF THE ASSET AT THE TIME IT WAS PURCHASED

2. Second, find all the suspect's *liabilities* that they had as of December 31 of the year you're targeting. This would be any financial obligation that the suspect is paying out to a creditor. It's important to note that these figures *are not to include* the monthly payments made toward the liabilities, but only refer to the *unpaid balance* listed on the liability during the specific time period you have requested. For example, if the suspect purchased a house for $200,000 and put a down payment of $125,000 on the home, he subsequently would owe $75,000 dollars on the unpaid balance of the mortgage. The unpaid balance is considered a *liability*, and if the unpaid balance is $75,000 on December 31 of 2002, then this is what you would use in your analysis. The $125,000 dollars used to secure the down payment of the house is now looked upon as an *asset* Some examples of liabilities would be:

    - the unpaid balance of the suspect's mortgage, and/ or second mortgage;
    - the unpaid balance of the suspect's vehicle(s), boat, etc.;
    - the unpaid balance on credit cards and/or installment accounts;
    - any bill that has an outstanding unpaid balance.

3. Once you have determined the suspect's net worth on December 31 of the year you are targeting, you will then need to subtract the total amount listed for *assets* from the total amount listed for *liabilities*. This will tell you if the suspect has a positive or negative net worth. If the

suspect's assets are more than their liabilities, then they have a positive net worth. The difference would then be added to your total of *expenditures* to reveal the suspect's *"portrayed available income"* for that period of time. If the suspect's liabilities are more than their assets then you would just put this figure to the side, as it does not represent any excess available income.

4. In order to get a suspect's true financial makeup, you will need to find the suspect's *expenditures*. It's important to note that expenditures will always reflect additional income, it's your job to determine if the money put toward these expenditures are from legitimate sources or illegal means (i.e., CDS distribution). At the end of this analysis you will effectively be able to determine this. To document a suspect's expenditure you will either need their exact amount or normal average approximate cost during a given period of time (i.e., the total amount paid for the electric bill from January 1 to December 31). This is an example of an expenditure that can be used to document money paid out during a given period of time.

These are just a few examples of expenditures, there will be more found throughout your investigation:

- *Mortgage Payments:* To get this you will most likely have to contact the mortgage company, or to be quiet about it, you can go to your local county court house and look up the down payment, purchase price, percentage rate, and monthly payment on the property in the land/deed records. By doing this, you are determining how much the suspect has paid out in mortgage payments during the year(s).
- *Payments on Credit Cards and Charge Accounts:* You can get this information from the credit-reporting agencies. Although once you find the companies who

the suspect has a credit card with, you will most likely have to subpoena each one asking for the date the account was opened, the current balance of the account, payment scheduling, and each month's payments received from the suspect up to date.

- *Auto Loan and Insurance Payments:* Retrieving this information can be done by obtaining the title information on all of the suspect's vehicles. This can be accessed through your state's Department of Motor Vehicles. The information you are seeking is the amount that the car was purchased for, the down payment placed on the car (including taxes and tags paid at time of sale if required), the amount the vehicle was financed for, and the percentage rate of the loan. You will also need to look at how much the suspect is paying a month for auto insurance coverage. The name of the auto insurance company can be found on the suspect's vehicle registration information or through the vehicle title paperwork held at your state's Motor Vehicle Administration.
- *Food:* This amount can be found through search warrants or trash rips. By taking food receipts, you can get an average amount spent per week/month. This in turn can be used in your analysis. Save the receipts for evidence in court later.
- *Clothing:* As with food, save the receipts for any clothing. If no receipts can be recovered a figure will need to be made to give an approximate value for the clothing. If the suspect has high dollar clothing, then try to come up with an amount by searching through clothing catalogs or the Internet. Document how you got your amount though; you will need to explain it in court later.
- *Rent:* This can be obtained from the suspect's landlord or grounds manager. If you need to be quiet about

the investigation then you will need to covertly find the amount that the apartment is renting for by portraying to the landlord or grounds keeper that you are seeking an apartment and was inquiring on how much the rent was.

- *Utilities:* This will be water bill, cable, electric, gas, etc., get a schedule of payments from these companies to use in your expenditure analysis.

- *Vacations:* Contact travel agencies for this information, due to prices always changing in this market. If the suspect had taken a vacation without the assistance of a travel agency, try and determine the cost of the trip (i.e., adding up approximate mileage from point A to point B, then throw in the approximate gas price of that time and get a figure to use) This is just one example of what expenses your suspect may have incurred. There may be lodging, meals, etc, that you would have to account for and possibly give an approximation on. Document it well for court later though.

- *Rental Cars/Merchandise:* As we all know, drug dealers often utilize rental cars as a form of transportation. This allows them the separation from liability due to the vehicle being used to facilitate the transportation of controlled dangerous substances. Rental vehicles also allow the suspect to remain somewhat anonymous due to the vehicle not being registered in their name, which hinders police from immediately making the identification of the owner/operator. Once you have identified which rental company supplied the vehicle in question you can obtain a copy of the rental agreement, which will display the identity of the person who had rented the vehicle. In addition, rental companies will supply you with records of every time the suspect has rented a vehicle and the amount that they paid. This in turn can be used in your financial analysis to show money paid out by the suspect. Another resource to inquire about is household merchandise that is rented. This is another expenditure commonly found used by drug dealers to limit their asset liability. Some items that would be rented are furniture, televisions, computers, etc. You would again need to obtain the rental contracts involving your suspect, which will identify how much they have spent each time to rent the merchandise. Most rental car and merchandise companies have a security section that can be contacted to obtain the information you are seeking. In some instances you can develop a working relationship with these companies so they would notify you automatically when the suspect obtains rented merchandise or vehicles from their business.

- *Miscellaneous Items Purchased:* This would be anything individually purchased by the suspect such as: chrome rims for their vehicle, or home improvements such as a deck or driveway, etc. You can usually find out how much an addition or major home improvement had cost the suspect by contacting your local land assessment office. The amount spent on the improvement will be listed in building permit paperwork along with a diagram of the project completed. The amounts for these items would also be included in the expenditures total.

REMEMBER TO ADD ONLY THE "POSITIVE NET WORTH" AMOUNT TO YOUR TOTAL OF EXPENDITURES TO GET THE SUSPECT'S "PORTRAYED AVAILABLE INCOME"

5. Next, total up all the expenditures that you have found. This total represents income that was obtained by the

suspect either through legitimate or illegal means. Once you have the total of the expenditures then you will need to locate any legitimate sources of income that the suspect may have. Some examples of legitimate sources of income are:

- legitimate employment
- an inheritance
- gifts received
- gambling/lottery winnings
- "cash hoards"

Once you have totaled up the suspect's legitimate income, you will need to subtract it from your total of expenditures. The difference between the two will show you exactly how much money the suspect has spent above and beyond their legitimate source of income.

6. Once your financial analysis is complete on the suspect you will need to document and investigate all leads involving "cash hoards" or "cash on hand"(i.e., case hoarded away in a shoe box, mattress, buried in the backyard, etc.), to prevent a cash hoard defense later in court. Some examples of what to look for are:

- evidence of gifts (in the form of money or other physical assets)
- inheritances received (check your county's registrar of wills or probate)
- insurance proceeds
- gambling/lottery winnings
- cash held for other people
- cash held by other individuals for the suspect

It's important to note that a cash hoard defense can be refuted in court by other evidence obtained throughout the investigation. Some forms of evidence that would be needed are:

- *Evidence that the suspect has a need to borrow substantial funds.* The thinking here is that if you can show that the suspect has a substantial amount of liabilities in the form of interest-bearing loans, then why would the suspect have money sitting around when he could pay off his/her debt.
- *Financial statements filed by the suspect that show no evidence of a cash hoard.* For example, bank account statements that show the suspect had no money in a checking or savings account at any point in time.
- *Evidence that purchases were deferred until funds could be accumulated.* For instance, items placed on "lay away" at local department stores because the suspect did not have the money to spend on it right away. Another is when you find that certain times of the month the suspect is excessively late on paying his bills.
- *Statements made by the suspect to business associates or third parties regarding the suspect's lack of cash.* Criminals love to talk, this is no secret. For this reason, talking with associates of the suspect may benefit you with statements previously made by the suspect to others concerning their financial stability.
- *And the suspect's initial admissions to law enforcement officer or others explaining that he/she has no money.* And lastly, when you place the suspect under arrest or detention and question him/her about the money found, and they tell officers that they have no money or very little.

EXAMPLE OF A NET WORTH ANALYSIS

FIRST EXAMPLE FOR NET WORTH ANALYSIS

(1) ASSETS:

3,000	equity in the home
5,000	paid on vehicle
10,000	in savings account
$18,000	assets

(2) LIABILITIES:

83,000	mortgage
35,000	vehicle loan
10,000	on credit cards
128,000	liabilities

(3) TOTAL DIFFERENCE = NET WORTH:

NET WORTH: $ -110,000

(if this was a positive amount instead of a negative amount, then you would add the difference of the positive amount to the expenditure's total to get your suspect's Yearly Portrayed Available Income A positive net worth represents "additional income." Because this is negative you have nothing to add to the expenditures amount.)

(4) MONTHLY EXPENDITURES:

$300 for food (average household monthly spending)
$700 for mortgage payment
$200 for electric
$100 home phone bill
$200 cell phone bill
$110 on credit card bill
$700 on car payment
$2310 a month x 12 months = $27,720 a year. (Portrayed Available Income)

(5) LEGITIMATE SOURCES(S) OF INCOME FOUND:

 $1600 a month from paycheck-after taxes (averaged out)

(6) TOTAL DIFFERENCE:

 $2310 monthly Expenditures

 -$1600 monthly Income

 $710 a month of unexplained income (approximate amount)

 OR

 $8,520 a yearly of unexplained income (approximate amount)

SECOND EXAMPLE FOR NET WORTH ANALYSIS
*Remember you're only looking at assets and liabilities during a specific year.

(1) ASSETS:

$30,000	equity in the home purchased 2002 (money paid into the home including down payment)
$25,000	paid on vehicle purchased 2002 (money paid into a vehicle including down payment, taxes and tags)
$90,000	placed in savings account during the 2002 year
$145,000	assets

(2) LIABILITIES:

$80,000	mortgage unpaid balance
$15,000	vehicle loan unpaid balance
$10,000	on credit cards unpaid balance
$105,000	liabilities

(3) TOTAL DIFFERENCE = NET WORTH:

 NET WORTH: $ +40,000

 (The suspect's net worth has proven to be positive instead of a negative amount. In this case you would add the difference of the positive amount to the expenditures total to get your suspect's Yearly Portrayed Available

Income A positive net worth represents "additional income," like from a paycheck or selling narcotics.

(4) MONTHLY EXPENDITURES:

$300 for food (average household monthly spending)
$700 for mortgage payment
$200 for electric
$100 home phone bill
$200 cell phone bill
$110 on credit card bill
$700 on car payment

$2310 a month x 12 months = $27,720 a year.

Add $40,000 from positive net worth to the yearly expenditures of $27,720, which equals to $67,720 is the suspect's "portrayed available income"

(5) LEGITIMATE SOURCES(S) OF INCOME FOUND:

$1600 a month from paycheck-After taxes (averaged out)
$1600 x 12 months = $19,200 of yearly legitimate income

(6) TOTAL DIFFERENCE:

$67,720 of Portrayed yearly available income
-$19,200 of legitimate source of income.

$48,520 a year of unexplained income

VEHICLE FINANCIAL INVESTIGATION CHECK LIST

SUSPECT INFORMATION				
1. NAME:				
2. ALIAS:				
3. AGE:	DOB:	RACE:	HGT:	WGT:
4. SSN:	FBI NO:		STATE ID:	

THINGS TO DO FOR VEHICLE FINANCHIAL INVESTIGATION

1. VEHICLE/ TRAILER/ BOAT/ AIRCRAFT:

☐ LIST THE VEHILCE OWNED OR SUSPECTED OF FINANCING BY THE SUSPECT:

➢ *VEHICLE INFORMATION*

MAKE: _____ MODEL: _____

BODYSTYLE: _____ YEAR: _____

REGISTRATION NO.: _____ STATE: _____

➢ *REGISTERED TO* (IF SAME AS SUSPECT WRITE "SAME")

NAME: _____

ADDRESS: _____

_____

DOB: _____ HGT: _____ WGT: _____

☐ START A SURVEILLANCE LOG ON VEHICLE. DOCUMENT WHO WAS OPERATING THE VEHICLE AND/OR WHERE IT WAS PARKED.

☐ GET PHOTOGRAPH OF VEHICLE TO INCLUDE IN CASE FILE. (FRONT AND SIDE PROFILE OF VEHICLE IF POSSIBLE)

☐ RUN A FULL MVA PRINTOUT ON VEHICLE AND REGISTERED OWNER OF VEHICLE. INCLUDE THIS IN FILE.

☐ OBTAIN A CERTIFIED COPY OF VEHICLES TITLE. INCLUDE THIS IN FILE.

*IF TITLE WORK SHOWS THE REGISTERED OWNER ONLY (WHO IS *NOT* THE SUSPECT). GO BACK TO THE PREVIOUS OWNERS TITLE WORK TO SEE IF THE SUSPECT HAD SOLD THE VEHICLE TO THE CURRENT OWNER.

OBTAIN THE FOLLOWING INFORMATION FROM THE TITLE WORK AND FINANCIAL INSTITUTION

➢ **TITLE PAPER WORK/ FINANCIAL INSTITUTE**

- **WAS VEHICLE PURCHASED:** NEW **OR** USED **(CIRCLE ONE)**

- WHAT YEAR WAS THE VEHICLE PURCHASED: _____

- WHAT WAS THE PURCHASE AMOUNT: $_____

- DOWN PAYMENT: **YES** OR **NO** AMOUNT: $_____

- DOWN PAYMENT PAID IN:

  ☐ **CASH**
  ☐ **CHECK**
  ☐ **MONEY ORDER**
  ☐ **OTHER** _____

- WAS THERE A TRADE-IN? IF SO LIST WHAT VEHICLE WAS EXCHANGED:

  MAKE: _____   MODEL: _____

  BODYSTYLE: _____   YEAR: _____

- HOW MUCH CREDIT WAS GIVEN FOR VEHICLE TOWARD THE PURCHASE PRICE? $_____.

  OR

  WAS THE TRADE-IN VEHICLES CURRENT LEIN PAID OFF BY DEALERSHIP: **YES** OR **NO**

- WAS THE VEHICLE PAID IN FULL AT THE TIME OF SALE? **YES** OR **NO**

- IF SO, WHAT WAS THE AMOUNT? $_____

- AMOUNT PAID IN:
  - ☐ **CASH**
  - ☐ **CHECK**
  - ☐ **MONEY ORDER**
  - ☐ **OTHER** _____

- WAS THE VEHICLE FINANCED? **YES OR NO**

- IF FINANCED LIST THE FINANCE COMPANY:

  NAME: _____

  ADDRESS: _____

  _____

  PHONE NO.: _____

- HOW MUCH WAS VEHICLE FINANCED FOR? $_____

- WHAT PERCENTAGE RATE: _____%

- WHAT IS THE TERM OF THE LOAN: _____MNTH/YRS

- WHAT WAS THE TOTAL AMOUNT PAID, OR THAT THE SUSPECT WILL PAY AFTER ALL PAYMENTS MADE: $_____

- WHAT IS THE MONTHLY PAYMENT? $_____

- IF PAID OFF, WHAT WAS THE DATE: _____

- HOW IS THE SUSPECT PAYING THE LOAN:
  - ☐ **CASH**
  - ☐ **CHECK**
  - ☐ **MONEY ORDER**
  - ☐ **OTHER** _____

- IF BY CHECK, WHOSE NAME IS ON THE CHECKS AND WHAT IS THE BANK NAME LISTED ON THE CHECKS USED TO MAKE THOSE PAYMENTS? _____

➢ **INSURANCE COMPANY**

- IF INSURED LIST THE INSURANCE COMPANY:

  NAME: _____

ADDRESS: _____

_____

PHONE NO.: _____

- HOW IS THE SUSPECT PAYING THE INSURANCE?

       ☐ **CASH**
       ☐ **CHECK**
       ☐ **MONEY ORDER**
       ☐ **OTHER** _____

- WHAT IS THE MONTHLY PAYMENT? $_____

- WHAT IS THE PAYMENT SCHEDULE?

       ☐ **WEEKLY**
       ☐ **MONTHLY**
       ☐ **YEARLY/PAID FULL**
       ☐ **OTHER PAYMENT**
          SCHEDUAL:

       _____

- IF BY CHECK, WHOSE NAME IS ON THE CHECKS AND WHAT IS THE BANK NAME LISTED ON THE CHECKS USED TO MAKE THOSE PAYMENTS? _____

- ARE PAYMENTS MADE IN PERSON, MAILED, OR DIRECT DEPOSITED? _____

- IF IN PERSON OR MAILED WHAT IS THE NAME AND/OR ADDRESS OF THE INDIVIDUAL MAKING THE PAYMENT?

NAME: _____

ADDRESS: _____

_____

- IF DIRECTLY DEPOSITED WHAT IS THE NAME AND ADDRESS OF THE BANK USED TO MAKE THE DEPOSIT?

NAME: _____

ADDRESS: _____

_____

PHONE NO.: _____

- IS THERE ANYONE ELSE WHO IS LISTED ON THIS INSURANCE AS DRIVERS?

NAME: _____

ADDRESS: _____

_____

PHONE NO.: _____

- DOES THE SUSPECT MAKE PAYMENTS FOR INSURANCE FOR OTHER PEOPLE AT YOUR AGENCY AND IF SO WHO IS THE PERSON AND LIST THE TYPE OF INSURANCE?

YES OR **NO**

1. NAME: _____

ADDRESS: _____

_____

PHONE NO.: _____

2. NAME: _____

ADDRESS: _____

_____

PHONE NO.: _____

3. NAME: _____

ADDRESS: _____

_____

PHONE No.: _____

- DOES THE SUSPECT OWN ANY OTHER TYPE OF INSURANCE OR BONDS THROUGH YOUR AGENCY? (i.e. construction bonds, renters insurance, business insurance, etc.)

YES OR **NO**

- WHAT KIND AND FOR WHAT? _____

_____

- HOW IS THE SUSPECT PAYING FOR THIS INSURANCE?

     ☐ **CASH**
     ☐ **CHECK**
     ☐ **MONEY ORDER**
     ☐ **OTHER** _____

- IF BY CHECK, WHOSE NAME IS ON THE CHECKS AND WHAT IS THE BANK NAME LISTED ON THE CHECKS USED TO MAKE THOSE PAYMENTS?_____

_____

- IF DIRECTLY DEPOSITED WHAT IS THE NAME AND ADDRESS OF THE BANK USED TO MAKE THE DEPOSIT?

NAME: _____

ADDRESS: _____

_____

PHONE No.: _____

- WHAT IS THE MONTHLY PAYMENT? $_____

- WHAT IS THE PAYMENT SCHEDUAL?

     ☐ **WEEKLY**
     ☐ **MONTHLY**
     ☐ **YEARLY/PAID FULL**
     ☐ **OTHER PAYMENT SCHEDUAL:**

_____

- WHAT IS THE VALUE OF THE INSURANCE POLICY OR BOND? $_____

- ARE PAYMENTS MADE IN PERSON, MAILED, OR DIRECTLY DEOSITED OR ADD TO SUSPECT'S ORIGINAL INSURANCE PAYMENT?_____

•   IF IN PERSON OR MAILED WHAT IS THE NAME AND/
    OR ADDRESS OF THE INDIVIDUAL MAKING THE PAYMENT?

    NAME: _____

    ADDRESS: _____

    _____

•   IS THERE ANYONE ELSE WHO IS LISTED ON THIS
    INSURANCE POLICY OR BOND?

    NAME: _____

    ADDRESS: _____

    _____

    PHONE NO.: _____

POST SEIZURE

➢   **CONTACT THE DEALERSHIPS THAT SOLD THE VEHICLE.**

    DEALER'S NAME: _____

    SALESMAN: _____

    ADDRESS: _____

    PHONE NO.: _____

☐   SHOW THE SALESMAN A PICTURE OF THE VEHICLE SO
    HE/SHE COULD TRY AND IDENTIFY THE VEHICLE.

☐   DID THE DEALER RECOGNIZE THE VEHICLE IN
    QUESTION? **YES** OR **NO**

☐   SHOW THE SALESMAN A PICTURE OF THE SUSPECT SO
    THEY CAN TRY AND IDENTIFY THE SUSPECT.

☐   DID THE DEALER RECOGNIZE THE SUSPECT IN
    QUESTION? **YES** OR **NO**

☐   INTERVIEW THE SALESMAN THAT SOLD THE VEHICLE.
    FIND OUT THE FOLLWING INFORMATION:

    ☐   WAS THERE ANYONE PRESENT WITH HIM OR HER?
        YES OR **NO**

NAME: _____

ADDRESS: _____

_____

PHONE NO.: _____

☐   IF TWO PEOPLE WERE INQUIRING ABOUT THE
    VEHICLE WHO SHOWED THE MOST INTEREST IN
    THE VEHICLE OR DID MOST OF THE TALKING?

    _____

☐   WHO TEST DROVE THE VEHICLE?

    _____

☐   GET ANY AND ALL DEALERSHIP PAPERWORK
    INCLUDING SERVICE WORK ORDERS FOR
    VEHICLE. MOST DEALERS WILL MAKE A COPY OF
    A PERSON'S DRIVER'S LICENCE AND KEEP IT IN
    THEIR FILE IF THE PERSON TEST-DRIVES A VEHICLE
    THAT WAS PURCHASED.

DOCUMENTATION NEEDED FOR SEIZURE FILE

1. FOUR PICTURES OF VEHICLE—FRONT, REAR, AND SIDE
    PROFILES. TAKE PICTURES OF ANY PRIOR DAMAGE TO
    VEHICLE. IF ANY DAMAGE TO THE EXTERIOR DOCUMENT
    IT IN YOUR REPORT.

2. INSPECT THE VEHICLE'S INTERIOR FOR ANY PRIOR
    DAMAGE AND NOTE IT IN REPORT.

3. DO INVENTORY SHEET OFF ALL MISC. ITEMS FOUND
    WITHIN

4. TAG KEYS WITH DESCRIPTION OF VEHICLE AND INCLUDE
    WITH CASE FILE.

5. INCLUDE DRIVING RECORD OF OWNER, PRINTOUT
    REGISTRATION INFORMATION OF THE VEHICLE, A WANTED
    CHECK OF THE VEHICLE, AND CERTIFIED TITLE WORK.

6. INCLUDE COPY OF A COPY OF YOUR CRIMINAL
    INVESTIGATION REPORT OR INCIDENT REPORT IN THIS
    FILE, AS WELL AS ANY NOTES TAKEN CONCERNING THE
    INVESTIGATION OF THE VEHICLE.

NOTES

(AGENCY LETTERHEAD)
VEHICLE INDEMNITY AGREEMENT

This agreement is made between _____

(NAME OF OWNER OR FIRM NAME)

_____

(ADDRESS)   (PHONE NUMBER)

and the _____

(INSERT YOUR AGECY NAME HERE)

The agreement is made in consideration of the return of a:

_____

(DESCRIPTION OF VEHICLE)

registered to _____

(NAME AND ADDRESS)

used in violation of the Controlled Substance Act, and for the consideration, the receipt of which is hereby acknowledged:

_____ being the _____

(FIRM OR PERSON INVOLVED)   (LIST THEIR INTEREST IN THE VEHICLE)

of the property as evidenced by a:

_____ dated _____

(TITLE, REGISTRATION,   (INSERT DATE LISTED ON

CONTRACT, NOTE NUMBER, ETC.)   PAPERWORK)

It is hereby agreed to unconditionally release and hold harmless the (INSERT YOUR AGENCY'S NAME HERE), its officers, employees, and agents from any and all claims, demands, damages, causes of actions or suits, of whatever kind and description, and wheresoever situated, that might now exist or hereafter exist by reason of or growing out of or affecting, directly or indirectly, the seizure or the return of the above described vehicle.

It is further incumbent upon the individual and/or firm to whom the above described property is being released to be aware of the provisions of state law (INSERT YOUR STATE'S LAW "INOCENT OWNER LAW"). This section of the state law provides that a claimant of any right of a seized vehicle may be called upon to prove that such "right, title, or interest was created without any knowledge or reason to believe that the vehicle, airplane, or vessel was being, or was to be, used for the purpose charged" In the event you and/or firm choose to authorize the future control of the above described property or any other vehicle, airplane, or vessel to the individual or individuals causing the seizure addressed in this agreement such vehicle, airplane, or vessel may be subject to forfeiture for any violation under state law regardless of your and/or your firm's right, title, or interest.

Executed in triplicate this _____ day of _____ 20 ____

Case No. : _____   _____
                                    (SIGNATURE AND DATE OF PERSON
                                    EXECUTING)

_____
(SIGNATURE AND DATE OF OFFICER)

                        _____
                        (TITLE OF OFFICER)

IN WITNESS HEREOF, the above-signed parties have read and understood fully the terms of this VEHICLE INDEMNITY AGREEMENT and so state by subscribing their names thereto.

          Subscribed and sworn to before me this _____ day
          of _____, 20 _____

                        _____
                        NOTARY PUBLIC SIGNATURE

My commission expires: _____

(AGENCY LETTERHEAD)
RESIDENCE INDEMNITY AGREEMENT

This agreement is made between _____

(NAME OF OWNER OR FIRM NAME)

_____

(ADDRESS)   (PHONE NUMBER)

and the _____

(INSERT YOUR AGECY'S NAME HERE)

The agreement is made in consideration of the return of :

_____

(DESCRIPTION OF RESIDENCE)

owned/rented to _____

(NAME AND ADDRESS)

used in violation of the Controlled Substance Act, and for the consideration, the receipt of which is hereby acknowledged:

_____ being the _____

(FIRM OR PERSON INVOLVED)   (LIST THEIR INTEREST IN THE
                                 RESIDENCE-OWNER/RENTER)

of the property as evidenced by a:

_____ dated _____

(DEED OR RENTAL CONTRACT)   (INSERT DATE LISTED ON
                                 PAPERWORK)

It is hereby agreed to unconditionally release and hold harmless the

_____

(INSERT YOUR AGENCY NAME HERE)

its officers, employees, and agents from any and all claims, demands, damages, causes of actions or suits, of whatever kind and description, and wheresoever situated, that might now exist or hereafter exist by reason of or growing out of or affecting, directly or indirectly, the seizure or the return of the above described property.

It is further incumbent upon the individual and/or firm to whom the above-described property is being released to be aware of the provisions of state law (INSERT YOUR STATE'S CONTROLLED SUBSTANCE CODE OR SECTION NUMBER). This section of the state law provides that a claimant of any right of a seized residence may be called upon to prove that such "right, title, or interest was created without any knowledge or reason to believe that the residence/property was being, or was to be, used for the purpose charged." In the event you and/or the firm choose to authorize the future control of the above described property or any other residence/property to the individual or individuals causing the seizure addressed in this agreement such residence/property may be subject to forfeiture for any violation under state law regardless of your and/or your firm's right, title, or interest.

Executed in triplicate this _____ day of _____ 20 ____

Case No.:_____   _____

                         (SIGNATURE AND DATE OF PERSON EXECUTING)

_____

(SIGNATURE AND DATE OF OFFICER)

                         (TITLE OF OFFICER)

IN WITNESS HEREOF, the above-signed parties have read and understand fully the terms of this RESIDENCE INDEMNITY AGREEMENT and so state by subscribing their names thereto.

                         Subscribed and sworn to before me this _____ day of _____, 20 _____

                         _____

                         NOTARY PUBLIC SIGNATURE

My commission expires: _____

(DEPARTMENT LETTERHEAD)

(Date)

(INSERT ADDRESS AND
POINT OF CONTACT NAME
OF THE DEPARTMENT YOU
ARE REQUESTING THE
RECORDS FROM)

Dear (Point of contact),

I would like to request a copy of the most recent Personal Property Return for Individuals and Firms for the following (INCORPORATED OR UNINCORPORATED) business:

(INSERT YOUR SUSPECT'S NAME, THE NAME THAT
THE BUSINESS TRADES UNDER, AND THE
ADDRESS OF THE BUSINESS HERE)

The requested information will be utilized for official law enforcement purposes only and will be treated as confidential material.

Please send this information to: (INSERT YOUR NAME AND ADDRESS)

If you have any questions regarding this request, please contact me at (INSERT YOUR PHONE NUMBER HERE). Thank you for your assistance.

Sincerely,

(SIGNATURE)
(YOUR NAME/RANK)
(YOUR DEPARTMENT)

(DEPARTMENT LETTERHEAD)

DATE

You will need to find out the address of the casino you wish to send the inquiry letter to.

Michael Sullivan
Division of Gambling Enforcement
Casino Investigation Unit
Richard J. Hughes Justice Complex
CN 047
Trenton, New Jersey 08625

Dear Sir:

The ***INSERT THE NAME OF AGENCY AND DIVISION*** arrested ***INSERT NAME OF SUSPECT***, DOB: ***INSERT DOB AND SOCIAL SECURITY NUMBER HERE FOLLOWED BY SUSPECT'S ADDRESS***. ***INSERT NAME OF SUSPECT*** was arrested for ***INSERT CDS CRIME AND SCHEDULE DRUG HERE*** which is a violation of the Maryland Code Annotated Criminal Law Article, Title 5 et seq. and Common Law Conspiracy to commit said crimes, dealing generally with controlled dangerous substances as amended and revised. A ***INSERT AMOUNT OF TIME FOR VIOLATION HERE*** year penalty for the violation may be imposed upon conviction of this crime.

Insert your state's criminal code or section number for controlled dangerous substances here.

During an interview with ***INSERT NAME OF SUSPECT*** <u>*he/she*</u> stated that <u>he/she</u> frequents the casinos in ***INSERT CITY THAT CASINO IS LOCATED IN***. ***INSERT NAME OF SUSPECT*** has a history of drug arrest and it's likely he is laundering his money through gambling.

The ***INSERT HERE THE NAME OF YOUR DEPARTMENT AND DIVISION*** are requesting a survey of each of the ***INSERT THE AMOUNT OF CASINOS IN THE AREA OR UNDER THEIR JURISDICTION*** operating casinos to determine if any information in the form of credit, cash deposits, player ratings, and/or complementaries exist for ***INSERT NAME OF SUSPECT* from *INSERT DATE HERE* to *INSERT DATE HERE*.**

Information received from the casino survey will possibly aid in revealing any assets of the subject(s) involved in this investigation.

Please direct your reply to:

INSERT NAME, ADDRESS, AND PHONE/FAX NUMBER OF INVESTIGATING OFFICER HERE

Thank you in advance for your continued cooperation.

Sincerely,

INSERT YOUR NAME, RANK DEPARTMENT AND DIVISION HERE

(AGENCY LETTERHEAD)
(FINCEN REQUEST MEMO)

ORIGINAL REQUEST:

Financial Crimes Enforcement Network
Attn: Director
2070 Chain Bridge Rd., Suite 200
Vienna, VA 22182

The (INSERT YOUR AGENCY) is investigating (INSERT YOUR SUSPECT'S NAME) who is suspected of (INSERT CRIME HERE) in (INSERT YOUR COUNTY or CITY, and STATE HERE). The investigation to date has revealed (INSERT BREIF NARRATIVE DEPICTING THE HIGHLIGHTS OF YOUR INVESTIGATION)

The (INSERT YOUR AGENCY) requests FinCEN's assistance to supply information concerning (INSERT YOUR SUSPECT'S NAME) consisting of all applicable commercial, financial and law enforcement databases. We are currently working with representatives of the (INSERT ALLIED AGENCY'S NAME) in connection with this investigation. For further details concerning this investigation please contact (INSERT YOUR NAME) at (INSERT YOUR PHONE NUMBER) or fax (INSERT YOUR FAX NUMBER)

Suspect Information: (NOT ALL INFORMATION IS NEEDED)

- date of birth
- Social Security Number
- address, etc.

Requesters Signature: _____ Supervisors Signature _____
                (NAME)   (NAME)
                (RANK)   (RANK)

Suspicious Transaction Matrix

Suspect Name: _____

Case Number: _____   **Page No:** _____ of _____

Report or Form	CTR (Currency Transaction Report)	CMIR (Currency & Monetary Instrument Report)	Form 8300
When Filed			
Who Filed			
Filed With			
NOTES			

Report or Form	CTR (Currency Transaction Report)	CMIR (Currency & Monetary Instrument Report)	Form 8300
When Filed			
Who Filed			
Filed With			
NOTES			

Report or Form	CTR (Currency Transaction Report)	CMIR (Currency & Monetary Instrument Report)	Form 8300
When Filed			
Who Filed			
Filed With			
NOTES			

(EXAMPLE OF VEHICLE *FACILITATION* APPLICATION FOR WARRANT)

APPLICATION AND AFFIDAVIT FOR SEIZURE OF MOTOR VEHICLE

TO: The Honorable _____, judge of the Circuit/District Court for ***INSERT NAME OF COUNTY HERE*** County, State of ***INSERT YOUR STATE HERE***.

I. Introduction

This application and affidavit relates to a ***INSERT YEAR MAKE, MODEL AND COLOR OF TARGET VEHICLE*** in color, displaying ***INSERT STATE REGISTRATION AND REGISTRATION NUMBER HERE***, registered to ***INSERT NAME OF SUSPECT OR REGISTERED OWNER'S NAME HERE***.

II. Expertise

The name of your affiant is ***INSERT YOUR NEME, RANK, AND DEPARTMENT HERE***, currently assigned to the ***INSERT YOUR UNIT/DIVISION ASSIGNED HERE***. Your affiant has been a police officer for over ***INSERT THE NUMBER OF YEARS YOU HAVE BEEN A POLICE OFFICER HERE*** year, and has completed the basic training requirements for the ***INSERT YOUR STATE'S POLICE COMMISION NAME HERE*** (i.e., Maryland Police Training Commission) at the ***INSERT THE NAME OF THE POLICE ACADEMY YOU ATTENDED*** Police Academy, ***INSERT THE CITY AND STATE THAT THE POLICE ACADEMY IS LOCATED IN***, in which a portion of the training involved the identification and detection of controlled dangerous substances. In addition, your affiant has obtained additional training in ***INSERT YOUR TRAINING AND PROFESSIONAL EDUCATION HERE***

Your affiant, ***INSERT YOUR NAME AND RANK HERE*** has authored and assisted in the execution of numerous search and seizure warrants during his tenure as a law enforcement officer. Your affiant ***INSERT YOUR NAME AND RANK HERE*** has also made controlled purchases and hand-to-hand drug transactions of controlled dangerous substances. Your affiant ***INSERT YOUR NAME AND RANK HERE*** has successfully arrested and obtained convictions for numerous persons concerning violations of the Controlled Dangerous Substance Laws. Furthermore, your affiant receives training on a daily basis working on drug investigations for the ***INSERT YOUR UNIT/DIVISION ASSIGNED HERE***.

III. Basis for application
In support of this application and the basis for probable cause, your affiant deposes and says (INSERT YOUR PROBABLE CAUSE HERE)

INSERT INVESTIGATION HERE
(SAMPLE INVESTIGATION BELOW)

In ***INSERT ONLY MONTH AND YEAR HERE OF WHEN YOU INITIATED YOUR INVESTIGATION*** the ***INSERT YOUR UNIT/DIVISION ASSIGNED HERE*** initiated an investigation into the violations of the controlled dangerous substance laws involving ***INSERT NAME, SEX, DOB, AND ADDRESS OF SUSPECT HERE***.

During the week of ***INSERT DATE OF THE FIRST DAY OF THE WEEK IN WHICH THE CONTROLLED BUY TOOK PLACE* *INSERT YEAR HERE***, the ***INSERT YOUR UNIT/DIVISION ASSIGNED HERE*** made a controlled purchase of ***INSERT TYPE OF DRUGS PURCHASED*** from ***INSERT NAME SUSPECT HERE***, by utilizing a confidential informant.

On a separate occasion, during the week of ***INSERT DATE OF THE FIRST DAY OF THE WEEK IN WHICH THE**

CONTROLLED BUY TOOK PLACE* *INSERT YEAR HERE*, the ***INSERT YOUR UNIT/DIVISION ASSIGNED HERE*** arranged for an additional controlled purchase of ***INSERT TYPE OF DRUGS PURCHASED*** from ***INSERT NAME SUSPECT HERE***, utilizing the confidential informant. During this time the confidential informant agreed to meet ***INSERT NAME SUSPECT HERE*** in the ***INSERT NAME OF CITY OR AREA*** area of ***INSERT NAME OF COUNTY AND STATE HERE***, to complete the transaction. As a result of their conversation, ***INSERT NAME OF SUSPECT HERE*** arrived at the meeting place driving his/her ***INSERT YEAR MAKE, MODEL AND COLOR OF TARGET VEHICLE*** in color, displaying ***INSERT STATE REGISTRATION AND REGISTRATION NUMBER HERE***. The confidential informant again subsequently purchased a quantity of ***INSERT TYPE OF DRUGS PURCHASED*** from ***INSERT NAME SUSPECT HERE***.

Your affiant ***INSERT YOUR NAME HERE***, avers that based upon the aforementioned investigation conducted from information supplied by the confidential informant in this case and the forgoing facts and circumstances, it is clear that ***INSERT NAME OF SUSPECT HERE*** used the ***INSERT YEAR MAKE, MODEL AND COLOR OF TARGET VEHICLE*** in color, displaying ***INSERT STATE REGISTRATION AND REGISTRATION NUMBER HERE*** to facilitate the sale of ***INSERT TYPE OF DRUGS PURCHASED***, a schedule ***INSERT SCHEDULE NUMBER HERE i.e., I, II, III, etc.*** controlled dangerous substance. ***INSERT NAME SUSPECT HERE*** also used the ***INSERT YEAR MAKE, MODEL AND COLOR OF TARGET VEHICLE*** to further his drug trafficking enterprise.

Insert your state's criminal code or section number for controlled dangerous substances here

For example: Two Thousand And Three

I accordingly believe that ***INSERT NAME SUSPECT HERE*** vehicle was used to facilitate the sale of controlled dangerous substances and is therefore forfeitable under the Maryland Code Annotated Criminal Law Article, Title 5 et seq. and Common Law Conspiracy to commit said crimes, dealing generally with controlled dangerous substances as amended and revised.

SUBSCRIBED AND SWORN TO, this _____ day of ***INSERT MONTH HERE*** in the YEAR OF OUR LORD, *Two Thousand and* _____.

Insert your information here

Affiant
Detective James A. Henning No.0140
Caroline County Sheriff's Department-CID
Caroline County Drug Task Force

Before me, a district/circuit court judge of the State of ***INSERT STATE HERE***, in and for ***INSERT NAME OF COUNTY HERE*** County, this _____ day of ***INSERT MONTH AND YEAR HERE***, personally appeared ***INSERT YOUR NAME AND RANK HERE***, personally known to me or properly identified, and he made oath that the contents of the a foregoing application and affidavit are true and correct to the best of his knowledge.

_____   _____
Time   **Judge**

(EXAMPLE OF VEHICLE *FACILITATION* WARRANT)

SEIZURE WARRANT

STATE OF *INSERT STATE NAME HERE*
INSERT COUNTY NAME HERE COUNTY

To: **INSERT YOUR NAME, RANK, AND DEPARTMENT HERE***, or any other law enforcement officer;

GREETINGS:

    WHEREAS, it appears to me, the subscriber, the Honorable _____, judge of the Circuit Court/District Court of **INSERT STATE HERE*** for **INSERT COUNTY HERE*** County, State of **INSERT STATE HERE***, by the written information of the affiant **INSERT YOUR LAST NAME HERE*** hereinafter named, which information is contained in the application and affidavit attached to this seizure warrant, and made a part hereof, that there is probable cause to believe:

    INSERT YEAR MAKE, MODEL AND COLOR OF TARGET VEHICLE* in color, displaying **INSERT STATE REGISTRATION AND REGISTRATION NUMBER HERE***, registered to **INSERT NAME OF SUSPECT OR REGISTERED OWNER'S NAME HERE***.

    The vehicle is owned by **INSERT NAME, AND ADDRESS OF SUSPECT HERE*** and was used to *facilitate* the sale of controlled dangerous substances, and I am satisfied that there is probable cause to believe that the vehicle was used to facilitate the sale of controlled dangerous substances, in violation of the Maryland Code Annotated Criminal Law Article, Title 5 et seq. and Common Law Conspiracy to commit said

Insert your state's criminal code or section number for controlled dangerous substance violations.

crimes, dealing generally with controlled dangerous substances as amended and revised and that a seizure warrant exist for said vehicle should be issued.

You are therefore commanded, with the necessary and proper assistance, to seize forthwith the vehicle herein above described, executing this warrant and making the seizure; and if upon executing this warrant, there are found persons in said motor vehicle then and there engaged in the commission of a crime, or crimes, arrest those so participating; leave a copy of this warrant and the application and affidavit in support thereof with an inventory of the property seized with the person from who said vehicle and/or property is seized, or, if no one is present at the time of said seizure, a copy of the aforementioned documents shall be left with the person apparently in charge of said automobile and/or property, or if none is present when this warrant is served, a copy of the aforementioned documents shall be left in a conspicuous place at the premises

Make sure that you have your inventory return and one of the original signed seizure warrants back to the judge within your states specified time limit.

from which said motor vehicle and/or property is seized, if practicable, or if not practicable, a copy of said documents shall be furnished to the owner of said vehicle and/or property promptly after the service of this warrant. Further, you are hereby ordered to return a copy of said warrant, application, and affidavit in support thereof together with an inventory of the property seized, to me within ten days after the execution of this warrant; or if not

*served, to return this warrant to me promptly
after it's expiration as required by law.*

WHEREOF, fail not at your peril and have you then and there this warrant. GIVEN under my hand this _____ day of ***INSERT MONTH HERE*** in the year of our Lord, ***INSERT THE YEAR HERE***.

_____   _____
Date and Time   Judge

(EXAMPLE OF VEHICLE *PROCEEDS* APPLICATION FOR WARRANT)

APPLICATION AND AFFIDAVIT FOR SEIZURE OF MOTOR VEHICLE

TO: The Honorable _____, judge of the Circuit/District Court for ***INSERT NAME OF COUNTY HERE*** County, State of ***INSERT YOUR STATE HERE***.

IV. Introduction

This application and affidavit relates to a ***INSERT YEAR MAKE, MODEL AND COLOR OF TARGET VEHICLE*** in color, displaying ***INSERT STATE REGISTRATION AND REGISTRATION NUMBER HERE***, registered to ***INSERT NAME OF SUSPECT OR REGISTERED OWNER'S NAME HERE***.

V. Expertise

The name of your affiant is ***INSERT YOUR NEME, RANK, AND DEPARTMENT HERE***, currently assigned to the ***INSERT YOUR UNIT/DIVISION THAT YOUR ASSIGNED TO HERE***. Your affiant has been a police officer for over ***INSERT THE NUMBER OF YEARS YOU HAVE BEEN A POLICE OFFICER HERE*** years, and has completed the basic training requirements for the ***INSERT YOUR STATES POLICE COMMISION NAME HERE*** (i.e., Maryland Police Training Commission) at the ***INSERT THE NAME OF THE POLICE ACADEMY YOU ATTENDED*** Police Academy, ***INSERT THE CITY AND STATE THAT THE POLICE ACADEMY IS LOCATED IN***, in which a portion of the training involved the identification and detection of controlled dangerous substances. In addition, your affiant has obtained additional training in: ***INSERT YOUR TRAINING AND PROFESSIONAL EDUCATION HERE***

Your affiant ***INSERT YOUR NAME AND RANK HERE*** has authored and assisted in the execution of numerous search and seizure warrants during his tenure as a law enforcement officer. Your affiant ***INSERT YOUR NAME AND RANK HERE*** has also made controlled purchases and hand-to-hand drug transactions of controlled dangerous substances. Your affiant ***INSERT YOUR NAME AND RANK HERE*** has successfully arrested and obtained convictions for numerous persons concerning violations of the Controlled Dangerous Substance Laws. Furthermore, your affiant receives training on a daily basis working on drug investigations for the ***INSERT YOUR UNIT/DIVISION ASSIGNED HERE***.

III. BASIS FOR APPLICATION

In support of this application and the basis for probable cause, your affiant deposes and says:

INSERT YOUR STORY HERE

IV. Conclusion

Your affiant ***INSERT YOUR NAME HERE***, avers that based upon the aforementioned investigation conducted from the forgoing facts and circumstances, it is clear that money spent by ***INSERT NAME OF SUSPECT HERE*** exceeds any known reported income. ***INSERT NAME OF SUSPECT HERE*** increase in wealth is not attributable to any known legitimate income and is probative evidence of **his/her** success in narcotics trafficking. I accordingly believe that ***INSERT**

Insert your state's criminal code or section number for controlled dangerous substances here

For example: Two Thousand And Three

NAME SUSPECT HERE* vehicle was purchased with proceeds traceable to the exchange of controlled dangerous substances and is therefore forfeitable under the Maryland Code Annotated Criminal Law Article, Title 5 et seq. and Common Law Conspiracy to commit said crimes, dealing generally with controlled dangerous substances as amended and revised.

SUBSCRIBED AND SWORN TO, this _____ day of ***INSERT MONTH HERE*** in the YEAR OF OUR LORD, *Two Thousand and* _____.

_____

Affiant

Insert your information here

Detective James A. Henning No.0140
Caroline County Sheriff's Department-CID
Caroline County Drug Task Force

Before me, a district/circuit court judge of the State of ***INSERT YOUR STATE HERE***, in and for ***INSERT YOUR COUNTY HERE*** County, this _____ day of ***INSERT THE MONTH AND YEAR HERE***, personally appeared ***INSERT YOUR NAME HERE***, personally known to me or properly identified, and he made oath that the contents of the a foregoing application and affidavit are true and correct to the best of his knowledge.

_____   _____
Time   Judge

(EXAMPLE OF *PROCEEDS* WARRANT)

SEIZURE WARRANT

STATE OF MARYLAND
CAROLINE COUNTY

To: ***INSERT YOUR NAME, RANK, AND DEPARTMENT HERE*** or any other law enforcement officer;

GREETINGS:
    WHEREAS, it appears to me, the subscriber, the Honorable _____, judge of the Circuit Court/District Court of ***INSERT STATE HERE*** for ***INSERT COUNTY HERE*** County, State of ***INSERT STATE HERE***, by the written information of the affiant ***INSERT YOUR LAST NAME HERE*** hereinafter named, which information is contained in the application and affidavit attached to this seizure warrant, and made a part hereof, that there is probable cause to believe:
    INSERT YEAR MAKE, MODEL AND COLOR OF TARGET VEHICLE in color, displaying ***INSERT STATE REGISTRATION AND REGISTRATION NUMBER HERE***, registered to ***INSERT NAME OF SUSPECT OR REGISTERED OWNER'S NAME HERE***.
    The vehicle was purchased by and is registered to ***INSERT NAME, SEX, RACE, DOB, AND ADDRESS OF SUSPECT HERE*,** allegedly with the proceeds obtained through the sale of controlled dangerous substances, and I am satisfied that there is probable cause to believe that the vehicle was purchased through the sale of controlled dangerous substances, in violation of the Maryland Code

Insert your state's criminal code or section number for controlled dangerous substance violations.

Annotated Criminal Law Article, Title 5 et seq. and Common Law Conspiracy to commit said crimes, dealing generally with controlled dangerous substances as amended and revised, and that a seizure warrant exist for said vehicle should be issued.

You are therefore commanded, with the necessary and proper assistance, to seize forthwith the vehicle herein above described, executing this warrant and making the seizure; and if upon executing this warrant, there are found persons in said motor vehicle then and there engaged in the commission of a crime, or crimes, arrest those so participating; leave a copy of this warrant and the application and affidavit in support thereof with an inventory of the property seized with the person from who said vehicle and/or property is seized, or, if no one is present at the time of said seizure, a copy of the aforementioned documents shall be left with the person apparently in charge of said automobile and/or property, or if none is present when this warrant is served, a copy of the aforementioned documents shall be left in a conspicuous place at the premises from which the said motor vehicle and/or property is seized, if practicable, or if not practicable, a copy of said documents shall be furnished to the owner of said vehicle and/or property promptly after the service of this warrant. Further, you are hereby ordered to return a copy of said warrant, application,

Make sure that you have your inventory return and one of the original signed seizure warrants back to the judge within your states specified time limit.

and affidavit in support thereof together with an inventory of the property seized, to me within ten days after the execution of this warrant; or if not served, to return this warrant to me promptly after it's expiration as required by law.

WHEREOF, fail not at your peril and have you then and there this warrant. GIVEN under my hand this _____ day of ***INSERT THE MONTH HERE*** in the year of our Lord, ***INSERT THE YEAR HERE***

_____   _____

       Date and Time   Judge

(EXAMPLE OF SAFETY DEPOSIT BOX AND BANK ACCOUNTS APPLICATION FOR WARRANT)

APPLICATION AND AFFIDAVIT FOR SEARCH AND SEIZURE WARRANT

TO: The Honorable _____, judge of the Circuit Court/District Court of ***INSERT YOUR STATE HERE***, for ***INSERT COUNTY NAME HERE*** County, State of ***INSERT YOUR STATE HERE***.

Insert your state's criminal code or section number for controlled dangerous substances here

Application is herewith made for a search and seizure warrant because there is probable cause to believe that, monies, records of accounts, and other proceeds as defined by Maryland Code Annotated Criminal Law Article, Title 5 et seq. and Common Law Conspiracy to commit said crimes, dealing generally with controlled dangerous substances as amended and revised, relating to the illegal distribution of controlled dangerous substances and dangerous substances are being, maintained and stored for safekeeping, at:

The ***INSERT NAME OF FINANCIAL INSTITUTION HERE*** Bank/Credit Union held under account/member number ***INSERT NUMBER HERE*** in the name of ***INSERT NAME OF SUSPECT OR INDIVIDUAL WHOM ACCOUNT'S NAME IS SET UP IN*,** social security number: ***INSERT NUMBER HERE***.

EXPERTISE

The name of your affiant is ***INSERT YOUR NEME, RANK, AND DEPARTMENT HERE*,** currently assigned to the ***INSERT YOUR UNIT/DIVISION ASSIGNED HERE***.

Your affiant has been a police officer for over ***INSERT THE NUMBER OF YEARS YOU HAVE BEEN A POLICE OFFICER HERE*** years, and has completed the basic training requirements for the ***INSERT YOUR STATES POLICE COMMISION NAME HERE*** (i.e., Maryland Police Training Commission) at the ***INSERT THE NAME OF THE POLICE ACADEMY YOU ATTENDED*** Police Academy, ***INSERT THE CITY AND STATE THAT THE POLICE ACADEMY IS LOCATED IN***, in which a portion of the training involved the identification and detection of controlled dangerous substances. In addition, your affiant has obtained additional training in: ***INSERT YOUR TRAINING AND PROFESSIONAL EDUCATION HERE***

BASIS FOR APPLICATION

In support of this Application, and the basis for probable cause, your affiant deposes and says:

INSERT YOUR STORY HERE

Based upon your affiant's training, experience, knowledge, and participation in financial investigations involving amounts of other controlled dangerous substances, I believe there is presently concealed within the accounts listed to ***INSERT NAME OF SUSPECT OR INDIVIDUAL WHOM ACCOUNT'S NAME IS SET UP IN***, monies; records of accounts, and other proceeds as defined by Maryland Code Annotated Criminal Law Article, Title 5 et seq. and Common Law Conspiracy to commit said crimes, dealing generally with controlled dangerous substances as amended and revised. The source of my information and the grounds for my belief are as follows:

Insert your states criminal code or section number for controlled dangerous substances here

Based upon my training, knowledge, experience, and participation in other financial investigations involving large amounts of controlled dangerous substances, I know:

That large-scale drug traffickers must maintain on hand large amounts of U.S. currency in order to maintain and finance their ongoing drug business;

That when drug traffickers amass large proceeds from the sale of drugs that the drug traffickers attempt to legitimize these profits. That your affiant knows to accomplish these goals, drug traffickers utilize domestic banks and their attendants services, securities, cashier's checks, money drafts, letter of credit, brokerage houses, real estates, shell corporations, and business fronts;

That the courts have recognized that unexplained wealth is probative evidence of crimes motivated by greed, in particular, trafficking in controlled dangerous substances.

Your affiant, therefore prays that a search and seizure warrant be issued authorizing him, with the necessary and proper assistance, to:

A. Enter and search the ***INSERT NAME OF FINANCIAL INSTITUTION HERE*** Bank/Credit Union held under account/member number ***INSERT NUMBER HERE*** in the name of ***INSERT NAME OF SUSPECT OR INDIVIDUAL WHOM ACCOUNT'S NAME IS SET UP IN***, social security number: ***INSERT NUMBER HERE*** and any and all accounts and/or safety deposit boxes in the name of, ***INSERT NAME OF SUSPECT OR INDIVIDUAL WHOM ACCOUNT'S NAME IS SET UP IN***

B. Open and search any safes, safety deposit boxes, drawers, compartments, or files in the nature thereof found in or upon the ***INSERT NAME AND ADDRESS OF FINANCIAL INSTITUTION HERE*** Bank/Credit Union, in the name of ***INSERT NAME OF SUSPECT OR INDIVIDUAL WHOM ACCOUNT'S NAME IS SET UP IN***.

C. Seize monies from account number(s): ***INSERT NUMBER HERE*** and/or all accounts, records, certificates, and other proceeds held at the ***INSERT NAME OF FINANCIAL INSTITUTION*** Bank/Credit Union in the name of and any other account in the name of ***INSERT NAME OF SUSPECT OR INDIVIDUAL WHOM ACCOUNT'S NAME IS SET UP IN***. This means that ***INSERT NAME AND ADDRESS OF FINANCIAL INSTITUTION ***, is to turn over all funds to the officer serving this search and seizure warrant by making a check payable to the ***INSERT YOUR DEPARTMENT'S NAME HERE*** for further civil/criminal proceedings.

D. Bring said evidence and/or paraphernalia before me, subscriber, or some other judge that of the state or county aforesaid, to be dealt with and disposed of according to law.

SUBSCRIBED AND SWORN TO, this _____ **day of *INSERT THE MONTH* in the YEAR OF OUR LORD,** *Two Thousand and* _____.

Affiant

Insert your information here

Detective James A. Henning No.0140
Caroline County Sheriff's Department-CID
Caroline County Drug Task Force

Before me, a district/circuit court judge of the State of ***INSERT STATE HERE***, in and for ***INSERT NAME OF COUNTY HERE*** County, this _____ day of ***INSERT MONTH AND YEAR HERE***, personally appeared ***INSERT YOUR NAME AND RANK HERE***, personally known to me or properly identified, and he made oath that the contents of the a foregoing application and affidavit are true and correct to the best of his knowledge.

_____   _____
Date and Time   Judge

(EXAMPLE OF SAFETY DEPOSIT BOX AND BANK ACCOUNT WARRANT)

SEARCH AND SEIZURE WARRANT

STATE OF ***INSERT STATE NAME HERE***
INSERT COUNTY NAME HERE COUNTY

To: ***INSERT YOUR NAME, RANK, AND DEPARTMENT HERE*** or any other law enforcement officer;

GREETINGS:
WHEREAS, it appears to me, the subscriber, the Honorable
_____, judge of the Circuit Court / District Court of ***INSERT YOUR STATE HERE*** for ***INSERT YOUR COUNTY HERE*** County, State of ***INSERT YOUR STATE HERE***, by the written information of the affiant ***INSERT YOUR NAME HERE*** hereinafter named, which information is contained in the application and affidavit attached to this warrant, and made a part hereof, that there is probable cause to believe that monies, records of accounts, and other proceeds as defined by Maryland Code Annotated Criminal Law Article, Title 5 et seq. and Common Law Conspiracy to commit said crimes, dealing generally with controlled dangerous substances as amended and revised are being, maintained and stored for safekeeping, at:
The ***INSERT NAME OF FINANCIAL INSTITUTION HERE*** Bank/Credit Union held under account/member number ***INSERT NUMBER HERE*** in the name of ***INSERT NAME OF SUSPECT OR INDIVIDUAL WHOM ACCOUNT'S NAME IS SET UP IN***, social security number: ***INSERT NUMBER HERE***.
I am satisfied that there is probable cause to believe that there is now being concealed certain property, namely monies, accounts, records of accounts and other traceable proceeds relating to illegal drug activities on the premises above-described and that the foregoing grounds for application for issuance of

the search warrant exist and is attached hereto and made a part hereof.

The name of your affiant is ***INSERT YOUR NAME, RANK, AND DEPARTMENT HERE***. Your affiant ***INSERT YOUR NAME HERE*** is currently assigned to the ***INSERT YOUR DIVISION/UNIT NAME HERE*** You are therefore, hereby commanded, with the necessary assistance to:

E. Enter and search the ***INSERT NAME OF FINANCIAL INSTITUTION HERE*** Bank/Credit Union held under account/member number ***INSERT NUMBER HERE*** in the name of ***INSERT NAME OF SUSPECT OR INDIVIDUAL WHOM ACCOUNT'S NAME IS SET UP IN***, social security number: ***INSERT NUMBER HERE*** and any and all accounts and/or safety deposit boxes in the name of, ***INSERT NAME OF SUSPECT OR INDIVIDUAL WHOM ACCOUNT'S NAME IS SET UP IN***

F. Open and search any safes, safety deposit boxes, drawers, compartments, or files in the nature thereof found in or upon the ***INSERT NAME AND ADDRESS OF FINANCIAL INSTITUTION HERE*** Bank/Credit Union, in the name of ***INSERT NAME OF SUSPECT OR INDIVIDUAL WHOM ACCOUNT'S NAME IS SET UP IN***.

G. Seize monies from account number(s): ***INSERT NUMBER HERE*** and/or all accounts, records, certificates, and other proceeds held at the ***INSERT NAME OF FINANCIAL INSTITUTION*** Bank/Credit Union in the name of and any other account in the name of ***INSERT NAME OF SUSPECT OR INDIVIDUAL WHOM ACCOUNT'S NAME IS SET UP IN***. This means that ***INSERT NAME AND ADDRESS OF FINANCIAL INSTITUTION ***, is to turn over all funds to the officer serving this search and seizure warrant by making a check payable to the ***INSERT YOUR**

DEPARTMENT'S NAME HERE* for further civil/ criminal proceedings.

H. Bring said evidence and/or paraphernalia before me, subscriber, or some other judge that of the state or county aforesaid, to be dealt with and disposed of according to law.

WHEREOF, fail not at your peril and have you then and there this warrant.

Make sure that you have your inventory return and one of the original signed seizure warrants back to the judge within your states specified time limit.	GIVEN under my hand this _____ day of ***INSERT MONTH HERE*** in the year of our Lord, ***INSERT YEAR HERE***. Further, you are hereby ordered to return a copy of said application / affidavit / search and seizure warrant, together with an inventory of the property seized, to me within ten days after the execution of this Warrant; or if not served, to return this warrant to me promptly after its expiration, as required by law.

_____   _____
Date and Time   **Judge**

(EXAMPLE OF LIFE INSURANCE SEARCH WARRANT APPLICATION)

APPLICATION AND AFFIDAVIT FOR SEARCH AND SEIZURE WARRANT

TO: The Honorable _____, judge of the Circuit/District Court for ***INSERT NAME OF COUNTY HERE*** County, State of ***INSERT YOUR STATE HERE***.

Application is herewith made for a search and seizure warrant because there is probable cause to believe that laws, monies, records of accounts, and other traceable proceeds as defined by Maryland Code Annotated Criminal Law Article, Title 5 et seq. and Common Law Conspiracy to commit said crimes, dealing generally with controlled dangerous substances as amended and revised, relating to the illegal distribution of controlled dangerous substances and dangerous substances are being, maintained and stored for safekeeping, at:

Insert your state's criminal code or section number for controlled dangerous substance violations.

The ***INSERT NAME OF LIFE INSURANCE COMPANY HERE*** Life Insurance Company, ***INSERT ADDRESS OF LIFE INSURANCE COMPANY HERE***, in the name of ***INSERT NAME OF SUSPECT OR INDIVIDUAL WHOM ACCOUNT'S NAME IS SET UP IN*** policy number ***INSERT POLICY NUMBER HERE***.

EXPERTISE

The name of your affiant is ***INSERT YOUR NAME, RANK, AND DEPARTMENT HERE***, currently assigned to the ***INSERT THE DIVISION/UNIT YOUR ASSIGNED TO HERE***. Your affiant has been a police officer for over

INSERT THE NUMBER OF YEARS YOU HAVE BEEN A POLICE OFFICER HERE, and has completed the basic training requirements for ***INSERT YOUR STATES POLICE COMMISION NAME HERE* (i.e., Maryland Police Training Commission), at the *INSERT THE NAME OF THE POLICE ACADEMY YOU ATTENDED*** Police Academy, ***INSERT THE CITY AND STATE THAT THE POLICE ACADEMY IS LOCATED IN***, in which a portion of the training involved the identification and detection of controlled dangerous substances. In addition, your affiant has obtained additional training in: ***INSERT YOUR TRAINING AND PROFESSIONAL EDUCATION HERE***

Your affiant, ***INSERT YOUR NAME AND RANK HERE*** has authored and assisted in the execution of numerous search and seizure warrants during his tenure as a law enforcement officer. Your affiant ***INSERT YOUR NAME AND RANK HERE*** has also made controlled purchases and hand-to-hand drug transactions of controlled dangerous substances. Your affiant ***INSERT YOUR NAME AND RANK HERE*** has successfully arrested and obtained convictions for numerous persons concerning violations of the Controlled Dangerous Substance Laws. Furthermore, your affiant receives training on a daily basis working on drug investigations for the ***INSERT YOUR UNIT/DIVISION ASSIGNED HERE***.

BASIS FOR APPLICATION

In support of this Application, and the basis for probable cause, your affiant deposes and says:

INSERT YOUR STORY HERE

Based upon your affiant's training, experience, knowledge, and participation in financial investigations involving amounts of other controlled dangerous substances, I believe there is presently concealed within the accounts owned by ***INSERT NAME OF SUSPECT OR**

INDIVIDUAL WHOM ACCOUNT'S NAME IS SET UP IN* at the ***INSERT NAME OF LIFE INSURANCE COMPANY HERE*** Life Insurance Company, monies; records of accounts, and other proceeds as defined by Maryland Code Annotated Criminal Law Article, Title 5 et seq. and Common Law Conspiracy to commit said crimes, dealing generally with controlled dangerous substances as amended and revised. The source of my information and the grounds for my belief are as follows:

Based upon my training, knowledge, experience, and participation in other financial investigations involving large amounts of controlled dangerous substances, I know:

That when drug traffickers amass large proceeds from the sale of drugs that the drug traffickers attempt to legitimize these profits. Your affiant knows that to accomplish these goals, drug traffickers utilize, domestic banks and their attendant services, securities, cashier's checks, money drafts, letter of credit, brokerage houses, real estate, shell corporations and business fronts; that the courts have recognized that unexplained wealth is probative evidence of crimes motivated by greed, in particular, trafficking in controlled substances;

Your affiant, therefore prays that a search and seizure warrant be issued authorizing him, with the necessary and proper assistance, to:

A. Enter and search the ***INSERT NAME OF LIFE INSURANCE COMPANY HERE*** Life Insurance Company for accounts in the name of ***INSERT NAME OF SUSPECT OR INDIVIDUAL WHOM ACCOUNT'S NAME IS SET UP IN***;

B. Seize all accounts, records, certificates, monies and other proceeds used in or obtained from the illegal distribution of controlled dangerous substances found in the ***INSERT NAME OF LIFE INSURANCE COMPANY HERE*** Life Insurance Company in the name of

INSERT NAME OF SUSPECT OR INDIVIDUAL WHOM ACCOUNT'S NAME IS SET UP IN;

C. Order ***INSERT NAME OF LIFE INSURANCE COMPANY HERE*** Life Insurance Company to deliver a check to the ***INSERT THE NAME OF YOUR PROSECUTOR'S OFFICE AND ADDRESS HERE*** for the cash value of policy number ***INSERT POLICY NUMBER HERE*** and any other policies owned by ***INSERT NAME OF SUSPECT OR INDIVIDUAL WHOM ACCOUNT'S NAME IS SET UP IN***. The check should be made out to the ***INSERT YOUR DEPARTMENT'S NAME HERE*** and be presented within forty-eight hours of this order.

D. Bring said evidence and/or paraphernalia before me, subscriber, or some other judge that of the state or county aforesaid, to be dealt with and disposed of according to law.

SUBSCRIBED AND SWORN TO, this _____**day of *INSERT THE MONTH HERE* in the YEAR OF OUR LORD,** *Two* **Thousand and**

Insert your information here

Affiant
Detective James A. Henning No.0140
Caroline County Sheriff's Department-CID
Caroline County Drug Task Force

Before me, a district/circuit court judge of the State of ***INSERT YOUR STATE HERE***, in and for ***INSERT YOUR COUNTY HERE*** County, this _____ day of ***INSERT THE MONTH AND YEAR HERE***, personally appeared ***INSERT YOUR NAME HERE***, personally known to me or properly identified, and he made oath that the contents of the aforegoing application and affidavit are true and correct to the best of his knowledge.

Date and Time   Judge

(EXAMPLE OF LIFE INSURANCE WARRANT)

SEARCH AND SEIZURE WARRANT

STATE OF MARYLAND
CAROLINE COUNTY

To: ***INSERT YOUR NAME, RANK, AND DEPARTMENT HERE***, or any other law enforcement officer;

GREETINGS:

WHEREAS, it appears to me, the subscriber, the Honorable _____, judge of the Circuit Court/District Court of ***INSERT YOUR STATE HERE*** for ***INSERT YOUR COUNTY'S NAME HERE*** County, State of ***INSERT YOUR STATE HERE***, by the written information of the affiant ***INSERT YOUR NAME HERE*** hereinafter named, which information is contained in the application and affidavit attached to this warrant, and made a part hereof, that there is probable cause to believe that monies, records of accounts, and other proceeds as defined by Maryland Code Annotated Criminal Law Article, Title 5 et seq. and Common Law Conspiracy to commit said crimes, dealing generally with controlled dangerous substances as amended and revised are being, maintained and stored for safekeeping, at:

Insert your state's criminal code or section number for controlled dangerous substance violations.

The ***INSERT NAME OF LIFE INSURANCE COMPANY HERE*** Life Insurance Company, ***INSERT ADDRESS OF LIFE INSURANCE COMPANY HERE***, in the name of ***INSERT NAME OF SUSPECT OR INDIVIDUAL WHOM**

ACCOUNT'S NAME IS SET UP IN* policy number
INSERT POLICY NUMBER HERE.

I am satisfied that there is probable cause to believe that there is now being concealed certain property, namely monies, accounts, records of accounts, and other traceable proceeds relating to illegal drug activities on the premises above-described and that the foregoing grounds for application for issuance of the search warrant exist and is attached hereto and made a part hereof.

The name of your affiant is ***INSERT YOUR NAME AND RANK HERE*.** Your affiant ***INSERT YOUR NAME HERE*** is currently assigned to the ***INSERT YOUR DEPARTMENT AND DIVISION/UNIT HERE*** You are therefore, hereby commanded, with the necessary assistance to:

E. Enter and search the ***INSERT NAME OF LIFE INSURANCE COMPANY HERE*** Life Insurance Company for accounts in the name of ***INSERT NAME OF SUSPECT OR INDIVIDUAL WHOM ACCOUNT'S NAME IS SET UP IN*;**

F. Seize all accounts, records, certificates, monies, and other proceeds used in or obtained from the illegal distribution of controlled dangerous substances found in the ***INSERT NAME OF LIFE INSURANCE COMPANY HERE*** Life Insurance Company in the name of ***INSERT NAME OF SUSPECT OR INDIVIDUAL WHOM ACCOUNT'S NAME IS SET UP IN*;**

G. Order ***INSERT NAME OF LIFE INSURANCE COMPANY HERE*** Life Insurance Company to deliver a check to the ***INSERT THE NAME OF YOUR PROSECUTOR'S OFFICE AND ADDRESS HERE*** for the cash value of policy number ***INSERT POLICY NUMBER HERE*** and any other policies owned by ***INSERT NAME OF SUSPECT OR INDIVIDUAL WHOM ACCOUNT'S NAME IS SET UP IN*.** The check should be made out to the ***INSERT YOUR DEPARTMENT'S NAME HERE*** and be presented within forty-eight hours of this order.

H. Bring said evidence and/or paraphernalia before me, subscriber, or some other judge that of the state or county aforesaid, to be dealt with and disposed of according to law.

WHEREOF, fail not at your peril and have you then and there this warrant.

GIVEN under my hand this _____

day of ***INSERT THE MONTH HERE*** in the year of our Lord, ***INSERT THE YEAR HERE***. Further, you are hereby ordered to return a copy of said application / affidavit / search and seizure warrant, together with an inventory of the property seized, to me within ten days after the execution of this warrant; or if not served, to return this arrant to me promptly after its expiration, as required by law.

Make sure that you have your inventory return and one of the original signed seizure warrants back to the judge within your states specified time limit.

_____   _____
Date and Time   Judge

(EXAMPLE OF BAIL BOND SEIZURE APPLICATION FOR WARRANT)

APPLICATION AND AFFIDAVIT FOR SEIZURE WARRANT

TO: The Honorable _____, judge of the Circuit Court/District Court of ***INSERT YOUR STATE HERE***, for ***INSERT YOUR COUNTY HERE*** County, State of ***INSERT YOUR STATE HERE***.

Application is herewith made for a seizure warrant because there is probable cause to believe that monies utilized as a cash bond to guarantee appearance at trial are in fact traceable proceeds relating to the illegal manufacturing, distribution, and possession with intent to distribute controlled dangerous substances, as defined in Maryland Code Annotated Criminal Law Article, Title 5 et seq. and Common Law Conspiracy to commit said crimes, dealing generally with controlled dangerous substances as amended and revised, relating to the illegal distribution and possession of controlled dangerous substances. The monies are being maintained and stored for safekeeping at the ***NAME OF COUNTY COURT AND IF IT IS DISTRICT OR CIRCUIT COURT*** court of ***INSERT STATE HERE*, *ADDRESS OF COURT*** The cash bond is being held for the appearance of ***NAME OF SUSPECT AND DOB***, criminal case tracking number: ***INSERT NUMBER HERE / AND ANY OTHER CASE NUMBERS ASSOCIATED WITH SUSPECT'S CASE***

Insert your state's criminal code or section number for controlled dangerous substance violations.

EXPERTISE

The name of your affiant is ***INSERT YOUR NAME, RANK, AND DEPARTMENT HERE***, currently assigned to the ***INSERT THE DIVISION/UNIT YOU'RE ASSIGNED TO HERE***. Your affiant has been a police officer for over ***INSERT THE NUMBER OF YEARS YOU HAVE BEEN A POLICE OFFICER HERE***, and has completed the basic training requirements for ***INSERT YOUR STATES POLICE COMMISION NAME HERE* (i.e., Maryland Police Training Commission)**, at the ***INSERT THE NAME OF THE POLICE ACADEMY YOU ATTENDED*** Police Academy, ***INSERT THE CITY AND STATE THAT THE POLICE ACADEMY IS LOCATED IN***, in which a portion of the training involved the identification and detection of controlled dangerous substances. In addition, your affiant has obtained additional training in: ***INSERT YOUR TRAINING AND PROFESSIONAL EDUCATION HERE***

Your affiant, ***INSERT YOUR NAME AND RANK HERE*** has authored and assisted in the execution of numerous search and seizure warrants during his tenure as a law enforcement officer. Your affiant ***INSERT YOUR NAME AND RANK HERE*** has also made controlled purchases and hand-to-hand drug transactions of controlled dangerous substances. Your affiant ***INSERT YOUR NAME AND RANK HERE*** has successfully arrested and obtained convictions for numerous persons concerning violations of the Controlled Dangerous Substance Laws. Furthermore, your affiant receives training on a daily basis working on drug investigations for the ***INSERT YOUR UNIT/DIVISION ASSIGNED HERE***.

BASIS FOR APPLICATION

In support of this application and the basis for probable cause, your affiant deposes and says:

INSERT YOUR STORY HERE

Based upon your affiant's training, experience, knowledge, and participation in financial investigations involving amounts of other controlled dangerous substances, your affiant knows:

That when drug traffickers amass large proceeds from the sale of drugs that the drug traffickers attempt to legitimize these profits. That your affiant knows to accomplish these goals, drug traffickers utilize domestic banks and their attendants services, securities, cashier's checks, money drafts, letter of credit, brokerage houses, real estates, shell corporations, and business fronts; that the courts have recognized that unexplained wealth is probative evidence of crimes motivated by greed, in particular, trafficking in controlled dangerous substances.

Therefore, as a result of your affiant's involvement in this investigation and your affiant's knowledge, training, and experience that there is probable cause to believe and your affiant does believe that the aforementioned monies involved are traceable proceeds relating to the illegal manufacturing, distribution, and possession with intent to distribute controlled dangerous substances, as defined in Maryland Code Annotated Criminal Law Article, Title 5 et seq. and Common Law Conspiracy to commit said crimes, dealing generally with controlled dangerous substances as amended and revised, relating to the illegal distribution of controlled dangerous substances and dangerous substances

| Insert your state's criminal code or section number for controlled dangerous substance violations. |

Your affiant, therefore prays that a search and seizure warrant be issued authorizing him, with the necessary and proper assistance, to:

A. Seize the ***INSERT AMOUNT OF MONEY HERE*** cash bond received from ***INSERT HERE WHO PUT DOWN THE MONEY*** for ***INSERT HERE WHO**

THE MONEY WAS PLACED DOWN FOR (SUSPECT)* as a guarantee for *his/her* appearance at trial for case number(s) ***INSERT NUMBER HERE / AND ANY OTHER CASE NUMBERS ASSOCIATED WITH SUSPECT'S CASE***, as traceable proceeds used in or obtained from the illegal distribution of controlled dangerous substances found in and held by the ***NAME OF COUNTY COURT AND IF IT IS DISTRICT OR CIRCUIT COURT***.

B. Bring said evidence and/or paraphernalia before me, subscriber, or some other judge that of the state or county aforesaid, to be dealt with and disposed of according to law.

SUBSCRIBED AND SWORN TO, this _____ **day of *INSERT THE MONTH HERE* in the YEAR OF OUR LORD,** *Two* **Thousand and** _____.

Insert your information here	**Affiant**
	Detective James A. Henning No.0140
	Caroline County Sheriff's Department-CID
	Caroline County Drug Task Force

Before me, District/Circuit Court of ***INSERT YOUR STATE HERE***, judge of the State of ***INSERT YOUR STATE HERE***, in and for ***INSERT YOUR COUNTY HERE*** County, this _____ day of ***INSERT THE MONTH AND YEAR HERE***, personally appeared ***INSERT YOUR NAME HERE***, personally known to me or properly identified, and he made oath that the contents of the a foregoing application and affidavit are true and correct to the best of his knowledge.

_____   _____
Date and Time   Judge

(EXAMPLE OF BAIL BONDS SEIZURE WARRANT)

SEIZURE WARRANT

STATE OF *INSERT STATE NAME HERE* *INSERT COUNTY NAME HERE* COUNTY

To: *INSERT YOUR NAME, RANK, AND DEPARTMENT HERE* or any other law enforcement officer;

GREETINGS:
WHEREAS, it appears to me, the subscriber, the Honorable _____, judge of the Circuit Court/District Court of *INSERT YOUR STATE HERE* for *INSERT YOUR COUNTY NAME HERE* County, State of *INSERT YOUR STATE HERE*, by the written information of the affiant *INSERT YOUR NAME HERE* hereinafter named, which information is contained in the application and affidavit attached to this warrant, and made a part hereof, that there is probable cause to believe that monies that monies utilized as a cash bond to guarantee appearance at trial are in fact traceable proceeds relating to the illegal manufacturing, distribution, and possession with intent to distribute controlled dangerous substances, as defined in Maryland Code Annotated Criminal Law Article, Title 5 et seq. and Common Law Conspiracy to commit said crimes, dealing generally with controlled dangerous substances as amended and revised, dealing generally with controlled dangerous substances, including narcotics, hallucinogenic and dangerous drugs are being, maintained and stored for safekeeping, at the *NAME OF COUNTY COURT AND IF IT IS DISTRICT OR CIRCUIT COURT* court of *INSERT YOUR STATE HERE*, *ADDRESS OF COURT* in the name of *NAME OF SUSPECT AND DOB*

I am satisfied that there is probable cause to believe that there is now being concealed certain property, namely monies, in the form of ***INSERT AMOUNT OF MONEY HERE*** cash bond are traceable proceeds relating to illegal drug activities on the above-described and that the forgoing grounds for application for issuance of the seizure warrant exist and is attached hereto and made a part hereof.

The name of your affiant is ***INSERT YOUR NAME AND RANK HERE***, of the ***INSERT YOUR DEPARTMENT HERE***. Your affiant ***INSERT YOUR NAME HERE*** is currently assigned to the ***INSERT YOUR DIVISION/UNIT NAME HERE*** You are therefore, hereby commanded, with the necessary assistance to:

C. Seize the ***INSERT AMOUNT OF MONEY HERE*** cash bond received from ***INSERT HERE WHO PUT DOWN THE MONEY*** for ***INSERT HERE WHO THE MONEY WAS PLACED DOWN FOR (SUSPECT)*** as a guarantee for *his/her* appearance at trial for case number(s) ***INSERT NUMBER HERE / AND ANY OTHER CASE NUMBERS ASSOCIATED WITH SUSPECT'S CASE***, as traceable proceeds used in or obtained from the illegal distribution of controlled dangerous substances found in and held by the ***NAME OF COUNTY COURT AND IF IT IS DISTRICT OR CIRCUIT COURT***.

D. Bring said evidence and/or paraphernalia before me, subscriber, or some other judge that of the state or county aforesaid, to be dealt with and disposed of according to law.

WHEREOF, fail not at your peril and have you then and there this warrant.

Make sure that you have your inventory return and one of the original signed seizure warrants back to the judge within your states specified time limit.

GIVEN under my hand this _____ day of ***INSERT THE MONTH HERE*** in the year of our Lord, ***INSERT YEAR HERE***. Further, you are hereby ordered to return a copy of said application / affidavit / search and seizure warrant, together with an inventory of the property seized, to me within ten days after the execution of this warrant; or if not served, to return this warrant to me promptly after its expiration, as required by law.

_____   _____
Date and Time   Judge

(EXAMPLE OF RETAIL STORE DEPOSIT MONEY SEIZURE APPLICATION FOR WARRANT)

APPLICATION AND AFFIDAVIT FOR SEARCH AND SEIZURE WARRANT

TO: The Honorable _____, judge of the Circuit Court/District Court of ***INSERT YOUR STATE HERE***, for ***INSERT YOUR COUNTY HERE*** County, State of ***INSERT YOUR STATE HERE***.

Application is herewith made for a search and seizure warrant because there is probable cause to believe that, monies, records of accounts, and other proceeds as defined by Maryland Code Annotated Criminal Law Article, Title 5 et seq. and Common Law Conspiracy to commit said crimes, dealing generally with controlled dangerous substances as amended and revised, relating to the illegal distribution of controlled dangerous substances and dangerous substances are being, maintained, and stored for safekeeping at:

> Insert your states criminal code or section number for controlled dangerous substance violations.

INSERT NAME AND ADDRESS OF BUSINESS HERE held under account/customer number ***INSERT NUMBER HERE*** in the name of ***INSERT NAME OF SUSPECT OR INDIVIDUAL WHOM ACCOUNTS NAME IS SET UP IN***,

EXPERTISE
The name of your affiant is ***INSERT YOUR NAME, RANK, AND DEPARTMENT HERE***, currently assigned to the ***INSERT THE DIVISION/UNIT YOUR ASSIGNED TO HERE***. Your affiant has been a police officer for over ***INSERT THE NUMBER OF YEARS YOU HAVE BEEN A POLICE OFFICER HERE***, and has completed the basic training requirements for ***INSERT YOUR STATES POLICE**

COMMISION NAME HERE* (i.e., Maryland Police Training Commission), at the ***INSERT THE NAME OF THE POLICE ACADEMY YOU ATTENDED*** Police Academy, ***INSERT THE CITY AND STATE THAT THE POLICE ACADEMY IS LOCATED IN*,** in which a portion of the training involved the identification and detection of controlled dangerous substances. In addition, your affiant has obtained additional training in: ***INSERT YOUR TRAINING AND PROFESSIONAL EDUCATION HERE***

Your affiant, ***INSERT YOUR NAME AND RANK HERE*** has authored and assisted in the execution of numerous search and seizure warrants during his tenure as a law enforcement officer. Your affiant ***INSERT YOUR NAME AND RANK HERE*** has also made controlled purchases and hand-to-hand drug transactions of controlled dangerous substances. Your affiant ***INSERT YOUR NAME AND RANK HERE*** has successfully arrested and obtained convictions for numerous persons concerning violations of the Controlled Dangerous Substance Laws. Furthermore, your affiant receives training on a daily basis working on drug investigations for the ***INSERT YOUR UNIT/DIVISION ASSIGNED HERE*.**

BASIS FOR APPLICATION

In support of this application, and the basis for probable cause, your affiant deposes and says:

INSERT YOUR STORY HERE

Based upon my training, knowledge, experience, and participation in other financial investigations involving large amounts of controlled dangerous substances, I know:

That large-scale drug traffickers must maintain on hand large amounts of U.S. currency in order to maintain and finance their ongoing drug business; that when drug traffickers amass large proceeds from the sale of drugs that the drug traffickers attempt to legitimize these profits. That your affiant knows to accomplish these goals, drug traffickers utilize domestic banks and their attendants services, securities, cashier's checks, money drafts, letter of credit, brokerage houses, real estates, shell corporations, and business fronts; that the courts have recognized that unexplained wealth is probative evidence of crimes motivated by greed, in particular, trafficking in controlled dangerous substances.

Your affiant, therefore prays that a search and seizure warrant be issued authorizing him, with the necessary and proper assistance, to:

I.   Enter and search the ***INSERT NAME AND ADDRESS OF BUSINESS HERE*** in the name of ***INSERT NAME OF SUSPECT OR INDIVIDUAL WHOM ACCOUNT'S NAME IS SET UP IN*,**

J.   Seize all accounts and money on deposits held at the ***INSERT NAME AND ADDRESS OF BUSINESS HERE***, in the name of ***INSERT NAME OF SUSPECT OR INDIVIDUAL WHOM ACCOUNT'S NAME IS SET UP IN***. This means that ***INSERT NAME AND ADDRESS OF FINANCIAL INSTITUTION ***, is to turn over all funds to the officer serving this search and seizure warrant by making a check payable to the ***INSERT YOU DEPARTMENT HERE*** for further civil/criminal proceedings.

K.   Bring said evidence and/or paraphernalia before me, subscriber, or some other judge that of the state or county aforesaid, to be dealt with and disposed of according to law.

    SUBSCRIBED AND SWORN TO, this _____**day of *INSERT THE MONTH HERE* in the YEAR OF OUR LORD,** *Two* **Thousand and** _____.

Insert your information here	**Affiant**
	Detective James A. Henning No.0140
	Caroline County Sheriff's Department-CID
	Caroline County Drug Task Force

Before me, a District Court of Maryland/Circuit Court, judge of the State of ***INSERT YOUR STATE HERE***, in and for ***INSERT YOUR COUNTY HERE*** County, this _____ day of ***INSERT MONTH AND YEAR HERE***, personally appeared ***INSERT YOUR NAME AND RANK HERE***, personally known to me or properly identified, and he made oath that the contents of the a foregoing application and affidavit are true and correct to the best of his knowledge.

_____	_____
Date and Time	Judge

(EXAMPLE OF RETAIL STORE DEPOSIT MONEY SEIZURE WARRANT)

SEARCH AND SEIZURE WARRANT

STATE OF *INSERT STATE NAME HERE*
***INSERT COUNTY NAME HERE* COUNTY**

To: ***INSERT YOUR NAME, RANK, AND DEPARTMENT HERE***, or any other Law Enforcement Officer;

GREETINGS:

WHEREAS, it appears to me, the subscriber, the Honorable _____, judge of the Circuit Court/District Court of ***INSERT YOUR STATE HERE*** for ***INSERT YOUR COUNTY HERE*** County, State of ***INSERT YOUR STATE HERE***, by the written information of the affiant ***INSERT YOUR NAME HERE*** hereinafter named, which information is contained in the application and affidavit attached to this warrant, and made a part hereof, that there is probable cause to believe that monies, records of accounts, and other proceeds as defined by Maryland Code Annotated Criminal Law Article, Title 5 et seq. and Common Law Conspiracy to commit said crimes, dealing generally with controlled dangerous substances as amended and revised, dealing generally with controlled dangerous substances, including narcotics, hallucinogenic and dangerous drugs are being, maintained and stored for safekeeping, at:

Insert your state's criminal code or section number for controlled dangerous substance violations.

INSERT NAME AND ADDRESS OF BUSINESS HERE held under account/customer number ***INSERT NUMBER HERE*** in the name of ***INSERT NAME OF SUSPECT OR INDIVIDUAL WHOM ACCOUNT'S NAME IS SET UP IN***,

I am satisfied that there is probable cause to believe that there is now being concealed certain property, namely monies, accounts, records of accounts and other traceable proceeds relating to illegal drug activities on the premises above described and that the foregoing grounds for application for issuance of the search warrant exist and is attached hereto and made a part hereof.

The name of your affiant is ***INSERT YOUR NAME AND RANK HERE***, of the ***INSERT YOUR DEPARTMENT NAME HERE***. Your affiant ***INSERT YOUR NAME HERE*** is currently assigned to the ***INSERT YOUR DIVISION/UNIT HERE***. You are therefore, hereby commanded, with the necessary assistance to:

L. Enter and search the ***INSERT NAME AND ADDRESS OF BUSINESS HERE*** in the name of ***INSERT NAME OF SUSPECT OR INDIVIDUAL WHOM ACCOUNT'S NAME IS SET UP IN***,

M. Seize all accounts and money on deposits held at the ***INSERT NAME AND ADDRESS OF BUSINESS HERE*,** in the name of ***INSERT NAME OF SUSPECT OR INDIVIDUAL WHOM ACCOUNT'S NAME IS SET UP IN***. This means that ***INSERT NAME AND ADDRESS OF FINANCIAL INSTITUTION***, is to turn over all funds to the officer serving this search and seizure warrant by making a check payable to the ***INSERT YOUR DEPARTMENT'S NAME HERE*** for further civil/criminal proceedings.

N. Bring said evidence and/or paraphernalia before me, subscriber, or some other judge that of the state or county aforesaid, to be dealt with and disposed of according to law.

WHEREOF, fail not at your peril and have you then and there this warrant.

GIVEN under my hand this _____ day of ***INSERT MONTH HERE*** in the year of our Lord, ***INSERT YEAR HERE***. Further, you are hereby ordered to return a copy of said application / affidavit / search and seizure warrant, together with an inventory of the property seized, to me within ten days after the execution of this warrant; or if not served, to return this warrant to me promptly after its expiration, as required by law.

> *Make sure that you have your inventory return and one of the original signed seizure warrants back to the judge within your state's specified time limit.*

_____   _____
Date and Time   Judge

(EXAMPLE OF A PETION TO ORDER CREDIT REPORT)

IN RE:
A SPECIAL
INVESTIGATION

- IN THE
- CIRCUIT COURT FOR
- ***INSERT NAME OF COUNTY HERE*** COUNTY

• • • • • • • • • • • • • • • • •

PETITION FOR DISCLOSURE OF CREDIT REPORT

Now comes ***INSERT NAME OF STATE'S ATTORNEY HERE***, state's attorney for ***INSERT NAME OF COUNTY*** County, respectfully petition this court for orders directing the ***INSERT NAME AND ADDRESS OF CREDIT— REPORTING COMPANY HERE*** to provide to ***NAME, ID, AND ADDRESS OF INVESTIGATOR*** full and complete credit and consumer reports on the below listed person for the years ***INSERT YEAR HERE*** to date, and for cause, states the following:

1. The aforementioned person(s) figure in an ongoing investigation by officers of the ***INSERT THE NAME OF YOUR DEPARTMENT HERE*** into criminal activity in ***INSERT NAME OF COUNTY*** County, Maryland.
2. ***INSERT YOUR INVESTIGATION HERE***
3. In order to gain a complete financial picture of the below-mentioned individuals, the ***INSERT THE NAME OF YOUR DEPARTMENT HERE*** needs to obtain credit reports from ***INSERT NAME AND ADDRESS OF CREDIT-REPORTING COMPANY HERE***
4. Section 604 of the Fair Credit Reporting Act (15 U.S.C. § 1681 *et seq.*) prohibits consumer reporting agencies such as the ***INSERT NAME OF CREDIT-REPORTING**

<u>COMPANY HERE*</u> from furnishing credit or consumer reports to anyone—even law enforcement or grand juries—except by court order.

WHEREFORE, the state respectfully requests this court to order the ***INSERT NAME OF CREDIT-REPORTING COMPANY HERE*** to provide to the ***INSERT THE NAME OF YOUR DEPARTMENT HERE*** full and complete credit and consumer reports on the below listed persons.

The state further requests that this court order ***INSERT NAME OF CREDIT-REPORTING COMPANY HERE*** not to post this court ordered inquiry to the above-mentioned files, and not otherwise to disclose to these person(s) the fact of said inquiry;

- NAME:
- ADDRESS:
- SOCIAL SECURITY NUMBER:

Respectfully submitted,

_____

Assistant State Attorney
For ***INSERT THE NAME OF YOUR COUNTY HERE*** County, Maryland

(EXAMPLE OF AN ORDER FOR CREDIT REPORT)

IN RE: • IN THE
A SPECIAL   • CIRCUIT COURT FOR
INVESTIGATION   • ***INSERT NAME OF COUNTY
                            HERE*** COUNTY

• • • • • • • • • • • • • • • • •

ORDER

Upon petition by the state's attorney for disclosure of credit and consumer reports, it is this ＿＿＿ day of ***INSERT MONTH AND YEAR HERE***.

ORDERED that ***INSERT NAME OF CREDIT-REPORTING COMPANY HERE*** provide to ***NAME, ID, AND ADDRESS OF INVESTIGATOR*** full and complete credit and consumer reports from ***INSERT YEAR HERE*** to date for the following individual: ***INSERT IFORMATON OF SUSPECT***

- NAME:
- ADDRESS:
- SOCIAL SECURITY NUMBER:

AND IT IS FURTHER O, that ***INSERT NAME CREDIT REPORTING COMPANY HERE*** not post this court-ordered inquiry to any of the named person's file or otherwise disclose to ***him/her*** the fact of this order or inquiry.

AND IT IS FURTHER ORDERED, that the petition and order be filed with the clerk of the Circuit Court for ***INSERT NAME OF COUNTY*** and a true test copy of the order be provided to the ***INSERT THE NAME OF YOUR**

DEPARTMENT HERE* for service upon ***INSERT NAME
CREDIT-REPORTING COMPANY HERE***.

_____

Judge:
Circuit Court for ***INSERT NAME OF
YOUR COUNTY HERE*** County,
State of Maryland

(PETITION FOR STATE TAX RECORDS)

IN RE: • IN THE
A SPECIAL • CIRCUIT COURT FOR
INVESTIGATION • (INSERT COUNTY), COUNTY

• • • • • • • • • • • • • • • • •

PETITION FOR ORDER AUTHORIZING

PRODUCTION OF TAX RECORDS

Now comes ***INSERT NAME OF STATES ATTORNEY HERE***, state's attorney for ***INSERT NAME OF COUNTY*** County, and ***INSERT NAME OF ASSISTANT STATES ATTORNEY HERE***, assistant state attorney for ***INSERT NAME OF COUNTY*** County, petition this court to sign an order directing the Custodian of Maryland Income Tax Records, State Treasury Building, Annapolis, Maryland 21401, to produce the Maryland Income Tax Records for the taxable years ***INSERT YEAR HERE*** to ***INSERT YEAR HERE*** for the below listed persons(s):

> Insert your state's tax section or code here. You can get this from your prosecutor's office

(INSERT THE SUSPECT'S INFORMATION BELOW)

- NAME:
- ADDRESS:
- SOCIAL SECURITY NUMBER:

1. ***INSERT FULL NAME OF SUSPECT(S)*** figures in an ongoing investigation by ***INSERT OFFICER'S**

NAME HERE* of the ***INSERT YOUR AGENCY HERE*** into criminal activity in ***INSERT NAME OF COUNTY*** County, Maryland.

2. Pursuant to the Annotated Code Of Maryland, Tax-General, Section 13-203 (b) the Custodian of the Maryland Income Tax Records shall not divulge such tax records unless directed to do so by proper judicial order.

3. The records are requested by the aforementioned officer in their official capacity and are necessary to conduct a through and complete investigation of a criminal matter.

4. ***INSERT YOUR PROBABLE CAUSE HERE***

WEREFORE, **the state prays this court sign the attached order.**

_____

Assistant State Attorney

For (INSERT COUNTY HERE) County, Maryland.

(ORDER FOR STATE TAX RECORDS)

IN RE:
A SPECIAL
INVESTIGATION

- IN THE
- CIRCUIT COURT FOR
- (INSERT COUNTY NAME) COUNTY

• • • • • • • • • • • • • • • • •

ORDER

The petition for order authorizing production of tax records having come before this Court; and

Insert your state's tax section or code here. You can get this from your prosecutor's office

IT APPEARING that the custodian of Maryland Income Tax Records shall not, in accordance with the Annotated Code of Maryland, Tax-General, Section 13-203 (b), disclose the requested information unless pursuant to proper judicial order; and

IT FURTHER APPEARING that good cause exists for the issuance of an order pursuant to the Annotated Cods of Maryland, Tax-General, Section 13-203 (b);

IT IS HEREBY ORDERED, this ***INSERT DATE***, day of ***INSERT MONTH AND YEAR***, that the custodian of the Maryland Income Tax Records deliver to ***INSERT NAME OF STATE'S ATTORNEY***, state's attorney for ***INSERT NAME OF COUNTY*** or ***HIS/HER*** authorized agent, ***INSERT OFFICER'S NAME HERE***, ***INSERT NAME AND ADDRESS OF OFFICERS AGENCY HERE***, all Maryland Income Tax Returns filed by the following person(s) for the taxable years ***INSERT YEAR HERE*** to ***INSERT YEAR HERE*** inclusive:

- NAME:
- ADDRESS:
- SOCIAL SECURITY NUMBER:

_____

Judge:
Circuit Court for **(INSERT COUNTY NAME)** County
State of Maryland

Investigation and Intelligence Gathering

The initiation of a drug investigation consists of receiving and verifying the information. Then conducting the planning and preparation that is deemed necessary to properly develop the case. By utilizing the investigative techniques listed in this chapter, you will most certainly be able to gather the necessary information needed to find a suspect's identity, location(s), corroborate informant information, and gather background / historical information on various aspects of the investigation such as information needed for search warrants, operations, and communications with in a drug organization.

INVESTIGATIVE TECHNIQUES

1) Utility and phone bills

Contact your local electric, gas, water, and phone company to reveal who is the subscriber (paying the bill) at the target residence. This will establish a connection between the suspect (s) and the home described in the search warrant. The information received from subscriber information can further corroborate your confidential informant or source's information pertaining to the occupants of the residence, and most importantly that the target resides at the residence or at least has a connection to that residence. Most electric and phone subscriber information will have the name of the subscriber's spouse and the employer of the subscriber which can be used to corroborate other information in the investigation. Of course you will most likely need a subpoena to receive this information.

In addition, if you notice large tanks alongside or behind the residence during your surveillance then this most likely means that the residence is being supplied with some sort of fuel/oil. Often the company's name supplying the fuel will be written on the tank itself. You can then make contact with the company and find out who resides or pays for the fuel at that residence. Your larger companies for electric, gas, and phone are usually territorial and service a large area, which will help in identifying who to contact for this information.

Subpoena language for obtaining cell/landline subscriber records:

Any and all listed, nonlisted, and/or nonpublished telephone numbers and associated numbers, billing/credit information and subscriber information pertaining to the following number(s): (insert the phone number of your target here). This information is needed to aid in the investigation of the following case: Criminal Investigation number: (insert your case number here). By faxing the required information to (insert your departments fax number here) can satisfy this subpoena. (Insert your name, rank, and department here), can answer any questions concerning said information and can be reached at (insert your department's phone number here).

Subpoena language for obtaining cell phone subscriber/ toll records:

Any and all listed, nonlisted, and/or nonpublished telephone numbers and associated numbers, billing/credit information and subscriber information pertaining to the following number(s): (insert the phone number of your target here). In addition, I would like to receive toll records, both incoming and **outgoing**, from the month of **(insert beginning month here and the year) to present.** This information is needed to aid in the investigation of the following case: Criminal Investigation number: (insert your case number here). If at all possible the toll records requested could be placed on disk in a format that is capable of being integrated into "PENLINK," it would better assist our investigation.(Insert your name, rank, and department here), can answer any questions concerning said information and can be reached at (insert your department's phone number here).

Subpoena language for obtaining electric/gas (fuel)/ water subscriber records:

Name(s), Address(es), phone number(s) and/or the subscriber(s) to the following residence: (insert the address of the suspect's residence here) to include any other information assigned or pertaining to said residence. This information is needed to aid in the investigation of the following case: Criminal Investigation number: (insert your case number here). Faxing the required information to (insert your departments fax number here) can satisfy this subpoena. (Insert your name, rank, and department here), can answer any questions concerning said information and can be reached at (insert your department's phone number here).

2) CAD (Computer-Aided Dispatch)

In today's law enforcement community every department utilizes some sort of computer-aided dispatch system. This is usually covered under the county government, emergency management database. Every residence in the county will be listed in this system. To access this information you will need to have the address of the target residence. Or in cases where an address is not visible through surveillance (which oftentimes individuals involved in narcotics violations will not have an address visible. This is done to further evade police detection and make our jobs just a little bit harder), use the addresses from the residences on both sides of the target; or if it is a rural area the next residence before and after. Then run the addresses through the CAD system where you can then pinpoint the exact address for the target residence. The usual information that can be retrieved from this system is the name of the occupant/owner, other occupants listed at the residence, the power company that provides utilities to the residence, and the telephone number listed there. Most of the time a brief physical description of the residence is included as well. This description can be included in the search and seizure warrant to corroborate your observations of the residence and informant information. This description further confirms that the target residence that you have under investigation is the same listed in the CAD system.

3) U.S. Post Office

Probably one of the best ways to determine if a target resides at a specific residence (next to physical surveillance of course) is checking through the U.S. Post Office for subscriber information. The Post Office utilizes special forms that are made just for this purpose (a sample Post Office Request Form is included at the end of this chapter). When making this inquiry only make contact with the postmaster on duty. By using this investigative technique the name of all individuals receiving mail at the target residence can be obtained This further confirms that the target is currently receiving mail at that residence on a daily basis. If you find that the target has a forwarding address to another residence this could mean one or two things: first, the target may be trying to avoid police detection and is causing a paper trail; in which you would need to connect the target through physical surveillance from the new address to the one under investigation. Or, sometimes in narcotics cases the target will only use the residence that's under investigation, as a base of operation to make the deals, or whatever violation that may be occurring, and keep the main supply (CDS) or money at he or she's other residence listed under the forwarding address. If this is the case with a little surveillance, putting the target at the new residence, the investigator should be able to obtain a document search warrant to look for evidence of the crime (see "document warrants" under the Search Warrants chapter).

In most rural areas, speaking with anyone at your local post office could jeopardize your investigation. This is due to the fact that everyone pretty much knows everyone in small towns and its human nature for people to talk. As a rule of thumb, unless you have a contact in the small town post office that you can trust; don't use them! To get around this, make contact with your states (or area) Postal Inspectors Office. The Postal Inspectors Office will retrieve the information you need and fax it back to you within a couple of days. By going this route you eliminate the chance of compromising your investigation.

4) Pictures

During your investigation you should also obtain a photograph of the target as well. This can be done through surveillance, police records, or in most states the Motor Vehicle Administration, which now have individuals photographs kept in a digital computer database. This is probably the easiest way to obtain a photograph of a target. Make contact with your states Motor Vehicle Administration to inquire how to obtain a picture of an individual. Once you get your picture of the target keep this with your case file. The picture will give a face to the name when conducting your surveillance or briefing the tactical team and other members when you go to execute the search warrant I have included an example letter to the Motor Vehicle Administration to retrieve photos of suspects at the end of this chapter. This letter format can be used in various states. But you should first confirm with the state that you are sending your inquiry to that no other information is needed.

You can also receive pictures of your suspects by contacting police agencies that have arrested the individual. Or you can retrieve a photo of a suspect from your county or states department of Probation and Parole if he/she has currently or previously been handled through their agency. And lastly the Division of Corrections routinely photographs prisoners for identification while they are incarcerated. But if your suspect does not have a criminal background (yet) go through your states Motor Vehicle Administration.

5) Criminal History and Motor Vehicle Information

Run a check through NCIC (National Crime Information Center) an your states local criminal records database. Information received from both databases can further your investigation by giving you information concerning past criminal charges of the target, the sentence received and if the target is currently on probation or parole. The investigator then can make contact with the agencies that charged the target and gather important details surrounding that particular case to use in there search warrants and briefings. Remember, if the target has a felony conviction on his/her record, and is found to be in either possession or in a house that has weapons accessible, then this is an additional felony charge. Researching past investigations involving the target may further your Investigation as to co-conspirators, vehicles used by the target to further his or her criminal activity, and other MOs (method of operation) previously used by the target. In some cases the target was initially charged with one crime but in court plead guilty to a lesser offence. This lesser offence would be the one listed on the criminal history. For example: Thomas Byron was arrested on May 15, 1999 for possession of cocaine according to the criminal history check. But when you contacted the agency that had arrested him for that charge you find out that Byron was initially arrested for Possession with intent to distribute cocaine and had taken a plea for the lesser charge of possession of cocaine.

By running a Motor Vehicle inquiry on your suspect you can receive a current address that can be used to corroborate information given by informants or sources.

In addition, you can also find what vehicles the suspect owns which will assist you during your surveillance to pinpoint the vehicles that the suspect may use/operate, or even establish a starting point for your financial investigation concerning the purchaser/payee of the vehicles.

6) Land/Property Records

An investigator can determine the owner of a residence by checking with the county tax / property assessment office. Most states have this information on the Internet as a matter of pubic record and can be retrieved twenty-four hours a day. The information you receive from this is: who the owner of the residence is, a physical description of the residence, acreage and the assessed value. Remember, the assessed value of the home will normally be lower then if an appraiser is hired by the owner to give an estimated value. In some cases a picture of the residence is kept in the main property file at the tax assessment office. If you need to confirm that the residence described in the database is the one under investigation, contact the office clerk and retrieve the picture from the file. Although the picture in the file could be quite older then the actual house that you have observed during your surveillance, you have none the less taken that extra step to corroborate that the address you are investigating is in-fact the same house.

In outdoor marijuana grow investigations this can prove to be a valuable investigative tool that could very well save you some headaches in court. This information can show you how the targets land is laid out on the tax map, and help you to distinguish areas occupied within the curtilage so as to not violate his/her Fourth Amendment rights. Remember, the Supreme Court has said a law enforcement officer can trespass on to a person's property. Just not onto the curtilage of the property. **(OPEN FIELDS DOCTRINE: U.S. v. Dunn, 480 U.S. 294, 107 S. Ct. 1134 (1987))** Refer to the surveillance chapter for additional information on the "Open Fields Doctrine"

7) Tips

Tips consist of confidential informants, confidential sources of information, and sources of information. Once a tip concerning a target is received, the investigator needs to document this information on some sort of tips form. If the information was received from a confidential informant then the tip should be documented on a CI contact sheet assigned to that particular CI and placed in his or her file. All information received from a CI should be kept on a CI contact sheet. This is because if the information is corroborated through surveillance or some other means, and is subsequently proven to be correct, it ultimately adds to the reliability and credibility of your informant, which is very important when it comes to trial. Once the tip has been properly documented the investigator needs to come up with some sort of filing system or database that will keep track of all the tips received. The tips you receive concerning a certain target should then be placed in your search warrant to show an ongoing pattern regarding sales, distribution of CDS or other crimes. As my training officer (Sgt. Ronald Crouch, Maryland State Police) always told me *"If it isn't documented, then it never happened."* It is imperative that all complaints or information received on a target are well documented. There will be a day in court when you will have to produce documentation of those tips you listed in your search warrant and will have to bring them before the court. Refer to the Informant Operations chapter for additional information and examples of a CI contact sheet and Tip Form.

8) Surveillance

While conducting surveillance, try to obtain a photograph of the front of the residence. This will assist the investigator when it comes to writing the search warrant, by allowing the investigator to look at the photograph and have an accurate description. The photograph would also be used in the briefing of the tactical team by giving the team an actual photograph of the residence that they are going to make entry on. This further eliminates mistakes of hitting the wrong house upon execution of the search warrant. When looking at the target residence try to locate an electric meter. More then one electric meter could be an indication that the residence is spilt up into apartments. If this is the case then make contact with your local electric company to inquire if there are more then one subscribers listed at that residence; and if the residence is broken into apartments. Then subpoena all subscribers at the apartment to find where your suspect lives. Look for dogs or tell tale signs of the presence of a dog such as a doghouse, kennel, and steaks in the ground with a chain attached to it, etc This information should then be forwarded to the entry team when a search warrant is executed. This way they will know that a dog is present in the home and be able to prepare for it accordingly.

In your surveillance of the residence, attempt to locate a vent pipe coming from the roof. This will tell you the approximate location of the bathroom and can prove most useful in narcotics cases where intelligence reveals that the target will attempt to destroy the CDS by flushing it down the toilet. It allows the entry team to attempt to secure the bathroom before the target can get to it. Another way to determine where a bathroom is located in a residence is to look for the window. Most bathroom windows are smaller or shaped different from the rest on the residences windows. In the event that a diagram cannot be obtained, an investigator can determine where certain rooms are in the residence through surveillance. Various window treatments can give an indication as to the area of the home. While conducting surveillance at night, utilizing the light from the interior shining through the windows, you can determine based on the time of night certain rooms in the residence. A living room light will be on during the evening hours as well as the kitchen and dinning room most likely. Late at night the bedroom lights will come on; this will give you at least some indication as to where certain rooms are within the target residence.

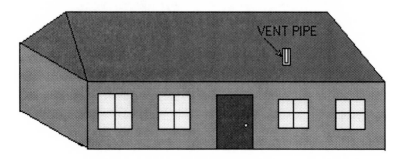

NOTE: If you have information that the target will (or has been known in the past) to flush the CDS down the toilet or otherwise destroy evidence to avoid detection by police, then this meets the exigent circumstance rule and should subsequently result in the investigator to ask for a "no knock" search warrant signed by the judge. (Check with your states laws concerning "no knock search warrants"). Refer to the Search Warrants Chapter for more on "no knock search warrants.

It is imperative that the investigator gets a good description of the residence. Some things to look for are:

A) Which door is primarily used as the main entrance into the residence, the front door or the back?

B) Is the doorknob on the left or the right side of the door? Does this door open inward or outward? (I have found that most doors on trailers / mobile homes open outward)

C) What color is the door? Are there any distinguishing features on the door such as windows, floral arrangements, etc.?

D) Is there any bolt locks visible or any other type of fortification on or around the door that would hamper a tactical entry?

E) Is there a screen door? If so, which side does it open to?

Try and identify and locate any countersurveillance utilized at the residence. Countersurveillance can be anything from the target peaking out the window every time a vehicle or person approaches the residence to a more organized form where individuals are strategically placed around the residence using two-way radios to communicate. Countersurveillance is primarily an organization or action that the target uses or has set up to be used as an early warning measure to evade police detection which ultimately would enhance the destruction of evidence. Remember any type of countersurveillance is an officer safety issue and should be articulated in the warrant, along with the destruction of evidence, as just that "an officer safety issue!" If countersurveillance is present at the residence or in the area then this does meet the exigent circumstances rule based on the above-listed reasons and should subsequently result in a "no-knock search warrant" to be obtained from the judge.

9) Layout or Diagram of a Residence

This can be obtained through police officers who have responded to the residence previously, confidential informants, and sources of information. For example: obtaining a diagram from a developer of prefabricated home that has the same floor plan as the target residence. The diagram will act as a guide for the tactical team during the execution of the warrant. It's also used to assist the case investigator with designating searching areas to other officers once within the residence.

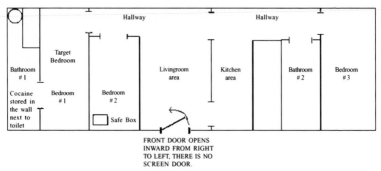

FRONT DOOR OPENS
INWARD FROM RIGHT
TO LEFT, THERE IS NO
SCREEN DOOR.

9234 Skyler Road, Denton, Maryland

10) Weapons Registration Check

Every state has a weapon registration / licensing division used to track individuals that own handguns, rifles, etc The investigator should run the target through this system to find out if the target owns any weapons. If the target does own weapons, this could be put in your search warrant to support a no knock warrant for officer safety. Make sure to notify the tactical team making the entry that there is weapons in the home and what type.

11) Social Security Administration:

The Social Security Administration can prove to be a valuable resource in locating suspects not only in your jurisdiction but also throughout the United States. The only draw back on using this method is that the suspect must be a *fugitive felon* in order for them to assist you. The information you will obtain will consist of the suspect's residence where their SSA checks are being sent and/or what the suspect is receiving social security for (i.e., disabled due to accident at work, etc.), and the schedule of payments that the suspect receives the checks.

To request this information you will need to contact your states Social Security Administration office to get their fax number. Once you have obtained the fax number, send them a fax:

- Attention: Resident Agent-in-Charge or Fugitive Felon Coordinator.
- At the top of your fax write: Request for Investigative Assistance
- Be sure to include the suspect's name, SSN, and your criminal case number.
- Lastly describe your case in one to two sentences (i.e., the suspect needs to be located due to an active felony warrant placed on him by this office for CDS distribution.)

12) Passports:

The United States Department of State Passport Services handles all inquires concerning passports. A passport is a very good way of obtaining vital information about your suspect due to the passport's security features to discourage individuals from making fraudulent alterations; ultimately ensuring that the information contained in the passport is true and accurate. Some of the information you can receive from passports are:

- location of suspect (address, or mailing address),
- physical Identifiers (date of birth, Social Security Number, etc),
- associates of the suspect (parents' names, emergency contacts),
- photograph, the subject's signature

Passports are needed to enter and exit a country, depending on what country you are visiting. While entering and exiting the country the passport is stamped, usually by a customs or immigration agency, which displays the time/ date they entered and/or left the country. Most passports today are digitized and can be accessed in a matter of hours.

Older passports that contain a standard Polaroid-style photo are recorded on paper and will require passport services to hand search the passport information at their records center. This will take approximately one week to access before you receive the information you need. In an event of an emergency though, an agent will be sent to the records center to do the hand search immediately, but this will only be done under exigent circumstances.

To obtain the information from passport services you will need to do the following:

- Send a letter (by mail) to the following address:
  Passport Services
  Research and Liaison Branch
  1111-19th Street, N.W.—Suite 500
  Washington DC 20524-1705

Or,

Contact the *Diplomatic Security Service (DSS)*, located in Washington DC, for them to guide you in the direction needed. The most recent phone number for Diplomatic Security Services is 202-955-0398. If it has changed dial the operator for further assistance.

*Note: The letter sent via mail should have your original signature on it or it will not be accepted. In addition, the letter should briefly state your reason for the request in about one to two paragraphs.

- At the same time, fax the letter you have sent through the mail to passport services so they can retrieve the information sought and fax it back to you in a timely fashion. They will still need the original letter you faxed, sent to them through the mail to be logged.

13) Immigration and Customs Enforcement (ICE):

Once known as Immigration and Naturalization Service (INS) has been combined with the United States Customs Service, under the Department of Homeland Security. This merger of agencies is now referred to as the Bureau of Immigration and Customs Enforcement, otherwise known as ICE. The immigration side of this bureau can assist your investigation by identifying the following about your suspect:

- the immigration status of a foreign national subject, whether they are in this country legally or not.
- if they have an FBI or State Identification Number,
- their current address according to their immigration files,
- any alias names used currently or in the past,
- or any alternate dates of birth and/or social security numbers used.

To retrieve this information make contact with your state's Immigration and Customs Enforcement office or you can contact the Law Enforcement Support Center (LESC), located in Williston, Vermont, through the following numbers: (open to receive twenty-four hours a day, seven days a week)

- Phone: (802) 872-6020
- Fax: (802) 228-1220
- Or you can send the *Law Enforcement Support Center* an NLETS message through your dispatch utilizing the following terminal keys:

  - Message Key "IAQ"
  - (PF1) NLE/INS
  - There are nine mandatory fields:

    - PUR/ (C for criminal, F for Firearm/Brady)
    - ATN/ (Name of Requestor)

- PHN/ (Requesting person's phone number)
- NAM/ (Name of subject)
- DOB/ (Date of birth of subject)
- SEX/ (Sex of subject male or female)
- POB/ (Must be two letter NCIC code for country)
- CUS/ (Custody status of subject yes or no)
- OFF/ (NCIC four digit offense code: this is the reason for the inquiry. When entering this offense always use the most serious)

14) Military Records and Information:

The "Defense Manpower Data Center" contains information on all military branches of the United States Government. This database can prove to be a valuable asset if you have a suspect that is in the military or had been a member in the past. The information you will be able to receive from this is:

- name/rank
- start date / discharge date
- DOB
- SSN last assignment
- occupation code (MOS)

You can access this information by putting your request on department letterhead and faxing it to the following phone number:

- (314) 801-9195

Or mail to the address below:

National Personnel Records Center
Military Personnel Records
9700 Page Avenue
St. Louis, MO, 63132-5100

Any other questions concerning military service records can be answered by calling the National Personnel Records Center at (314) 801-0800.

15) Vessel/Boat Checks:

The United States Coast Guard captures all information concerning the documentation of vessels that are five net tons or more that are used in fishing activities on navigable waters of the United States or in the Exclusive Economic Zone (EEZ) or used in coastwise trade. Vessels involved in this activity must be documented unless otherwise exempted. Coastwise trade consists of the transportation of merchandise, passengers, or towboats operating between points in the U.S. or the Exclusive Economic Zone. This usually consists of vessels that are twenty-six feet long or larger. All information concerning these vessels are kept in the United States Coast Guard, National Documentation Center Database The information that can be gained by using this database are:

a. ownership
b. the name of the vessel
c. the sizes of the vessel
d. the vessel's official number
e. its hailing port
f. the vessels description
g. and it's registered use (recreation, charter, business, etc.)

To obtain the information on the vessel you are targeting, make contact with the National Documentation Center at the following number:

• 800-799-8362, dial 0 to speak with an operator.

When making your inquiry over the phone, personnel will only confirm or deny the vessel's ownership. So you will need to have your suspect already identified in order to access the information over the phone.

To make a more thorough inquiry into the vessels ownership or purpose, you will need to request the vessels **Certificate of Documentation** which can only be done by mail. To retrieve this information, fax your request to (304) 271-2405 on your department's letterhead identifying yourself, briefly describing your suspect, and purpose of the investigation (i.e., drug trafficking), and that all fees pertaining to such request be waived.

When looking at vessels or boats that do not fit the above criteria, contact your state's Department of Natural Resources or agency in charge of monitoring and regulating watercraft. By doing this you can usually retrieve the following information:

- owner name and address
- the boat number
- boat size
- a basic description and horsepower
- and the year that it was registered in.

16) Federal Aviation Administration (FAA):

Large-scale drug traffickers utilize a variety of methods to smuggle drugs into the country. One such common method is the use of aircraft to land in rural airports, makeshift landing strips, or airdrops (dropping shipments of narcotics from the air without landing) in inconspicuous locations. If you have a situation such as this you will need to contact the Federal Aviation Administration. By making your inquiry with the FAA you will be able to receive the following information:

- all records pertaining to licensed airmen/pilots,
- whether your suspect is licensed,
- all records pertaining to registered aircraft, amateur built aircraft, and ultralight aircraft.

You can receive this information by contacting the FAA's law enforcement telephone line at: (405) 954-3784 and speaking with a representative about your investigation or information you wish to obtain.

17) Parole and Probation (P&P):

Your local Parole and Probation (P&P) Department can prove to be a valuable resource in uncovering information about your suspect if he/she is on probation or recently paroled. Their records pertaining to individuals under their supervision are constantly updated and can help in corroborating information obtained in your investigation and further positively identify your suspect. The following information can be obtained from their records:

- the physical address of your suspect,
- who resides at the residence with him/her,
- whether they have recently failed drug testing
- what drugs showed up in the drug testing,
- photographs of the suspect
- where they currently work, or if they are unemployed
- any monthly monitoring fees paid by the suspect (Financial Inv.)
- the agent's notes pertaining to meetings with the suspect or home visitations. You can educate the suspect's Probation/Parole Agent on what to be aware of while conducting home visitations. If the suspect is allegedly manufacturing methamphetamine at his residence or on his property, make the Parole/Probation Agent be aware of any chemical smells or other foul-smelling substance in the air. Depending on your investigation and/or sources of information concerning the suspect, this could be what brings you over the hurdle for probable cause to obtain a search warrant. In addition, they will be able to give you a layout of the suspect's residence, and if there are dogs or kids present.

- any and all restrictions placed on the suspect by the court (i.e., abstinence from alcohol or to stay away from a certain residence, business, area, etc.). If you have this information ordered by the court early in the investigation, and witness the suspect violating the court order, you will have probable cause to conduct an on view arrest of the suspect. Better yet, document the violation you observed and report it back to the suspect's Parole/Probation Agent so a warrant can be issued for his/her arrest for the violation of the court order. You can then set up a surveillance or informant operation so that you arrest him on the P&P violation warrant when you have reason to believe that he/she is holding or distributing CDS.

18) Department of Corrections (DOC-Local Jail/State Prison):
   What better place to gather intelligence on suspects than the "Devils Den" itself? Jails, detention centers, and state prisons harbor the very people that we put away on a daily basis. Because of these corrections facilities are a wealth of information and cannot only provide information on your suspect, but also his/her associates. The information that can be found through correctional facilities records are:

- nicknames of the suspect
- cellmates
- group associations, i.e., Hell's Angels, Arian Nation, etc.
- any internal violations committed while incarcerated
- Call List: While your suspect is incarcerated on a violation, contact the correctional facility to retrieve the phone records belonging to your suspect. Often correctional facilities will issue individual pin numbers to inmates in order to use the phone while incarcerated. This is meant to log the phone numbers

called out by the inmates. By obtaining this call list you will be able to see who your suspect is calling by obtaining subscriber information on each of the phone numbers captured on the list. This will usually lead you to unknown associates in the suspect's organization.

- Visitor List: Just like the call list at correctional facilities, a record is created to document the people who visit the suspect. This is a great way to unveil previously unknown associates in the suspect's criminal organization.

- Prisoner Mail: Another way of revealing associates of your suspect is through his mail/correspondence that he or she receives or sends while incarcerated. Capturing the information utilizing a Prisoner Mail Identification form does this. If you notify the warden or superintendent of the correctional facility that the suspect is incarcerated in, they will direct that all mail/correspondence names and addresses, both incoming and outgoing be recorded on this form, similar to a standard mail cover. This is usually conducted in one-month intervals unless other wise directed. Once you have received the list of names/address you can then start investigating these individuals as to their connection to the suspect's criminal organization. Refer to a Prisoner Mail Identification form at the end of this chapter.

(EXAMPLE OF POST OFFICE REQUEST FOR BOX HOLDER / SUBSCRIBER INFORMATION)

(DEPARTMENT LETTERHEAD)

Postmaster

_____

City, State, ZIP Code

Date:_____

**Request for change of address or box holder
Information needed for service or legal process**

Please furnish the new address or the name and street address (if a box holder) for the following:

Name: _____

Address: _____

NOTE: The name and last known address are required for change of address information. The name, if known, and post office box address are required for box holder information.

The following information is provided in accordance with 39 CFR 265.6(d)(6)(ii). There is no fee for providing box holder information. The fee for providing change of address information is waived in accordance with 39 CFR 256.6(d)(1) and (2) and corresponding Administrative Support Manual 352.44a and b.

1. Capacity of requester (e.g., process server, attorney, party representing himself):

   _____

2. Statute or regulation that empowers me to serve process (not required when requester is an attorney or a party acting _pro se_—except a corporation acting _pro se_ must cite statute):

   _____

3. The names of all known parties to the litigation:

   _____

4. The court in which the case has been or will be heard:

   _____

5. The docket or other identifying number if one has been issued:

   _____

6. The capacity in which this individual is to be served (e.g. defendant or witness): _____

Warning

The submission of false information to obtain and use change of address information or box holder information for any purpose other than the service of legal process in connection with actual or prospective litigation could result in criminal penalties including a fine of (1) up to $10,000 or imprisonment, or (2) to avoid payment of the fee for change of address information of not more than five years, or both (title 18 U.S.C. section 1001).

I certify that the above information is true and that the address information is needed and will be used solely for service of legal process in connection with actual or prospective litigation.

_____   _____

Signature   _Address_

_____   _____

Printed Name   _City, State, ZIP Code_

FOR POST OFFICE USE ONLY
____No change of address order on file.
BOX HOLDERS POSTMARK NEW ADDRESS or NAME and STREET ADDRESS
____Not known at address given   _____
____Moved, left no forwarding address   _____
____No such address.   _____

(EXAMPLE OF DRIVER'S LICENSE PHOTO REQUEST LETTER)

(Department Letterhead)

Date: _____

(Put the name of person that the letter goes to here)
(Name of department here. i.e., Motor Vehicle Administration)
(Address of department here)
(Fax number)
(Office number)

Dear **(Name of person letter goes to)**,

Please fax me a picture of the following person (s) needed for an ongoing criminal investigation. Our fax number is **(insert your fax number here)** Thank you for your time and assistance with this matter.

1) Name:
   Address:
   DOB:
   Race:
   Sex:
   License No.:

Thank you,

(Insert your name, title, and ID No. here)
(Insert your department name here)
(Insert your unit/division name here)

PRISONER MAIL IDENTIFICATION FORM

DIRECTIONS FOR INSTITUTION PERSONEL:

1. LIST THE NAMES AND ADDRESSES ON ALL MAIL/CORRESPONDENCE/ PACKAGES FORWARDED TO OR SENT BY THE LISTED INMATE.
2. ONCE THE DURATION HAS EXPIRED RETURN TO SUPERINTENDENT OR HIS/HER DESIGNEE FOR FURTHER DISPOSITION.

INMATE INFORMATION

NAME: _____ *HOUSEING LOCATION:* _____

SENT ▨ *RECEIVED* ▨ *OFFICER'S INITIALS* _____ *ID NO.:* _____	**NAME:** _____ **ADDRESS:** **DATE:** _____ _____ _____ _____	**MAIL** ▨ **PACKAGE** ▨ **CORRESPONDENCE** ▨ **CONTRABAND FOUND** ▨
SENT ▨ *RECEIVED* ▨ *OFFICER'S INITIALS* _____ *ID NO.:* _____	**NAME:** _____ **ADDRESS:** **DATE:** _____ _____ _____ _____	**MAIL** ▨ **PACKAGE** ▨ **CORRESPONDENCE** ▨ **CONTRABAND FOUND** ▨
SENT ▨ *RECEIVED* ▨ *OFFICER'S INITIALS* _____ *ID NO.:* _____	**NAME:** _____ **ADDRESS:** **DATE:** _____ _____ _____ _____	**MAIL** ▨ **PACKAGE** ▨ **CORRESPONDENCE** ▨ **CONTRABAND FOUND** ▨
SENT ▨ *RECEIVED* ▨ *OFFICER'S INITIALS* _____ *ID NO.:* _____	**NAME:** _____ **ADDRESS:** **DATE:** _____ _____ _____ _____	**MAIL** ▨ **PACKAGE** ▨ **CORRESPONDENCE** ▨ **CONTRABAND FOUND** ▨
SENT ▨ *RECEIVED* ▨ *OFFICER'S INITIALS* _____ *ID NO.:* _____	**NAME:** _____ **ADDRESS:** **DATE:** _____ _____ _____ _____	**MAIL** ▨ **PACKAGE** ▨ **CORRESPONDENCE** ▨ **CONTRABAND FOUND** ▨

PAGE 1 OF _____. DOCUMENT FROM _____ TO _____

OFFICIAL MAKING REQUEST:_____

PRISONER MAIL IDENTIFICATION
FORM CONTINUED

SENT ▨ RECEIVED ▨ OFFICER'S INITIALS _____ ID NO.: _____	NAME: _____ ADDRESS: DATE: _____ _____ _____	MAIL ▨ PACKAGE ▨ CORRESPONDENCE ▨ CONTRABAND FOUND ▨
SENT ▨ RECEIVED ▨ OFFICER'S INITIALS _____ ID NO.: _____	NAME: _____ ADDRESS: DATE: _____ _____ _____	MAIL ▨ PACKAGE ▨ CORRESPONDENCE ▨ CONTRABAND FOUND ▨
SENT ▨ RECEIVED ▨ OFFICER'S INITIALS _____ ID NO.: _____	NAME: _____ ADDRESS: DATE: _____ _____ _____	MAIL ▨ PACKAGE ▨ CORRESPONDENCE ▨ CONTRABAND FOUND ▨
SENT ▨ RECEIVED ▨ OFFICER'S INITIALS _____ ID NO.: _____	NAME: _____ ADDRESS: DATE: _____ _____ _____	MAIL ▨ PACKAGE ▨ CORRESPONDENCE ▨ CONTRABAND FOUND ▨
SENT ▨ RECEIVED ▨ OFFICER'S INITIALS _____ ID NO.: _____	NAME: _____ ADDRESS: DATE: _____ _____ _____	MAIL ▨ PACKAGE ▨ CORRESPONDENCE ▨ CONTRABAND FOUND ▨

PAGE _____ OF _____

Consent Searches

Consent searches are a recognized exception to the written warrant requirement and a valuable tool in the fight against crime. It allows the ability for the investigating officer to conduct a search of a willing individual without a search warrant or where the necessary requisite for probable cause to get a search warrant cannot be established at that time. Any items located during a properly administered consent search can and will be used in court to support criminal charges brought forth by law enforcement officials.

Once an individual gives officers consent to search an area or desired item, that individual ultimately relinquishes their Fourth Amendment right to be free from unreasonable search and seizures executed by law enforcement. A blank consent to search form is placed at the end of this chapter for your review.

To conduct a properly administered consent search the officer must first establish the following requirements:

- ***FREELY, INTELLIGENTLY, AND VOLUNTARILY GIVEN:*** That the suspect was *not persuaded* by officers to consent to the search. It must be given in a manner to show the court that the consent was *"uncontaminated by any duress* (show of force) *or coercion, express* (verbally) *or implied"* (inferred consent from the *conduct* or *actions* of the person from which consent is being asked of). (United States v. Morrow, 731 F.2d 233 [4th Cir. 1984] [quoting United States v. Vickers, 387 F.2d 703, 706 (4th Cir. 1967)] and Channel v United States, 285 F.2d 217, 219 [9th Cir. 1960]). In all consent to search cases, *"the* *question whether a consent to a search was in fact voluntary or was the product of duress or coercion, express or implied, is a question of fact to be determined from the totality of the circumstances"* (Schneckloth v. Bustamonte, 412 U.S. 218, 222, 93 S. Ct. 2041, 2045 [1973]).

EXAMPLES OF WHERE "CONSENT" WAS NOT FREELY, INTELLIGENTLY, AND VOLUNTARILY GIVEN

The defendant was held at gunpoint by several officers outside of his trailer and ordered to get on his knees and place his hands on his head. During this time officers asked the defendant for consent to search his trailer. The court will find that this was not a freely given statement by the defendant due to the above actions displayed by law enforcement during their inquiry of the defendant to get consent to search.

In another example, while officers talk to the defendant they make the statement that if he does not consent to a search, they would get a search warrant that will allow them to tear the walls apart and ransack the house. This is clearly a show of duress on law enforcements part and should be avoided at all cost.

QUESTION ASKED BY THE SUSPECT: WHAT IF I SAY NO?

Oftentimes a suspect will ask the question to police *"What will happen if I say no to the consent?"* To answer this properly is imperative when the case comes to trial. The officer should reply *"If consent is denied, I **could** apply for a search warrant if I have probable cause upon which a warrant could be issued."* For an example of a similar case refer to *United States v. Kaplan*, 895 *F.2d* 618, 622 (9th Cir. 1990). In that case the suspect asked the question, the officer simply replied with his available options. By the officer merely informing the suspect of his lawful alternatives, the courts have found this not to be coercive. Refer also to *State v. Prevost*, 690 *A.* 2d 1029, 141 N.H. 647 (1997).

FACTORS THE COURT USES TO DETERMINE IF THE CONSENT WAS VALID

• ***Custodial situations:*** Although the courts tend to treat persons under arrest as more susceptible to coercion or duress, not every consent in this instance will be viewed unreasonable (United States v. Watson, 423 *U.S.* 411 [1976]). For example: If the suspect is under arrest and consent is desired to further the investigation, the officer should:

- Remove the handcuffs from the suspect *(only if it is safe)* On the other hand, the courts have routinely found that an officer can lawfully obtain consent from an individual who is handcuffed and this still not be found to be coercive in nature. Refer to *United States v. Kozinski*, 16 *F.* 3d 795 (7th Cir. 1994). In every case officer safety should and will be the foremost important factor when it comes to a judge's decision at trial.
- Have one officer speak to the suspect,
- With no weapon visible (if possible)
- In a room or location where they can be alone (one on one), to further inquire about receiving consent to search the desired location.

This is all done to avoid an environment free of coercion in the courts mind. In addition, this should all be documented in your police report as detailed as possible—down to the tone of your voice.

• **A *display of force* by police:** Threats of force or use of force will inevitably lead the courts to find the consent to search involuntary. To prevent this from happening the following should be adhered to:

- Speak to the suspect in a normal conversational tone, *not* in an authoritative manner. In essence you are simply wining and dinning them with your tone of voice.
- *Do not* have your gun displayed or pointed at the suspect when asking consent.
- And lastly, try to have a one-on-one conversation with the person you're asking consent of. This is due to the courts finding that more than one officer speaking to a suspect while asking for consent has been deemed an intimidating show of authority and coercive in nature.

The person's mental and emotional state: If the consenting party is so intoxicated by alcohol or drugs to the point where rational intellect or free will cannot be exhibited then the court will most likely find the consent involuntary. This is not to say that a lawful consent cannot be obtained from an individual under the influence of drugs or alcohol. On the contrary, it's only when the person is clearly "out of it" and is barely in a cognitive state. Refer to *United States v. Gay*, 774 *F.* 2d 368, 377 (10th Cir. 1985). A way of establishing a person's state of mind when under the influence of drugs or alcohol is to ask questions similar to the ones below:

- Do you know that you are talking to the police?
- Do you know and understand why we are here talking to you?
- Do you know where you are right now?
- Do you know your full name, age, and date of birth?
- Do you in fact know that you are giving police consent to search your car, truck, house, or person, etc.?

By asking question similar to the ones above you are establishing the suspect's state of mind. In addition, you need to document your questions and the suspect's answers to those questions in your report for trial purposes.

WHO MAY CONSENT TO A SEARCH

THIRD PARTIES: A third party may give consent to search a specific location, item or area, if the third party has "common authority," which is in effect mutual use of the property by persons generally having joint access or control for most purposes. See United States v. Matlock, 415 U.S. 164, 94 S. Ct. 988 (1974). Third party examples: caretaker, family member, friends etc., but they must have mutual use of the property and joint access. Further, the areas deemed "common areas" (which are areas given joint access to all parties of the residence or at least the consenting party) and the consenting parties' personal area itself could only be searched. If an officer goes into a room of the residence which is not normally accessed by the consenting party then any item in that room deemed to be evidence pertaining to a crime, can and will be thrown out during trial based on the exclusionary rule. Some typical common areas are: living rooms, hall bathrooms, kitchens, garages, etc. basically any room "commonly" used by all parties at said residence or individuals that have routine access of the residence.

To establish if authority exists by a third party the officer should "look for indicia of actual authority" (United States v. Saadeh, 61 F.3d 510, 517 [7th Cir. 1995]). "The question is not who comes to the door so much as it is whether whoever appears there projects an aura of authority upon which one can reasonably rely" (Id. [quoting United States v. Rosario, 962 F.2d. 733, 738 (7th Cir. 1992)]). In fact, the officer should ask more than the mere question, "Do you live here?" Questions that the officer should address to the third party are:

- Do you have a key to the residence? If so may I see it? (Make sure the key fits the front door or to the property you wish to search.) If not, how do you routinely gain access in and out of the property? (Show me!)
- Do you live here?
- How long have you lived here?
- What relationship do you have to the primary owners of the property?
- Do you have access to the entire property or just certain common areas?
- Where is your room in the residence?
- Do you utilize or routinely occupy any other individual's rooms within the residence? If so, in what capacity have you done this and on what frequency?

The above-listed questions should be included in your report and explained in detail at trial. This should clearly, put you over the hurdle of obtaining the Third Party Consent when it comes to trial later.

Example: You arrive at a residence that you suspect being involved in the distribution of drugs. Upon your arrival you knock on the door and are greeted by an individual who claims to be a friend of the family who has been staying with the owners for several weeks. After introducing yourself, you ask consent to search the residence for any illegal drugs. Once consent is granted, you begin inquiring as to the common areas he has routine access to and begin your search of the residence. Located in the living room you find several baggies of marijuana in a wooden chest with a small caliber handgun.

HOTEL/MOTEL PERSONNEL: Once an individual's rental period for a room has expired, that individual's Fourth Amendment rights terminate as well. In this, management, hotel personnel or law enforcement may enter the previously rented room and conduct a search of the premises.

Example: John Doe is a suspect who has been reported to utilize hotel rooms to distribute drugs. During the course of your investigation you find that your suspect had rented a hotel room at the Holiday Inn and has been there all night. The night attendant reported that a lot of foot traffic has been seen going in and out of the room since his arrival. A few hours later the suspect checks out of the hotel (permanently) and leaves the area in his vehicle. Before hotel staff enters the room, you position an officer at the door to secure the room, then immediately ask and retrieve consent from the hotel manager to search the room for any evidence of drug use or distribution. Upon entry you smell the odor of burning marijuana. Located in the bathroom trash can is numerous gallon-size plastic baggies containing marijuana residue. After retrieving the evidence, you then go type up an arrest warrant for John Doe based on the evidence that you found.

SPOUSAL CONSENT: Husbands and wives who reside together at a residence and share or have routine access over an area for which each exhibits common authority over can give permission to search—even if the other spouse is not present or denies the consent. Only areas that each spouse has routine care, custody or control over can be searched in the absence of its rightful owner or against their objection. An example of this is if the wife does the laundry and puts his clothes away in the draw or hangs up her husband's clothes in his closet. This shows that the wife has routine access over that area and can ultimately give consent even if it is not an area strictly belonging to her.

Example: Officers respond to a residence to ask consent to search for drugs based on an anonymous tip. A female who claims to be the wife of the suspect greets them at the door. They find through questioning that her husband is at work and will not be home for hours. During your encounter with the wife you ask her for consent to search the residence. The wife agrees and directs your attention to the various areas they share joint custody and/or access over. A search of the master bedroom closet revealed a large plastic baggie containing marijuana on the top shelf.

SHARED APARTMENTS (ROOMMATES): When talking about apartments and roommates the courts have come to the conclusion that "one ordinarily assumes the risk that a co-tenant might consent to a search, at least to all common areas and those areas to which the other has access" (United States v. Ladell, 127 F. 3d 622,624 [7th Cir. 1997]). On the other hand though, the officer must clearly establish that the roommate has routine access over the other tenant's room or personal area. For example, if roommate A gives permission to search roommate B's room, some information that the officer will need to establish is whether roommate A has clothes in roommate B's closet, or that roommate A utilizes roommate B's bedroom to study in, or use of B's computer. These are just a few of the examples that an officer will need to establish when conducting a consent search involving roommates.

THIRD PARTY CONSENTS CONCERNING VEHICLES AND RENTALS: In this day and age the use of rental vehicles or vehicles operated by third parties who are not present during a stop have become all too commonplace in the transportation of drugs and/or other illegal items on our highways. When officers are confronted with this type of situation, the main thing to establish is whether the driver has any "standing" (an individuals right to make a legal claim) in the vehicle in question.

When dealing with rental cars, this can be established through the rental agreement. If the actual renter of the vehicle is not present then the driver and the occupants in the vehicle legally have no standing to challenge the validity of a search, or more specifically a consent search later in trial

In some states, such as Maryland, it is an arrestable offence to be operating a rental vehicle and not listed on the rental agreement. In fact most rental companies have provisions in their rental contracts, which state that the vehicle is to be driven only by persons authorized to do so and then only by those listed on the rental contract itself. Refer to your states case law to see if this is similar.

Various courts throughout the country have ruled that persons who drive rental cars and are not the authorized renter listed on the rental contract have no legal standing to challenge the validity of the search due to the fact that they have no legal expectation of privacy in that vehicle. Refer to United States v. Dunkley, 911 *F*.2d 522 (11th Cir. 1990); and United States v. Riazco, 91 *F.* 3d 752 (5th Cir. 1996); United States v. Matlock, 415 *U.S.* 164, 94 *S. Ct.* 988 (1974); United States v. Wellons, 32 *F* 3d 117, 119 and *n.*4 (4th Cir. 1994); and United States v. Roper, 918 F. 2d 885, 887-88 (10th Cir. 1990).

Further, when dealing with suspect's utilizing rental vehicles, the officer should ask to see the rental agreement. If the rental agreement does not have the driver listed as an authorized person to possess or operate said vehicle, then he clearly has no standing to object to a search of said vehicle. In addition, as mentioned before, in some states this is an arrestable offence, so the passenger compartment can be search incident to arrest anyway. Often the officer will find that the driver will not possess the rental agreement for the vehicle and claim to be the authorized renter. First, being the renter of the vehicle or at the very least an authorized operator, he or she most certainly had been told to keep said rental agreement in the vehicle at all times by the rental company. That this does not save the driver from not being searched like most suspects would assume. Secondly, this should be used in the officer's reasonable suspicion to go further in the investigation.

CONSENT OF MINORS: When conducting consent searches, officers will sometimes come across minors who are home alone without parental supervision. This does not necessarily make the search invalid if you seek consent to search the home. Although age is looked at during trial as an element to determine if consent to search was given willingly and intelligently, minority status by itself does not prevent one from giving consent. This situation would be handled in the same manner as the "spousal consent" and the "third party consent" scenarios, but attention should be given to the age and mentality of the minor you are asking consent of. A small child of twelve may not have the mentality and maturity to make an independent decision like a sixteen-year-old teenager would. For an example of this type of consent refer to Commonwealth v. Maxwell, 505 Pa. 152, 477 A. 2d 1309 (1984).

ERRONEOUS CONSENT: There have been situations where officers seeking consent to search a residence, indeed have received that consent from an individual whom initially had portrayed himself or herself to have such authority to give the consent. Then through investigation it was later learned that the individual did not have such authority. In this situation, the Supreme Court Of The United States ruled in *Illinois v. Rodriguez*, 497 U.S. 177, 110 S. Ct. 2793 (1990) that this does not necessarily violate the defendant's Fourth Amendment rights pertaining to illegal search and seizure. The court explained: "As with other factual determinations bearing upon search and seizure, determination of consent . . . must 'be judged against an objective standard: would the facts available to the officer at the moment . . ." warrant a man of reasonable caution in the belief that the consenting party had authority over the premises? . . . If not, then warrantless entry is unlawful unless authority actually exists. But if so, the search is valid" (Id. at 2801). Refer also to United States v. Matlock, 415 *U.S.* 164, 94 *S. Ct.* 988 (1974).

LOCKED CONTAINERS AND COMPARTMENTS: When conducting consent searches often officers will find glove compartments, luggage, and/or other containers within a vehicle that are locked, preventing the opening of that item. It is important for the officer to know that when he or she asks for consent to search, the consent which is given is for the entire area or vehicle asked to be searched—this includes items that are secured with a lock.

In *Florida v. Jimeno*, 500 *U.S.* 248, 111 S. Ct. 1801 (1991), the Supreme Court explained, "We see no basis for adding this sort of superstructure to the Fourth Amendment's basic test of objective reasonableness. A suspect may of course delimit as he chooses *the scope* (what items or area he or she allows you to search) of the search to which he consents. But if his consent would reasonably be understood to extend to a particular container, the Fourth Amendment provides no grounds for requiring a more explicit authorization (Id.).

In *United States v. Martinez*, 949 F.2d. 1117 (11th Cir. 1992), it was well understood by the suspect Martinez that the police wanted to search her "mini-storage unit" for drugs. General consent was given, where police subsequently searched the storage unit. In their search they noticed a 1949 Dodge parked inside. The court in this case upheld police officers prying open the locked trunk of the vehicle to search for narcotics. In their reasoning they explained that "When an individual gives a general statement of consent without express limitations, the scope of a permissible search in not limitless. Rather, it is constrained by the bounds of reasonableness: what a police officer could reasonably interpret the consent to encompass . . . . Permission to search a specific area for narcotics, for example may be construed as permission to search any compartment or container within the specified area where narcotics may be found" (Id. at 1119-1120).

Comparing a consent search to a search warrant the court held that "a general consent to search a specific area for specific things includes consent to open locked containers that may contain the objects of the search, in the same manner that such locked containers would be subject to search pursuant to a valid warrant" (Id. at 1120).

"As to prying open the trunk, the record does not show, and Martinez does not allege, that it involved [the] 'mutilation' [of the automobile]. Indeed, . . . forcing open locked compartments or containers has been held to be within the scope of general warrant searches and consent searches" (Id. At 1120-1121).

CONSENT TO SEARCH PERSONS: When talking about consent to search one's person the courts have consistently held that it should be looked at as if there was a search warrant involved. In this they explained that it is no more invasive than the typical pat-down frisk for weapons described by the Supreme Court in *Terry v. Ohio.* Once an officer comes across an item he or she reasonably believes to be contraband based on their training, knowledge, and experience, they can then affect the arrest pursuant to a lawfully permitted consent search. Refer to United States v. Rodney, 956 *F.*2d 295 (D.C. Cir. 1992); United States v. Broxton, 926 F.2d 1180, 1181 (D.C. Cir. 1991); United States v. Wright, 924 F.2d 545, 546 (4th Cir. 1991), and United States v. Winfrey, 915 F.2d 212, 215-16 (6th Cir. 1990).

(INSERT YOUR DEPARTMENT'S NAME HERE)

CONSENT TO SEARCH AND SEIZE

I, _____ herby authorize _____
(Name of person consenting search)   (Name of Officer)
of the (insert your department's name here) and any other law enforcement
officer designated to assist, to conduct a complete search of _____

_____

(Through description of residence, property, vehicle, etc.)

_____

located at _____

_____

_____

(Thorough description of location and/or complete address)

I further authorize the above member(s) of the (insert your department's
name here) to remove any letters, documents, papers, material, or other
property, which is considered important to the investigation, provided that
I am subsequently given a receipt for anything that is removed.

I have knowingly and voluntarily given my consent to search the
above-described location without fear, threat, or promise either expressed
or implied. Furthermore, I understand that I have a Constitutional right to
refuse to consent to this search and that any items seized may be used
against me in a court of law.

WITNESS: _____   X_____

_____   (Signature of person consenting search)

ITEMIZED LIST OF ARTICLES TAKEN AS EVIDENCE

Item Number	INCLUDE THOROUGH DESCRIPTION, QUANTITY, WHERE AND BY WHOM FOUND		
Rank-Signature- I.D.#:		Case#:	Date:

(INSERT YOUR DEPARTMENT'S NAME HERE)

EVIDENCE INVENTORY FORM

Primary Location: _____ Page: ____ of ____

List item number, specific location, and description for items seized.

Item No. ____ _____

_____

Item No. ____ _____

_____

Item No. ____ _____

_____

Item No. ____ _____

_____

Item No. ____ _____

_____

Item No. ____ _____

_____

Item No. ____ _____

_____

Item No. ____ _____

_____

_____

(Seizing Officer's Signature)

DISTRIBUTION OF COPIES
Issuing judge
Officer
Recipient

Writing Search Warrants

Search warrants are an intricate part of narcotics investigations and solely rely on the Fourth Amendment of the Constitution. The Fourth Amendment states the following:

> *The right of the people to be secure in their persons, houses, papers, and effects, against unreasonable searches and seizures, shall not be violated, and no warrants shall issue, but upon probable cause, supported by oath or affirmation, and particularly describing the place to be searched, and the persons or things to be seized*

The purpose of obtaining a search and seizure warrant is to have a neutral and detached magistrate review the facts of the investigation and subsequently determine if there is probable cause for the search or not. This is a method of checks and balance that our judicial system uses to ensure that there is a probability that a crime has occurred or is occurring. By obtaining a search warrant, you shift the burden of proof over to the defendant to prove that the evidence was illegally obtained. For this reason it is obvious the benefits to obtaining a search and seizure warrant when at all possible in your investigations.

When writing a search and seizure warrant it must contain the following in order to be lawful:

- Must be issued (signed) by a *neutral and detached judicial magistrate (judge).*

- Posses an *adequate showing of probable cause* to both search and seize the items or person(s) sought, which is supported and sworn to under oath by a police officer in an affidavit. This is where you explain your investigation and how it is connected to the defendant(s).
- And lastly, the warrant *must describe with particularity* the place to be search and the items or persons to be seized. It is important to note that when writing a search warrant you need to be specific in the location you wish to search and the items you are searching for. The items listed in your warrant should only be those that you have probable cause to believe will be found at that specific location and not what you would "like to find." This is referred to as "The Scope of the Search Warrant." Seizing any items other than what is particularly described in your warrant is considered out of the scope of the warrant and will certainly fall within the exclusionary rule and subsequently not be admissible in court. In many instances you will find that there are numerous items that you are searching for. In this case you will list the general items you wish to locate (i.e., electronic equipment) followed by the phrase "including but not limited to," and follow this up with several of the items that you believe to be found at this location. This will indicate to the judge that there is more items sought related to the items listed and are to be captured under that general category of items.

There are two types of search warrants that you will use in narcotics investigations: a standard search warrant and a document search warrant.

1. *Standard Search and Seizure Warrant:* This is your typical search and seizure warrant used to search homes, vehicles, or persons for controlled dangerous substances and other forms of evidence at locations where there is a

direct link to the suspect's distribution practices. For example: a suspect's home, business, or vehicle that he/she is dealing from shows a direct link to that suspect's distribution operation. In essence, any location where the suspect is literally using that particular place as a base of operation to distribute drugs from. This includes the suspect's body if it is a street dealer. The following examples are separated into the affidavit and the search warrant.

EXAMPLE OF STANDARD
SEARCH WARRANT AFFADAVIT

Start off with the salutation to the judge. Be sure to include whether it is a circuit court or district court judge, and what county they are sitting for.

TO: The Honorable _____,
Judge of the Circuit Court/District Court of Maryland, in and for Caroline County, State of Maryland.

This paragraph explains:

(1) The crimes that are occurring,
(2) What code or article said violations are found under —i.e., Maryland Code annotated Criminal Law Article, Title 5 et seq. and Common Law Conspiracy to commit said crimes, dealing generally with controlled dangerous substances as amended and revised,
(3) And the address of the residence/ business, and/or description of the suspects or vehicles
(4) Lastly give a brief description of the residence with detailed directions to the target. To start your directions use a landmark or major highway.

Application is herewith made for a search and seizure warrant in that there is probable cause to believe that evidence relating to the crimes of distribution of controlled dangerous substances, possession of controlled dangerous substances with the intent to distribute, and possession of controlled dangerous substances, as defined in the Maryland Code Annotated Criminal Law Article, Title 5 et seq. and Common Law Conspiracy to commit said crimes, dealing generally with controlled dangerous substances as amended and revised are being violated in and upon a certain residence identified as: 123 North Sixth Street, Denton, Caroline County, Maryland; the vehicle identified as: a white four-door 2001 Ford Taurus bearing Maryland registration ABC-123, VIN No. 123BDB46R11H585397; and the individual identified as Jonathon Michael Doe, DOB: 08/14/84, W/M, 6' 00", 200 lbs. The residence is described as a white two-story single-family home with a black-colored roof. Directions to said residence are from the Denton, Sixth Street entrance, off of Maryland Route 404, follow in to the town limits of Denton for approximately a half mile. Said residence is located on the right side of the roadway directly across the street from Fresh Foods Deli convenience store.

Said residence is further described as having a covered porch positioned on top of a concrete slab, with several steps leading up to the porch. There are several dark-colored shutters flanking each along the front and two brick chimneys positioned in the window center of the roof. The main door to the residence is a standard home door located along the front, which appears to open inward with a metal storm door attached. Furthermore, the dwelling afore described can be positively identified by your affiant Henning.

This paragraph gives the overall description of the entire residence or vehicle. This is where you would go into as much detail as possible. For example: describing chimneys, doors, porches, and sheds, etc. Lastly, make sure that you put in this paragraph that you can positively identify this residence.

Expertise

The name of your affiant is James Henning, detective, Caroline County Sheriff's Department, Criminal Investigation Division, currently assigned to the Caroline County Drug Task Force. Your affiant has been a police officer for over six and a half years, and has completed the basic training requirements for the Maryland Police Training Commission at the Anne Arundel County Police Academy, Davidsonville, Maryland, in which a portion of the training involved the identification and detection of controlled dangerous substances. Your affiant attended a one-day seminar on Drug Interdiction / Hidden Compartments in vehicles, sponsored by the United States Department of Justice—Drug Enforcement

Administration (DEA), Maryland State Police, and the Virginia State Chesapeake Bay Bridge Tunnel Police Academy. Your affiant also has completed fifty-six hours of instruction in Basic Criminal Investigation Techniques through Eastern Shore Criminal Justice Academy. Your affiant annually attends eighteen hours of in-service training for law enforcement officers, which included search and seizure law, Maryland case law, and various criminal law updates. Your affiant attended a total of 160 hours (4 weeks) in Basic Drug Investigators school sponsored by the United States Department of Justice-Drug Enforcement Administration (DEA), which included confidential sources, case initiation and development, conspiracy investigations, domestic drug trends, diversion investigations, drug field testing, drug identification and pharmacology, street drugs and trafficking patterns, postal drug investigation, interview and interrogation, asset forfeiture and sharing, clandestine laboratory investigations, highway interdiction, tactical street operations, and vehicle containment and arrest. Furthermore your affiant is a graduate of the "Top Gun" Academy, for undercover drug investigators, sponsored by the Army National Guard, Multijurisdictional Counter Drug Task Force, which included but not limited to confidential informant and source management; case initiation, development, and investigation; Maryland case law; search and seizure law; undercover surveillance

List all law enforcement training, specialized training, and experience in this paragraph. Also mention college education (if any) with the type of degree you received or in the absence of a degree how many credits you have earned and in what major area of study. In addition state that "you receive training on a daily basis as a uniform police officer on patrol or a detective conducting CDS-related investigations on a daily basis." In essence this is where you sell yourself to the judge to back up your affidavit and let him/her know that you know what you're talking about and trying to convey.

techniques; conspiracy investigations; domestic drug trends; diversion investigations; drug field testing; drug identification and pharmacology; street drugs and trafficking patterns; postal drug investigations; interview and interrogation; asset forfeiture and sharing; clandestine laboratory investigations; highway interdiction; tactical street operations; and vehicle containment and arrest.

Your affiant, Det James Henning has authored and assisted in the execution of numerous search-and-seizure warrants during his tenure as a law enforcement officer. Your affiant Henning has also made controlled purchases and hand-to-hand drug transactions of controlled dangerous substances. Your affiant Henning has successfully arrested and obtained convictions for numerous persons concerning violations of the Controlled Dangerous Substance Laws, and has been declared an "expert" on several occasions in the Caroline County Judicial system regarding the investigations, sales, distribution, and identification of controlled dangerous substances. Furthermore, your affiant receives training on a daily basis working on drug investigations for the Caroline County Drug Task Force.

Continuation of above experience.

This section is where the officer explains the events and the investigation that was conducted, which further supports the probable cause for the search-and-seizure warrant. This paragraph is where articulation is important so as to convey your investigation properly to the judge. Refer to the proceeding paragraphs as to what corroboration and investigative methods should be included in this section.

BASIS FOR APPLICATION

In support of this application and the basis for probable cause, your affiant deposes and says:

Numbering each paragraph allows an easier time of locating specific information, especially in court.

The first paragraph should list the very first time you received information on the suspect. This is usually from a tip given by a confidential informant or anonymous source. Be sure to qualify the informant information given for each tip included in the affidavit. Refer to the informant operations section for methods of qualifying informant information. In addition, remember to always refer to the CI as "it" instead of him or her. This gives anonymity to your informants and keeps the bad guys guessing. Lastly, give your CI's a number like CI No. No.1, CI No. No.2, etc. This keeps the CIs in order and allows you to easily refer back to them throughout the affidavit. When you have more than one informant it is wise to keep a separate list (out of the case file) as to what the CI's true identity is in relation to the CI's number, i.e., CI No. No.1-Jeffery Palmer, CI No. No.2-Rick Diggs...This is used as a reference if needed later.

1. On April 16, 2002, your affiant received information from a confidential informant during an in person interview and who was properly identified, hereinafter referred to as CI No.1, who explained that an individual known to it as John Doe is distributing quantities of cocaine and marijuana to the Caroline County, Maryland area. CI No.1 described John Doe as a light-skinned African-American, male, approximately 6' 00" in his late teens. That CI No.1 personally knows John Doe to live at 123 North Sixth Street, Denton, Maryland, and to routinely use this residence as a base of operation to store, contain, and distribute controlled dangerous substances. In addition, CI No.1 has personally witnessed on numerous occasions John Doe not only distributing amounts of controlled dangerous substances from his residence, but also from his vehicle described as a white-colored Ford Taurus that has chrome rims. Further, CI No.1 has also witnessed John Doe to utilize other people's vehicles in an effort to evade police detection while distributing controlled dangerous substances throughout the area.

2. CI No.1 has consistently provided information concerning controlled dangerous substance violations in the area, which your affiant have been able to corroborate, thereby establishing the credibility of CI No.1. Members of

various law enforcement agencies have known CI No.1 for approximately three years. During that time, CI No.1 has given information, which has led to the issuance of three arrest warrants as well as four search and seizure warrants, all resulting in successful prosecution and convictions. CI No.1 is familiar with the use, packaging, and appearance of controlled dangerous substances, which has been verified by members of the Caroline County Drug Task Force through their training, knowledge, and experience. Further, CI No.1 has never given any fraudulent information to members of the Caroline County Drug Task Force or any other allied Law Enforcement agency to the best of my knowledge. CI No.1 is deemed a credible and reliable confidential informant by the Caroline County Drug Task Force based on its successful and accurate history while assisting law enforcement in various criminal investigations.

This paragraph is a continuation of the first. After every informant tip you need to put in the qualifications of that informant. There are many variations of this which are described in more detail in the informant operations section

3. On September 26, 2002, your affiant received information from Officer Mark Thomas, Denton Police Department, who stated that for a period of about one month he had conducted surveillance of the residence located at 123 North Sixth Street, Denton, Caroline County, Maryland, and observed numerous individuals responding to said residence and subsequently entering, only to leave moments later. That the majority of these individuals had been the subject of prior

Police information from allied agencies are very reliable and valuable information that can be added into your affidavit. Be sure to personally contact the officer giving the information to inquire on any other details that may be beneficial to the investigation.

Sometimes information is received that needs to be explained based on your training, knowledge, and experience to clarify what your investigation has revealed that would otherwise seem to the lay person to be unimportant. Basically this is where you clarify what has occurred for the judge. You can also refer back and forth to information received from CIs or other parts of your investigation to corroborate each piece of information listed information.

CDS investigations/arrests in the past by either himself or other local law enforcement. Officer Thomas believes based on his training, knowledge, and experience that the distribution of controlled dangerous substances is occurring at said residence and are suspected of continuing to this date. Further, Officer Thomas stated that Jonathon Doe, who is known to Denton Police Department, and the Caroline County Drug Task Force, through previous related CDS investigations, resides at said residence and routinely operates a white Ford Taurus with chrome rims bearing Maryland registration 123-ABC. In addition, the Denton Police Department has observed Jonathon Doe on numerous occasions in said vehicle and noticed him to be the sole operator on every instance.

4. Your affiant knows based on my training, knowledge, and experience that individuals involved in the distribution of controlled dangerous substances will often have a high volume of people responding to and from their residence, either in vehicles or on foot, for the purposes of purchasing controlled dangerous substances. That these individuals will stay at the dealer's residence for short periods of time to complete the transactions then exit the residence and leave the area.

5. During the month of October 2002, your affiant conducted cursory surveillance of 123 North Sixth Street, Denton, Caroline County, Maryland. Your affiant found that the residents along North Sixth Street, Denton, Caroline County, Maryland usually set their household garbage out along LeGates Lane, which is an alleyway that runs along the back of said residence, to be taken away on Tuesday(s) of each week. More specifically, your affiant noted that the household garbage containers utilized by the residents of 123 North Sixth Street, Denton, Caroline County, Maryland, would normally be placed at the roadside along LeGates Lane, for collection on Tuesdays; which is clearly outside the curtilage of the residence along a public access roadway.

6. On October 8, 2002, members of the Caroline County Drug Task Force, and your affiant, responded to the residence of 123 North Sixth Street, Denton, Caroline County, Maryland, for the purposes of retrieving the trash from said residence. Upon arrival your affiant noted that the garbage containers (bags) utilized by 123 North Sixth Street, Denton, Caroline County, Maryland, had been placed at the edge of the roadway along LeGates Road, where the garbage is commonly recovered by refuse collection personnel. Your affiant found that there were several garbage bags that were tied tightly in a knot at the top with no exterior damage exposed. It should be noted that in order to retrieve the garbage bags your affiant had to travel on the public roadway and did not leave the boundaries of the pavement of that public roadway.

7. A search of the household garbage retrieved by me revealed several miscellaneous documents with the address of 123 North Sixth Street, Denton, Maryland, PO Box 81. In addition, a designer dog tag with the name John Doe inscribed on it and loose cigar/tobacco shavings were found lying loose within said garbage. Your affiant knows based on his training, knowledge, and experience that loose tobacco shavings are indicative of CDS (marijuana) paraphernalia use. Your affiant has found on numerous occasions that users of marijuana will often cut out the tobacco from a cigar and subsequently refill the cigar with marijuana. This is commonly referred to on the street as a "blunt." Further inspection of the garbage bags revealed several suspected marijuana seeds, a small amount of marijuana, and numerous plastic baggies with their corners cut or twisted off.

> Again, explain the situation according to your training, knowledge, and experience. This is basically telling the reader that this is a known fact in the drug trade based on your prior experience in the same situations.

> Trash rip operation.,

8. The manner in which the plastic baggies were found indicated to your affiant based on his training, knowledge, and experience that they had been used in the *production and packaging* of controlled dangerous substances specifically for the illicit purposes of street-level sales and distribution of same.

Be sure to state that the evidence was field-tested and if it was positive for marijuana, cocaine, etc. A field test is not necessary but will only corroborate your experience. Refer to "United States v. Russell", United States Court of Appeals, 655 F. 2d. 069 (D.C. Cir.1981)

9. The above-described suspected marijuana located was field-tested utilizing the ODV reagent field-test kit, which produced a positive result for the presence of marijuana—a schedule I controlled dangerous substance.

Example of corroborating the previous information as mentioned before.

10. Surveillance conducted by Officer Thomas of the Denton Police Department, and the plastic baggies, and suspected marijuana located in 123 North Sixth Street's household garbage, independently corroborated the information given by CI No.1, in reference to illicit CDS activity occurring at the residence of 123 North Sixth Street, Denton, Caroline County, Maryland.

11. On October 11, 2002, as a result of obtaining the above-listed information, your affiant caused a computer inquiry through the Maryland Motor Vehicle Administration (MVA), Federal Bureau of Investigation (FBI), and the Criminal Justice Information System (CJIS), concerning the suspect Jonathon Doe, with the following results:

MVA:

Investigative methods to corroborate your CI's information, police information, surveillance, etc.

Jonathon Michael Doe
123 N. 6th Street, PO Box 81, Denton, Maryland, 21629
White Male, 6'-00", 200 lbs.,
DOB: 08/14/84, Soundex No.: D-201-115-488-685
Valid class "C", Maryland driver's license

CRIMINAL: Adult: No history listed.

CAROLINE COUNTY DRUG TASK FORCE
07/20/01

1) Possession of marijuana
2) Possession of Paraphernalia

DISPOSITION: **Handled on intake through the Department of Juvenile Services. Substance tested positive for marijuana, a schedule I CDS.**

---

12. On October 12, 2002, your affiant caused an inquiry through the Denton Post Office in reference to subscriber(s) / box holder information at the residence of 123 North Sixth Street, PO Box 81, Denton, Caroline County, Maryland, 21629. As a result of this inquiry your affiant received the following information:

    Name: **Jonathon Michael Doe**
    Address: **PO Box 81, 123 N. 6th Street, Denton, Caroline County, Maryland, 21629**

13. During the month of October 2002, your affiant again conducted cursory surveillance of 123 North Sixth Street, Denton, Caroline County, Maryland. Your affiant found that the residents along North Sixth Street, Denton, Caroline County, Maryland usually set their household garbage out along

LeGates Lane, which is an alleyway that runs along the back of said residence, to be taken away on Tuesday(s) of each week. More specifically, your affiant noted that the household garbage containers utilized by the residents of 123 North Sixth Street, Denton, Caroline County, Maryland, would normally be placed at the roadside along LeGates Lane, for collection on Tuesdays; which is clearly outside the curtilage of the residence along a public access roadway.

14. On October 15, 2002, members of the Caroline County Drug Task Force, and your affiant, again responded to the residence of 123 North Sixth Street, Denton, Caroline County, Maryland, for the purposes of retrieving the trash from said residence. Upon arrival your affiant noted that the garbage containers utilized by 123 North Sixth Street, Denton, Caroline County, Maryland, had been placed at the edge of the roadway along LeGates Road, where the garbage is commonly recovered by refuse collection personnel. Your affiant found that there were several garbage bags that were tied tightly in a knot at the top, with no exterior damage exposed. It should be noted that in order to retrieve the garbage bags your affiant had to travel on the public roadway and did not leave the boundaries of the pavement of that public roadway.

15. A search of the household garbage retrieved by your affiant revealed

2nd Trash Rip Operation

several miscellaneous documents with the name Jonathon Doe written on them and the address of 123 North Sixth Street, Denton, Maryland, PO Box 81. Further inspection of the garbage bags revealed two suspected marijuana cigarettes, and numerous plastic baggies with their corners cut or twisted off— most of which contained suspected cocaine residue inside.

16. Again, the manner in which the plastic baggies were found indicated to your affiant based on my training, knowledge, and experience that they had been used in the *production and packaging* of controlled dangerous substances specifically for the illicit purposes of street level sales and distribution of same.

17. The above-described suspected marijuana cigarettes located were field-tested utilizing the ODV reagent field-test kit, which produced a positive result for the presence of marijuana—a schedule I controlled dangerous substance. The plastic baggies containing the suspected cocaine residue was field-tested utilizing the NIK field test swab, which produced a positive result for the presence of cocaine; a schedule II controlled dangerous substance.

18. On July 3, 2003, your affiant received information from a confidential source of information, herein after referred to as CS No.1, during an in-person interview where they were properly identified, that Jonathon Doe is continuously distributing

controlled dangerous substances, namely cocaine and marijuana to the surrounding Caroline County area. CS No.1 described Jonathon Doe as a light-skinned African-American male, heavy build, in his late teens. According to CS No.1, Jonathon Doe lives at a residence described as a two-story, white-colored, single-family home, located along Sixth Street, Denton, Maryland, positioned directly across the street from the convenience store, Fresh Foods Deli. CS No.1 went on to explained that it has personally witnessed on numerous occasions Jonathon Doe utilize his vehicle, as well as vehicles belonging to others, to transport and distribute said controlled dangerous substance to various individuals in the area. CS No.1 explained that Jonathon Doe routinely operates a white four-door Ford Taurus with chrome wheels. Further, CS No.1 stated that it has personally overheard conversations from Jonathon Doe, between Doe and other individuals in his organization, that he (Jonathon Doe) utilizes his home to store and contain illegally gained currency from the sales of controlled dangerous substances and that the currency and portions of the controlled dangerous substances are kept their to evade detection by police.

> Confidential source information

19. *CS No.1 has provided information concerning individuals involved in controlled dangerous substance violations in the area, which your affiant has been able to corroborate, thereby*

establishing the credibility of CS No.1. CS No.1 is familiar with the use, packaging, and appearance of controlled dangerous substances, which has been verified by members of the Caroline County Drug Task Force through their training, knowledge, and experience. CS No.1 has assisted members of various Law Enforcement agencies in the past. During that time, CS No.1 has given information, which has led to the arrest two individuals. CS No.1 has never given any fraudulent information to members of the Caroline County Drug Task Force or any other allied Law Enforcement agency to the best of my knowledge. The Caroline County Drug Task Force has deemed CS No.1 a credible and reliable confidential source of information.

In this paragraph you will be establishing the credibility of the confidential source. Be sure to refer to the informant operations chapter for detailed examples.

20. On September 13, 2003, at approximately 12:05 a.m., Mark Thomas, Denton Police Department observed Jonathon Doe operating the previously described Ford Taurus in the Sixth and Market Street area of Denton, Caroline County, Maryland, with a passenger in the vehicle as well. During this time, Officer Thomas noticed a minor traffic violation and conducted a traffic stop on the vehicle.

Police information from allied agencies concerning the suspect's involvement in narcotics should be used in your affidavit to show that the suspect is predisposed to drugs or is associated with individuals involved in drugs.

During the traffic stop, Officer Thomas noticed a strong odor of burning marijuana emanating from within said vehicle, based on his training, knowledge, and experience. As a result, a search was conducted which produced small quantities of suspected marijuana on the floorboards of the vehicle and a small partially burnt suspected marijuana cigarette located in the ashtray. Officer Thomas also located a plastic baggie containing suspected marijuana on the ground next to the rear tire of Jonathon Doe's vehicle. Officer Thomas noticed that the baggy of suspected marijuana was dry having no wetness or moisture on it. Officer Thomas noted that it had been raining on and off all night and that it had been raining lightly throughout the traffic stop. Officer Thomas subsequently issued citations to Jonathon Doe and his passenger where they were subsequently released at the scene.

21. On September 25, 2003, your affiant received information from a confidential informant, herein after referred to as CI No.2, during an in-person interview where said CI was properly identified, who stated that John Doe is continuously distributing controlled dangerous substances, namely cocaine and marijuana to the surrounding Caroline County area. CI No.2 described John Doe as a light-skinned African-American male, approximately 5' 11" to "5' 12", heavy build, in his late teens. CI No.2 explained that it personally knows John Doe to reside at a residence described as a two-story white-colored single-family home located along Sixth Street, Denton,

Confidential informant No.2's information

Maryland, positioned directly across the street from the convenience store, Fresh Food Deli. CI No.2 went on to explain that it has personally witnessed on numerous occasions John Doe utilize his residence and vehicle, as well as other vehicles to transport and distribute said controlled dangerous substance to various individuals in the area. That John Doe routinely frequents the Goose Creek convenience store parking lot to distribute quantities of controlled dangerous substances, while utilizing his vehicle or others as previously described. In addition, the CI has observed John Doe in possession of large amounts of cocaine and marijuana while at Doe's residence packaged for the street-level sales and distribution. The CI further stated that John Doe routinely operates a white four-door Ford Taurus with chrome wheels.

22. CI No.2 has provided information concerning individuals involved in controlled dangerous substance violations in the area, which your affiant has been able to corroborate, thereby establishing the credibility of CI No.2. CI No.2 is familiar with the use, packaging, and appearance of controlled dangerous substances, which has been verified by members of the Caroline County Drug Task Force through their training, knowledge, and experience. Members of various law enforcement agencies have

Again, qualify your sources of information immediately after listing their information

known CI No.2 for approximately one year. During that time, CI No.2 has given information, which has led to the apprehension of two individuals who were the subject of arrest warrants. In addition,

CI No.2's cooperation has also led to the issuance of one search and seizure warrant, all resulting in successful prosecution and convictions. CI No.2 has never given any fraudulent information to members of the Caroline County Drug Task Force or any other allied law enforcement agency to the best of my knowledge. CI No.2 is deemed a credible and reliable confidential informant through the Caroline County Drug Task Force.

23. On October 29, 2003, your affiant again caused an inquiry through the Maryland Motor Vehicle Administration (MVA) and the Denton Post Office as to any changes to John Doe's driver's license information or physical mailing address. As a result, all information has remained the same since last checked on October 10 and 11, 2002

24. During the week of October 26, 2003, your affiant repeatedly conducted cursory surveillance of John Doe's residence located at 123 North Sixth Street, Denton, Caroline County, Maryland. As a result, your affiant noted that a white-colored Ford Taurus with chrome rims bearing Maryland registration 123-ABC was parked in the driveway alongside or behind said

---

Continuation of informant qualification

Make sure to update your information if you had originally researched it several months or years earlier.

Surveillance logs should be used to document the exact date and time that you had made your observations. This is due to the fact that the defense attorneys will try to say that your observations were wrong or some other twist to make it look like you're lying or that you don't know what you're talking about. With a surveillance log you will be able to effectively document the dates, times, and activity to back up your statement or show that the suspect is lying. **Remember: if it's not documented it never happened!** Refer to the surveillance chapter for an example of a surveillance Log".

residence. Further corroborating confidential informant and database information that John Doe is residing at said residence.

25. During the week of November 1, 2003, members of the Caroline County Drug Task Force and your affiant met with CI No.2 at a predetermined location in Caroline County for the purpose of CI No.2 performing a controlled purchase of a controlled dangerous substance from John Doe while at Doe's residence. CI No.2 had previously ordered a quantity of cocaine from Doe and was advised to meet at Doe's residence to complete the transaction. Your affiant subsequently caused a complete and thorough search of CI No.2 and the vehicle to be used by the CI No.2. No controlled dangerous substances or United States currency were located. The CI was then given an amount of U.S. currency from the task force official advanced funds used for the purchase of controlled dangerous substances.

26. Detective Robert Bell, Caroline County Drug Task Force, and your affiant took up a position where we could maintain surveillance on the suspect's residence and on the CI's path going to and from said residence. The CI subsequently arrived at said residence and was greeted at the front door by an African-American male. During this surveillance I noticed a white Ford Taurus bearing Maryland

Be sure to record this conversation if the informant is testifying. If the informant is *not* *testifying do not* record this conversation due to this being able to be introduced into evidence at trial.

Controlled buy operation utilizing a confidential informant

registration 123-ABC parked in the driveway of said residence; the same vehicle this investigation has determined to be owned and routinely operated by the suspect John Doe. After several minutes, the CI exited said residence and left the area, responding directly to the predetermined location to meet with task force personnel. Upon contact with the CI, it handed your affiant a plastic baggie, which contained a quantity of suspected cocaine. At no time did said CI come in contact with any other person prior to or after leaving the designated meeting location. Your affiant again caused a complete and thorough search to be conducted of the CI and the CI's vehicle, which were found to be free of any controlled dangerous substances or United States currency.

Continuation of controlled buy

Your affiant spoke to the CI who advised your affiant that it had made contact with John Doe at the front door of the residence and was permitted access inside. As a result of their contact, the CI purchased a quantity of suspected cocaine from John Doe. After their conversation, the CI left and returned directly to the predetermined location. At that time contact with said CI was terminated.

The debriefing of the informant after the controlled buy. Be vague enough so that the suspect will not relate your informant to this buy.

27. The suspected cocaine was field tested utilizing the NIK Swab field-test system for cocaine, which yielded a positive indication for the presence of cocaine—

a schedule II controlled dangerous substance.

28. Your affiant avers, that based upon the aforementioned investigation conducted by receiving corroborating information supplied by CI No.1, CI No.2, and the CS, pertaining to the illegal distribution of controlled dangerous substances concerning Jonathon Michael Doe; the past criminal arrest for possession of marijuana; the incident involving Jonathon Doe while operating his motor vehicle, as previously described, where quantities of marijuana were located as well as the burning odor of suspected marijuana emanating from said vehicle; Officer Mark Thomas's observations of a large amount of foot traffic going in and out of said Jonathon Doe's residence, typical of illicit drug distribution practices; the previous two searches of his household garbage, which contained trace amounts of suspected cocaine, marijuana, and related paraphernalia used in the packaging, distribution, and sales of controlled dangerous substances; the aforementioned controlled purchase of suspected cocaine from Jonathon Doe while at his residence of 123 North Sixth Street, Denton, Caroline County, Maryland; all leads your affiant to believe based on your affiant's training, experience, and knowledge as an experienced member of the Caroline County Drug Task Force, that probable cause exists for a search and seizure

This paragraph sums up your entire probable cause and clearly illustrates to the judge why you believe that the suspect is involved in criminal activity.

warrant, and that the laws relating to the illegal distribution and possession with intent to distribute controlled dangerous substances, as hereinbefore cited, are being violated and will continue to be violated in and upon the premises, person(s) and vehicle located at 123 North Sixth Street, Denton, Caroline County, Maryland.

29. Further, your affiant avers that controlled dangerous substance traffickers maintain books, records, receipts, notes, ledgers, airline tickets, money orders, and other papers relating to the transportation, ordering, sale, and distribution of controlled substances; that controlled dangerous substance traffickers commonly "front" (provide drugs on consignment) CDS to the clients. That the aforementioned books, records, receipts, notes, ledgers, etc., are maintained where the traffickers have ready access to them; that it is common for drug dealers to secrete contraband, proceeds of drug sales, and records of drug transactions in secure locations within their residences, businesses and/or their vehicles for their ready access and to conceal from law enforcement authorities. That the persons involved in drug trafficking conceal in their residences, businesses, and vehicles caches of drugs, amounts of currency, financial instructions, precious metals, jewelry, and other items of value and/or proceeds of drug transactions; and evidence of financial transactions relating

This paragraph clearly explains what types of **documents** that are typically found in drug distribution organizations. This will not change and should be included in all search warrants involving narcotics. You will be asking the judge at the conclusion of this search warrant to search for all of these items mentioned.

to obtaining, transferring, secreting, or the spending of large sums of money made from engaging in narcotics-trafficking activities; that when drug traffickers amass large proceeds from the sale of drugs that the drug traffickers attempt to legitimize these profits. Your affiant knows that to accomplish these goals, drug traffickers utilize, domestic banks and their attendant services, securities, cashier's checks, money drafts, letter of credit, brokerage houses, real estate, shell corporations and business fronts.

Continuation of the above paragraph

30. Therefore, as a result of your affiant's involvement in this investigation and your affiant's expertise in the investigation of narcotics and dangerous drugs, your affiant believes there is presently concealed within the aforesaid premises and vehicle(s) listed in the heading of this affidavit those items which have been previously mentioned as commonly found among drug traffickers and ultimately constitute evidence that relate to the illegal distribution and possession with intent to distribute controlled dangerous substance, monies, records or accounts, ledgers, books, receipts, bank statements, and other proceeds as defined in the Maryland Code Annotated Criminal Law Article, Title 5 et seq. and Common Law Conspiracy to commit said crimes, dealing generally with controlled dangerous substances as amended and revised.

Be sure to mention your states code or section number for narcotics violations.

This paragraph contains evidence relating to computers, electronics, cell phones, pagers, etc. Notice the amount of detail that goes into describing the various computer and electronic peripherals. This is due to the technology that criminals utilize in their drug distribution organizations. In addition, it is imperative to include the wording "and the contents therein" in this paragraph. Because if this is not in this paragraph then you would need to write a separate search warrant to gain access to the data/electronic information within all the mentioned electronic devices. This paragraph should be placed in all your affidavits as a catch all for electronic

Continuation of electronic evidence and peripherals.

31. That electronic equipment, such as computers, telex machines, facsimile machines, currency counting machines, telephone answering machines, cell phones, pagers, PDAs/computers, and related manuals are used to generate, transfer, count, record and store the information described above. Additionally, computer software, tapes and discs, *and the contents therein*, that contain the information generated by the aforementioned electronic equipment will need to be seized and examined, including but not limited to any and all electronic data processing and computer storage devices, such as central processing units, internal and peripheral storage devices such as fixed disks, external hard disks, floppy disk drives and diskettes, tape drives and tapes, optical storage devices, optical readers and scanning-devices, CD-ROM drives and compact disks and related hardware, digital cameras and digital storage media, operating logs, software and operating instructions or operating manuals, computer materials, software and programs used to communicate with other terminals via telephone or other means, and any computer modems, monitors, printers, etc, *that may have been used while engaging in the distribution of cocaine and or any other CDS-related activity, as defined in the Annotated Code of Maryland, as amended and revised.*

32. In addition, your affiant knows that CDS traffickers commonly maintain addresses and/or telephone numbers in books, papers, cell phones, pagers, PDAs or computers, which reflect names, address and/or telephone numbers of their associates in the trafficking organizations. Furthermore, your affiant Henning knows through training, knowledge, and experience that drug traffickers take or cause to be taken photographs, or videographic images of themselves, their associates, their property, and their product, and that these traffickers usually maintain these photographs or videographic images in their possession.

This paragraph explains that you are trying to look for additional individuals in the suspect's organization by searching for addresses or photographs stored or logged in books, computers, cell phones, etc.

33. Also, in support of this application, your affiant Henning avers that these individuals involved in the use and sales of controlled dangerous substances will also use their vehicles and/or outbuildings to conceal controlled dangerous substances not only from the police, but also from other dealers and addicts at the residence. That it has been your affiant's experience in searching residences and persons for drug violations, that your affiant and other law enforcement officers have

Be sure to reiterate various facts of the case to back up what you're asking to search for. For example: in this paragraph you're asking to search vehicles at the residence. CIs have stated that John Doe uses his vehicles to transport the CDS from one location to another.

Here you're asking to search in vehicles and outbuildings that are located on the property.

on numerous occasions found controlled dangerous substances in outbuildings and vehicles located at the residence, where the vehicles were either registered to or under the immediate control of the residence. In addition, this investigation has revealed through information obtained by two separate and distinct confidential informants that Jonathon Doe will routinely transport controlled dangerous substances while utilizing motor vehicles to further his illicit criminal enterprise and evade police detection.

34. That the prior experience of your affiant indicates that narcotic/drug dealers/users have, carry, and use firearms to protect their operations. This protection is both from the police and other drug dealers/users who may try to seize the drugs or moneys gained from the operation. These firearms include handguns, rifles, shotguns, and semi/fully automatic weapons, and related equipment such as, but not limited to, ammunition, magazines, bayonets, bipods, tripods, ocular and laser-sighting scopes, etc. These weapons allow the drug dealer/user to operate freely and openly, also enabling them to retaliate against anyone they feel threatened by. The possession of these weapons is an extension of the narcotic operation and/or conspiracy being conducted.

This paragraph lists the known fact that guns and drugs go together. Because of this you're asking the judge to locate and seize evidence relating to weapons and their related equipment. This is an important paragraph that needs to be added into all your affidavits.

This is where you would place the paragraph to ask for a no knock warrant. Refer to the end of this Affidavit for an example paragraph to be placed directly after this one.

If seeking a no knock warrant, you will need to replace this "A", with the sample "A" at the end of this affidavit. Only if your state requires you to specifically ask for one.

This is where you would ask specifically to search for the items you expect will be found at the location.

Your affiant Henning, therefore prays that a search and seizure warrant be issued authorizing him, with the necessary and proper assistance, to:

A. Enter and search the residence and outbuildings identified as 123 N. Sixth Street, Denton, Caroline County, Maryland; the vehicle identified as a white four-door 2001 Ford Taurus bearing Maryland registration 123-ABC, VIN No.: 123BDB46R11H585397; (as completely described above); as well as any motor vehicles that are located on said property, and/or any motor vehicles under the immediate control of Jonathon Michael Doe.

B. Search the person and clothing of Jonathon Michael Doe, DOB: 08/14/84, B/M, 6' 00", 200 lbs.; as well as any other persons found in or upon said premises that may be participating in violations of the statutes hereinbefore cited, and who may be concealing evidence, paraphernalia, and controlled dangerous substances.

C. Open and search any safes, boxes, bags, luggage, compartments, storage units or things in the nature thereof, found in or upon said premises, outbuildings, and vehicles.

D. Seize all evidence, paraphernalia, controlled dangerous substances, papers, evidentiary items, books, records, receipts, notes, ledgers and other papers relating to the transportation, ordering, purchase, and distribution of controlled dangerous substances. Papers, tickets, notes, schedules, receipts, and other items relating to domestic and international travel. Books, records, receipts, bank statements and records, money drafts, letters of credit, money order and cashier's checks, receipts, passbooks, bank checks, safe deposit box keys, and other items evidencing the obtaining, secreting, transfer, and/or concealment of assets and the obtaining, secreting, transfer, concealment and/or expenditure of money United States currency, precious metals, jewelry, and financial instruments, including stocks and bonds in amounts indicative of the proceeds of illegal narcotics trafficking. Photographs of co-conspirators, of assets, and/or controlled substances. Indicia of occupancy, residency, and/or ownership of the premises described above, including, but not limited to, utility and telephone bills, canceled envelopes, and keys. Receipt for items evidencing the expenditure of the proceeds of drug distribution including, but not limited to, clothing, furniture, and electronic equipment. Receipts, bills, and money used in or incidental to the conduct or operation of controlled dangerous substance violations found in or upon said premises, outbuildings and vehicles.

E. Search and seize any weapons such as handguns, rifles, shotguns, ammunition, and related equipment such as, but not limited to, magazines, bayonets, bipods, tripods, ocular and laser-sighting scopes, etc, in addition to any and all electronic equipment, such as, but not limited to, computers, telex machines, facsimile machines, currency counting machines, telephone answering machines, pagers, PDAs, cell phones, and related manuals used to generate, transfer, count, record and/or store the information described above. Additionally, computer software, tapes and discs, *and the contents therein,* that contain the information generated by the aforementioned electronic equipment will need to be seized and examined, by persons qualified to do so, and in a laboratory setting, including but not limited to any and all electronic data processing and computer storage devices, such as central processing units, internal and peripheral storage devices such as fixed disks, external hard disks, floppy disk drives and diskettes, tape drives and tapes, optical storage devices, optical readers and scanning—devices, CD-ROM drives and compact disks and related hardware, digital cameras and digital storage media, operating logs, software and operating instructions or operating manuals, computer materials, software and programs used to communicate with other terminals via

This is where you would ask specifically to search for the items you expect will be found at the location.

telephone or other means, and any computer modems, monitors, printers, etc., *that may have been used while engaging in the distribution of controlled dangerous substances, and or any other controlled dangerous substance related activity*;

F. Arrest all persons found in or upon said premises who are participating in violations of the statutes hereinbefore cited.

G. Bring said persons, evidence, and paraphernalia before me, subscriber, or some other judge that of the state or county aforesaid, to be dealt with and disposed of according to law.

SUBSCRIBED AND SWORN TO, this _____ day of November in the YEAR OF OUR LORD, *Two Thousand and Three*.

Affiant

Detective James A. Henning No.0140
Caroline County Sheriff's Department—CID
Caroline County Drug Task Force

Confirmation by the judge that the officer was properly identified and that he/she had sworn to the affidavit under penalty of perjury.

Before me, a district/circuit court judge of the State of Maryland, in and for Caroline County, this _____ day of November, 2003, personally appeared Det James A. Henning, personally known to me or properly identified, and he made oath that the contents of the aforegoing application and affidavit are true and correct to the best of his knowledge.

Time   *Judge*

"NO KNOCK SEARCH WARRANTS: No knock search warrants are used to achieve the element of surprise on the suspect when executing the search warrant. During a normal search and seizure warrant execution you would need to knock and announce your police presence before entering the dwelling. With a no knock warrant the police are justified to simply enter the residence without the need to knock and announce their police presence. It's important to note that some jurisdictions are bound by their states constitution to not execute no knock warrants. The officer will need to contact their prosecutors' office to inquire if your state's constitution allows such a warrant to be executed in this manner.

No knock warrants are to be only used in exigent circumstances, which need to be clearly justified based on your investigation of the suspect. In the states that allow no knock warrants, i.e., Maryland, there are certain criteria that need to be met in order to execute this type of warrant. Some examples of situations that would justify an exigency to conduct a no knock warrant are:

1. *Destruction of evidence:* By obtaining statements made by the suspect directed to the CI, that he/she would attempt to discard or destroy any evidence if confronted by the police enables the no knock clause to be initiated. In addition, you can incorporate information through past encounters with the police where the suspect attempted to destroy or discard the evidence when approached or chased.

2. *Officer Safety:* If the suspect has a violent history of assaults, murder, or armed robbery, etc., then there

is a possible threat to the well-being of the officer's executing the search warrant. Another way that this criteria is met, is if you have done surveillance on the suspect's residence and you identify several individuals, either through photos, personal knowledge, or vehicle registration checks, and confirm through their criminal history that they themselves have been the subject of a violent crime then this also raises to the level of a no knock warrant. In addition if the CI explains that the suspect carries or has access to a weapon, this would also allow the investigator to obtain a no knock warrant.

3. *Countersurveillance:* The fact that the suspect continually looks out his windows for police, uses two-way radios, or performs "heat runs" (random saturation of the area to locate the presence of law enforcement) prior to buys occurring would validate the investigator to ask for a no knock warrant. This all shows a form of countersurveillance used by the suspect.

4. *Fleeing and Eluding Police:* If the suspect has been known in the past to flee from the police upon sight, whether on foot or in a vehicle, this will

meet the requirements for the no knock warrant requirement.

EXAMPLE OF INFORMATION NEEDED FOR "NO KNOCK" PARAGRAPH

PARAGRAPH EXAMPLE

35. That your affiant Henning, through the use of surveillance, confirmed that individuals involved in the illegal use and distribution of controlled dangerous substances, frequent the aforementioned residence and that these individuals have been arrested in the past for crimes of violence: Don Douglas Jones, has been arrested on two counts of resisting arrest; Antwain Bennett has been arrested for battery, first-degree attempted murder, and reckless endanger, wear and carry a handgun; Larry Cornell has been arrested for one count of battery. In addition, your affiant Henning was advised by CI No.2 and CSI No.1 that individuals distributing controlled dangerous substances at the aforementioned residence utilize persons as lookouts. These lookouts monitor for police presence in an effort to conceal their activity in anticipation of police intervention so they may discard any evidence if a police presence is detected, and/or to protect their product and proceeds. Further, CS No.1 explained that Don Douglas Jones has made the statement that a member of the

Be sure to document in the body of the affidavit the date, time, and location of the information contained in your no knock paragraph. This is just an example of what to put in your paragraph. Basically any of the four previous mentioned situations can be used here to justify your no knock clause and or service.

police department is going to get "shot" if the police do not back off with patrols in the Brooklyn, Federalsburg area.

ITEM "A" NO KNOCK EXAMPLE

If required by your state judges to ask for a no knock warrant, you would replace the first item A with this one that includes the bold print. Maryland leaves the discretion of executing a no knock warrant with the officer, based on the investigation and/or specific events just prior to the execution of the search warrant that justify a no knock entry.

A. Enter and search, **without the need for a knock or the announcement of a police presence,** the residence and outbuildings identified as 123 N. Sixth Street, Denton, Caroline County, Maryland; the vehicle identified as a white four-door 2001 Ford Taurus bearing Maryland registration 123-ABC, VIN No.: 123BDB46R11H585397; (as completely described above); as well as any motor vehicles that are located on said property, and/or any motor vehicles under the immediate control of Jonathon Michael Doe.

EXAMPLE OF THE SEARCH WARRANT

STATE OF MARYLAND
CAROLINE COUNTY

To: Detective James Henning, Caroline County Sheriff's Department, or any other law enforcement officer;

GREETINGS:

WHEREAS, it appears to me, the subscriber, the Honorable _____, judge of the Circuit Court/District Court of Maryland for Caroline County, State of Maryland, by the written information of the affiant Henning hereinafter named, which information is contained in the application and affidavit attached to this warrant, and made a part hereof, that there is probable cause to believe that a felony or misdemeanor is being committed, in that the laws relating to the illegal manufacturing, distribution, possession with the intent to distribute, and possession of controlled dangerous substances, as defined in the Maryland Code Annotated Criminal Law Article, Title 5 et seq. and Common Law Conspiracy to commit said crimes, dealing generally with controlled dangerous substances as amended and revised are being violated in and upon a certain residence identified as 123 North Sixth Street, Denton, Caroline County, Maryland; the vehicle identified as a white four-door 2001 Ford Taurus bearing Maryland registration ABC-123, VIN No.: 123BDB46R11H585397; and the individual identified as Jonathon Michael Doe, DOB: 08/14/84, W/M, 6' 00", 200 lbs. The residence is described as a white two-story single-family home with a black-colored roof. Directions to said residence are from the Denton, Sixth Street entrance, off of Maryland Route 404, follow in to the town limits of Denton for approximately a half mile. Said residence is located on the right side of the roadway directly across the street from Fresh Foods Deli convenience store.

Said residence is further described as having a covered porch, positioned on top of a concrete slab, with several steps leading up to the porch. There are several dark-colored shutters flanking each along the front and two brick chimneys positioned in the window center of the roof. The main door to the residence is a standard home door located along the front, which appears to open inward with a metal storm door attached. Furthermore, the dwelling afore described can be positively identified by your affiant Henning.

Notice that this portion is the exact same as what's listed in the affidavit. This will always remain the same.

I am satisfied that there is probable cause to believe that there is now being concealed certain property, namely controlled dangerous substances, including narcotics, hallucinogenic, and/or dangerous drugs on the person, premises, and vehicle described above and that the foregoing grounds for a search warrant exist.

The name of your affiant is James A. Henning, detective of the Caroline County Sheriff's Department, Criminal Investigation Division. Your affiant Henning is currently assigned to the Caroline County Drug Task Force. You are therefore, hereby commanded, with the necessary assistance to:

A. Enter and search the residence and outbuildings identified as 123 N. Sixth Street, Denton, Caroline County, Maryland; the vehicle identified as a white four-door 2001 Ford Taurus bearing Maryland registration 123-ABC, VIN No.: 123BDB46R11H585397; (as completely described above); as well as any motor vehicles that are located on said property, and/or any motor vehicles under the immediate control of Jonathon Michael Doe.

B. Search the person and clothing of Jonathon Michael Doe, DOB: 08/14/84, B/M, 6' 00", 200 lbs; as well as any other persons found in or upon said premises that may be participating in violations of the statutes hereinbefore cited, and who may be concealing evidence, paraphernalia, and controlled dangerous substances.

C. Open and search any safes, boxes, bags, luggage, compartments, storage units or things in the nature thereof, found in or upon said premises, outbuildings, and vehicles.

D. Seize all evidence, paraphernalia, controlled dangerous substances, papers, evidentiary items, books, records, receipts, notes, ledgers, and other papers relating to the transportation, ordering, purchase, and distribution of controlled dangerous substances. Papers, tickets, notes, schedules, receipts, and other items relating to domestic and international travel. Books, records, receipts, bank

If seeking a no knock warrant, you will need to add the phrase in here in here. Refer to sample A at the end of the affidavit.

This is where you would ask specifically to search for the items you expect will be found at the location. Notice that this is the exact same as what is listed in the affidavit. This will always be the same.

statements and records, money drafts, letters of credit, money order and cashier's checks, receipts, passbooks, bank checks, safe deposit box keys, and other items evidencing the obtaining, secreting, transfer, and/or concealment of assets and the obtaining, secreting, transfer, concealment and/or expenditure of money. United States currency, precious metals, jewelry, and financial instruments, including stocks and bonds in amounts indicative of the proceeds of illegal narcotics trafficking. Photographs of co-conspirators, of assets, and/or controlled substances. Indicia of occupancy, residency, and/or ownership of the premises described above, including, but not limited to, utility and telephone bills, canceled envelopes, and keys. Receipt for items evidencing the expenditure of the proceeds of drug distribution including, but not limited to, clothing, furniture, and electronic equipment. Receipts, bills, and money used in or incidental to the conduct or operation of controlled dangerous substance violations found in or upon said premises, outbuildings and vehicles.

E. Search and seize any weapons such as handguns, rifles, shotguns, ammunition, and related equipment such as, but not limited to, magazines, bayonets, bipods, tripods, ocular and laser-sighting scopes, etc., in addition to any and all electronic equipment, such as, but not limited to, computers, telex machines, facsimile machines, currency counting machines, telephone answering machines, pagers, PDAs, cell phones, and related manuals used to generate, transfer, count, record and/or store the information described above. Additionally, computer software, tapes and discs, *and the contents therein*, that contain the information generated by the aforementioned electronic equipment will need to be seized and examined, by persons qualified to do so, and in a laboratory setting, including but not limited to any and all electronic data processing and computer storage devices, such as central processing units, internal and peripheral storage devices such as fixed disks, external hard disks, floppy disk drives and diskettes, tape drives and tapes, optical storage devices, optical readers and scanning—devices, CD-ROM drives and compact disks and related hardware, digital cameras and digital storage media, operating logs, software and operating instructions or operating manuals, computer materials, software and programs used to communicate with other terminals via telephone or other means, and any computer modems, monitors, printers, etc., *that may have been used while engaging in the distribution of controlled dangerous substances, and or any other controlled dangerous substance related activity*;

F. Arrest all persons found in or upon said premises who are participating in violations of the statutes hereinbefore cited.

Continuation of items asking to search for.

G. Bring said persons, evidence, and paraphernalia before me, subscriber, or some other judge that of the state or county aforesaid, to be dealt with and disposed of according to law.

WHEREOF, fail not at your peril and have you then and there this warrant.

GIVEN under my hand this day of November in the year of our Lord, 2003.

Notice that the search warrant return is to be given back within ten days. This may be different in your state. Check with your local prosecutor's office to determine the exact time limit for your inventory return.

Further, you are hereby ordered to return a copy of said application / affidavit / search and seizure warrant, together with an inventory of the property seized, to me within ten days after the execution of this warrant; or if not served, to return this warrant to me promptly after its expiration, as required by law.

_____   _____

        Date and Time   Judge

2. *Document Warrant:* This warrant is used specifically to locate documents relating to the distribution of controlled dangerous substances. Some of the documents you would be looking for are:

- drug ledgers
- receipts of items paid in cash
- bank account statements
- and other hidden assets

There are many more items listed in a document warrant, which go hand in hand to locate evidence of hidden assets. Refer to the document warrant example and exhibit for a complete list.

Although a document warrant is a search warrant by nature, it is used in a different way. A document warrant is meant to search for "documentary" evidence at locations where the suspect is known (through investigation and surveillance) to reside, routinely frequent, or own. Unlike the standard search warrant, the suspect *does not* need to use this location to distribute the drugs, rather the suspect need only be associated to that location and that there is likelihood that items such as documentary evidence pertaining to the crime of distribution and possession of controlled dangerous substances are present at that location.

The great aspect of a document search warrant is that documents can be hidden or kept anywhere—well, so can drugs! The majority of the time when executing document search warrants, officers will find CDS or related paraphernalia hidden among such items.

EXAMPLE OF DOCUMENT
WARRANT AFFADAVIT

TO: The Honorable _____, judge of the Circuit Court/District Court of Maryland, for *INSERT NAME OF COUNTY HERE* County, State of Maryland.

> This paragraph briefly explains the type of evidence expected and your states article, title, or code for CDS violations.

Application is herewith made for a search and seizure warrant because there is probable cause to believe that laws, monies, records or accounts, ledgers, books, receipts, bank statements, and other proceeds as defined by *Maryland Code Annotated Criminal Law Article, Title 5 et seq. and Common Law Conspiracy to commit said crimes, dealing generally with controlled dangerous substances as amended and revised* are being violated, maintained, and stored for safekeeping at the following address;

> Be sure to put in you states article, title, or code for controlled dangerous substances.

> This paragraph lists the description and basic information of the location and/or vehicle that you wish to search

INSERT THE ADDRESS AND THE DECRIPTION OF HOUSE/BUSINESS OR OTHER TYPE OF LOCATION HERE, County, Maryland. And in the following vehicle;

YEAR OF VEHICLE, MAKE, MODEL, COLOR in color, Maryland Registration: XXXXXXX, VIN: XXXXXXXXXXXX. *INSERT DIRECTIONS TO THE LOCATION HERE* Furthermore, the *INSERT IF IT'S A HOUSE/BUSINESS OR OTHER TYPE OF LOCATION HERE* and vehicle afore described can be positively identified by your affiant *INSERT YOUR LAST NAME HERE*

List all you're training that you have received since you began your career in Law Enforcement and any college

EXPERTISE

The name of your affiant is *INSERT YOUR NAME HERE AND THE NAME OF YOUR AGENCY AND UNIT/DIVISION ASSIGNED WITH*. *NEXT FILL IN ALL YOUR TRAINING KNOWLEDGE AND EXPERIENCE*

Be sure to include the information that links your suspect to the location that you are seeking to search

BASIS FOR APPLICATION

In support of this Application, and the basis for probable cause, your affiant deposes and says: *INSERT THE FACTS OF YOUR INVESTIGATION HERE*

Based upon your affiant's training, experience, knowledge, and participation in financial investigations involving amounts of other controlled dangerous substances, I know:

1. That drug traffickers very often place assets in names other than their own to avoid detection of these assets by government agencies;
2. That drug traffickers very often place assets in corporate entities in order to avoid detection of these assets by government agencies;
3. That even though these assets are in other persons' names, the drug dealers actually own and continue to use these assets and exercise dominion and control over them;
4. That narcotics traffickers maintain books, records, receipts, notes, ledgers, airline tickets, money orders, and other papers relating to the transportation, ordering, sale, and distribution of

controlled dangerous substances. That narcotics traffickers commonly "front" (provide drugs on consignment) CDS to their clients. That the aforementioned books, records, receipts, notes, ledgers, etc., are maintained where the traffickers have ready access to them;

5. That it is common for large-scale drug dealers to secrete contraband, proceeds of drug sales, and records of drug transactions in secure locations within their residences and/or their businesses for their ready access and to conceal from law enforcement authorities;

6. The persons involved in large-scale drug trafficking conceal in their residences and businesses caches of drugs, large amounts of currency, financial instructions, precious metals, jewelry, and other items of value and/or proceeds of drug transactions, and evidence of financial transactions relating to obtaining, transferring, secreting, or the spending of large sums of money make from engaging in narcotics trafficking activities;

7. That when drug traffickers amass large proceeds from the sale of drugs that the drug traffickers attempt to legitimize these profits. He knows that to accomplish these goals, drug traffickers utilize domestic banks and their attendant services, securities, cashier's checks, money drafts, letter of credit, brokerage houses, real estate, shell corporations, and business fronts;

In this paragraph you're laying it out to the judge how drug dealers operate and the items and documents that they commonly utilize.

8. That marijuana and/or other CDS traffickers commonly maintain addresses or telephone numbers in books or papers which reflect names, addresses and/or telephone numbers of their associates in the trafficking organizations;

9. That drug traffickers take or cause to be taken photographs of them, their associates, their property, and their product. That these traffickers usually maintain these photographs in their possessions;

10. That the courts have recognized that unexplained wealth is probative evidence of crimes motivated by greed, in particular, trafficking in controlled substances;

Continuation of above explanations

11. That based on my training and experience, I know that drug traffickers commonly have in their possession, that is on their person, at their residences and/or their businesses, firearms, including but not limited to handguns, pistols, revolvers, rifles, shotguns, machine guns, and other weapons. Said firearms are used to protect and secure a drug traffickers property. Such property may include, but is not limited to, narcotics, jewelry, narcotic paraphernalia, books, records, U.S. currency, etc.

Therefore, as a result of you affiant's involvement in this investigation and his expertise and experience in the investigation of narcotics and dangerous drugs, your affiant believes there is presently concealed within the aforesaid premises and vehicle listed in the heading of this affidavit those items which are set forth in Exhibit A, attached, which items constitute evidence that relate to the illegal distribution and possession with intent to distribute controlled dangerous substance, monies, records or accounts, ledgers, books, receipts, bank statements and other proceeds as defined by Maryland Code Annotated Criminal Law Article, Title 5 et seq. and Common Law Conspiracy to commit said crimes, dealing generally with controlled dangerous substances as amended and revised

> This paragraph sums up the above information and reiterates the issues at hand

Your affiant, therefore prays that a search and seizure warrant be issued authorizing him, with the necessary and proper assistance, to:

I. Enter and search the premises and vehicle as completely described above;

J. Open and search any safes, boxes, bags, compartments, computers or things in the nature thereof *and the contents therein,* that contain the information generated by the aforementioned electronic equipment, found in or upon said premises and vehicle;

K. Seize all property listed in Exhibit A, attached hereto.

L. Bring said evidence and/or paraphernalia before me, subscriber, or some other judge that of the state or county aforesaid, to be dealt with and disposed of according to law.

> The itemized list to the right is what you are asking the judge to allow you to perform and search for. **Refer to "Exhibit A" at the end of the affidavit.**

SUBSCRIBED AND SWORN TO, this _____ **day of** *ENTER MONTH HERE* **in the YEAR OF OUR LORD,** *Two Thousand And Two (ENTER APPROPRIATE YEAR).*

This is the conclusion of the affidavit

_____
Affiant
ENTER TITLE / NAME / AND ID NUMBER
ENTER AGENCY / UNIT-DIVISION ASSIGNED

Confirmation by the judge that the officer was properly identified and that he/she had sworn to the affidavit under penalty of perjury.

Before me, a district court of Maryland/ circuit court, judge of the State of Maryland, in and for *ENTER COUNTY NAME* County, this _____ day of *ENTER MONTH/ YEAR*, personally appeared *ENTER YOUR TITLE AND NAME HERE*, personally known to me or properly identified, and he made oath that the contents of the a foregoing application and affidavit are true and correct to the best of his knowledge.

_____   _____
Date and Time   Judge

EXAMPLE OF DOCUMENT WARRANT "EXHIBIT LIST"

> This should be printed out on a separate piece of paper and attached to the affidavit and the warrant to be made a part of each.

EXHIBIT A
PROPERTY TO BE SEIZED

1. Books, records, receipts, notes, ledgers, and other papers relating to the transportation, ordering, purchase, and distribution of controlled dangerous substances.

2. Papers, tickets, notes, schedules, receipts, and other items relating to domestic and international travel.

3. Books, records, receipts, bank statements and records, money drafts, letters of credit, money order and cashier's checks, receipts, passbooks, bank checks, safe deposit box keys, and other items evidencing the obtaining, secreting, transfer, and/or concealment of assets and the obtaining, secreting, transfer, concealment and/or expenditure of money.

4. United States currency, precious metals, jewelry, and financial instruments, including stocks and bonds in amounts indicative of the proceeds of illegal narcotics trafficking.

5. Photographs of co-conspirators, of assets, and/or controlled substances.

6. Indicia of occupancy, residency, and/or ownership of the premises described above, including, but not limited to, utility and telephone bills, canceled envelopes, and keys.

7. Receipt for items evidencing the expenditure of the proceeds of drug distribution including, but not limited to, clothing, furniture, and electronic equipment.

8. Any electronic equipment, such as computers, telex machines, facsimile machines, currency counting machines, telephone answering machines, and related

manuals used to generate, transfer, count, record and/or store the information described above. Additionally, computer software, tapes, and information generated by the aforementioned electronic equipment.

9. Any controlled dangerous substances.

EXAMPLE OF DOCUMENT WARRANT

STATE OF *INSERT STATE HERE*
***INSERT COUNTY HERE* COUNTY**

To: **INSERT YOUR NAME AND RANK HERE*, *INSERT THE NAME OF YOUR AGENCY HERE**, or any other law enforcement officer;

GREETINGS:

WHEREAS, it appears to me, the subscriber, the Honorable _____, Judge of the Circuit Court/District Court of *INSERT STATE NAME* for *INSERT COUNTY'S NAME* County, State of *INSERT STATE NAME*, by the written information of the affiant *INSERT YOUR NAME HERE* hereinafter named, which information is contained in the application and affidavit attached to this warrant, and made a part hereof, that there is probable cause to believe that a felony or misdemeanor is being committed, in that the laws monies, records, or accounts, ledgers, books, receipts, bank statements, and other traceable proceeds as defined by *Maryland Code Annotated Criminal Law Article, Title 5 et. seq. and Common Law Conspiracy to commit said crimes, dealing generally with controlled dangerous substances as amended and revised* are being violated, maintained, and stored for safekeeping, at

> This paragraph briefly explains the type of evidence expected and your states article, title, or code for CDS violations. This will be the same as in the affidavit.

> Be sure to put in you state's article, title, or code for controlled dangerous substances.

This paragraph lists the description and basic information of the location and/or vehicle that you wish to search. This will be the same as in the affidavit

INSERT THE ADDRESS AND THE DECRIPTION OF HOUSE/ BUSINESS OR OTHER TYPE OF LOCATION HERE, County, Maryland. And in the following vehicle: *LIST YEAR OF VEHICLE, MAKE, MODEL, COLOR* in color, Maryland Registration: XXXXXXX, VIN: XXXXXXXXXXXX. *INSERT DIRECTIONS TO THE LOCATION HERE* Furthermore, the *INSERT IF IT'S A HOUSE/ BUSINESS OR OTHER TYPE OF LOCATION HERE* and vehicle afore-described can be positively identified by your affiant *INSERT YOUR LAST NAME HERE*.

I am satisfied that there is probable cause to believe that there is now being concealed in a certain premises, which items constitute evidence that relate to the illegal distribution and possession with intent to distribute controlled dangerous substance, monies, records or accounts, ledgers, books, receipts, bank statements, and other traceable proceeds as defined by *Maryland Code Annotated Criminal Law Article, Title 5 et seq. and Common Law Conspiracy to commit said crimes, dealing generally with controlled dangerous substances as amended and revised*, in the above-described residence and that the foregoing grounds for application for issuance of the search warrant exist and is attached hereto and made a part hereof.

The name of your affiant is *_INSERT YOUR NAME AND RANK HERE_*, of the *INSERT THE NAME OF YOUR AGENCY AND UNIT/DIVISION ASSIGNED WITH*. Your affiant *_INSERT YOUR NAME_* is currently assigned to the *INSERT THE NAME OF YOUR AGENCY AND UNIT/DIVISION ASSIGNED WITH*. You are therefore, hereby commanded, with the necessary assistance to:

A. Enter and search the premises as completely described above;

B. Open and search any safes, boxes, bags, compartments, computers or things in the nature thereof **and the contents therein,** that contain the information generated by the aforementioned electronic equipment, found in or upon said premises and vehicle;

C. Seize all property listed in Exhibit A, attached hereto;

D. Bring said evidence and/or paraphernalia before me, subscriber, or some other judge that of the state or county aforesaid, to be dealt with and disposed of according to law.

WHEREOF, fail not at your peril and have you then and there this warrant.

GIVEN under my hand this _____ day of *_ENTER MONTH HERE_* in the year of our Lord, *_ENTER APPROPRIATE YEAR_*.

Notice that the search warrant return is to be given back within ten days. This may be different in your state. Check with your local prosecutor's office to determine the exact time limit for your inventory return.

Further, you are hereby ordered to return a copy of said application/affidavit/search and seizure warrant, together with an inventory of the property seized, to me within ten days after the execution of this warrant; or if not served, to return this warrant to me promptly after its expiration, as required by law.

Date and Time	Judge

SEALING SEARCH AND SEIZURE WARRANTS

The state attorney's/prosecutor's office is the only law enforcement entity that can petition the court to have a search and seizure warrant sealed from the suspect and from the general public record. The sealing of a search warrant allows anonymity about the specifics of the investigation and hides informant information from the suspect to prevent immediate or possible disclosure. This should only be used under circumstances that would lead you to believe that divulging the search warrant application to the suspect would hinder other ongoing investigations or pose a serious risk to the safety of officers or informants involved. There is a time limit for which you will need to give the suspect a copy of the application concerning his/her case. For example: in Maryland you will need to serve the application to the suspect within thirty days of executing the search warrant. Check with your local prosecutor's office on the requirements for sealing a search warrant. Refer to the end of this chapter for examples of a petition and order to seal a search warrant.

THE "GOOD FAITH" EXCEPTION TO SEARCH WARRANTS

What is the "good faith" exception? And how does it apply to law enforcement officers. The good faith exception is exercised when an officer, through his investigation, develops what he believes to be probable cause to receive a search warrant. And in that belief the officer has the search warrant reviewed and subsequently signed by a neutral and detached magistrate, which then becomes a valid court order to complete the officer's objective within the "scope" of the warrant's parameters. The search warrant, under the good faith exception will remain valid, even if later the court found certain information used in the affidavit turned out to be wrong. This is true, so long as the officer's assertions contained in the affidavit that was submitted to the judge was perceived to be truthful and to the best of the officer's knowledge at the time he submitted the warrant to the judge, and including up to the time the officer execute the warrant itself. If later found that the officer attempted to mislead or lie to the court in the affidavit that was given to the judge for review, all evidence obtained as a result of said search warrant would be discarded and subsequently fall under the "exclusionary rule."

When talking about situations such as this, there are two landmark United States Supreme Court cases that deal with the good faith exception to the exclusionary rule:

- United States v. Leon, 468 U.S. 897, 104 S. Ct. 3405 (1984), and
- Massachusetts v. Sheppard, 468 U.S. 981, 104 S. Ct. 3424 (1984)

"The basic purpose of the Exclusionary Rule is to deter police misconduct, not to punish the errors of judges and magistrates. It is neither intended nor able to cure the invasion of the defendant's rights, which he has suffered. The rule thus operates as a judicially drafted remedy designed to safeguard, through its deterrent effect on the police, Fourth Amendment rights generally rather than as a personal constitutional right of the person so affected" (Id. Leon).

Therefore, when a police officer, acting in objective *good faith*, has obtained a search warrant from a judge and has acted within its scope, there is no police misconduct, and thus, nothing to deter (suppress later in court)" (Id. Leon at 3431). "Penalizing the police officer for the judge's error cannot logically contribute to the deterrence of Fourth Amendment violations" (Id.).

It is important to note that this is a federal guideline and is subject to restrictions by the state courts in their constitutions. The state courts can provide a greater protection to the privacy interest of their citizens than that afforded under the parallel provisions of the United States Constitution. Be sure to check with your local prosecutor's office for further information.

PETITION TO SEAL APPLICATION
AND AFFIDAVIT FOR

SEARCH AND SEIZURE WARRANT

Be sure to check with your prosecutor's office to find out what article or section number that deals with sealing a search warrant, and the period that the warrant can be sealed for.

*The State of ***INSERT YOUR STATE HERE***, by ***INSERT THE STATE'S ATTORNEY/PROSECUTOR'S NAME WHO IS APPLYING FOR THIS***, state's attorney for ***INSERT THE NAME OF YOUR COUNTY HERE*** County, respectfully petitions that this honorable court seal the attached application and affidavit for search and seizure warrant for a period of thirty days pursuant to Article 27, Section 551(d) of the Maryland Annotated Code, Maryland Rule 4-601(b) and corresponding Criminal Law Articles and in support hereof states:*

1. Disclosure of the contents of the application and affidavit for the attached search and seizure warrant at the time it is executed could jeopardize the persons providing the information contained in the application and affidavit;
2. Individuals associated with the targets of the attached search and seizure warrant are targets of ongoing criminal investigations particularly involving controlled dangerous substance violations;
3. Divulging the contents of the application and affidavit for the attached search and seizure warrant could jeopardize the ongoing criminal investigations being conducted by the Kent County Drug Task Force;

WHEREFORE, the State of ***INSERT YOUR STATE HERE*** respectfully petitions that this honorable court seal the

attached application and affidavit for search and seizure warrant
for a period of thirty days.

***INSERT NAME OF STATE'S
ATTORNEY/PROSECUTER HERE***
State's Attorney for ***INSERT NAME OF
COUNTY HERE*** County

ORDER TO SEAL APPLICATION AND AFFIDAVIT FOR SEARCH AND SEIZURE WARRANT

*Upon consideration of the State of ***INSERT YOUR STATE HERE*** petition to seal the application and affidavit for search and seizure warrant, it is hereby*

Be sure to get the article or section number that deals with sealing a search warrant, and the period of time that the warrant can be sealed for

ORDERED, pursuant to Article 27, Section 551(d) of the Maryland Annotated Code, Maryland Rule 4-601(b) and the corresponding Criminal Law Article, this ____ day of ***INSERT THE MONTH AND YEAR HERE***, that the attached application and affidavit for the search and seizure warrant be sealed for a period of thirty days, and it is

FURTHER ORDERED that at the expiration of the thirty days the application and affidavit will be served upon the individuals residing at the warrant location and all other persons searched and arrested pursuant to the attached search and seizure warrant.

The Honorable *INSERT THE NAME OF THE JUDGE HERE*
Judge of the District/ Circuit Court

Evidence Collection and Processing

When dealing with the collection of evidence at a search warrant (crime scene), or consent search, it is imperative that a through and proper documentation of the area is completed. The officer needs to recreate, in words, the crime scene so that later at trial it is properly conveyed to the judge or jury. The slightest mistake made at the crime scene, no mater how trivial it may seem, will most likely allow a defense attorney to blow it out of proportion to confuse a jury into swaying toward the defense.

The following procedures are to be used as a guide for the officer to conduct a thorough and complete crime scene investigation, geared toward narcotics situations.

1. ***DOCUMENT TIMES:***

    The investigating officer should document the following events:

    - the time the *search warrant was executed,*
    - the time you physically *entered the residence,*
    - the time that *Miranda Rights were given to the suspect(s),*
    - and the time you *exited the residence (completed the crime scene).*

    The above-listed times are imperative when it comes to trial. On the stand, the officer will most certainly need

to testify to their actions conducted at the scene. Having the exact time of the above-listed events will map out for the court the various actions taken during your search. In addition, an officer that has specific times documented will most certainly add to his or hers credibility in the eyes of the court. The rule of thumb is *"if it isn't documented, it never happened"*
SO DOCUMENT EVERYTHING!

2. ***CRIME SCENE LOG:***

A crime scene log is just a piece of paper that is used to write down specific information concerning placement and the location of the individuals on scene. The following are things the officer should document once the scene is secured after initial entry:

- ***DOCUMENT THE LOCATION OF SUSPECTS:*** If a SWAT team was used, be sure to write down the name of the SWAT officer who found or detained each individual. In addition, document where each individual was found upon entry and what action did that individual display when the team made entry (i.e., ran down the hall, sitting at kitchen table, lying in bed, etc.) This is very important when it comes to trial. For example, your SWAT team enters the house and detains several individuals inside. You enter the residence and find cocaine sitting on the living room table and several suspects scattered throughout the residence, nowhere near the CDS. How can you put any or all suspects in proximity of the CDS? Contact the members of the SWAT team and find out each suspect's initial location upon entry. After asking the members of the team you find that one of the suspects who you made contact with in the back bedroom was in fact the one sitting at the table upon entry bagging the cocaine. The SWAT member advised that he had ran from the SWAT team upon entry and made it to the back bedroom where he was subsequently detained. The others were found in separate rooms. Now you know that by asking your team members the suspect's initial location upon entry, you can positively identify whom to charge and accurately document the suspect's proximity to the CDS and their subsequent actions in your report. Be sure to name the team members that gave you that information in your report in the event he is needed later at trial.

- *ASSIGN PERSONEL TO EACH AREA:* Once the SWAT team has cleared and all individuals are detained and positioned in a "safe area" (an area that has been previously checked for contraband and weapons) the investigator should assign his personnel to their perspective areas to begin the search. For example, send one person to search the bedroom, another to search the bathroom, etc. It is very important that each officer searching knows not to disturb any of the items found, unless absolutely necessary. If the item is moved or disturbed (i.e., unloading a handgun) then the searching officer should notify the seizing officer of his actions. This in turn will be documented in your notes to depict the original status of the evidence and who altered it.

3. *CRIME SCENE SEARCH PATERNS:* The following search patterns should be used to effectively search specific areas indoors and outdoors.

- *STRIP METHOD (OUTDOOR):* This method is commonly used for outdoor scenes involving a team of searchers. It is completed by setting up lanes or strips for the searchers to follow. By doing this, each searcher can scan their strip/lane thoroughly. A strip is designated by each searcher standing with their arms out to the sides, at arm's length of one another. This is a very good method to use when looking for evidence such as baggies of drugs thrown away by a suspect while chasing them. Refer to the diagram below.

STRIP METHOD

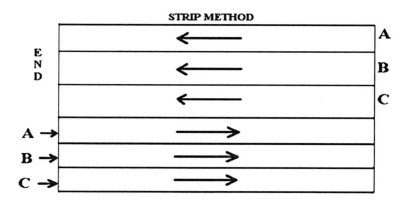

- *GRID METHOD (OUTDOOR):* The grid method is similar to the strip method, only you complete two passes in different directions to complete the search. This is the most thorough method of searching because you are going over the area twice, thus considerably reducing the risk that an evidence item would be overlooked. To complete this search you will need to conduct a strip search first of the area. Once the first search is complete you will then conduct a second strip search orienting your team at right angles to your initial strip search. Although tedious and time consuming, this method will ensure that no evidence was missed at the scene. Refer to the diagram below.

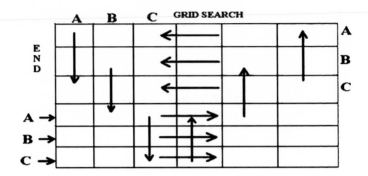

- ***ZONE METHOD (INDOOR AND OUTDOOR):***
  This method is commonly used by officers searching
  residences and automobiles. In this, you will simply
  divide up an area in four quadrants. Then assign your
  designated officers to search each section. If an area
  calls for additional personnel to search, the quadrants
  can be divided up into four additional sections. The
  purpose of this is to ensure that each officer
  thoroughly searching his or hers designated area.
  Refer to the diagram below.

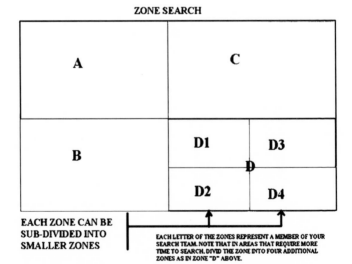

ZONE SEARCH

EACH ZONE CAN BE SUB-DIVIDED INTO SMALLER ZONES

EACH LETTER OF THE ZONES REPRESENT A MEMBER OF YOUR SEARCH TEAM. NOTE THAT IN AREAS THAT REQUIRE MORE TIME TO SEARCH, DIVID THE ZONE INTO FOUR ADDITIONAL ZONES AS IN ZONE "D" ABOVE.

- **SPIRAL METHOD (OUTDOOR):** The spiral method is meant to search large-scale areas to locate objects that easily stand out. This is done by the search team starting in the center of the crime scene and making a spiral path outward. The spiral method is not to be used on indoor searches; rather the zone method is the most through in those instances.

1. **DOCUMENT THE LOCATION OF CDS/ITEMS:** Once the seizing officer is certain that all evidence is located, the documentation of the evidence comes next.

    1. *PHOTOGRAPH THE AREA:* Take general pictures of each room or area to document the condition of the scene before your assigned personnel collecting evidence disturbed it. Another method used is video taping the scene in the same way. Both methods of documenting the scene are acceptable and equally useful.

    2. *PHOTOGRAPH THE ITEM:* After conducting the search of the area and locating all the items of evidence. The seizing officer will need to photograph the location and the specific item that is considered evidence. Include in the photo, rulers, photo scales, and number markers. The original position and condition of the evidence may become an issue later in court.

    3. *LAYOUT SKETCHES:* These drawings illustrate the location and relationship of the various items of evidence and assist in orientating the reader of the reports as to the layout of the residence or area in question. Measurements are not important in layout sketches, as the purposes of these sketches are to provide a visual framework for the photographs taken. The sketch is initially hand drawn on scrap paper while at the scene and can be transformed into

more detail later. Make sure to document on the sketch the locations where the suspects were initially found upon entry, not after the scene is secure. Below is an example of a crime scene layout sketch.

1324 Rolling Brook Road, Denton, MD

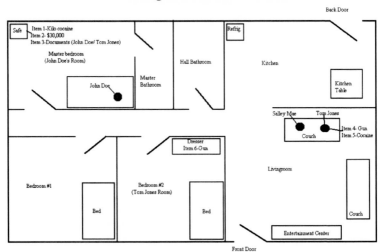

2.   *THE RECORDING AND COLLECTION OF EVIDENCE:*

- Be sure that the item is photographed and documented on the layout sketch and evidence inventory (list) return form before collection. The evidence inventory return is just a list and description of the items you have seized, the location, and item number given to that piece of evidence. An example inventory entry is: *"Item No.1: One glass smoking device, suspected CDS pipe, containing suspect marijuana residue; located in the master bedroom nightstand, top draw."* This is then turned into the judge within your state's specified time limit per statutory guidelines (i.e., Maryland's statutory time limit is within ten days from the time the warrant is served). A blank evidence inventory return form, both cover sheet and inventory list, is included at the end of this chapter.

- When collecting evidence the seizing officer should mark their initials on the item of evidence itself whenever possible. If this is not practical for reasons of size, shape, contamination, etc., then the container in which the evidence is found or stored should be marked with the officer's initials. When giving the evidence you marking you should only use permanent markers. Ballpoint or felt-tip pens tend to rub off or fade. In addition, a citizen turning in an item of evidence should be initialed by that citizen followed by the officer's initials who subsequently received the item.

- And most importantly, keep all evidence separated in different bags to avoid cross-contamination. Unless a group of items are located in the same container. A rule of thumb is: "If it's found together, it stays together." The reason for this is that the evidence has been found mixed with other evidence so the cross-contamination cannot be helped. For instance, you locate several pipes found together in a jewelry box that appear to have some sort of residue inside suspected CDS. For evidence collection purposes, the several pipes are going to be logged under one item number. You log all three pipes under item No.1, and place it in the bag. When you get back to the office to complete the packaging process, you will individually package each pipe in their own individual plastic bag (a bag cut to the size of the item, then heat sealed closed) and label the pipes individually, items No.1, 1A, and 1B. So as you can see, the pipes were found together and kept together when logged in at the crime scene. But back at your office, you will need to break them down into specific item numbers so the lab knows which item to test and which one not to.

ESTABLISHING POSSESSION OVER EVIDENCE

Oftentimes when officers execute search warrants or consent searches at residences or within vehicles, there are several individuals in the immediate area of a piece of evidence or no one present at all. This causes a problem when it comes to determining whom to place under arrest for the violation. It is for this reason you would need to investigate further and search for other forms of evidence that would make a connection to the suspect(s), actually, constructively, or jointly.

1. ***ACTUAL (DIRECT) POSSESSION:*** This is the most easiest to prove due to the fact that the suspect would physically possess the evidence on their person. An example of this is the suspect having a bag of cocaine in his/her pocket.

2. ***CONSTRUCTIVE POSSESSION:*** Is the ability to reduce an object (evidence) to actual possession. Constructive possession can be shown through *direct or circumstantial evidence* Establishing two factors accomplishes this by showing that the suspect possessed a reasonable *knowledge* and *control over the item or location* The item needs not be in the actual possession of the suspect but within his/her reach or in a location where they are storing it for future use. There are many ways of showing that a person was in constructive possession of an item.

   DISTANCE/PROXIMITY: The distance that an item is located from the suspect's position. An example is finding a bag of marijuana stuffed down in between a sofa cushion where the suspect was sitting upon entry. Or locating a bag of cocaine under the driver's seat of the suspect's vehicle for which he had just been driving. Another example that is more often encountered is, several individuals sitting around a table with cocaine on it. In this instance, every person technically possesses the knowledge of the drugs on the table and can easily exercise power and control over the substances themselves. It's important to note though that in some instances the mere presence or association to the location will not establish constructive possession. In other words, knowledge and control means more than "being where the action is," when your talking about a group of individuals allegedly involved. The officer should investigate each individual separately and take note of subtle observations and information obtained from each. To establish constructive possession to the item when distance/proximity is at issue, you will need to prove that not only did the individual know of the item, but was in a position or had the ability to exercise control over said item. Knowledge of the items existence is meant in terms of either directly or circumstantially, where the courts have established that knowledge of the item in question can be evaluated under what a reasonable person would determine. In that, the court takes a common sense approach to evaluating the totality of the circumstances to make its determination whether the individual was in a position to exercise domain or control over the evidence.

Case Concerning Distance, Proximity, and Association

United States v. Caballero
United States Court of Appeals
712 F. 2d 126 (5ᵗʰ Cir. 1983)

This case dealt with the defendant's mere presence or association with those who actually possessed or controlled the illegal substance and whether it rose to the level of constructive possession of marijuana.

The court clearly made it known that the mere presence or association of an individual with those who are found to be in actual possession or control over a controlled substance *will not* automatically result in a constructive possession situation. That the presence at a residence, or simply his/her proximity to the drug, is alone insufficient to establish constructive possession. To establish constructive possession, the government must show not only that the individual knew of the presence of the *drugs*, "but that he was in a position to exercise dominion and control over them" (United States v. Dingle, 114 F.3d. 307, 310 [D.C. Cir. 1997]).

CLOTHING: When searching in a room where evidence is located, take note of the various clothing in that location. An example would be if CDS is located in a metal box in the bedroom closet, the officer should document the style of clothing hanging up. In this case if you notice that within this closet there are all male clothing present or items belonging to the male party, then this would show that the suspect has control over this area. To go a step further, document the size of the shirts or pants and compare them to your suspect. This will strengthen your constructive possession evidence when it comes to trial.

Case Concerning Clothing

United States v. James
United States Court of Appeals
764 F. 2d 885 (D.C. Cir. 1985)

Police learned that the defendant was selling quantities of cocaine from his Washington DC residence. A search warrant was obtained and subsequently executed. As the officers knocked and announced their presence, they heard from within what they believed to be a person running down the backstairs. They immediately gained entry and made their way down the hallway to the basement. They found that the basement was separated in two distinct areas—a washroom on one end and the other a makeshift bedroom that had a sheet draped from the ceiling enabling privacy for sleeping quarters. While in the sleeping quarters part, they observed an individual trying to hide behind a bookcase, who was later identified as Thomas James. After subduing James they had him get dressed to be brought upstairs with the rest of the people located in the house. James went to a rack that had numerous articles of clothing hung from it and retrieved several articles of clothing. A search of the rest of the clothing that was hanging revealed 10,780 milligrams of marijuana laced with PCP in one of the jackets, and in another article of clothing there were seven tinfoil packets containing a total of 2,420 milligrams of marijuana laced with PCP. Additional items of CDS were located scattered in various hiding location found in the sleeping quarters area. It is important to note that the clothing hanging on this rack, for which the defendant James had retrieved several garments from, were all the same basic size that matched an individual of James's size and build.

The court recognized that "proximity may, under certain circumstances, amount to constructive possession" that "possession of a narcotic drug may be either actual or constructive . . . Constructive possession may be shown through direct or circumstantial evidence of dominion and control over the contraband . . . and may be found to exist where the evidence supports a finding that the person charged with possession was knowingly in a position, or had the right to exercise 'dominion or control' over the drug" (Id. [quoting United States v. Lawson, 682 F.2d 1012, 1017 [D.C. Cir. 1982]).

DOCUMENTS: The placement of documents in and around a location where CDS is found can show control over a certain item. While searching these locations, the officer should document and seize papers that have the name of individuals listed on them. An example would be located in a spare bedroom;

inside of a book bag you find numerous quantities of drugs along with a scale and packaging materials. You find a pay stub in one of the pockets of the bag that has the name of your suspect written on it. This shows constructive possession over the items located in the bag.

STATEMENTS/OBSERVATIONS: Oftentimes talking with the suspect or individuals located at the scene will give you the ability to associate constructively the possession of an item in question. Of course after Miranda Rights are read to the suspect, inquire as to access to the residence and how long they have lived or stayed at that location. In other instances, individuals besides the suspect located at the scene may explain who in fact possessed the evidence, basically playing them against each other, seeing who will tell on whom!

In addition to speaking with the suspects, take note of their behavior: Do they appear to be under the influence of a controlled substance? Does their breath smell like smoke after they have told you that they are not a smoker? Or is there a white-colored residue (suspected cocaine) under their nostrils? These observations should be documented along with other information to properly show constructive possession.

3. **JOINT CONSTRUCTIVE POSSESSION:** Is when more then one person has possession of an item at the same time. Joint possession is most commonly found when an item is located in a common area (residence or vehicle) where access is "jointly" shared—showing that both parties involved, each possessed the knowledge and control over the specific item. For example: Police raid a residence and find in the living room next to the television stand a one-foot tall water bong. The fact that the item was found in a common area immediately apparent to *all individuals residing at the residence*, as well as having ready access to the item itself, shows that they shared jointly the possession of the item.

OTHER CASES CONCERNING CONSTRUCTIVE POSSESSION

- U.S. v. Brett,
  United States Court of Appeals,
  872 F.2d 1365 (8th Cir. 1989)
  "The holder of the key, be it to the dwelling, vehicle or motel room in question, has constructive possession of the contents therein" (Id. at 1369 n.3).
- U.S. v. Zabalaga,
  United States Court of Appeals,
  834 F.2d 1062 (D.C. Cir. 1987)
  "Explained that the keys to a locked car where drugs were found indicated constructive possession."
- U.S. v. Perlaza,
  United States Court of Appeals,
  818 F.2d 1354 (7th Cir. 1987)
  "Keys to a motel room where drugs were seized indicated constructive possession."
- U.S v. Martinez,
  United States Court of Appeals,
  588 F.2d 495 (5th Cir. 1979)
  "Key to the trunk of a car found sufficient even when defendant was not the owner of the car nor in the car at the time contraband was found."

METHODS USED TO MAKE YOUR CASE

1. *USE OF ULTRAVIOLET LIGHT:* An alternate light source can be used when attempting to locate trace evidence of cocaine on various items such as skin, clothes, carpets, etc. Cocaine hydrochloride (powder) and crack cocaine will fluoresce under an ultraviolet light source and immediately become apparent to the officer. This method works best on carpets when searching vehicles. An officer

looking for trace evidence of drug use can utilize the
ultraviolet light source and scan the floorboards of the
vehicle. Oftentimes users will leave behind crumbs (small
pieces) caused by breaking apart the crack cocaine,
which become scattered throughout the vehicle over
time. If not for the use of the light source it would most
likely go undetected. You can obtain these light sources
at local specialty shops such as Radio Shack or other
electronic stores. A particular lens that can be placed
on the end of an officer's flashlight is called the Blue
Max lens. This lens converts the standard spectrum of
light to ultraviolet. The officer then needs to use
eyewear/goggles that have *amber* lenses to assist in the
observations.

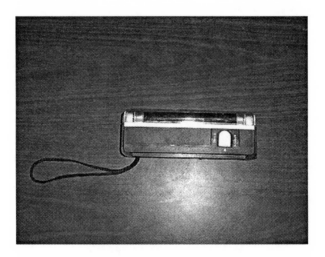

2. *FUMING TANK:* Superglue or Cyanoacrylate Fuming is
a method of making fingerprints visible on nonporous
surfaces. As a result of this method the fingerprints will
appear white in color along the surface you are fuming.
The superglue clings to the oils present in the fingerprint
and actually turns it into a permanent cast. In this form it
can be dusted, lifted, and photographed, or even washed

with laser sensitive dyes such as Rhodamine 6G and viewed with lasers or other alternate light sources. Many items found on search warrants and trash rips can be fumed for latent prints. In regards to evidence from trash rips, this method allows the investigator to identify the individual who had control over the evidence in question.

A fuming tank is a container that allows items/ evidence to be fumed for latent prints. Although there are many different styles of fuming tanks on the market, you can build one yourself as an aid in your investigations. All you need is the following materials:

- an aquarium
- a heating source like a coffee cup warmer or hot plate
- aluminum foil ashtrays or aluminum foil made into a tray
- and a piece of wood or plastic to make a cover that completely seals the top to keep all fumes inside.

Start off with an aquarium of your choice. It can be any size you desire, but remember that the bigger the tank, the more superglue you will need to completely fill the space within.

Next, construct a top that is able to complete a seal to prevent the fumes from leaking out. Wood, plastic, or Plexiglas will suffice. A small notch in the lid will need to be made to allow for the electric cable leading from the heating element.

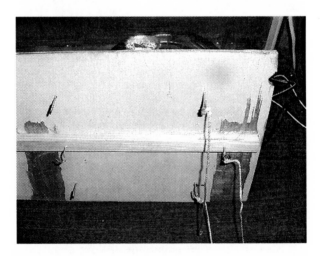

On the lid you can place hooks attached with string so items can be suspended within the tank and ensure that all surfaces are treated.

Then place an aluminum foil (disposable) ashtray on the heating element. You can also use standard household aluminum foil and mold it into a tray, as shown above in the picture. This is what will hold the superglue in place while it is heating up.

Once your evidence is in place within the tank, turn the heating element on. Place a quarter-sized amount of superglue on the tray You do not want to have the heater so hot that it will burn the glue. The optimal temperature is when you notice fumes rising from the tray ultimately filling the tank. After forty-five minutes to an hour, you will notice white-colored fingerprints over the item you have just processed. At this point you will need to package the evidence and forward it to the crime lab for further latent identification. It is important to note that evidence processed in this fashion should not be placed in plastic bags and forwarded to the lab. Instead, place the item in a paper bag, which will better preserve the evidence you have just processed.

WARNING: Cyanoacrylate fuming can be hazardous to your health if vapors are inhaled. At all times, proper ventilation should be used to prevent overexposure. In addition, do not attempt to process your evidence in this manner around open flames.

3. *MAGNETIC FINGERPRINT POWDER:* Oftentimes an officer will come across a drug ledger or some other paper document of interest. Standard fingerprint methods will not work properly. In this case, the use of magnetic fingerprint powder will give the desired results by revealing identifiable latent prints. The device used to complete this task is called a Magna Brush, which utilizes magnetic filings. When you have a document that needs to be processed, lay the document on a nonmetal surface (preferably wood) and dip the Magna Brush into the filings. Next, lightly brush the surface. You will immediately notice latent fingerprints appear on the document that can be later compared to your suspect.

4. *CASTINGS (SHOE PRINTS):* In outdoor marijuana growing operations, suspects will commonly leave subtle clues. One such clue is footprints left at the scene by the suspect. In less then thirty minutes you can obtain a cast of the suspect's shoe, which will later help in positively identifying the suspect and further strengthen your case in court. There are two materials used for casting of footwear and tire impressions—Plaster of Paris or dental stone. Dental stone will produce finer detail in your impressions and is inherently a stronger material when set. Both materials will produce casts of sufficient quality for the lab to conduct comparisons. Below are directions on preparing the impression for casting, while using Plaster of Paris.

    Preparation of the impression: Make up a retention wall to surround the impression. It is important that your retention wall is not higher than two inches due to the fact that it will interfere with pouring the cast. A retention wall can be easily made out of cardboard. Next, locate small twigs/sticks that will be used to strengthen and support the cast in its final state. The foot impression in its initial state is fragile and extreme care is to be used. A trick of the trade used to strengthen the impression before the plaster is added is to spray the impression with hairspray. *Do not* use the aerosol hair spray. Instead use the pump version. Aerosol sprays will damage the impression due to the force of the spray coming out.

Mixing the plaster:

- Get a two-pound coffee can or a container of the same size and fill it one-third of the way with water.
- Slowly add the plaster into the container, mixing slowly with a paddle, careful to avoid lumps and bubbles.
- Continue to stir till the plaster reaches the consistency of pancake batter. This should all be done next to where your impression is located, due to this material will start to harden. A mix too thick will harden quickly; a mix to thin will take forever to dry. A typical footprint will consume four pounds of plaster, a quart of water, and thirty minutes to set.

Pouring the plaster mix: *Next comes pouring the plaster mix into the impression. Use an old clipboard or large putty spatula to assist in the pouring of the material.*

- Hold the clipboard, or putty spatula approximately two inches above the imprint and slightly tipped at an angle.
- Then pour the plaster mixture on top of the impression, starting at the edge (heel or toe portion), careful not to cause any waves in the plaster.
- Then place the twigs/sticks on top of the first layer of plaster.
- If needed, an additional batch of plaster can be made and poured on to the first layer when it has firmed up.

- Lastly, when the material has firmed up, inscribe your initials and item number on the top for identifying marks.

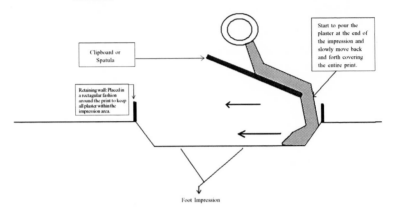

Foot Impression

Final Product: Once the cast has been made and successfully removed allow it to dry for twenty-four to forty-eight hours or longer if necessary. Do not attempt to remove soil or clean the cast because this will cause damage to the impression and not accurately depicted the exact impression left at the scene.

5. *HIDDEN COMPARTMENT CABLES:* Sgt. Michael Lewis of the Maryland State Police, Drug Interdiction Unit, developed this method of uncovering hidden compartments in vehicles, which has since proved invaluable in this field of narcotics investigation. The cables are meant to bypass the hidden compartment's electronic concealment system by connecting the cables directly to the battery of the vehicle and the other end connected to the motor controlling the compartments entry or hydraulics system.

Making the cables is simple enough. Go to your local electronics store, such as Radio Shack, and get at least ten feet of electrical wire. Next, get two small alligator clips and to large alligator clips. Attach the smaller clips to one end and the larger clips to the other end. When a compartment is located, place the larger clips on the vehicles battery. Then run the cable to the compartment's motor or hydraulic system. You may have to strip back the motor's wires to get a good connection. Once the cable is connected and power is supplied directly to the compartment's motor, it should open to reveal the hidden contents inside. If you hear a humming or buzzing sound from the suspected compartment, reverse the cable's positive and negative clips. This should correct the problem and cause the compartment to unlock/open.

(INSERT YOUR DEPARTMENT'S NAME HERE)

SEARCH WARRANT INVENTORY
REPORT AND RETURN

The attached list constitutes an official inventory of those items seized from:

_____

_____

(persons, premises, conveyance)

, as a result of a district/circuit court search warrant, being executed on _____ at _____ a.m./p.m.

                (Date)   (Time)

This search warrant inventory was prepared by: _____ and in the presence of: _____.

(Seizing Officer)   (Witness)

I hereby acknowledge receipt of a copy of the attached inventory as presented to me by: _____.

                        (Seizing Officer)

_____   _____   _____

(Signature of Recipient)   (Date)   (Time)

☐ Note: Check block if location of search warrant was unoccupied and copy left in conspicuous location.

This section to be completed only on official return

I swear that this inventory is a true and detailed account of all the property taken by me on the warrant.

_____
(Signature of Officer)

Subscribed and sworn to and returned before me this:_____ day of _____ 20_____.

_____
District/Circuit Court Judge in and for
_____ County, Maryland.

DISTRIBUTION OF COPIES
Issuing judge
Officer
Recipient

(INSERT YOUR DEPARTMENT'S NAME HERE)

EVIDENCE INVENTORY FORM

Primary Location: _____ Page: _____ Of _____

List item number, specific location, and description for items seized.

Item No. _____ _____

_____

Item No. _____ _____

_____

Item No. _____ _____

_____

Item No. _____ _____

_____

Item No. _____ _____

_____

Item No. _____ _____

_____

Item No. _____ _____

_____

Item No. _____ _____

_____
(Seizing Officer's Signature)

DISTRIBUTION OF COPIES
Issuing judge
Officer
Recipient

References

Miller, Gary J. (1997). *Drugs and the Law (Second Edition)*. Fl: J&B Gould Publications.

Bloom, R. & Brodin, M. (1996). *Criminal Procedure, Examples & Explanations (Second Edition)*. New York: Aspen Publishers Inc.

Ogle, Robert R. (1995). *Crime Scene Investigation & Physical Evidence Manual (Second Edition)*.

Lyman, Michael D. (1993). *Practical Drug Enforcement, Procedures and Administration*. Fl: CRC Press.

Holtz, Larry E. (2001). *Contemporary Criminal Procedure, Court Decisions for Law Enforcement*. Fl: J&B Gould Publications.

*Author's Note: the case law found in this manual was obtained largely in part through the above listed publication "Contemporary Criminal Procedure." I recommend that all members of law enforcement obtain Larry Holtz's manual as it has proven to be an invaluable addition to my reference collection. All material used with express permission through the author and publisher.

Index

CPSIA information can be obtained
at www.ICGtesting.com
Printed in the USA
FFOW03n0546040118
44338736-43988FF